# THEORIES OF CAREER DEVELOPMENT

*Second Edition*

# THEORIES OF CAREER DEVELOPMENT

## Samuel H. Osipow

THE OHIO STATE UNIVERSITY

PRENTICE-HALL, INC., *Englewood Cliffs, New Jersey*

Printed in the United States of America

ISBN: 0-13-913442

Library of Congress Catalog Card Number: 73-3859

10 9 8 7 6 5 4

PRENTICE-HALL INTERNATIONAL, INC., *London*
PRENTICE-HALL OF AUSTRALIA, PTY. LTD., *Sydney*
PRENTICE-HALL OF CANADA, LTD., *Toronto*
PRENTICE-HALL OF INDIA PRIVATE LIMITED, *New Delhi*
PRENTICE-HALL OF JAPAN, INC., *Tokyo*

To Sondra, Randall, Jay, Reva, and David

# Contents

# Preface to
# the Second Edition

Most of the comments I felt appropriate to make in the preface to the first edition of this book still seem suitable to me. Career development has continued to be an important process in the lives of individuals and in society. Federal programs are burgeoning in recognition of the importance of systematically fostering growth in awareness and decision-making skills in connection with educational and vocational choices. In addition, much attention has been placed on the problems and concerns of workers in various stages of their careers.

The need for a revised edition of this volume seems clear to me. In the five years since the completion of the first edition, literally hundreds of studies have been conducted and published dealing with issues of concern to vocational psychologists and others interested in the theoretical and practical aspects of career development. The integration of these new findings into the earlier edition seemed imperative. Even though relatively few new theoretical positions have been created during the five-year period since the first edition, most of the existing theoretical positions have been substantially tested and shaped in the intervening time, and some new applications developed.

Because of the essentially unchanged structure of theoretical thinking in this field, however, the basic organization of the book is the same as the first edition. What differs is the inclusion of new research findings, and modifications, where appropriate, in the implications, evaluations, and applications with respect to the theories that these new findings suggest.

The explosion of research in vocational development and behavior is such that there is always the risk that some important research finding has been overlooked. Hopefully, this danger has been held to a minimum. In the interest of finally reaching enough closure to produce a manuscript to send to the publisher, the systematic literature search ended in March, 1972. Certain additional material published later than that was included because it was specifically brought to my attention by its author or a colleague, or by means of the publication process of the *Journal of Vocational Behavior*. The *Journal of Vocational Behavior* material for 1972 and 1973 is known to me because of my role as its editor, one of the fringe benefits of such a role being that of maintaining a close view of the literature.

As in any work, many individuals deserve acknowledgment for their help. Since this volume is based on the framework of the first edition, those who helped me then continue to deserve thanks. Specifically helpful in the preparation of the revised edition were W. Bruce Walsh, Donna Nagely, John Valley, John Hartung, Keith Taylor, Anne Simon, and Gladys Hosansky. My wife, Sondra, has once again contributed to this volume by means of her general support in the management of our family activities during hectic times, by her editorial critique of the material, and by her willingness to step in where needed during emergencies. My sons Randall and Jay have also contributed to the work by last-minute help in assembling materials, running errands, typing, and proofreading, all of which is gratefully appreciated and, hopefully, will contribute to their own career development. Others — students, secretaries, colleagues — have also helped in various ways, and, though they deserve recognition, are so numerous as to be impossible to single out for thanks here.

Finally, The American Psychological Association, Academic Press, The College Entrance Examination Board, *The Counseling Psychologist*, and the Bureau of Publications of Teachers College of Columbia University are to be thanked for their willingness to permit me to quote extensively from their publications.

S.H.O.

# Preface to the First Edition

Since Adam and Eve left the Garden of Eden, man has been required to earn his daily bread. The meaning and variety of work in which he has engaged over the centuries and across various cultures have differed, depending upon the particular context. However, the generally distasteful attitude man has held toward his daily work has not changed. To be poor meant to work long and hard simply to stay alive. To be wealthy meant to have someone do your work for you. Only relatively recently have social scientists clearly recognized that man accomplishes more by his daily work than the maintenance of his bodily needs and that Western man derives considerable psychological gratification from his work, despite his chronic complaints.

As one attempts to define work it becomes increasingly clear that definitions confined to economic and societal factors alone do not include the wide variety of behaviors involved. Work is partly an attitude in the mind of a person toward the activity in which he is engaged at the moment. One man's work is another man's play. It is clear that working holds an important place both in society and in the psychological lives of individuals.

Our civilization has evolved to the point that, in Western society at least, man possesses an element of choice concerning the activity with which he will occupy himself. Though the variety of work from which any given man may choose varies from broad to narrow, one of the most highly prized freedoms in our culture is the right to decide what kind of work one will do, for whom, and when. Although men do not always exercise this freedom, they value the potential of choice highly.

It is not surprising in a society in which many people have the opportunity to choose their careers, and in which the broad significance of work is recognized, that attempts to understand the decision-making processes involved in career development should be made. Early attempts to understand career decisions were largely unsystematized and empirical, but more recently theorists have become concerned with the problem and have turned their attention to questions of career development.

The purposes of this book are several. First, an attempt will be made to fill the need that exists for an examination and evaluation of current theoretical and empirical findings relevant to the vocational decision-making process. It is important to realize that theories of career development are not theories in the traditional sense. They do not conform to all the particular requirements of theories following the physical science model. We would be wise to keep in mind that the physical science model may not be suitable to the study of behavior. Nevertheless, current theories of career development are not full-blown but rather are theory "fragments" which attempt to integrate and systematize a portion of human behavior with respect to a specific human problem. The current theories of career choice are the prototypes of future theories and serve much the same functions that theories in the more sophisticated sciences do. This book, then, describes and assesses the major theories of career choice and related research.

Juxtaposing one theory with another leads to a second function. A comparison of the similarities and differences of the theories becomes possible, allowing judgments to be made as to relative strengths and weaknesses of the theories. A further purpose of this book is to attempt to synthesize some general theoretical statements which might integrate the more useful and effective constructs of the various theoretical positions, as well as to identify the ingredients common to most of the theories. Finally, this book has been written with an eye toward the needs of the practicing counselor. The procedures involved in vocational counseling currently vary from the extreme of no more than the interpretation of a standard battery of interest and ability measures on one side to the extreme of extended psychotherapy on the other. Little guidance exists to help the counselor sort and select appropriate procedures. It seems likely that a sufficient theoretical basis relevant to the conduct of vocational counseling exists to be of use to the counselor. What appears to be lacking is the means of translating the theory into explicit terms useful to counselors. Thus, the fourth purpose of this book is to consider the theories with respect to their implications for career counseling.

Thus, we hope to describe and clarify the various theoretical conceptions about career development that have been proposed, to assess them with respect to their adequacy as theories, examine and evaluate research relevant to them, synthesize and integrate the variety of approaches that currently exist, and examine their potential utility for counseling.

The decision of which theories to discuss is not independent of the degree of development of each of these theoretical approaches. For example, a great deal of writing and research has been conducted in recent years concerning the developmental and personality approaches and less in the trait-factor and sociological models. Such emphasis cannot be ignored. Theories have been included for detailed discussion on the basis of the impact they have had in counseling practice and research. Thus, in the developmental approach the models of Ginzberg and his associates and Super and his associates are considered in detail, since they have significantly influenced vocational counseling during the 1950s and 1960s. Other, less well-known approaches, representative of the developmental approach, will be woven into the larger discussions about the major approaches.

Of the personality models, the work of Holland and that of Roe will be discussed in detail, as well as the assorted empirical findings of other researchers which will be reported with Holland's and Roe's work as reference points. In addition, the research directed at identifying personality traits of people in specific occupations will be treated at length. The psychoanalytic theories of vocational choice will also be discussed. The sociological theories will be treated briefly as a unit, since they are essentially nontheories in the sense that B. F. Skinner's concepts of behavior are nontheoretical (nonexplanatory) and since they do not attempt to organize the data descriptive of career choice in the way that other, more typical theories and models ordinarily do. Finally, consideration of the trait-factor approach to career choice is included in discussions about other approaches to vocational decision-making since assessment procedures are generally imbedded in most career development theories.

A number of people helped to shape my ideas about these theories and the way that I have organized and expressed these ideas in this book. Especially influential has been Donald H. Ford, whose critical review of each chapter has played a major role in increasing the clarity and vividness of the manuscript. Providing balance have been the comments of James A. Gold, who read the entire manuscript from the point of view of the graduate student. Anne Roe, John Holland, and Donald E. Super were gracious enough to read and comment upon the chapters concerning their views of career development. Edward J. Polder contributed useful comments concerning several of the chapters. My wife, Sondra, read the entire manuscript with a critical, wifely eye and made many constructive comments concerning exposition. The generally stimulating atmosphere provided by my colleagues on the staff of the Division of Counseling of the Pennsylvania State University between 1961 and 1967 is in no small way responsible for the execution of this book. The work was significantly facilitated by the opportunity for reading and reflection provided by five months spent as Visiting Research Associate at the Center for Research in Careers of the Harvard Graduate School of Education in 1965. Finally, I must thank Miss Nancy Andrews, who typed the final copy of the manuscript and provided excellent clerical support, and Mrs. Myrtle Ely Moon, who typed the early and difficult-to-read drafts of the work.

I would also like to thank the *Journal of Counseling Psychology*, *The American Psychologist*, the College Entrance Examination Board, and the Bureau of Publications of Teachers College of Columbia University for their permission to quote extensively from their publications.

# THEORIES OF CAREER DEVELOPMENT

# Introduction

## SCIENCE AND COUNSELING

**Goals of Science**

It is generally agreed that the goals of science include the understanding, prediction, and control of some kind of natural phenomena. In the natural sciences, theoretical advances have led to increased physical and biological control of the world around us. This increased control, in turn, has generally improved, or at least immensely altered, man's environment. People are healthier, live longer and more comfortably; machines do more and more of the routine work that must be done; communications are improving at a phenomenal rate even though they are already unbelievably rapid; and we have embarked upon the adventure of space travel, all as a consequence of our scientific establishment. The science of psychology is rapidly developing the theoretical structure, empirical base, and technological knowledge which permit it to predict and control human behavior with increasing efficiency and effectiveness. A reader of B. F. Skinner (1953) cannot help but be impressed with the many examples from daily life illustrating the techniques through which simple and even complex behaviors can be manipulated.

While there is undoubtedly a great deal about human behavior that is not clearly understood, the development of psychology as a science seems to be following the development of older sciences (Sarton, 1952) in that applications and technology follow closely on the heels of each empirical or theoretical advance. As a consequence, many of the most widely accepted principles concerning human behavior have already been applied to a variety of human endeavors. For example, it was very quickly discovered that research in human visual perception has implications for the design of complex control equipment operated by human beings. In another context, we see that data derived from

1

the operant conditioning studies of pigeons led to the development of principles which have influenced and vitalized the development of programmed instruction and assorted mechanical teaching devices. The detailed study of the arrangement of working conditions for human beings leading to the specialty of industrial psychology is built upon principles of learning and personality theory, theories which have a bedrock of empirical observation and experimental data. Psychotherapy rests on a similar body of theory and data, though the arrangement of that body and the emphasis given to aspects of it are different from industrial psychology since applications in psychotherapy are sought with respect to the diagnosis and treatment of disordered behavior. Much of the educational practice of Western society is based on the psychological theory and research in the area of learning and human development. A lengthy catalog of applied psychology could be compiled to illustrate the diverse uses of our knowledge about human behavior.

Of course, the applications of the basic study of human behavior made in the fields of counseling, clinical, industrial, and other psychological specialties are clearly incomplete. Consumers of psychological data, including psychologists themselves, are often quick to point out gaps in basic and applied knowledge and inconsistencies in expert opinion. Criticisms notwithstanding, many demands are made on psychologists by the public, suggesting that many of the applications of the study of human behavior are very useful indeed.

## A Definition of Theory

Theory in social and behavioral science has its roots in the more mature physical sciences. The theoretical structures which have served physical scientists stand as the models that have guided the shape that psychological theories have taken. Hence, it is important that the groundwork be laid for an accurate understanding of the role and character of theory in general before we undertake a discussion and evaluation of theories of career development.

*Role of theory.* As is to be expected when treating highly abstract topics, some disagreement exists among theoreticians as to the proper role of theory (Allport, 1955; Marx, 1951). Despite the differences of opinion, several common elements basic to theory construction stand out. Traditionally, theory has served as a generalized statement designed to facilitate broad conceptualization about natural events. Theories relate what would otherwise be a number of disparate empirical observations. Ideally, one theory should serve as a basis for conceptualization about all events; in practice, many theories exist, separated in a number of scientific disciplines and further subdivided into theories to deal with events within the disciplines.

It should be pointed out that although theory begins with the observation of events, it becomes more complex as it brings together diverse happenings and permits, by deduction, predictions to be made about other events involved in the framework under observation. Thus, theories lead to "deduced theorems" which, in turn, can be translated into research whose predictive value partly allows the appraisal of the validity of the theory (Allport, 1955). In this sense theory serves as a tool of the scientist. Also important in comparing theories is the recognition that theories should differ in the predictions made within the same framework; if they do not, then, in fact, one theory exists where two were orginally thought to be. Ultimately, it is the empirical and not the logical or philosophical difference between theories that is important (Marx, 1951).

Not to be ignored is the part that theories play in understanding events. At their best, theories produce "new understandings" about the universe; a good theory clarifies events and leads to further predictions about related events. It must be recognized that explanation in science refers to an increasing detail in describing events, yet a detail that grows in generality as it increases in specificity. According to Marx (1951) two types of explanation exist in science. *Reductive explanation* describes the functional role of phenomena at a level of description more fundamental than observation of the phenomena themselves would permit. Explaining human behavior in terms of physiological processes is an example of reductionistic explanation. *Constructive explanation*, on the other hand, consists of the description of phenomena in terms of constructs or hypotheses. The intervening variables used to account for an apparent relationship between two sets of events are examples of constructive explanation. In the end, both types of explanation come down to description at some level. It is in the adequacy and generality of the description that theories may differ.

*Evaluating theories.* It becomes possible to assess theory in terms of the degree to which it fulfills the roles just discussed (Allport, 1955). Do the data, such as they exist, support the predictions that grow from the theory? While it is true that theories are not "proven or disproven" on the basis of experimentation, the adequacy of a theory is inferred from the degree to which tests of the predictions yield expected results. How general is the theory? Judgments about the adequacy of a theory should, at least in part, consider the range of the phenomena the theory is capable of integrating and explaining. How well does the theory explain the phenomena it deals with? Does it lead to new understandings of events? How operational is the theory? How available are the constructs of the theory to immediate experimental work? How explicit are the referents of the theory? Does the theory possess logical consistency? Obviously, an illogical theory is not useful. The degree to which the theory can parsimoniously deal with events is important. A good theory should cover the widest possible range of phenomena with a minimum of postulates.

## Psychology and Theory

It becomes apparent from the preceding discussion that all theory is imperfect, a fact that is sometimes overlooked by zealous psychologists seeking to "prove" theories. It should properly be assumed that theories will eventually die and be replaced by newer theories that deal with observed events in a more general and useful way than their predecessors. The misapplication of theory and the excessive interest that some psychologists show in theory construction have led other psychologists to view theorizing as undersirable and premature. Still other psychologists have complained that the physical science model applied to behavior theory is inappropriate and has created unnecessary difficulties in psychological conceptualization and research.

Despite these views, it seems likely that some of the problems stemming from psychological theory are not exclusively the result of the theories themselves. Many of the difficulties in generating applications for human endeavor based on psychological theory lie with the consumers as well as the producers of theory. For example, many educators have been disappointed in the lack of utility of learning theory for educational practice, despite the relatively long history of learning theory in the brief span of formal psychological theory. Until recently, however, many of the attempts to apply learning theory to educational practices were uninspired. There are signs now, however, in the use of programmed instruction, concept formation, language development, and the like, that new ideas based on psychological theory are taking hold in the field of educational methods. Furthermore, these new ideas use psychological data and theory boldly, thus offering the potential to improve educational methods more significantly than any idea since the invention of the printing press.

## Applying Theory to Human Problems

Applied psychologists have often said that theory is useful if one is required to do no more than solve abstract hypothetical problems, but when faced with warm-blooded people in trouble or in need of assistance in decision-making, theory must be left at the interview door and the applied psychologist must assume an eclectic position, even if it means working intuitively. Such an argument is countered by theoretically minded practitioners who answer that to work blindly is to invite error and waste. Perhaps the most reasonable answer to both claims for and against the usefulness of theoretical formulations underlying counseling is analogous to the discussion by Rodgers (1964) on differences between academic and professional training for psychotherapists. Rodgers suggests that, depending upon the goals one has and the assumptions one makes about the problems with which psychologists deal, either kind of training might appear to be good or bad.

Thus, he points out, when faced with the question of what sort of treatment is appropriate for a schizophrenic, the academician answers that he will begin a research project to study the question and that possibly, with luck, in x number of years he might be able to make a recommendation based on the results of his reasearch. The professional, on the other hand, must develop the best possible plan of action, regardless of limitations, on the basis of the data he has available at present. Each psychologist seriously criticizes the approach of the other; the professional attacks the academician for being heartless and indifferent to human misery, as well as for being unrealistic, while the academician criticizes the professional for being slipshod and misleading in his methods and lacking in scientific integrity by jumping to premature conclusions. Actually, both are sincerely acting within the framework of their own job roles. It is the professional's job to do the best he can with the tools available for people in immediate difficulties, all the while recognizing that his best efforts are imperfect. Similarly, it is the academician's job to investigate thoroughly every question posed to him and to be wary of drawing premature conclusions. Indeed, if either party did otherwise, he would then be acting in violation of his professional obligations.

Returning to the question of theoretical utility in counseling with the academic versus professional training controversy in mind, it is not unreasonable to suggest that current theoretical formulations in vocational psychology are imperfect, largely unvalidated, and suggestive of minimal yet varying practical applications, yet at the same time holding potential for the future sophistication of vocational counseling. Counselors must deal with the here and now, which might frequently force them to work outside a theoretical context. To do so and meet with some degree of success is both necessary and remarkable, but not ideal.

## The Role of Theory in Vocational Psychology

What is the proper role of theory in vocational psychology? Practitioners of counseling have often been disappointed in the lack of relevance of psychological theory, both basic and "applied," to their general practice. Theoretical applications to practice have often been attempts to apply fragments of behavior theory to counseling problems, but as a result of their fragmentation they have limited their viability by damming themselves from the flow of the mainstream of behavior theory. Other attempts at building theories directly applicable to counseling interviews have suffered from a narrowness of purpose or have generally been too sterile, as a result of their sweeping style, to produce valid techniques for vocational counseling. The pendulum has swung back and forth between the slogan of "round pegs in round holes" and existential conceptions of man's role in the world of work.

The solution of many counselors to this problem of theoretical weakness has been to work without systematic theory. The consequences of counseling without a theory are frequently overlooked. Eclectic counselors work intuitively and often feel they have accomplished some worthwhile purpose if they have listened sympathetically to someone's difficulties. Surely, professional training should result in something more than skill in sympathetic listening. Furthermore, counselors without theoretical orientations must of necessity find it difficult to integrate the many disjointed research findings into some meaningfully organized body of knowledge.

## Implicit and Explicit Theories

Close examination of interview procedures is likely to reveal that every counselor has ideas about his cases and conducts his interviews on the basis of his ideas. Counselors must have some notions about how human behavior works because they cannot proceed without them. What may vary, however, is the degree to which counselors make their ideas explicit and systematic or implicit and probably less systematized.

The counselor who possesses implicit notions about his client's behavior may be unable to describe clearly the basis of his own behavior to an observer because his ideas have never been explicitly verbalized to himself. Such a counselor is probably hard pressed to explain his actions in an orderly fashion, indicating why he acted as he did and what effects he hoped to achieve as a result of his actions, not because he has no basis for his behavior but because he has never had the occasion to describe formally the antecedents of his own counseling procedures. When asked about a case, it is likely that he responds in terms of fragments of his underlying ideas and has rarely, if ever, been required to set out all the pieces of his theory and interpret them to show someone else in an orderly and systematic fashion. As part of his justification for the rejection of any system, he may explain that he is aware of no system that is entirely correct, and he prefers to use certain aspects of many theories. In making this type of judgment, a counselor runs the risk, however, of confounding system-based technique with system-based conceptualization. That is, while counseling procedures derived from a particular theoretical system may apply to other systems, the effectiveness of the procedures is likely to depend upon the manner and timing of their introduction. Since the application of the procedures is likely to be specified in a well-developed counseling theory, the use of such procedures may make little sense out of context. The counselor who follows an explicit theory of behavior is guided in his hypotheses about his client's behavior and possesses a common conceptual thread which connects his disparate professional experiences.

Thus, one type of criticism directed at the prematurity of vocational development theory (Crites, 1965) seems to miss the point of theory. Theory correctly precedes or accompanies empirical knowledge and orients a body of knowledge while it is in its development. How counselors use theory and the essential ingredients of a theory are correctly subject to various interpretations (Hewer, 1963; McCabe, 1958), but a strong case can be made for the usefulness of theory, even in the primitive stages of the development of a discipline.

Considering the differences between the highly systematic counselor and the unstructured counselor, it would appear that the major issue is not whether or not a counselor uses theory in his work, but rather to what degree he is explicit and systematic in his use of theory. Unfortunately, the issue between explicit and implicit theory use has been obscured by the people who assert that the application of theory to behavioral concerns is premature. At the very least, theory stimulates research and gives direction to activity, and at its best, it may integrate highly diffuse data into some meaningful whole. Others, arguing that no single current theory is adequate for vocational counselors, are probably correct but have no real substantive basis for their position since no one has in fact compared the theories in a direct and orderly fashion.

**Results of Failure to Apply Theory to Counseling**

As a result of the difficulty of organizing research findings, combined with the distaste of counselors for such tasks and their lack of time, counseling is left with many notions about career development that have gone more or less unchallenged. Some of the ideas are holdovers from folklore pertaining to vocational choice, such as, for every man there is a job that should fit him better than any other job. One probable reason for the persistence of many of these ideas, which sound plausible in some cases but which imply many unverified hypotheses, is that often no systematic study or research has been made on these questions. It is highly likely that the lack of research has resulted from a scarcity of systematic thinking about career development.

Among the concepts about vocational counseling that go more or less unchallenged is the notion that occupational information, i.e., pamphlets, films, visits to factories and offices, and speakers representing various career fields, facilitates occupational choice by better informing youth about the "facts" pertaining to careers. However, many questions can be raised about the role of occupational information in vocational counseling. How does this information accomplish the task of facilitating career choice? Under what conditions does it do so? Does occupational information provide useful data for all students at all times in the early stages of their career decision-making? Are there circumstances when occupational information obscures rather than enlightens students about careers?

Some of the few pertinent research findings raise questions about the effects of certain practices in occupational information, suggesting that the process is not as simple as it appears to be (Osipow, 1962; Rauner, 1962; Samler, 1961). Other questions about factors in career choice may be raised. Do people think in terms of careers or entry jobs, school subjects and college majors or industries, when they choose their "occupation"? Do people select careers because of the security they offer or is promise for growth a more important factor? What are the characteristics of those who choose careers because of the security they offer as opposed to the ambitious risk-takers? Are some people activity oriented and others success oriented and if so, why, and how do we identify the different types? Once identified, do we counsel them differently? Is appropriateness of vocational choice a useful outcome criterion of counseling (Gonyea, 1962)? How effective are counselors in this regard (Gonyea, 1963)? Do counselor recommendations about educational-vocational plans really result in greater academic success for students when the recommendations are followed (Marks, Ashby, and Zeigler, 1965)?

How does adolescent physical development influence vocational interest (Hulslander, 1958)? The question of interests is difficult to cope with without a theoretical framework. For example, a counselor may be faced with (1) a student who says he has no interests, (2) a student who says he possesses various interests but cannot decide from among them which to follow, or (3) a student who complains of an inability to implement his interests into a behavior pattern that translates them into successful performance. Faced with such problems, the counselor must ask himself a number of questions about the nature of interests. What are interests, anyway? When the first student complains that he has no interests, what does he mean? Doesn't everybody have interests? Or does he really mean that he cannot see the connection between his interests and the various career patterns that are evident to him?

What does the undecided student mean when he complains of an inability to commit himself to a career pattern? When do people decide on careers? Just what is meant by a career decision? When should certain decisions be made? Is indecisiveness a general behavior pattern or is it restricted to career choices? Does indecision refer to a strong distaste for a realistic second choice? Some research by Holland and Nichols (1964), Ashby, Wall, and Osipow (1966), and Osipow, Ashby, and Wall (1966) sheds light on indecisiveness as a factor in career decisions, but few investigators have studied it. What about the student who cannot perform adequately in the field of his interest? Is the problem a matter of aptitude or commitment? What the counselor decides to do when faced with such situations depends upon his ideas and conceptions about interests, what they are, how they are acquired, what factors determine career patterns in the normal course of events, and what circumstances can prevent a pattern from crystallizing as it should. Questions such as these, viewed in a cohesive theoretical framework, may be systematically studied. Furthermore, the results of research obtained in such a context are more likely to be integrated into counseling practice than results of research that do not stem from theory.

## The Effect of Theory on Counseling

What the counselor decides to do when confronted with career choice questions depends upon the estimate he has of the source of the problem and the precise nature of its behavioral correlates. The remedy he applies to the situation will be chosen in terms of what he thinks is needed to correct the situation. Thus, if he decides that career choice is a process of matching oneself against jobs or positions in terms of interests and aptitudes, he will arrange, wherever possible, opportunities for his client to explore a variety of positions. Typically he will do this by using a sequence of several techniques. First, he will introduce procedures designed to enable his client to clarify the details concerning himself. Reflection, clarification, interest and aptitude tests, and questions such as "Who are you?" are all procedures which contribute to the clarification of self. Self-clarification, however, not being a sufficient condition for career choice by itself, the counselor also turns his attention to the clarification of various career patterns, either specifically in terms of positions, or more generally in terms of abstract career titles. Procedures such as reading occupational literature, visiting plants, offices, and professional establishments, and hearing discussions and lectures on careers by their practitioners are designed to implement this goal.

Following these two clarification procedures, the final step is the matching of the self with the career through interview procedures and the subsequent initial decision of career direction in terms of education, or job, or both. Let us suppose, however, that our counselor decides that career development is not appropriately conceptualized in terms of a matching of interests and aptitudes with occupations. Suppose our counselor theorizes that career development is an elaboration and extension of the self. His counseling efforts will probably be directed toward creating an interview environment which is conducive to self-exploration and self-expression, and he is likely to conclude that the introduction of tests, inventories, and occupational information will inhibit the process of self-discovery and expression. The task as he sees it is very different from that of our first counselor and is likely to be a longer process with a less explicit outcome.

A third counselor might assess his client's inability to make independent vocational decisions and conclude that the client is an obsessive-compulsive personality and that his inability to make a vocational decision can best be remedied through psychotherapy designed to identify and remove the sources of the obsessive-compulsive behavior. Although some research (for example, Strupp, 1958) has suggested that successful clinical psychologists employ procedures more like one another than unsuccessful ones, the possibility that even successful psychologists employ different procedures with different kinds of cases must not be ignored. Strupp's conclusion can lead to error as to where one focuses his observations. It is as if, after observing men and women, the conclusion was drawn that they are alike, since both sexes have a head, two ears, two eyes, and so on, ignoring the very significant differences. Differences may be maximized or minimized, depending upon one's vantage point. The point, then, is that counselors with different theoretical persuasions will think differently about their cases and are very likely to have different expectations and procedures as a result.

## CAREER DEVELOPMENT THEORY

Any attempt to categorize models of behavioral phenomena of any kind runs the risk of oversimplification. Nevertheless, some classification of the assorted explanatory motifs is a prerequisite for intelligible discussion about them. Obviously, a variety of labels can be used to identify the models, and the models can be categorized in many different ways. Thus, some arbitrariness is involved in the particular manner in which these models are described here. For our purposes, four distinct approaches to thinking about career counseling appear to fall into place.

*Trait-factor theories.* The oldest theoretical approach has been known by a variety of names, most commonly the trait-factor approach. This system assumes that a straightforward matching of an individual's abilities and interests with the world's vocational opportunities can be accomplished, and once accomplished, solves the problems of vocational choice for that individual. Some of the original trait-factor theorists who influenced thinking about vocational psychology are Parsons (1909), Hull (1928), and Kitson (1925). Within this model several special approaches have developed over the years. The vocational testing movement has grown from the trait-factor point of view. Thus, interest inventories such as the Strong Vocational Interest Blank (SVIB) and the Kuder Preference Record (KPR), and aptitude tests such as the Differential Aptitude Test and the Guilford-Zimmerman Aptitude Survey are based on the trait-factor stream of thought. Currently, the trait-factor model has been absorbed into other approaches to vocational counseling, and few practitioners of vocational counseling today are pure trait-factor adherents, though a recent paper by Hewer (1963) illustrates the procedures implemented by a counselor with a trait-factor orientation. The development of the trait-factor approach has been summarized by Williamson (1965).

*Sociology and career choice.* A second approach might best be referred to as the sociological model of career development. Other descriptive names for the position have been the reality or accident theory of vocational choice. This approach has as its central point the notion that circumstances beyond the control of the individual contribute significantly to the career choices he makes, and that the principal task confronting the youth (or older person, for that matter) is the development of techniques to cope effectively with his environment. This approach is illustrated in the writings of Caplow (1954), Hollingshead (1949), and Miller and Form (1951). (See also Harmony, [1964] for a case study illustrating the sociological approach to conceptualizing career choice.)

*Self-concept theory.* A third approach actually weaves two models into one and can be called either the developmental or the self-concept theory. This position grows out of the early work of Buehler (1933), and more recently, the work of Super (1957), Samler (1953), and Ginzberg and his associates (1951) on the one hand and Carl Rogers and client-centered counselors on the other (1951). The approach holds as its central theses that (1) individuals develop more clearly defined self-concepts as they grow older, although these vary to conform with the changes in one's view of reality as correlated with aging; (2) people develop images of the occupational world which they compare with their self-image in trying to make career decisions; and (3) the adequacy of the eventual career decision is based on the similarity between an individual's self-concept and the vocational concept of the career he eventually chooses.

*Vocational choice and personality theories.* A fourth category might be called the personality approach to the study of career development. Here, the ideas range from elaborate lists of needs inherent in the process of vocational choice (Hoppock, 1957) and the detailed personality types for career areas described by Holland (1959) to the assorted empirical studies of Small (1953), Schaffer (1953), Roe (1957), and many others on the particular personality factors involved in career choice and career satisfaction. There are also the many research projects on the personality characteristics of people in different vocations, the life styles of various professionals, psychopathology associated with professional activity, and the specific needs of workers in particular industries or jobs. The general hypothesis underlying these studies is that workers select their jobs because they see potential for the satisfaction of their needs. A corollary hypothesis is that exposure to a job gradually modifies the personality characteristics of the worker so that, for example, accountants eventually become like one another if indeed they were not similar in personality to begin with.

Although it can be argued that other arrangements of the approaches to conceptualizations about career choice might be made, even the splinter points of view, such as the psychoanalytic, may be fit into the general scheme described above. The reader must avoid concluding that these types of models are independent of one another. They are closely intertwined and in many instances draw heavily upon one another both in terms of actual practice and in empirical research. For example, in the self-concept or developmental approach, part of the image of self-concept is based on tests which reflect the trait-factor approaches; also, Roe's personality theory of career choice includes many developmental factors.

## PLAN

The discussion of the theories is carried out in four general sections. First, a statement is made of the general nature and scope of the theory and its basic thesis. Next, the results of research stimulated by the theory or relevant to it are discussed and evaluated. Then the implications of the theory for the specific conduct of career counseling are considered. Finally, the theory is evaluated and the expectations for future development are discussed.

Each theory is evaluated with respect to the criteria pertinent to a good theory which were discussed earlier. The theories are considered in the light of their comprehensiveness, their logical consistency, the degree to which they increase our understanding of the events under consideration, how operational they are, and the degree to which predictions derived from them are borne out. In addition, the applications growing from each theory are discussed and evaluated, along with new proposals about the roles these theories may play in practical affairs not originally suggested by their authors.

It is evident that the research and observational data on which a certain portion of the theories are evaluated are subject to limitations imposed by the problem of criterion definition. No attempt has been made here to resolve the many difficulties involved in clearly stating desirable behavioral outcomes of counseling, even though the problem has a certain relevance to the application of the theory. Some of the research that is considered is based on counseling procedures generated by theories which should lead to specific predictable case outcomes. Since criterion problems concerning case outcome deserve detailed attention in themselves, however, no extensive discussion seems appropriate here. It should be sufficient to state that without adequate criteria, outcome studies are entirely without meaning.

Important distinctions must be made concerning the differences among vocational selection, preference, and attainment. These differences are particularly well illustrated by Vroom (1964), who points out that vocational preference is the answer a counselor receives from a student to the question, "What career would you like to follow?" Vocational preference differs from vocational selection, since selection is a behavioral entity (broader than verbal), reflecting individual action and acceptance of consequent outcome. Finally, there is vocational attainment, which is reflected in the actual position the individual holds. It is obvious that while vocational preference, selection, and attainment may be identical within a given person, they need not be. Preference carries with it the concept of what would be done assuming all things are possible; selection includes the results of the compromises the individual makes in the face of his perceived limitations; and attainment reflects the ability of the individual to implement his selection.

# SUMMARY

Work holds an important place in human behavior, and consequently the varieties of work and the ways men choose their work in Western culture have attracted the interest of behavioral scientists. In this introduction, an attempt was made to illustrate the role that theory in general plays in the development of science and technology and, in particular, in the development of approaches to vocational psychology. As a corollary to the role theory plays in vocational psychology, the implications of counseling without an explicit theoretical base were discussed.

The direct comparison between current theoretical modes of thought in vocational psychology is a primary purpose of this book. Other goals include an attempt to catalog the assorted techniques suggested by the major theories of vocational choice and an attempt to generate a synthesis of current research and theory in vocational psychology that will be of use to the practicing counselor in his daily interactions with the public.

The existing theories of career development were assigned to one of four categories: the trait-factor theories, the sociological theories, the self-concept or developmental theories, and the personality-in-career theories. Furthermore, several criteria were described against which each of the theories discussed in the book will be evaluated. Each theory will be assessed in terms of its comprehensiveness with respect to career development, the degree to which it explicitly states propositions concerning the process of career decision-making, and its internal consistency.

# REFERENCES

Allport, F. *Theories of perception and the concept of structure.* New York: Wiley, 1955.

Ashby, J. D., Wall, H. W., and Osipow, S. H. Vocational certainty and indecision in college freshmen. *Personnel and Guidance Journal,* 1966, *44,* 1037-1041.

Buehler, Charlotte. *Der menschliche Lebenslauf als psychologisches Problem.* Leipzig: Hirzel, 1933.

Caplow, T. *The sociology of work.* Minneapolis: University of Minnesota Press, 1954.

Crites, J. O. Review of D. V. Tiedeman and R. P. O'Hara, "Career development: choice and adjustment." *Contemporary Psychology,* 1965, *10,* 80-81.

Ginzberg, E., Ginsburg, S. W., Axelrad, S., and Herma, J. L. *Occupational choice: an approach to a general theory.* New York: Columbia University Press, 1951.

Gonyea, G. G. Appropriateness of vocational choice as a criterion of counseling outcome. *Journal of Counseling Psychology,* 1962, *9,* 213-219.

Gonyea, G. G. Appropriateness of vocational choices of counseled and uncounseled college students. *Journal of Counseling Psychology,* 1963, *10,* 269-275.

Harmony, Mary. A vocational biography. *Vocational Guidance Quarterly,* 1964, *13,* 37-40.

Hewer, Vivian. What do theories of vocational choice mean to a counselor? *Journal of Counseling Psychology,* 1963, *10,* 118-125.

Holland, J. L. A theory of vocational choice. *Journal of Counseling Psychology,* 1959, *6,* 35-45.

Holland, J. L., and Nichols, R. C. The development and validation of an indecision scale: the natural history of a problem in basic research. *Journal of Counseling Psychology,* 1964, *11,* 27-34.

Hollingshead, A. B. *Elmtown's youth.* New York: Wiley, 1949.

Hoppock, R. *Occupational information.* New York: McGraw-Hill, 1957.

Hull, C. L. *Aptitude testing.* Yonkers-on-Hudson, New York: World, 1928.

Hulslander, S. C. Aspects of physical growth and evolution of occupational interest. *Personnel and Guidance Journal,* 1958, *36,* 610-615.

Kitson, H. D. *The psychology of vocational adjustment.* Philadelphia: Lippincott, 1925.

McCabe, G. E. When is a good theory practical? *Personnel and Guidance Journal,* 1958, *37,* 47-52.

Marks, E., Ashby, J. D., and Zeigler, M. L. Recommended curricular changes and scholastic performance. *Journal of Counseling Psychology,* 1965, *12,* 17-22.

Marx, M. H. The general nature of theory construction. In M. H. Marx (Ed.), *Psychological theory.* New York: Macmillan, 1951.

Miller, D. C. and Form, W. H. *Industrial sociology.* New York: Harper & Row, 1951.

Osipow, S. H. Perceptions of occupations as a function of titles and descriptions. *Journal of Counseling Psychology,* 1962, *9,* 106-109.

Osipow, S. H., Ashby, J. D., and Wall, H. W. Personality types and vocational choice: a test of Holland's theory. *Personnel and Guidance Journal,* 1966, *45,* 37-42.

Parsons, F. *Choosing a vocation.* Boston: Houghton Mifflin, 1909.

Rauner, Theresa M. Occupational information and occupational choice. *Personnel and Guidance Journal,* 1962, *41,* 311-317.

Rodgers, D. A. In favor of separation of academic and professional training. *American Psychologist,* 1964, *19,* 675-680.

Rogers, C. R. *Client-centered therapy.* Boston: Houghton Mifflin, 1951.

Roe, Anne. Early determinants of vocational choice. *Journal of Counseling Psychology,* 1957, *4,* 212-217.

Samler, J. Toward a theoretical base for vocational counseling. *Personnel and Guidance Journal,* 1953, *32,* 34-35.

Samler, J. Psycho-social aspects of work: a critique of occupational information. *Personnel and Guidance Journal,* 1961, *39,* 458-465.

Sarton, G. *A history of science.* Cambridge: Harvard, 1952.

Schaffer, R. H. Job satisfaction as related to need satisfaction in work. *Psychological Monographs,* 1953, *67,* No. 14 (Whole No. 364).

Skinner, B. F. *Science and human behavior.* New York: Macmillan, 1953.
Small, L. Personality determinants of vocational choice. *Psychological Monographs,* 1953, *67,* No. 1 (Whole No. 351).
Strupp, H. H. The performance of psychiatrists and psychologists in a therapeutic interview. *Journal of Clinical Psychology,* 1958, *14,* 219-226.
Super, D. E. *The psychology of careers.* New York: Harper & Row, 1957.
Vroom, V. *Work and motivation.* New York: Wiley, 1964.
Williamson, E. G. *Vocational counseling: some historical, philosophical, and theoretical perspectives.* New York: McGraw-Hill, 1965.

# Roe's
# Personality Theory
# of Career Choice

Anne Roe, trained as a clinical psychologist, became involved in the field of career development through her research on the personality traits of artists. Her studies of the personality factors related to artistic creativity led her to conduct a major series of investigations into the characteristics of eminent scientists. The fact that her husband, George Gaylord Simpson, is a famous evolutionist and that she spent a substantial portion of her life in the company of successful scientific scholars was probably not coincidental to her decision to study scientists.

While a formal series of theoretical statements is only a relatively recent event (Roe, 1957; Roe and Siegelman, 1964), the research which heavily influenced the development of Roe's point of view about vocational choice was conducted almost ten years earlier. The theory grew out of a series of investigations into the developmental backgrounds and personalities of research scientists in various specialties and is summarized in several monographs (Roe, 1951a; 1951b; 1953). From her findings, Roe concluded that major personality differences exist between physical-biological and social scientists, primarily in the type of interactions they have with people and things. A second conclusion she drew was that the personality differences that do exist between various kinds of scientists are in some part the result of influences of child-rearing practices.

## THE THEORY

The theory proposes that every individual inherits a tendency to expend his energies in some particular way. This innate predisposition toward a manner of expending psychic energy combined with various childhood experiences molds

15

the general style an individual develops to satisfy his needs throughout his entire life. The resulting style has specific and major implications for career behavior. It is the relationship between the genetic factors and early childhood experiences on the one hand and vocational behavior on the other that Roe's theory attempts to make explicit.

Roe's theory, recently revised (Roe and Siegelman, 1964), has three important components. She utilizes two major personality theories in deriving the propositions of her theory. The influence of Gardner Murphy (1947) is implicit in her use of the concept of canalization of psychic energy and in her basic assumption that experiences of early childhood are likely to be related to vocational choice. A second major personality theme which is significantly related to her theory of vocational choice is "need" theory, specifically, Maslow's (1954). The third major component in her formulations, the notion of genetic influences on vocational decisions as well as in the development of need hierarchies, is explicitly woven into her discussion.

The theory itself seems to have two levels. The first level is in the form of general statements that in themselves are very difficult to test empirically. This portion of the theory states that each individual's genetic background underlies his abilities and interests, which in turn are related to vocational choice. Further, each individual expends his psychic energy in a manner not entirely under his control, and this involuntary expenditure of energy, which is presumably genetically determined, is influential in the development of the individual's abilities. Combined with the expenditure of the psychic energy is the development of need primacies based partly on early frustrations and satisfactions and partly on genetic factors such as outlined by personality theorists, particularly Maslow (1954). Maslow, it should be pointed out, assumes that the needs of humans may be arranged in a hierarchy, with the need for the satisfaction of lower-order needs, such as hunger, thrist, and oxygen, being greater than the need for such higher-order satisfactions as love, affection, knowledge, and self-actualization. A prerequisite to the expression of a need is the satisfaction of the needs which are more basic in the needs hierarchy. Thus, love would not emerge as a strong need in a starving man.

Genetic factors and need hierarchies combine to influence the selection of a vocation, as a part of their effect on the total life pattern. The degree of motivation toward the attainment of a vocational goal is a product of the arrangement and intensity of the individual's particular need structure. The degree to which an individual is motivated along a particular vocational line may thus be inferred from his accomplishments. In other words, given "equal" endowments genetically, differences in occupational achievement between two individuals may be inferred to be the result of motivational differences which, theoretically, are likely to be the outcome of different kinds of childhood experiences. There is the suggestion that some interaction between genetic and environmental factors occurs, but the theory fails to attempt to cope with the details of the nature of that interaction.

The second level of the theory pertains to the manner in which the development of patterns and strengths of the basic needs are affected by childhood experiences. The interactions that Roe describes in this portion of her theory are more explicit and are more open to empirical validation than the general statements concerning psychic energy and genetic structure of personality. Three specific propositions emerge: (1) Needs that are routinely satisfied do not become unconscious motivators. (2) Higher-order needs, in the sense of Maslow's self-actualization need, will disappear entirely if they are only rarely satisfied. Lower-order needs, in the Maslovian sense, will become dominant motivators if they are only rarely satisfied; in the event they become dominant motivators, they will block the appearance of higher-order needs. (3) Needs that are satisfied after unusual delay will become unconscious motivators under certain conditions. The influencing conditions are the strength of the need, the amount of delay between the arousal of the need and its satisfaction, and the value that the satisfaction of the need has in the individual's immediate environment.

Thus, it is the second portion of the theory that contains the features that make it distinctive from personality theory in general and from other theories of vocational choice. Reflection upon the circumstances under which needs might be satisfied or frustrated in early childhood brings one directly to those principal agents of childhood gratification and frustration, the parents. Consequently, Roe proposes that child-rearing practices relate directly to both the kinds of needs satisfied and the delay involved in their gratification.

## Modes of Child Rearing

Several specific child-rearing techniques have been described, all of which have to do with the manner in which the parents interact with the child. One type of parent exercises his attention very directly on the child, either overprotecting him or making excessive demands upon him. A second parent tends to avoid the child, either neglecting his physical requirements or, more significantly, rejecting the child emotionally. A third parental style is one of acceptance, either of a casual, unconcerned nature or of a loving nature. Roe specifies how these parental styles affect the satisfaction of the child's needs. The overprotective parent will fully and quickly satisfy the child's physiological needs, but he will be less prompt to gratify the child's demands for love and esteem and, where the child's demands are met, will reward behavior that is socially desirable. Furthermore, the overprotective parent teaches the child to place a great deal of emphasis on the speed with which his needs are gratified. Thus, the child is fully and quickly gratified at the lower-need levels; but higher-order needs, such as love, esteem, and a sense of belonging, are connected to dependency on others and conformity. On the other hand, while the overdemanding parent shares many practices with the overprotective parent, he differs in several important aspects. Similar to the overprotective parent, he indulges the child's physical needs promptly and more than adequately. Also like the overprotective parent, he imposes conditions on the love he offers the child. This love he offers in return for conformity and achievement. The child's needs for information and understanding are also acceptable and gratified, but only under specific circumstances where they contribute to the achievement of the child, as the parent sees such achievement.

The rejecting kinds of parents have some explicit effects on the needs of their children. Those parents who ignore the physical well-being of their children, within certain limits, probably do not injure their children as much as parents who withhold love and esteem under all conditions. Roe, unclear on the differential effects of these two kinds of rejecting parents with respect to the resulting needs hierarchies of the children, points out that unless the rejected children see others treated in a different way, they will suffer from a stunted, but not necessarily distorted, development.

Finally, the accepting parents, both the loving and casual types, offer satisfactory gratification of their children's needs at most levels. Although the two types of parent will differ somewhat in the way in which they will provide for the gratification of their children's needs and also in the degree to which they will gratify their offspring's needs, the personality that results from accepting parental techniques is able to seek the gratification of his needs at all levels.

**Early Experiences, Needs, and Adult Behavior**

What is the relationship between these various practices, the resulting needs hierarchies, eventual adult behavior patterns in general, and vocational selection in particular? Figure 1.1 is a representation of the relationship of careers resulting from needs hierarchies and the child-rearing procedures that produce certain needs hierarchies. The scheme is basically in terms of the degree to which an individual is oriented toward persons or not toward persons. Thus, according to Roe's (1957) occupational classification,[1] people in service occupations are primarily oriented toward persons and probably come from a home which generated a loving, overprotecting environment, while scientists tend not to be oriented toward persons and come from a cold home atmosphere where rejection and avoidance of the child predominated. The home atmosphere influences the *type* of vocational activities, while such items as the genetic structure and the involuntary pattern of expenditure of psychic energy influence the occupational *level* the worker achieves. Such factors as the intensity of needs, influenced by the early environment, may raise the occupational level

---

[1] Roe's classification system has been the subject of research in its own right as well as in connection with its relation to the theory. Roe, Hubbard, Hutchinson, and Bateman (1966) and Roe and Hutchinson (1969) attempted to validate the psychological aspects of classification systems in terms of observed occupational changes made over a period of years. Osipow (1966), with a similar purpose, examined the consistency of an individual's occupational preferences according to occupational field. The results of these studies provide some support for Roe's notion that adjacent occupational fields are more closely related psychologically than distant ones. Meir (1973), on the basis of a smallest space analysis of Roe's occupational classification, concludes that Roe's psychological assumptions underlying the system are basically sound.

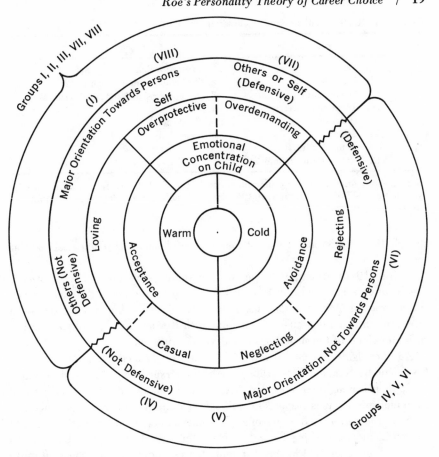

FIGURE 1.1 Schematic representation of Roe's theory. (From Anne Roe, Early determinants of vocational choice. *Journal of Counseling Psychology*, 1957, 4, 216. Copyright 1957 by the American Psychological Association, and reproduced by permission.)

because of an increase in motivation, but such an increase can only be within the limits set by the genetic factors influencing intelligence, combined with the socioeconomic background of the individual.

Roe and Klos (1969) have further modified Roe's original conception of the occupational classification from a cylindrical to a conical shape. This change was made to indicate that regardless of field, low-level jobs are more similar to one another psychologically than high-level jobs are to one other. The cone places the higher-level positions at the wide top, which implies greater differentiation psychologically for a level-one (high) worker in science from a level-one worker in arts and entertainment than between level-five workers in those fields. At its bottom, the cone narrows to reflect that lower-level work differs more as a function of the context within which it occurs than as a function of its inherent characteristics. In other words, a sweeper in a lab does not have psychological experiences very distinctive from a clean-up man in an artist's studio,

TABLE 1.1. Roe's Classification of Occupations and Levels

| Groups | Levels |
|--------|--------|
| I. Service | 1. Professional and managerial (1) |
| II. Business | 2. Professional and managerial (2) |
| III. Organization | 3. Semiprofessional and small business |
| IV. Technology | 4. Skilled |
| V. Outdoor | 5. Semiskilled |
| VI. Science | 6. Unskilled |
| VII. General cultural | |
| VIII. Arts and Entertainment | |

Source: From Anne Roe, Early determinants of vocational choice, *Journal of Counseling Psychology*, 1957, *4*, 217. Copyright 1957 by the American Psychological Association, and reproduced by permission.

though the scientist and the artist inhabit very different psychological environments.

Meir's (1970) attempt to examine the spatial structure of Roe's original classification system led him to conclude that the structure of the classification system was adequate for the higher occupational levels but not for the lower levels, an observation which is consistent with Roe and Klos' (1969) attempt to revise the shape of the structure from a cylinder to a cone.

Another significant modification in the occupational classification scheme of Roe made by Roe and Klos (1969) lies in the arrangement of the eight occupational fields along two axes. One axis reflects an orientation to purposeful communication versus resourceful utilization while the other axis is concerned with an orientation to interpersonal phenomena as opposed to an orientation to natural phenomena. Using Figure 1.2 it is, thus, possible to "plot" the location of an occupational field in this differentiated psychological space in relation to the basic wheel depicting Roe's theory (Figure 1.1).

## Summary

The theory attends to every important aspect of vocational selection. The development of needs influences the general vocational context, that is, toward others or not toward others. The factors in the early environment that influence the development of needs are clearly specified. The manner in which a normal individual develops is indicated, as are several ways that normal development may become misdirected. Motivation is largely the result of the intensity of needs, which is a function of the degree of deprivation of an individual combined with his genetic structure. Finally, the level of vocational activity (complexity and responsibility) is largely the product of the genetic differences between people which result in differences in intelligence and in the ways they attempt to manipulate various aspects of their environment. Conceivably, then, careful appraisal of an individual's childhood and his perception of his parents'

*Orientation to Purposeful Communication*

GENERAL
CULTURAL    ideas

enlightening people

     demonstrating     SCIENCE
     mastery or principle    "laws"

cooperative     TECHNOLOGY     independence
relations       mechanics       of relations

sustaining people or nature

polite     attending to method     OUTDOOR
relations                 nature

systematizing performance

ARTS AND ENTERTAINMENT
tastes

friendly     ORGANIZATION
relations      standards

BUSINESS CONTACT
persuasive
technique

*Orientation to*
*Interpersonal*     SERVICE     personal     *Orientation to*
*Relations*       needs        relations     *Natural Phenomena*

*Orientation to Resourceful Utilization*

Hypothesized horizontal dimension — Role performer's orientation to
    *interpersonal relations natural phenomena*
Hypothesized vertical dimension — Role performer's orientation to
    *purposeful communication resourceful utilization*
Hypothesized "key data" are listed near each occupational group

FIGURE 1.2. Occupational groups ordered by role performers' orientations to people, key data, and natural phenomena. (From Anne Roe and D. Klos. Occupational classification. Reprinted with permission from *The Counseling Psychologist*, 1969, 1(3), 92.

attitudes toward him plus an accurate assessment of his aptitudes should lead one to predict with accuracy the general occupational class he will pursue. Or, after the fact, people in different occupations on the same level should report childhood environments that differ, according to the system described by Roe.

# RESEARCH

There are two kinds of research relevant to the evaluation of Roe's theory. The first type is represented by investigations conducted by Roe herself, prior to her formal statement of the theory. The results of these studies guided her thinking about personality factors important to career choice. The other kind of research relevant to Roe's theory was conducted after the model was formally stated. Such research was primarily conducted by other investigators to evaluate Roe's theory by devising studies which predicted certain classes of vocational events based on the propositions of the theory and then assessing the degree to which the predictions correlated with those events.

## Preliminary Studies

The research conducted by Roe prior to the development of her theory does not subject her position to rigorous test, since much of it is descriptive and, in any event, the theory was not developed fully enough to test. Nevertheless, it is relevant to consider the design of her studies and the generalizations she drew from the results, since the research she conducted during the period prior to the publication of her theory had a significant influence on the direction and shape of the theory. The research was primarily a series of investigations into personality characteristics, background factors, aptitude, and intellectual abilities as they related to vocational choice. The results are reported in a series of papers, but the main findings are summarized in several monographs on the characteristics of men who have outstanding reputations in the physical, biological, and behavioral sciences.

Roe's studies had two general themes. The first study consisted of the assessment of the results of several group projective and ability tests administered to biologists, physicists, and chemists. From these studies she was able to report differences and similarities in responses to the Rorschach Inkblot Test, in some cases the Thematic Apperception Test (TAT), and on certain ability tests (Roe, 1949a; 1950; 1951c; 1951d; 1952a; 1952b; 1949b; 1951a; 1951b; 1953) for scientists in different fields. The second step in her research program was her investigation of the characteristics and backgrounds of eminent scientists. Her procedures in these studies were at first to select men judged to be outstanding in their field by their peers and then to enlist their cooperation in her schedule of interviews and tests. Detailed interviews were conducted in which topics such as family background, early experiences, psychosocial development, religious experiences and beliefs, and work experiences were discussed thoroughly. In addition, tests of verbal-spatial-mathematical abilities were administered, as well as two personality measures, the TAT and the Rorschach Inkblot Test. Comparisons between scientists in different fields were then made with respect to the data collected.

Of major significance to the development of her theory were the generalizations she drew from the interviews. By and large, she concluded that these groups of eminent scientists had childhood experiences which differentiated them from one another. For example, an unusual number of the eminent biologists she studied came from families broken either by divorce or the death of one parent. None of the social scientists came from a home permanently broken by parental conflict, though several were broken by a parent's death. The biological scientists reported more than the usual amount of difficulty in psychosexual development. Both the physical and biological scientists seemed somewhat distant in their relations with their parents and siblings, in contrast to the behavioral scientists (psychologists and anthropologists), who reported more interaction, though not necessarily positive, with their families. The parents of the social scientists were more overprotective and overcontrolling than those of the physical and biological scientists. The anthropologists, in particular, were often openly rebellious and hostile in their interactions with their parents.

Age at first commitment to their eventual vocation varied considerably for the different scientific groups. The physical and biological scientists tended to make their decisions earliest, the anthropologists and psychologists later. Of course, there was a wide range in age at the time of choice and considerable overlap among the groups. Nevertheless, the general trend for psychologists was to decide in college or later, while a few anthropologists decided in high school, and a larger number of physical and biological scientists decided in high school. (The parallel with Holland's theoretical predictions about the clarity and time of emergence of choice for different types of students is remarkable, as shall be seen in a later chapter.)

Also of interest is the finding that a prolonged illness leading to personal isolation during childhood seemed to play a significant role in development, especially among the theoretical physicists. Finally, as would be expected from a group of eminent professionals, all men scored very high on all the abilities measures, with the social scientists having the highest mean score on the verbal test, the physical scientists scoring highest on the spatial and mathematical tests (the mathematical test was not appropriately difficult for the physical scientists), and the social scientists scoring lowest on the mathematical test. All the eminent scientists impressed Roe with their unusual dedication to their work and the role their professional activities play in providing gratification for them. It would not be improper to infer that their dedication to their profession was closely related to their unusual vocational achievements, although, as Roe points out, such an inference is weakened by the lack of similar data on "less eminent" scientists to serve as a comparison group.

Roe's findings led her to conclude that there are distinctions in the personality characteristics of men in different vocations, that men in different vocations report qualitatively different childhood experiences, and that the major distinction between vocational orientations is in the dimension of interest toward persons or not toward persons. These conclusions played a significant role in fashioning the theory of vocational choice she later formulated.

*Evaluation.* The validity of Roe's studies of eminent scientists is dependent on the accuracy of the retrospective report of the scientists about their parents' attitudes and behaviors toward them, the early influences on their preferences and interests, feelings about themselves and other people, and also on Roe's interpretations of the interview material that revealed the scientists' recollections. Of course, some of Roe's conclusions were based on judgments she made about the scientists on the basis of Rorschach and TAT protocols. However, numerous problems exist in research based on projective tests, since the validity of the interpretations based on these tests has been questioned, as well as the reliability of responses to projective items. Furthermore, tests such as the Rorschach are primarily oriented toward the diagnosis of psychopathology and have questionable utility in work with normal populations. Results based on Rorschach tests are likely to emphasize personality disorders rather than normal personality patterns.

Some question may be raised concerning the degree to which generalizations can be made about career choice for people based on studies of outstanding figures. Roe's eminent scientists were clearly unusual people. It is also unfortunate that Roe did not attempt to integrate her research program explicitly into the existing stream of research in child development. Despite these limitations, the studies were imaginative and very useful as pilot work in the study of the interaction between childhood experiences, personality development, and vocational choice.

## Other Research

A good test of the usefulness of a theory lies in its ability to stimulate research designed to test it. Roe's relatively young theory has been successful in terms of such a criterion. The first study specifically designed to test Roe's theory was conducted by Grigg (1959). He chose to investigate differences in childhood recollections about parental treatment among women studying mathematics and science as compared with women studying nursing. He predicted that the mathematics-science majors would recall a "colder, less attentive" parental attitude than would the nursing students. Grigg compared the answers to a 15-item questionnaire about recollections of parental reactions during childhood, feelings of acceptance as a child, and father's and mother's reactions to the responsibilities of parenthood of 24 women graduate nursing students and 20 women graduate students in chemistry, physics, and mathematics. In addition, he inquired into their general interests during childhood.

The results indicated that no differences existed between the two groups in the child-parent interaction recollections or parental role acceptance. Grigg did find, however, that the women in the mathematics-science fields had been more interested as children in things and gadgets than were the nursing students, who were more interested in companionship. Grigg concluded that his results failed to support Roe's theory, since Roe's model predicts that differences in childhood experiences with parents along the cold-warm, accepting-rejecting dimensions should be related to such divergent careers as science and nursing.

Hagen (1960) assessed Roe's theory using a longitudinal approach. Using a large sample (245) of Harvard sophomores first contacted between 1938 and 1942, he used family history data that pertained to vocational, social, personal, and medical information. Parents, and at times other individuals, provided retrospective information about the subjects' childhood personality and parental child-rearing practices. Data were also obtained concerning the subjects' current practices in rearing their own children. These subjects were also required to respond to open-ended questionnaires concerning their attitudes and adjustment concerning their work.

The subjects' childhood experiences based on the family history data were then rated independently on Roe's categories of child-rearing practices by two judges. The judges agreed in their assignment of practices to categories in 70 percent of the sample. The 30 percent of Ss whose parents' child-rearing practices were not consistently evaluated were not used in the research. Then each subject's occupation was assigned to a category within Roe's vocational classification scheme and several predictions were made. It was predicted that people in service occupations come from a protecting childhood climate, people in business contact or general cultural occupations from a demanding climate, people in outdoor occupations from a rejecting climate, and people in technological fields from a casual climate. The results indicated that when childhood climate was paired with current occupation, only one of the child-rearing categories was significantly related to current vocation. Half the people from casual atmosphere were in appropriate occupations, which proved to be significant beyond the .01 level of probability, but the sample was very small, and in view of the lack of predictive success for the other categories, Hagen concluded that Roe's theory was not supported by the data.

Assessing Roe's theory on the agreement between childhood parental practices and the productions of orientations toward persons or not toward persons, Hagen still failed to find results corroborating Roe's theory. Of 112 subjects classed in the demanding or overprotective categories, 69 were in vocations oriented toward persons and 43 in careers not oriented toward persons. Of the 42 Ss from rejecting, neglecting, or casual environments, only 16 were in occupations not oriented toward persons (which is where the theory predicted they should be), while 26 were in fields where orientation toward persons was predominant. These distributions failed to be significant, leading to the conclusion that the data fail to support Roe's model in even the broadest way. Hagen points out that the possible inadequacy and inaccuracy of the background data might have contributed to his failure to find support for Roe's theory.

Nevertheless, some theoretical limitations seem likely, most significantly the fact that a variety of orientations is possible within a career so that a scientist may not be oriented toward persons and work in a laboratory, or he may be oriented toward persons and teach, or administer research projects.

Kinnane and Pable (1962) devised a study primarily concerned with the investigation of another model of career development (Super, 1957, which is discussed elsewhere), but several of the hypotheses they tested related very closely to Roe's theory. Kinnane and Pable were interested in identifying the relationship between family background and work-value orientations of adolescents. Their sample of 121 eleventh grade boys responded to a biographical inventory devised by Super and Overstreet (1956) designed to assess variables in family background such as cultural stimulation, family cohesiveness, social mobility, and adolescent independence. To provide added data Kinnane and Pable developed a scale measuring materialistic atmosphere in the home. They also used the Work Values Inventory (WVI) and another instrument devised by Super and Overstreet (1960). The latter two instruments rounded out the information necessary to assess home-family influences on the one hand and resulting work-value orientations on the other. The hypothesis of particular relevance to Roe's theory is their prediction that an orientation toward persons develops in a home atmosphere of warmth. A warm home is characterized by parental concern for their children, with some possiblity of parental overprotection or overcontrol. Upon examining the correlation between work values and family background, they found a significant correlation between family cohesiveness and an orientation toward working conditions and associations. Such a finding is consistent with Roe's position, though it does not rule out other theories. A finding that was unexpected and which is difficult to explain is that a materialistic orientation was correlated with family cohesiveness to an even greater extent than orientation to people. The study possesses one major shortcoming, as the authors point out. A stronger test of the hypotheses would result from a comparison between work values and biographical factors if the measures of each were more independent of one another. When such measures are as closely connected to each other as in Kinnane and Pable's study, there is some risk that the subjects' perceptions of one factor may influence their response on the other in a spurious manner.

Another approach to the evaluation of Roe's theory was devised by Utton (1962), who proposed the hypothesis that individuals in people-oriented occupations would report more "altruistic love" toward humanity than people in occupations that are essentially nonperson-oriented. He further predicted that the subjects in person-oriented occupations would recall warmer early childhood experiences than subjects in nonperson-oriented careers. His subjects were 33 female social workers and 25 female occupational therapists representing the person-oriented occupations, and 41 female dieticians and 28 female laboratory technicians representing the nonperson vocational orientations.

To test the first hypothesis he administered the Allport Inventory of Values

(AIV), which he found differentiated the two groups significantly on the Social Scale, confirming the hypothesis that the person-oriented subjects were more altruistic in their concern for others than the nonperson-oriented subjects. His second hypothesis was assessed by devising and administering a Childhood Experience Rating Scale (CERS) primarily measuring the warmth recalled from childhood experience. He found that the CERS scores of women who had scored above the mean for women in general on the Social Scale of the Allport Inventory of Beliefs (AIB) were no different from the CERS scores of women who had scored below the mean on the Social Scale. Furthermore, he found that the CERS scores were the same for subjects in both person- and nonperson-oriented careers. Utton did, however, find that when the SVIB scores of subjects with B or higher scores in their field were examined and their CERS backgrounds compared, some differences were evident, but not always differences that were consistent with his predictions. Social workers and occupational therapists with B or higher on the appropriate SVIB scale did have higher CERS scores than social workers and occupational therapists with less than B SVIB scores for their occupations. However, occupational therapists and dieticians were similar to each other in their recollections of their childhood experiences, whereas social workers and laboratory technicians resembled one another closely. (Thus, the findings are not consistently related to Roe's theory and consequently generate questions about the adequacy of the suggestion of the theory that a warm-cold dimension in childhood exerts an influence on the later choice of a vocation.)

Switzer, Grigg, Miller, and Young (1962) designed a study attempting to correct some of the deficiencies that Grigg's (1959) earlier study possessed with respect to the adequacy of his instrument to measure childhood experiences. Switzer and his associates predicted that ministerial students, representative of a person-oriented career, would perceive their parents as more demanding and less rejecting of them in childhood than would chemistry majors, representing a nonperson-oriented field. They studied 40 graduate students in theology, 40 undergraduate students in theology (called ministerial), and 40 undergraduate chemistry majors, all of whom represented themselves as certain of their vocational choice. A questionnaire designed to measure the demanding and rejecting aspects of the attitudes they recalled their parents having held toward them during their childhood was administered to the subjects.

The findings did not reflect any consistent relationship between occupational selection and parental attitude. In fact, some of their results were the reverse of theoretical expectations. For example, Switzer and his associates found that the ministerial and theological students reported more rejecting experiences than the chemistry majors did, and again the ministerial and theological students scored lower on the overdemanding scales than the chemists. Each of these findings is the opposite of what Roe's theory predicts. As with other research, however, the adequacy of the inventory measuring parental reactions and the memory of the respondents might be questioned. It could be, for instance, that the ministerial and theological students, being more socially perceptive than chemists, might have accumulated richer childhood recollections subject to more rigorous standards of parent-child interaction than the chemists.

Reasoning that jobs do not always possess the same characteristics even though they have the same titles, Levine (1963) controlled the social interaction within an occupation by having subjects from ten occupational groups which covered a wide range of social interaction possibilities. He predicted that people with a strong "human orientation" will be found in occupations where a high degree of social interaction is necessary. He also predicted that people who see their jobs as requiring considerable social interaction will rate themselves higher on scales measuring the possession of social manipulation skills than people in low social interaction jobs. To test these hypotheses, he developed a scale to assess the social requirements of jobs, a brief questionnaire (ten items) to measure the Ss' tendency toward human or nonhuman approaches to problem solving, and another brief questionnaire (three items) on which the Ss rated themselves with respect to their possession of manipulative skills.

His findings indicated some support for the first hypothesis, that people with a high degree of human orientation are likely to be found in occupations demanding social interaction. Thus, he found that salesmen were significantly different from all his other groups in the degree of human orientation indicated by their higher scores, while accountants were significantly lower in human orientation than social workers, draftsmen, laboratory technicians, and electrical engineers. The second hypothesis was not supported. Although questions can be raised about the adequacy of the execution of the study — for example, the reliability of a ten-item, human-nonhuman, problem-solving orientation questionnaire and a three-item questionnaire on rating of manipulative skills — Levine's results support Roe's broad conception of the dichotomous work orientation of toward persons/not toward persons. However, the results shed no light on how, or even if, background factors influence the development of social or nonsocial preferences classified in terms of Roe's taxonomical system. Jones (1965) also observed that his subjects expressed their occupational preferences fundamentally in terms of occupations oriented toward or away from people.

Green and Parker (1965) designed a study using adolescents as a sample to overcome the problems which previous investigators encountered concerning the retrospective reconstruction of childhood experiences. Seventh grade boys and girls, living with their parents, were given Roe and Siegelman's Parent-Child Relations Qeustionnaire, modified for use with seventh graders. The responses to this inventory provided data about the current home atmosphere of the children which were then related to the person or nonperson orientation of their occupational preferences. The results suggest that for boys the perception of either parent as warm and supporting results in person-oriented occupational choices, while for girls, cold parental relationships result in nonperson career choices. Curiously, boys do not make nonperson-oriented choices in a cold environment nor do girls from a warm environment make person-oriented career plans. Nevertheless, these findings offer more support for Roe's theory than most other studies and point to the importance of gaining current data about parental treatment of children in such studies. It would be interesting to follow these subjects as years go by to see, first, how constant their perceptions of parental treatment are, and second, how these perceptions continue to be related to the orientation of their career decisions.

Crites (1962) tested the hypothesis that a continuum of the importance of interpersonal relations exists for occupations. He required 100 students to rank eight occupational fields with respect to the degree that the fields required interpersonal relations with people as the main work activity of the job. The resulting empirical scale did not correlate significantly with the theoretical scale derived from Roe's model. Crites concluded that Roe's theoretical scale was not as valid as the empirically derived scale that he developed, at least so far as the ordering of judgments about job orientation toward persons or not toward persons is concerned. Although the differences between the two orders is slight, errors in Roe's theory in the degree of importance that person orientation has for a career field might be partially responsible for the failure of research to validate Roe's position.

Another study with important implications for Roe's theory was an attempt to construct a Family Relations Inventory (FRI) which might test the theory more effectively. Brunkan and Crites (1964), critical of the efforts that have been made by other investigators to test Roe's theory by using background information questionnaires of uncertain reliability and doubtful validity, have worked systematically to develop a more effective instrument with which to assess family background factors that might be related to vocational choice. However, in Brunkan's (1965) attempt to apply the instrument to test Roe's theory once again, no systematic connection between early environment and orientation of occupational choice was found. Brukan administered the FRI to 298 college undergraduate male students enrolled in psychology courses. Scores on the FRI were related to the category of the occupational choice in Roe's system and from this he predicted that the occupational choices would reflect the warmth or coldness of the family environment. None of these predictions was supported. Thus, even with a more carefully developed instrument to assess family environment, the data fail to support Roe's theory.

Appleton and Hansen (1969) administered the Roe-Siegelman (1964) parent-child questionnaire, the Kuder CH Social Service scale, and 40 items restated from the Edwards Personal Preference Schedule reflecting the nurturance, succorance, and dominance scales to 173 high school males and females in order to examine the relation between occupational plans and Roe's theory. The findings of this research did not reflect any significant relationship between reports about parent-child relations and vocational orientation. Appleton and Hansen speculate that these negative results can, at least in part, be attributed to deficiencies in the questionnaires, but the results add further to the questions about the validity of the theory. In another study, Byers, Forrest, and Zaccaria (1968) predicted that clergymen differ from a "men-in-general" group in the way they recall early parental relations. Some of the predicted differences were observed; for example, the clergymen recalled more father-avoidance on the Family Relations Inventory than the normative group, but in general, the statistical relationships are weak and do not provide strong theoretical support.

More recently, however, some positive support for the theory has been produced by Medvene (1969; 1970). In one study, Medvene (1969) found significant relations between perceived home atmosphere and vocational choice for 461 male graduate students in psychology. In another study (Medvene, 1970) he found that person-oriented students more frequently came from homes where there was acceptance of and emotional concentration on the child than non-person-oriented students. He further found that students in different specialties within psychology describe their family background in different terms. In previous research concerning Roe's theory few "within occupational" distinctions have been made, though there are data (De Coster and Rhode, 1972) indicating substantial intraoccupational differences in accountants' personality traits as a function of specialty and age. The failure to consider such differences could account for lack of support for Roe's theory, since the mixture of various personality types in one field might cancel the opportunity to observe the effects of personality on career.

Kriger (1972) applied a modified version of Roe's theory to the study of career versus homemaker orientation in women. Kriger reasoned that for women the most critical career decisions reside in career versus homemaking commitments. Thus, Kriger predicted that women in female-dominated occupations will report parents' attitudes toward them as overprotective, while women in male-dominated occupations will report recollections of more casual and accepting parental attitudes. To test these predictions, Kriger studied the responses of three groups of 22 women each on the Parent Attitude Research Instrument (PARI) and their need achievement scores as determined by the Edwards Personal Preference Schedule. The three groups of women represented homemakers, women in female-dominated occupations, and women in male-dominated occupations. Kriger observed that women in male-dominated occupations were highest in achievement need, followed by women in female-dominated occupations and then homemakers. She also found relationships between parental practices and career orientation; the field and level of a woman's occupation seem to be a function of her achievement orientation, which, in turn, was apparently related to her perception of the treatment she received from her parents. Kriger concluded that instead of developing an orientation toward or not toward people, parental treatment affects girls in a way that orients them toward homemaking or toward a career in that a controlling atmosphere leads to a homemaking orientation, while casual treatment leads toward a career.

Over the years since she first published her theory, Roe has recognized the limitations that a general series of statements about parent-child interactions have in predicting adult behavior. She and a collaborator (Roe and Siegelman, 1964) report an attempt to identify the role that needs play in the development of interests and to clarify the nature of childhood experiences that influence the kinds of interests adults acquire. In the design of the study, Roe and Siegelman made explicit statements about certain antecedent conditions (childhood experiences) which should lead to particular sets of subsequent events (adult interests). Three factors emerged from a factor analysis of childhood experiences that have been included as part of the antecedent conditions: loving-rejecting (LR), casual-demanding (CD), and overattention (O). In addition to these factors, eight group scores derived from a biographical inventory have been included as part of the antecedent and subsequent conditions. These group scores include stress (GS I), closeness to parents (GS II), early social activity (GS III), present socializing (GS IV), parents' interest and energy (GS V), dominance of parents (GS VI), present acceptance of parental values (GS VII), and identification with parents (GS VIII). This combination of parent-child relations and other childhood experiences results in a more sophisticated and sensitive formulation about the nature and the development of needs and the role that different combinations of experiences play in their development. Thus, both interactions of different parental styles and their intensity can be combined to replace the six categories of Roe's earlier theory.

The study conducted by Roe and Siegelman attempted to tie the three antecedent factors and relevant group scores to a series of subsequent events (adult activities). These events were assessed by the administration of several inventories and questionnaires to a sample of 24 male and 25 female engineers, 22 male and 23 female social workers, and 142 Harvard University seniors representing a wide variety of academic concentrations. The questionnaires included information about the subject's general interests, his occupational interests (assessed by the career chosen or followed, depending on his status as a student or professional, and by scores on the California Occupational Interest Inventory), and several measures of personality and orientation toward or not toward persons. The personality measure that was finally used in the study represented factor A (Cyclothymia-Schizothymia) of the Cattell 16 PF test.

The general hypotheses that Roe and Sielgelman investigated were related to the effect that early personal experiences have on adult interest patterns. They hypothesized that the degree of adult person orientation is a function of the extent and satisfaction of early personal relations. Using Roe and Siegelman's experimental terms, the hypothesis was that factors LR and O, and GS II and GS III (closeness to parents and early social activity) would correlate positively with the subsequent measures of person orientation. Roe and Siegelman also predicted that there would be some Ss who would be person-oriented as adults, although they had experienced early rejection. Finally, it was predicted that early nondemanding but adequately nurturant (casual) personal relations do not affect the degree of adult person orientation.

Roe and Siegelman conclude that their findings generally support their major hypotheses, although the results point up some surprising events. They found that factor O, taken separately for each parent, and factor LR for the mother correlate positively with subsequent measures of personal orientation. More significantly, they found that memories about early social experience (GS III) seemed to be the most important of the group scores in the relationship with later person orientation. Thus, the combination of LR plus O and GS III is the most effective set of antecedent conditions for producing later person orientation. As predicted, the factor CD (casual-demanding) was found to be unrelated to the degree of adult person orientation.

It was also found that occupational choice and present leisure interests are unrelated to the antecedent measures. This finding carries with it very significant implications for Roe's theory of vocational choice. It would suggest that while Roe's theory may be valid in accounting for the way that childhood experiences affect adult person orientation, the feature of person orientation itself might not be very important to vocational choice. Such a conclusion, however, is slightly tempered by the comparisons between engineers and social workers on the antecedent variables. There appear to be few differences between the early experiences of female engineers and social workers. More differences exist in antecedents for male engineers and social workers but, interestingly, the differences contradict those stated in the theory. Male social workers often had stressful or dissatisfying early personal experiences and seem to have entered social work or to have become person-oriented in an effort to discover what had been wrong with their relations with other people. The engineers, rather than rejecting people, merely seem to have been following their natural inclinations. Roe and Siegelman conclude that while occupational choice, at least for social workers and engineers, seems to be related to personality characteristics such as person or nonperson orientation, similar childhood experiences do not systematically lead to the same choice. Male social workers and female engineers appear to have had more stressful childhood experiences than male engineers and female social workers, and this seems to be in some way related to their later attempts to defy social vocational norms.

Roe and Siegelman drew several generalizations from the results of their study. First, they concluded that the amount of early social experience seems to be related to the amount of later person orientation. Second, they suggest that the hypothesis that particular kinds of early parent-child interactions will affect vocational choice in a certain way is too specific to be valid, since parental interaction with their children is not constant, and one parent will often behave in a manner that will offset the impact which the behavior of the other parent has on the child. Finally, they point out the importance that factors such as the labor market, an individual's socioeconomic background, his education and abilities, and chance may play in the choice of a specific vocation.

Such conclusions are not inconsistent with the observation that while person-nonperson orientations are influenced by early childhood experiences, such orientations seem remotely related to occupational choice. However, Roe and Siegelman's conclusions leave the status of theory in vocational selection in disarray, since their suggestion that vocational selection is largely a function of chance factors discourages further attempts to systematize the role that personal developmental factors play in vocational selection.

One final development deserves mention. Two recent attempts to devise interest inventories based on Roe's theory have been made. While these are still too new to be fully evaluated, they offer promise for the continued vitality of some of Roe's ideas. The first of these is the Hall Occupational Orientation Inventory, which is based on the development of psychological needs in occupational terms (Hall, 1968). The results of one study based on this inventory are encouraging (Hall, Shappell, and Tarrier, 1971). A second new instrument has been developed by Meir (described in Meir and Barak, 1973), which requires respondents to indicate their preferences for occupational titles by field and level according to the Roe classification. The result is a simply derived set of data describing the degree to which a student's interests are focused by level and field, thus indicating to the counselor the nature of the counseling task required by the individual. A companion instrument based on occupationally oriented course titles without the levels component is also available.

*Evaluation.* Several general shortcomings in the research methodology are apparent. The data upon which judgments were made about the nature of early parental behaviors toward children were essentially unreliable. To base what is the crux of the research design on retrospective data, whether reported through interviews or, worse, through short, unvalidated questionnaires is highly risky. Furthermore, the samples studied were either very small or included occupational groupings of such a specific nature as to make generalization almost impossible. Other deficiencies exist. Many of the studies used students as the sample and, without making it explicit, were really using occupational preferences and selection rather than occupational attainment as the criterion against which early experiences were compared.

Finally, none of the investigations adequately attempted to handle the problem of parental inconsistencies in child-rearing patterns and the effect on subsequent personality development and vocational choice. To fail to do so ignores the confounding effects that differences between parents in child-rearing attitudes have on personality development, as well as ignoring effects of changing parental attitudes toward child-rearing practices as the children grow older. These two factors alone are important variables for study within a theoretical context stressing childhood and parental practices. Despite these shortcomings, the evidence is very strong against the likelihood that Roe's theory as originally proposed is an adequate representation of the crucial features of vocational development.

One major modification in the theory could be worth exploring. It has been suggested that early childhood experiences, somewhat along the lines mentioned by Roe, could be one source of influence on the development of cognitive styles. These styles, in turn, may be related to a variety of personality functions, which in their own right, could have some impact on many behaviors, among them those associated with career development. In other words, Roe may have been on the right track in trying to relate early experience to personality development and vocational choice, but the variables she chose to emphasize are too diffuse and the gaps between early experience, personality development, and vocational choice too great. The introduction of numerous intervening variables into this chain of events could infuse new life into the theory and make it more testable (Osipow, 1970).

## STATUS

### The Implications for Counseling

Is Roe's theory of vocational choice useful in suggesting counseling procedures? Roe makes no explicit recommendations, in either her original theoretical statement or her later revised statement, that are relevant to counseling. Despite her failure to do so, however, it is possible to infer certain implications. Her first theoretical statement has more potential impact for counseling since it carries with it a strong statement that vocational choice is closely related to personality characteristics developed during early childhood. Her revised statement of theory has fewer implications for counseling practice, since the relationship between personality factors, their manner of development, and vocational choice seems less clear as a result of research. Roe and Siegelman's conclusion that chance plays a greater role in career choice than suggested in the earlier theoretical statement reduces the contribution counseling may make to career development.

Considering the early formulation alone, it can be seen that if the needs structure of an individual is related to his vocational choice in the sense that he selects his vocation with an eye toward the satisfaction of his needs, then counseling would logically be aimed at helping the individual effectively understand his needs, identify occupations in which his needs can best be satisfied, and, if necessary, help him overcome circumstances which might have thwarted the development of his needs structure. This last feature deserves elaboration. For individuals whose background has caused their needs hierarchies to halt at a relatively low level, counseling might resemble psychotherapy aimed at reliving and learning to understand childhood patterns of gratification. Thus, if an individual was the child of overdemanding parents and found that his needs structure developed in a way that led him to seek approval from other significant people, counseling might be directed to help him in understanding the stunting of his needs, developing higher-order needs, and acquiring the techniques to satisfy such needs.

Translating Roe's theory into counseling procedures for a typical vocational choice case results in a series of activities oriented toward the identification of a student's psychological needs structure and then matching the resulting hierarchy of needs with those offered by various occupations. Thus, a counselor would assess his client's needs through interview procedures or some relevant inventory.

He might than assess the student's family background to determine whether or not the individual has had a reasonably normal family background in terms of the development of his needs. If the interviews reveal that the student was at an appropriate (to his background) point in the development of his needs, two choices would be open to the counselor. He could try to help the student evaluate the potential of various fields for the satisfaction of his current needs, or he could try to help the student further evolve his needs hierarchy through interview procedures. These procedures would probably emphasize the client's perceptions of his parents' attitudes toward him, the kinds of gratifications they provided him, and the conditions they imposed for gratification. Thus, the student might become aware of forces in his background that stunted or misguided his developing needs system and correct it accordingly. Unfortunately, however, the theory fails to explicate the interview procedures with which to accomplish such a task.

What procedures would the revised theory suggest for counseling? As a result of Roe and Siegelman's conclusion that economic and chance factors are important, the revised position would logically place more emphasis on occupational information designed to help the student make the most expeditious use of his abilities. Needs would not be ignored, however, but would be considered more in terms of satisfaction within an acceptable socioeconomic framework. Since Roe and Siegelman concluded that person-nonperson orientation is not directly related to vocational choice, less emphasis would be placed on that aspect of needs. In neither the original not revised formulation, however, is counseling practice accorded much concern.

## Evaluation

Several general observations may be made about the overall tone of Roe's theory. The model possesses a very strong psychoanalytic tone, which is modified somewhat by the introduction of Maslow's hierarchy of needs. The theory has stimulated considerable research activity. The results of most of the research, however, have not supported the specifics of Roe's model. What remains after attempts at empirical validation is a general statement that individuals are either person- or nonperson-oriented in their interests and that their orientation influences the choice of their vocation. Roe and Siegelman's study, however, generates some doubt about even this mild conclusion.

Roe's propositions concerning the effects of parent-child interactions on the development of needs hierarchies—which in turn influence, among other behaviors, vocational choices—possess several ambiguities which contribute to the inability of investigators to validate the theory empirically. Assume, for example, that the parental acceptance of children's behavior represents a normal and desirable interaction between children and their parents. If all parent-child interactions were normal and Roe's theory correct, we would eventually have only restricted classes of vocational choice. Do most scientists come from families that deemphasize interpersonal relations? Such is the implication of Roe's theory. Roe and Siegelman (1964) found, however, that male engineers seemed to be following their natural inclinations rather than choosing engineering as a reaction to parental treatment.

Another difficulty arising from Roe's propositions about the impact of parent-child interactions on vocational choice lies in the impurity of parental behavior styles. Parents do not uniformly reject or overprotect or love their children. What are the effects of such mixtures on children's needs? What are the effects of differences between the parents themselves on the child's developing needs hierarchy? One parent might be loving and the other overdemanding. Although in the revised theory (Roe and Siegelman, 1964) some serious attempts were made to resolve this dilemma, the results are not entirely satisfactory. Finally, parental attitudes themselves are not likely to be constant across the various stages of childhood development. How old are children when parental behaviors began to lose their impact on the development of needs? The age must be young or still another parent-child variable confounds the predictions of the theory.

How does the theory stand in terms of fulfilling the requirements of a desirable theory? Certainly, the model is comprehensive. It includes in its scope not only vocational decision-making but general personality development as well. In fact, the later version of the model is described in terms that make it seem more like a fragment of a personality theory than a theory of vocational choice. The theory rates well on the feature of explicitness. Roe carefully states propositions and the behavioral implications of each proposition. Furthermore, the propositions are logical and suggest new ways of interpreting and predicting vocational behavior. She traces in detail the features of normal personality development which lead to appropriate vocational selection. She suggests clearly the circumstances under which personality development will become misdirected and result in inappropriate vocational choice.

Is the theory operational? The numerous attempts to test the theory make it appear to be operational, but the ambiguous results of the research suggest that the theory may not be as open to testing as it might appear. The inability of investigators to put the theory to a rigorous test is probably the result of the ambiguities in Roe's theory discussed above and partly the result of the difficulty of adequately assessing parent-child interactions many years after they have occurred. Are children's perceptions of parental attitudes toward them enough to influence personality development to the extent Roe suggests? If so, then the accuracy of recollections may be unimportant since the perceptual recall might be the main factor influencing a person's style of life. Such a question is not easily resolved even through the use of longitudinal studies.

The theory has little to say about procedures useful in vocational counseling. If one were to judge the adequacy of the theory only on those procedures the theory explicitly recommended, the model would be inadequate, since no procedures are suggested. Inferences about techniques that can be drawn from the general nature of the theory suggest few procedures different from other, less systematic approaches to counseling. ⌐The theory presents no goals for counseling, no recommendations with respect to useful or suitable counseling techniques or procedures, and no descriptions of desirable behaviors or sequences of behavior.⌐ Some inferences might be made concerning the origin of deviant vocational patterns, but no remedial measures are recommended. Consequently, there is nothing built into the theory that would lead to evaluation studies. The only likely goals that are suggested by the theory are that counseling should help an individual identify his basic needs, remove blocks retarding the development of his needs hierarchy, and develop techniques to satisfy his needs. No procedures to accomplish these ends are recommended.

Roe's model of vocational choice contains many of the elements of a good theory. While Roe's theory was not the first explicit attempt to develop a theoretical understanding of career behavior, her theory has come as close to dealing comprehensively with the topic as any other. Furthermore, Roe was one of the first theorists to include in detail the intuitively appealing notion of the role that personality plays in vocational behavior. That research provides little empirical support for the theory does not detract from the appeal the theory has in the abstract. It may be that while the propositions of Roe's theory possess significant theoretical validity, they encompass so little of the actual variance involved in career development that they fail to possess practical significance. Unless it is possible to develop the premise that parental treatment influences some stream of intervening variables (such as cognitive style), it is difficult to see how the theory can prove viable. The theory is somewhat useful at the present stage of theoretical development in vocational choice, but has few applied implications in its current state and little empirical support. Consequently, without a major revision it is not likely to have a growing impact on vocational counseling in future years.

# REFERENCES

Appleton, G. M., and Hansen, J. C. Parent-child relations, need-nurturance, and vocational orientation. *Personnel and Guidance Journal*, 1969, *47*, 794-799.

Brunkan, R. J. Perceived parental attitudes and parental identification in relation to field of vocational choice. *Journal of Counseling Psychology*, 1965, *12*, 39-47.

Brunkan, R. J., and Crites, J. O. An inventory to measure the parental attitude variable in Roe's theory of vocational choice. *Journal of Counseling Psychology*, 1964, *11*, 3-11.

Byers, A. P., Forrest, G. G., and Zaccaria, J. S. Recalled early parent-child relations, adult needs, and occupational choice. *Journal of Counseling Psychology*, 1968, *15*, 324-328.

Crites, J. O. An interpersonal relations scale for occupational groups. *Journal of Applied Psychology*, 1962, *46*, 87-90.

De Coster, D. T., and Rhode, J. G. Analysis of certified public accounting subgroup and accounting student personality traits using the California Personality Inventory. *Journal of Vocational Behavior*, 1972, *2*, 155-162.

Green, L. B., and Parker, H. J. Parental influence upon adolescents' occupational choice: a test of an aspect of Roe's theory. *Journal of Counseling Psychology*, 1965, *12*, 379-383.

Grigg, A. E. Childhood experience and parental attitudes: a test of Roe's hypothesis. *Journal of Counseling Psychology*, 1959, *6*, 153-156.

Hagen, D. Careers and family atmosphere: a test of Roe's theory. *Journal of Counseling Psychology*, 1960, *7*, 251-256.

Hall, L. G. *Hall Occupational Orientation Inventory*. Chicago: Follett, 1968.

Hall, L. G., Shappell, D. L., and Tarrier, R. B. An application of Roe's vocational choice model: inventory, counseling goals and strategies. *The School Counselor*, 1971, *19*, 43-48.

Jones, K. J. Occupational preference and social orientation. *Personnel and Guidance Journal*, 1965, *43*, 574-579.

Kinnane, J. F., and Pable, M. W. Family background and work value orientation. *Journal of Counseling Psychology*, 1962, *9*, 320-325.

Kriger, Sara Finn. Need achievement and perceived parental child-rearing attitudes of career women and homemakers. *Journal of Vocational Behavior*, 1972, *2*, 419-433.

Levine, S. Occupation and personality: relationship between the social factors of the job and human orientation. *Personnel and Guidance Journal*, 1963, *41*, 602-605.

Maslow, A. H. *Motivation and personality*. New York: Harper & Row, 1954.

Medvene, A. M. Occupational choice of graduate students in psychology as a function of early parent-child interactions. *Journal of Counseling Psychology*, 1969, *16*, 385-389.

Medvene, A. M. Person-oriented and non-person-oriented occupations in psychology. *Journal of Counseling Psychology*, 1970, *17*, 243-246.

Meir, E. I. Empirical test of Roe's structure of occupations and an alternative structure. *Journal of Counseling Psychology*, 1970, *17*, 41-48.

Meir, E. I. The structure of occupations by interests – a smallest space analysis. *Journal of Vocational Behavior*, 1973, *3*, 21-31.

Meir, E. I., and Barak, A. A simple instrument for measuring vocational interests based on Roe's classification of occupations. *Journal of Vocational Behavior*, 1973, *3*, in press.

Murphy, G. *Personality: a bio-social approach to origins and structure*. New York: Harper & Row, 1947.

Osipow, S. H. Consistency of occupational choice and Roe's classification of occupations. *Vocational Guidance Quarterly*, 1966, *14*, 285-286.

Osipow, S. H. Some cognitive aspects of career development. In Evans, E. (Ed.), *Adolescents: readings in behavior and development*. Hinsdale, Ill.: Dryden, 1970.

Roe, Anne. Analysis of group Rorschachs of biologists. *Journal of Projective Techniques*, 1949, *13*, 25-43. (a)

Roe, Anne. Psychological examinations of eminent biologists. *Journal of Consulting Psychology*, 1949, *13*, 225-246. (b)

Roe, Anne. Analysis of group Rorschachs of physical scientists. *Journal of Projective Techniques*, 1950, *14*, 385-398.

Roe, Anne. A psychological study of eminent biologists. *Psychological Monographs*, 1951, *65*, No. 14 (Whole No. 331). (a)

Roe, Anne. A psychological study of eminent physical scientists. *Genetic Psychology Monograph*, 1951, *43*, 121-239. (b)

Roe, Anne. A study of imagery in research scientists. *Journal of Personality*, 1951, *19*, 459-470. (c)

Roe, Anne. Psychological tests of research scientists. *Journal of Consulting Psychology*, 1951, *15*, 492-495. (d)

Roe, Anne. Analysis of group Rorschachs of psychologists and anthropologists. *Journal of Projective Techniques*, 1952, *16*, 212-224. (a)

Roe, Anne. Group Rorschachs of university faculties. *Journal of Consulting Psychology*, 1952, *16*, 18-22. (b)

Roe, Anne. A psychological study of eminent psychologists and anthropologists and a comparison with biological and physical scientists. *Psychological Monographs*, 1953, *67*, No. 2 (Whole No. 352).

Roe, Anne. *The psychology of occupations*. New York: Wiley, 1956.

Roe, Anne. Early determinants of vocational choice. *Journal of Counseling Psychology*, 1957, *4*, 212-217.

Roe, Anne, Hubbard, W. D., Hutchinson, T., and Bateman, R. Studies of occupational history. Part I: Job changes and the classification of occupations. *Journal of Counseling Psychology*, 1966, *13*, 387-393.

Roe, Anne, and Hutchinson, T. Groups of the Roe system. *Journal of Counseling Psychology*, 1969, *16*, 390-395.

Roe, Anne, and Klos, D. Occupational classification. *The Counseling Psychologist*, 1969, *1*, 84-92.

Roe, Anne, and Siegelman, M. The origin of interests. *The APGA Inquiry Series*, No. 1, Washington, D.C.: American Personnel and Guidance Association, 1964.

Super, D. E., and Overstreet, Phoebe I. *The vocational maturity of ninth grade boys.* New York: Bureau of Publications, Teachers College, Columbia University, 1960.

Switzer, D. K., Grigg, A. E., Miller, J. B., and Young, R. K. Early experiences and occupational choice: a test of Roe's hypothesis. *Journal of Counseling Psychology*, 1962, *9*, 45-48.

Utton, A. C. Recalled parent-child relations as determinants of vocational choice. *Journal of Counseling Psychology*, 1962, *9*, 49-53.

# 2

# Holland's Career Typology Theory of Vocational Behavior

Holland's theory of vocational selection represents a marriage between two streams of thought in vocational psychology, one of them popular and the other novel. The popular conception that Holland employs in his theory is an elaboration of the hypothesis that career choices represent an extension of personality and an attempt to implement broad personal behavioral styles in the context of one's life work. The novel feature that Holland introduces is the notion that people project their views of themselves and the world of work onto occupational titles. By the simple procedure of allowing individuals to express their preference for, or feelings against, a particular list of occupational titles, Holland assigns people to modal personal styles which have theoretical implications for personality and vocational choice.

Holland's conception of career development grew from his experiences with people involved in making career decisions. He observed that most people view the vocational world in terms of occupational stereotypes. Instead of concluding that such stereotyping confuses people and causes vocational counselors extra difficulty, Holland turned the stereotyping process to his advantage by assuming that it is based on the individual's experience with work, thus being based on reality and possessing a high degree of accuracy and utility. Holland hypothesized that where the individual possesses little knowledge about a particular vocation, the stereotype he holds reveals information about him, much in the manner a projective test presumably exposes personality dynamics. Consequently, Holland set out to develop a list of occupational titles that would be useful as a device onto which a person could project his preferred life style.

# THE THEORY

## Occupational Environments

Holland's original theoretical statement (1959) was somewhat modified as a result of his own research testing the theory (1962; 1966a; 1973). In the original statement, Holland proposed that a finite number of work environments exists within the American society. These environments are the realistic (farmers, truck drivers, and so on), the investigative (chemists, biologists), the social (social workers, teachers), the conventional (bookkeepers, bank tellers), the enterprising (salesmen, politicians), and the artistic (musicians, artists).

## The Developmental Hierarchy

The developmental hierarchy is represented by the individual's adjustment to the six occupational environments. Everyone is required to adjust to each of the environments and develop certain skills with reference to the setting. The six types of adjustment stemming from the developmental hierarchy represent major life styles and patterns of relationships between the individual and his world. The most typical way an individual responds to his environment is, of course, his modal personal orientation. The six orientations were referred to by the same names as the occupational environments in earlier versions of the theory, but were renamed by Holland later (1962; 1971). The original names are in parentheses in the following descriptions of the orientations.

The *Realistic* (Motoric) orientation is characterized by aggressive behavior, interest in activities requiring motor coordination, skill and physical strength, and masculinity. People oriented toward this role prefer "acting out" problems; they avoid tasks involving interpersonal and verbal skills and seek concrete rather than abstract problem situations. They score high on traits such as concreteness, physical strength, and masculinity, and low on social skill and sensitivity.

The *Investigative* (Intellectual) persons' main characteristics are thinking rather than acting, organizing and understanding rather than dominating or persuading, and asociability rather than sociability. These people prefer to avoid close interpersonal contact, though the quality of their avoidance seems different from their Realistic colleagues.

The *Social* (Supportive) people seem to satisfy their needs for attention in a teaching or therapeutic situation. In sharp contrast to the Investigative and Realistic people, Social people seek close interpersonal situations and are skilled in their interpersonal relations, while they avoid situations where they might be required to engage in intellectual problem solving or use extensive physical skills.

The *Conventional* (Conforming) style is typified by a great concern for rules and regulations, great self-control, subordination of personal needs, and strong identification with power and status. This kind of person prefers structure and order and thus seeks interpersonal and work situations where structure is readily available.

The *Enterprising* (Persuasive) people are verbally skilled, but rather than use their verbal skills to support others as the Social types do, they use them for manipulating and dominating people. They are concerned about power and status, as are the Conventional people, but differ in that they aspire to the power and status while the Conventionals honor others for it.

The *Artistic* (Esthetic) orientation manifests strong self-expression and relations with other people indirectly through artistic expression. Such people dislike structure, rather prefer tasks emphasizing physical skills or interpersonal interactions. They are intraceptive and asocial much like the Investigatives, but differ in that they are more feminine than masculine, show relatively little self-control, and express emotion more readily than most people.

### The Role and History of Developmental Hierarchies

Holland does not explicitly discuss the manner in which these modal orientations develop. Presumably, the development of the styles corresponds to the general notions surrounding personality development of other theorists, that is, the personality at a given point in time is a result of genetic and environmental influences. Such a statement is far too general to be of value in understanding personality development, particularly for counselors who may be involved in tasks of correcting misdirected development. Holland does, however, indicate the way in which these modal orientations influence vocational behavior once the orientations have been clearly established. If one orientation is clearly dominant over the others, the individual will seek an occupational environment that corresponds to the orientation.

The practical, hard-headed young male will thus choose to become an engineer and the aggressive, verbal, ambitious boy will easily decide that law is the career for him. If two or more orientations are the same or nearly the same in their strength, the individual will vacillate in his selection of an occupational environment. A girl characterized by a mixture of detached thought about problems, avoidance of close interpersonal relations, a tendency to organize combined with desire to exert self-control and considerable desire to be emotionally expressive may one day choose to be a biologist and next decide that the graphic arts are most suitable for her. If environmental factors interfere with the implementation of the first clear-cut orientation, then the individual will seek an occupational environment appropriate to his second strongest orientation. A student blocked in his attempts to implement his Investigative choice of oceanography because his financial resources will not support him through the necessary graduate training might well select the field of mechanical engineering representing his second major orientation, the Realistic. However, if the hierarchy of orientations is not well ordered beyond the first one, then vacillation in the selection of an occupational environment will occur, just as if the first two orientations were not clearly different in their strength.

## The Level Hierarchy

The modal orientation exerts a clear influence on the particular occupational environment an individual chooses or whether or not he experiences indecision. The question of the level within an occupational environment that the individual chooses is a function of several other variables, entitled the level hierarchy. The level hierarchy is defined in terms of the individual's intelligence and his self-evaluations. Intelligence is inferred from relevant tests and presumably, for the purposes of this theory, has the usual social and genetic antecedents. Generally, the gross manipulations of this variable are outside of the control of the person making the vocational choices. Gross misperceptions of intelligence are possible, but would probably enter into the other half of the level hierarchy equation, self-evaluation. The self-evaluation, which might operationally correspond to a scale such as the Occupational Level scale of the Strong Vocational Interest Blank, is itself a function of the person's life history, such as his social status, his economic condition, his level of education, and his health. It seems, however, that when defined in this way, the factors which contribute to the development of a person's self-evaluations are not independent of the factors which go toward influencing his intelligence, and vice versa.

## Interaction between Level and Developmental Hierarchies

The process then, is something like this: a person gradually evolves a modal personality orientation which leads him, at the appropriate points in time, to make educational decisions which have implications for a specific occupational environment. As he takes steps to implement his decisions, the level hierarchy that he has developed over the years leads him to gravitate toward a career within the appropriate occupational environment that is at a skill level equivalent to his abilities and achievements. The adequacy of his decisions and the amount of difficulty he encounters in the process of making them are related to his knowledge about himself and the world of work. If he has a vague idea of what occupational environments exist, he will have difficulty in selecting one; if he has contradictory self-evaluations, he will vacillate in the level he selects.

The smoothness of his decisions is affected by the clarity of the structure of his developmental hierarchy. Thus, if life circumstances (unspecified by the theory) result in an uncrystallized developmental hierarchy, difficulty will be encountered in selecting an occupational environment, and the individual will change from one environment to another. Other environmental factors will also influence the ease with which the selection of an occupational environment exists, but these are more extra-individual than those already mentioned. Some examples are family factors, such as aspirations and occupational history, which might result in pressures toward a particular occupational environment; financial resources; general economic conditions in society; and educational opportunities.

Others of a similar sort would exert some influence on the content of the environment eventually chosen.

Not only does the particular dominant personal orientation influence the career choice a person makes, but the *pattern* of the orientations within the individual's hierarchy exerts a significant influence. That is, two students with the same major orientation will choose similar fields, but the stability of their choice is a function of the order of the other five orientations in their personal hierarchy. If the order is consistent, the choice is likely to be stable, all other factors held constant; if the pattern is inconsistent for that occupational environment, then the choice is likely to be unstable. For example, a research engineer with the order Realistic, Enterprising, Conventional, Social, Artistic, and Investigative is likely to be less stable in the pursuit of his research specialty than another research engineer whose hierarchy is Realistic, Investigative, Artistic, Social, Enterprising, and Conventional. The latter would represent what might be a more typical pattern for research engineers.

Holland originally did not elaborate upon what patterns are typical for certain fields and what patterns are not. Presumably, that is an empirical question and can be answered with respect to patterns indicating stability within the large category of occupational environments, or the more specific category of particular occupations within certain occupational environments. The question of typical versus atypical ordering assumes further importance since the order affects an individual's success in his chosen field as well as his stability, according to the theory. Recent publications of Holland's (e.g., *The Job Finder*) in connection with the *Self-Directed Search* do present pattern data.

In addition to success, Holland proposes that typical patterns of hierarchies for an occupational environment reflect the intensity of the choice and thus provide some predictive data about the potential persistence of the individual in that area. The less typical the pattern of the hierarchy, the less intense the choice, and consequently, the less persistent the person is likely to be in his efforts to implement it. This feature, however, is not clearly distinguishable from stability.

### Other Influences on Career Choice

In addition to the concept of self-evaluation, which, it will be recalled, was one of the two critical variables contributing to the individual's level hierarchy, Holland introduced a concept known as *self-knowledge*. Self-knowledge refers to the amount and accuracy of information an individual has about himself. It differs from self-evaluation, which refers to the worth the individual attributes to himself. However, these two constructs are not clearly differentiated. They seem to be highly interdependent; they might well refer to two parts of the same phenomenon. Holland apparently introduces these two separately to permit himself to predict the adequacy of vocational choice for people who have self-evaluations based closely on accurate self-knowledge, as opposed to those whose vocational choices are partially based on self-evaluations founded on inadequate self-knowledge.

Holland states that the adequacy of occupational choice is largely a function of the adequacy of self-knowledge and occupational knowledge. The greater the amount and accuracy of information the individual has about each, the more adequate is his choice. Such a conception is reminiscent of the early, and still useful, trait-factor notion of round pegs fitting best in round holes. He explicitly includes other important environmental features, such as social pressures and opportunities available in society. His theory, however, does not assume that these influence people in random ways. Rather, he suggests that people with well-structured developmental hierarchies will be less affected by outside pressures than people possessing ambiguous personal hierarchies. Such a notion is an extension of his analysis concerning the effects of the hierarchy pattern on the stability and intensity of the choice and success the individual has in implementing it. He also expresses the importance that social pressures in early adolescence and childhood experiences with parents (similar to Roe, 1957) have in influencing vocational choices. Since such influences occur before the stable hierarchy of personal orientation develops, these experiences are likely to influence the shape of the hierarchy rather than influence choices after the hierarchy is developed. These two early experiences are as close as Holland comes to explaining how personal orientations actually develop.

# RESEARCH

Almost all the early attempts to validate the theory through research conducted by Holland and his associates used a population of National Merit Scholarship finalists, but recent efforts have studied more representative groups. Holland's approach to the study of vocational selection within his theoretical framework is very comprehensive. His research has frequently been longitudinal, and he has attempted to assess a wide variety of personal, family, social, and achievement correlates that are pertinent to his theoretical construction. A basic feature in the research has been the idea that occupational titles possess a considerable amount of stimulus value to people and that these titles, while stereotypic, are congruent with reality. More important, Holland proposes to use responses of Like versus Dislike to occupational titles as projective data about the respondent on the assumption, probably valid, that vocational preferences represent more than "what interests" the individual, that they represent a major facet of his personality (Holland, 1961). Certainly, the history of the use of the SVIB and Kuder Preference Record (KPR) leads to such an inference.

The Vocational Preference Inventory (VPI) (Holland, 1958), actually developed *prior* to the theory, is a personality inventory very intimately tied to vocational interests. Until the recent development of the *Self-Directed Search*, the VPI has been the primary tool for the measurement of the personality types. The inventory consists of 300 occupational titles to which the subject is instructed to express his interest or disinterest. In an early form of the test the items were scored in terms of several scales: physical activity, intellectuality, responsibility, conformity, verbal activity, emotionality, reality orientation, and acquiescence. These early scales were developed on an *a priori* basis. Later, by statistical methods assessing internal consistency, six additional scales were added: control, aggressiveness, masculinity-femininity, status, heterosexuality, and infrequency. Further research and validation finally resulted in a system that included ten personality scales (physical activity, intellectuality, responsibility, conformity, verbal activity, emotionality, control, aggressiveness, masculinity-femininity, and status) and three response set scales (infrequency, acquiescence, and number omitted).

In Holland's theory, only some of the scales apply to the modal personal orientations. These are physical activity for Realistic, intellectuality for the Investigative type, responsibility for the Social type, conformity for the Conventional, verbal activity for the Enterprising, and emotional for the Artistic (Holland, 1962). In other research validating the VPI, Holland (1960) has studied its relationship to the Cattell Sixteen Personality Factor Questionnaire (16 PF). The resulting intercorrelations between the VPI and the 16 PF suggest that the VPI possesses sufficient concurrent validity to be of use.

**Design of Research**

*Samples.* Holland's research on his theory is characterized by observing members of several large samples whose behavior is studied by means of multiple observations over moderate to long time spans. Students participating in the National Merit Scholarship program have served as one such population in the research. Generally, the procedure has been to select a sample randomly, frequently the size of one-sixth of the students in the population, though sometimes a smaller fraction, and to enlist their cooperation in the research. Usable returns from such procedures have ranged from about 84 percent, at most, to about 66 percent, at least. Holland's work has been strengthened by his use of several samples in his investigations. Since considerable duplication exists in his design of studies, the result is an unusual amount of replication of his findings.

*Instruments.* The key instrument in Holland's early research is the Vocational Preference Inventory (VPI), which was described earlier. Holland has used this device in several studies to assign to his subjects personal orientations which served as independent variables. After scoring the VPI on the six scales relevant to personal orientations, Holland took the scale on which the highest score was earned, called that the high point code, and assigned the subject to the appropriate group. Where the VPI was employed in his research, such a procedure was generally used, though there is one exception. In studying the effects of the patterns of orientations, Holland did attend to the rest of the code beyond the high point (Holland, 1962).

Holland did use other approaches to the assignment of subjects to personal types. In one study, he assigned subjects to personal orientation categories by using their scores on six selected scales of the Strong Vocational Interest Blank, each of which discriminated the VPI scores most efficiently for one of the six personal orientations. He used the aviator scale to correspond to the Realistic orientation, the physicist scale for the Investigative, the social science teacher scale for Social, accountant scale for Conventional, sales manager for Enterprising, and musician for Artistic (Holland, 1963). In a third study, Holland and Nichols (1964) assigned their subjects to one of the six personal orientations by classifying the students' initial major field preference during the senior year into one of the six types.

In his search for relationships between the VPI and other variables and for correlates of the personal orientations, Holland and his collaborators have employed an extremely wide variety of tests, inventories, and questionnaires. Some of these instruments are standard and well known in the psychological literature, while many were custom-made instruments developed by the National Merit Scholarship Corporation for use in studying the Merit Scholars. Among the instruments used were the Cattell Sixteen Personality Factor Questionnaire; the Gough Differential Reaction Schedule; selected scales from Barron's Inventory of Personal Philosophy; selected items from Strodtbeck's Value Scale entitled the Mastery Scale; a Deferred Gratification Scale developed from the National Merit Student Survey; the Ghisellie Self-Description Inventory; the Creative Activities Scale, based on data from the National Merit Student Survey related to activities and hobbies requiring or exhibiting unusual originality; the Parental Attitude Research Instrument (PARI); student self-evaluations on selected traits; fathers' ratings on goals and traits they value in their offspring; family background information; the Minnesota Multiphasic Personality Inventory (MMPI); selected scales (Femininity, Socialization, and Social Presence) of the California Psychological Inventory (CPI); and numerous National Merit questionnaires which revealed information concerning student daydreams, activities, and personality tendencies.

### General Correlates of the Personal Orientation

Holland has published numerous reports of the findings of the behavioral, educational, and vocational correlates of the personal orientations. The first report (Holland, 1962) is very comprehensive, and since the students were assigned to a personal orientation on the basis of their high point code on the VPI, we shall use the results of that report as the base line of correlates of the personal orientations and add the results of the other studies which used different assessment techniques at a later point in the discussion.

The descriptions of modal personal orientations are based on empirical findings. Because of some sex differences in response to the tests and vocational plans, Holland did not summarize his findings for males and females combined, but summarized them for males only. The personality correlates of the girls in his sample are similar to those of the boys, however.

*Personal traits.* Table 2.1 summarizes the characteristics of the six personal orientations reported by Holland in his first major study. Examination of Table 2.1 reveals considerable similarity between the characteristics of the various personal orientations. While it is difficult to see patterns in those findings, there is some basis for grouping the Realistic and Investigative students together; the Social, Enterprising, and Conventional, as a second group; and the Artistic as a type by itself. Such a grouping does not suggest that the types do not cross these lines, however. Thus, the Realistic types were similar to the Intellectual type in personality characteristics, different from the Investigatives in their hobbies and activities, were mainly similar to the Artistic and Investigative in the factors that most influenced their vocational decision. The Social and Enterprising types and to some extent the Conventional types had personality scores similar to each other, but typically they had different interests and hobbies and only partially similar self-evaluations. Where the background of the Social type particularly differed from those of the Conventional and Enterprising is in fathers' ambitions for their sons.

Other features enter into these categories. The Investigative types were less likely to change their college majors, while the Social types were most likely to do so. The Enterprising were the second most likely to change the direction of their college studies. The aspirations and daydreams of the students of the various types also differed, as one would expect they would. The Artistic and Investigative types aspired to graduate study and the Investigative subjects engaged in daydreams reflecting learning and achievement content, whereas the Social types daydreamed about helping other people and the Enterprising wove fantasies about money and status.

In his four-year follow-up study, based on selected scores on the SVIB (which were mentioned earlier in this chapter), Holland (1963) found substantially the same characteristics as in his earlier study based on the high point VPI codes. Some supplementary characteristics were found, however. The Realistic subjects again rated themselves low on leadership, originality, achievement drive, sociability, expressiveness, and perseverance, while they gave themselves high ratings on athletic ability and practical-mindedness. The Investigative group scored high on originality (their earlier self-ratings on originality were high), and rated themselves low on leadership, popularity, achievement drive, sociability, aggressiveness, practicality, expressiveness, self-confidence, self-understanding, and perseverance. The Social rated themselves high on the same traits as in the earlier study, and in addition their ratings on popularity, dependability, self-understanding, and perseverance were high in the later study. The Conventional subjects rated themselves high on dependability and neatness in addition to the high traits reported in the earlier study and low on originality. The Enterprising subjects' self-rating added originality, popularity, drive to achieve, expressive-

TABLE 2.1. Correlates of Personality Orientation

| Type | Heroes | Personality Characteristics | Self-rating | Activities | Father's Values | Mother's Attitudes | Vocational Influences |
|---|---|---|---|---|---|---|---|
| R | Byrd Edison | unsociable, mature, masculine, extroverted, persistent | leadership (low) popularity (low) expressiveness (low) | experimental hobbies, industrial arts, fishing, hunting, bowling | ambitious | unsociable, suppressive | self-examination |
| I | Curie Darwin | unsociable, masculine, radical, self-sufficient, dedicated to scholarly work, introverted, persistent | originality (high) cheerfulness (low) | chemistry, general science, chess | curious | permissive, passive | self-examination |
| S | Churchill Schweitzer | sociable, cheerful, adventurous, conservative, feminine, dominant, dependent, responsive | leadership, speaking skills, sociability, practical-minded (all of these high) | social studies, history, school offices, debate, church work, foreign languages | self-controlled | not reported | other persons |
| C | Baruch | conforming, masculine, conservative, dependent, playful, extroverted, responsible | popularity, neatness, conservatism, practical-minded, cheerfulness (all of these high) | cards, bowling | happy and well adjusted | authoritarian | not reported |
| E | Ford Churchill | sociable, dominant, cheerful, adventurous, conservative, dependent, impulsive, non-intellectual, playful, extroverted | leadership, sociability, aggressiveness, practical-minded, cheerful, self-understanding (all of these high) | business subjects, motoring, movies, bowling | popular, happy, and well adjusted | authoritarian | other people |
| A | Picasso Eliot | immature, effeminate, paranoid, introverted | self-control, independence, expressiveness, self-understanding (all of these high) | English, drama, music, art, school publications, debate, photography, foreign languages | curious, independent | less authoritarian than other mothers | self-examination |

Source: From J. L. Holland, Some explorations of a theory of vocational choice: I. one- and two-year longitudinal studies, *Psychological Monographs*, 1962, 76, 26.

ness, self-confidence, and perseverance to their earlier estimation of their strengths. Finally, the Artistic students rated themselves low on leadership, popularity, sociability, aggressiveness, neatness, conservatism, practical-mindedness, cheerfulness, and self-confidence and evaluated themselves high on originality and scholarship.

In a major longitudinal investigation of more than 3500 male college students from 28 colleges and universities, Holland (1968a) accumulated extensive data describing competencies by type. The Realistic males possessed technical competencies and rated themselves high on mechanical abilities; the Investigative males, scientific competencies and high self-ratings in mathematics; the Social students had social-educational competencies and rated themselves high in their understandings of others; the Conventional had high business competencies and high self-ratings in conservatism; the Enterprising had high leadership competencies and self-ratings in popularity; and the Artistic had high artistic competencies and self-ratings in originality. These competencies and self-ratings seem generally consistent with the theoretical implications of the various types.

*Hobbies and extracurricular activities.* Once again, Holland (1962) found some sex differences in his sample. Males varied in their hobbies and activities according to their high point code, while females varied systematically only with respect to their activities. The Realistic code subjects were active in sports, student government, and scouting; the Investigative subjects were not unusually active in any activities. The Social were active in religious and community service activities, the Conventional in theatricals, musical groups, and student government; the Enterprising were involved in sports and community service, and the Artistic in debate, theater, and school newspapers. Hobbies were arts, crafts, domestic arts, and photography for the Realistic; collecting, reading, study, and scientific projects for the Investigative; domestic arts for the Social; collecting, music, and sports for the Conventional; collecting, sports, and writing for the Artistic. Patterns of a similar nature were found between personal orientations for girls and hobbies and interests. Thus, differential interest and activity patterns for the boys by personal orientation exist, but their meaning in the development of the personality patterns of the subjects is not clear. Some of the activities and hobbies seem intuitively related to the modal orientations, but many cross type lines. Furthermore, there is no way to decide from Holland's data whether these activity patterns are the impetus for differing personality orientations in the first place or outcomes of other influences on personality.

*Vocational daydreams.* One of the imaginative approaches Holland took with respect to studying the correlates of the personal orientations was the investigation of daydreams about vocations. He asked this question in his first study (1962) over a one- and two-year period, in his four-year follow-up study (1963), and again in a third study (1963; 1964). Once again, some stable differences were found distinguishing the vocational daydreams of the boys in the sample according to their personal orientation. Again, more differences were found for the males than for the females. In the first study, Holland reports that the

Investigative daydreamed of "achievement and learning," the Social about "helping others," and the Enterprising about "money, status, success, and leadership." Except for an inexplicable finding that the Artistic daydreamed about "helping others," data on the four-year follow-up study show similar trends in vocational daydreams.

Holland also reports that subjects in Realistic and Investigative college majors report more consistent vocational daydreams through their adolescence than students making choices in the other categories. The Realistic and Investigative types daydreamed almost exclusively about Realistic and Investigative vocations, while the other subjects daydreamed about Realistic, Investigative, and other vocations. Holland suggests that this finding may parallel the general finding that students in Realistic and Investigative fields tend to be more stable in their vocational choices during college than students whose choices are in the other categories.

*Vocational images.* Along with assessing differences in daydreams about vocations, Holland (1963; 1964) inquired into the images his subjects held of people in various occupations. Selecting one occupation to represent each occupational environment, Holland found that his subjects' images of these occupations were much as would be expected. Engineers were characteristically viewed as "practical" by males and "intelligent" by females; physicists were clearly stereotyped by both males and females as "intelligent"; teachers were typed as "underpaid" by boys and as "dedicated" by girls; accountants were seen as "dull" by males and "precise" by females; business executives as "intelligent" by males and "very busy" by females; and artists as "creative" by both boys and girls.

To report findings simply in the above terms might be misleading, however. Some of the images seem to be vivid and universally held; for example, 56 of the boys and 65 of the girls thought physicists were "intelligent," but only 12 of the boys characterized business executives as "intelligent" and 19 of the girls described them as "very busy." In both the examples, however, the characteristics reported above is the view most commonly held. Thus, images of business executives are much less stereotyped than are those of physicists. It is also important to note that the characteristics were derived not from data based on a list of characteristics subjects were required to check, but from a semiprojective statement, such as "Engineers are ————," a format which is likely to result in a minimum degree of stereotyped responses.

In another study (1964), Holland asked his subjects to describe their impression of the typical person in their chosen profession by checking relevant adjectives from a list presented to them. Some consistency exists in the results of both studies of vocational images; for example, the Realistic subjects characterized the typical person in their chosen profession as practical-minded. The difference in format results in some additional data, however. Some of the personality types emitted a greater variety of images than others. The Realistic subjects described their chosen fields as employing people high on practical-mindedness and with considerable mechanical ability. The Social listed people high on emotional stability, understanding of others, and nine more traits. They only rated two traits to a low degree. The Realistic subjects reported that people in their fields are low on no less than ten traits. Similar trends are evident in the other orientations. These results suggest, for example, that the Realistic careers have a vivid positive stereotype (few characteristics) and a vague negative stereotype (many traits listed) while the Social are the reverse, a clear negative stereotype (two traits listed) and a vague positive stereotype (11 traits indicated).

*Achievement patterns.* Full data about occupational choice must reasonably include information about the degree to which people are able to implement their choices. Holland has included such data by examining the achievement, both academic and in other relevant areas, of people expressing different high point codes in his 1962 report and different SVIB scores in his 1963 report. In nonacademic achievement areas, Holland found that Social and Enterprising boys held many school offices while Realistic and Conventional boys held few. He interpreted this finding as consistent with the predicted differences in the degree of interpersonal skill held by these types. Girls with Social high point codes earned higher ranks in Girl Scouts than girls with other high point codes, while Social and Investigative girls earned better grades in high school than other girls. In college, the Social students once again held more elective student offices than other groups and in general achieved more than other types.

Further follow-up data on collegiate achievement resulted from Holland's four-year longitudinal study (1963). Predictions that Social and Enterprising orientations are positively related to leadership in college and that scientific achievement is positively related to Investigative orientation and somewhat to Realistic orientation were both generally supported. The only deviation was that the Enterprising, rather than Artistic orientation, seemed related to artistic achievement. An artistic modal orientation did not correlate positively with artistic achievement.

### Relations between Types

Though satisfied with the predictive efficiency of the original classification system, Holland's experience with the data he and others had collected over the years made him attempt to increase the subtlety and sensitivity of the system by moving increasingly to multidigit classifications. He found that his classification system could be extended to two digits and still maintain good predictive validity (Holland, 1966). Over time, however, it has become increasingly clear that the types are related to each other differentially. In a manner very similar to Roe, Holland began to explore the idea that some of the occupational environments are more psychologically similar than others. The results of a major investigation into the relationships between the six types (Holland, Whitney, Cole, and Richards, 1969) indicate that the types may be presented in a crude hexagon. The outer rim of the hexagon reveals the psychological relationship between environments. Highly correlated environments, similar to one another, are closer together than those with low correlations. Realistic is close to Investigative on the one hand and Conventional on the other (correlations of 0.46 and 0.36, respectively) but fairly remote from Social, which is completely across the hexagon and correlates 0.21. Artistic is next to Investigative and Social (correlations of 0.34 and 0.42) but very distant from Conventional across the hexagon (correlation of 0.11). While the shape would not conform exactly to the hexagon if plotted in scale, it is close enough to be intriguing, and to lend vitality to Holland's attempt to relate the environments to one another differentially.

### Parental Influences on Personal Orientations

Although the statement of the theory did not include a formulation about the events that shape the particular personal orientation that an individual develops, Holland has chosen to investigate classes of events that might bear on the subject. One of the classes of most significance is that of parental influence. We have already studied one theorist who maintains that parent-child interactions are the crucial variable in the development of personality traits which influence later vocational behavior (Roe, 1957). Holland chose to look into parental behaviors in two ways (1962). First, he developed the Parental Attitude Research Instrument (PARI), which was administered to the mothers of the National Merit sample of 1959. The PARI, based on the work of Schaefer and Bell (1958), assesses the degree to which mothers hold attitudes such as intrusiveness, equalitarianism, martyrdom, and so on. The findings indicated that the student personal orientations were related to some of the attitudes held by their mothers. For example, students in the Conventional mode had mothers possessing the most authoritarian attitudes, followed in order by those students in the Enterprising, Realistic, Artistic, Social, and Investigative groups. Generally, however, the correlations were low and, except for authoritarian attitudes, generalizations about them are difficult to make.

The approach taken to the study of the fathers' influence on behavior was somewhat different. Each father in the 1959 sample was asked to rank nine goals he held for his child and also his hopes for his child's eventual income. The results indicate that fathers of sons in the Realistic category valued ambition in their sons and hoped their income would be considerable. Fathers of boys in the Investigative category valued curiosity, Social fathers valued self-control, Conventional fathers hoped their sons would be "happy and well adjusted," fathers of boys in the Enterprising group wished happiness and adjustment plus popularity for their sons, and fathers of sons in the Artistic category valued curiosity and independence. Findings for girls, though not as vivid, were in the same general direction.

To test the implicit assumption the theory makes that people with the same personal high point codes should be the product of similar backgrounds, Holland (1962) compared the high point code of the student with that of his father's occupation, parents' education (years), student birth order, and number of children in the family. Only the category of the father's occupation and category of the son's high point code were significantly related. Other data indicated that father's and son's personal orientations are similar; the father's high point code was significantly related to son's high point code, though several inversions in the data are evident.

The question of causality recurs when the above data are examined. Thus, while concurrent data about the relationship between parental attitudes and values and student high point codes and personal orientations can be viewed as interesting, they do not clearly demonstrate that parental attitude factors are a primary influence on the particular pattern of personal styles an individual develops. The only rigorous test of such a hypothesis must be predictive in design. Nevertheless, one can speculate from these findings that parental behavior creates environments which exert a powerful influence on the personal characteristics of their offspring and that one consequence of the influence is the particular vocational environment the children select. However, such speculation is nothing new in the history of developmental psychology, which has always assigned a major role to the parents. What is new is the shape of the variables Holland chooses to study and the direct connection he tries to make with vocational choice.

Holland did attempt to resolve an issue concerning parental influence with which Roe's theory has difficulty, the question of the effects of parental inconsistency on the vocational behavior of the offspring. Classifying the parents with respect to the degree of authoritarianism or democracy they espouse, he reports that parents who hold consistently democratic ideas toward their children tend to produce sons who are likely to choose scientific careers, while parents holding consistently authoritarian attitudes and values are likely to produce sons selecting Realistic careers, such as engineering or, surprisingly, a Social occupation. It is interesting to recall that Roe and Siegelman (1964) found that male social workers had been more distant from their mothers than engineers and female social workers.

### Personal Orientations and Vocational and Educational Choices

*The choices made.* Holland's theory leads to the prediction that individuals will choose occupations consistent with their personal orientations. For example, Realistic people will select careers in a Realistic occupational environment. Using career choice, instead of career attainment, as the dependent variable, Holland studied the relationship between the category of personal orientation and the occupational environment of the field for which a person stated a preference. The assignment of a career field to a particular orientation was made largely on an intuitive basis but, in at least one case, intuition was tempered by empirical findings. Engineering, which intuitively would fit into the Investigative category, was coded as Realistic when it was observed that most engineers' high point codes on the VPI were Realistic rather than Investigative.

Comparing high point code and category of first career choice (Holland, 1962), the results are clear and highly consistent with theoretical expectations. A majority of Realistic, Investigative, and Social subjects chose careers in the appropriate fields. Enterprising Ss chose as many careers in the Realistic area as in the Enterprising, but those two categories constitute a majority of choices for them. Only for the Artistic and Conventional groups does the theory fall down. Artistic Ss chose more Investigative occupations than any other type, not inconsistent with the other findings of similarity between Artistic and Investigative Ss. What is difficult to explain is the finding that Artistic Ss chose Realistic and Social fields more frequently than Artistic careers, and Enterprising occupations as often as Artistic ones. Perhaps these results reflect a cultural bias against artistic careers for talented young men. The Conventional group also failed to conform to expectations. They chose a preponderance of Investigative careers, followed by Realistic, Enterprising, Social, in that order, before Conventional. For this finding, explanations are difficult to generate.

What about second and third occupational preferences? Theoretically, these should conform to the principal personal orientation of the chooser. Holland found, by and large, findings similar to those between first choices and high point code. Most second and third vocational choices were in fields consistent with the major personal orientation of the chooser, and where they were not, they were in a highly related area. As in other parts of his research, Holland found highly similar trends for girls, though his data for girls in the Realistic category are based on an extremely small sample and must be viewed cautiously.

The results of Holland's four-year study (1963) are not clear. It will be recalled that personal orientation in this study was based on the Ss' score on selected SVIB scales. The problem Holland encountered was that his correct predictions, based on the SVIB scores, often did not exceed the predictive efficiency of the base rates of entry into gross occupational categories. For example, he found that about one-third of his sample entered scientific fields, and thus, he was as likely to be correct in predicting that all his subjects would enter a science field on the base rate expectation as on the SVIB scores.

*Stability of choice.* Holland assessed the stability of vocational choices by examining his samples in several ways. He studied the relationship between the student high point codes and successive vocational choices; he compared the high point codes of students who changed majors with those who did not, and he studied the institution's influence on change in the major field. He found that when he examined the first three vocational preferences expressed by the students and grouped the sample into nonchangers (whose three choices all fell into the same environmental orientation) and changers (whose choices fell into two or more categories), his data became more sensitive to the vocational behavior of the students. Thus, if a student had the high point code relevant to the Realistic category and his vocational choice was consistent with it, then it was highly likely that his successive occupational preferences would fall into the Realistic orientation. But a student who said he wanted to be an engineer (Realistic) with a high point code in Investigative was likely to express second and third vocational preferences outside of the Realistic environment, presumably in the Investigative area (Holland, 1962).

Other data indicate that when major fields are designated simply as science versus nonscience, boys' changes in major field seem to be a function of their high point code rather than their first choice. Thus, Social Ss change more frequently than other Ss, while Investigative Ss change fields least often, and these changes are independent of field (Holland, 1962; 1963). In a later study (1963), Holland used an *a priori* basis for deciding which combinations of high point codes are consistent with each other and which are not. For example, he says code 12 (Realistic-Investigative) is a consistent code, since Realistic and Investigative people share many interests, activities, and personal traits, However, code 23 (Investigative-Social) is inconsistent because too many differences exist in the environment and character of these two types. Examining changes of major field in this context, Holland concluded that consistency in code is related to stability of vocational choice.

In another study (Holland and Nichols, 1964), the prediction was tested that remaining in a field is associated with the possession of attributes similar to those of the typical student in the field. To examine this hypothesis, each vocational group, in effect, served as its own control. Students were examined as a function of the group which they originally entered, making it possible to identify differences, if any, between those who departed and those who remained. In general, the prediction was supported, though Holland and Nichols point out that the resulting correlations are low, and some inversions exist. Of significance, however, is their final interpretation that change of preferred field is the outcome of a multivariate input combining personality and achievement factors.

Holland's insight into significant variables related to vocational choice stability led him to study student-institution interactions and their effect on the continuity of vocational choice. In his first study (1962), he classified each college attended by Ss in his sample into one of the six environments. These classifications were two-digit codes; the first digit was based on the most common personal orientation of the freshman class vocational choices, the second digit on the second most frequent category. A two-way classification between an individual student's high point code and the institutional code was then made, with the expectation that Ss in colleges with institutional characteristics similar to their own would receive reinforcement for their orientation and would thus be less likely to change their major fields than students in colleges with characteristics inconsistent with their personal orientation. Although his findings did not support the prediction, one interesting result did occur. He found that students, whatever the category of their first occupational choice, were significantly more likely to change their major field if they attended an institution with a predominantly Social environment. That is, a science student was more than twice as likely to change his major field during his freshman year if he were in a Social college than if he were in a non-Social college.

Further refining his attempts to isolate the influence of colleges on student vocational stability in a later study (1963), Holland developed a four-point stability score which assessed four important features connected with stability and examined the students' stability of choices across these four features. A student received one point for each of the following characteristics that applied to him: possessing a high point code congruent with the college; having a consistent college code; being a science major; possessing a consistent two-digit code. Classed further into nonchangers and changers, the results indicated a strong relationship between high stability scores and stability of choice. In his sample of males, no Ss scoring four (the maximum) changed field (N = 15); about half of the sample scoring two changed and half did not (N = 46 and N = 42, respectively); twice as many Ss scoring 0 changed than did not change (N = 6 and N = 3, respectively). Evidently, then, a third variable must be added to the list of relevant features influencing vocational attainment: achievement, personality orientation, and environmental factors (for example, college characteristics).

In an extensive, longitudinal study of more than 3500 male and 4200 female college students in 28 schools, Holland (1968a) was able to draw some generalizations about choice stability defined in terms of college major. In this study students with Realistic, Social, and Conventional high point codes appear to express very predictable vocational role choices. Overall, when student vocational choice was predicted from the highest VPI score and checked eight months later, the "hit" rate ranged from 21.5 percent to 51.4 percent, while predictions based on the students' original vocational choices and checked eight months later were correct from 63.2 percent to 71.2 percent. Obviously, original choices were better predictors than VPI scores. Holland and Whitney (1968) point out that since about half the males and 60 percent of the females did not change their vocational choice over an 8- to 12-month period in college, one would have a good accuracy rate in predicting that a student's choice would be unchanged. However, the important information is how well the classification system and its instruments permit accurate prediction of choices made by those students who do make changes. If the uncertain students can be sorted out from the more certain ones, and predictions made based on their VPI scores, the eventual vocational decisions of these uncertain students may be enhanced.

On the basis of his large longitudinal study of stability of choices, Holland (1968a) made two other observations of interest. First, he found that the homogeneity or sharpness of a VPI profile is related to stability for male but not female students. Inferences about this observation for women are difficult to make (the problems in understanding the career development of women will be discussed in a later chapter). For men, however, it does seem clear that homogeneity of interest is related to crystallization and commitment.

Second, Holland found that the higher a student's choice is in the hierarchy of types in his college, the greater is the probability that he will be satisfied (and, presumably, stable) with his choice. This observation is consistent with results of earlier studies.

Cole, Whitney, and Holland (1971) conducted a study designed to examine the relationship among the occupational groups in the context of Holland's system. One question they specifically asked was whether the congruence of an individual's interest to those of other people in his chosen field was related to his vocational stability. The Vocational Preference Inventory was administered to two large samples (6,000 and 12,000); more than half the first sample was followed up a year after original data collection. A principal components analysis of the VPI data was computed. The resulting factor loadings were manipulated to locate the six factor scores over six points; these, in turn, were projected onto the resulting plane, resulting in a two-dimensional representation of the six points. The result of these various manipulations is that occupations can be mapped as a function of their relationship to one another, as shown in Figure 2.1. Cole, Whitney, and Holland used this configuration to define job similarity (the distance between the occupational groups in question on the planar configuration), congruence of an individual and an occupation (again, defined in terms of distances on the configuration), the stability of a vocational choice (the distance between the old and new preference where a large distance indicates instability), and differentiation of interests (a person with a dominating interest pattern would have a profile far removed from the center of the plane, while one with diverse interests would have a profile near the plane's center). With occupational preference stability defined in these terms, congruence and stability were found to be significantly correlated (0.454). In addition, it was found that differentiation of interests was negatively correlated with stability, a finding somewhat inconsistent with the usual expectation that the emergence of a dominating interest pattern would result in an increase in occupational preference stability.

## The Level Hierarchy

It will be recalled that the theory included a set of statements which led to some expectations about the occupational level to which a student would aspire. This level hierarchy was hypothetically an additive function of self-evaluation and intelligence. In the 1962 study, Holland tested his formulations about the level hierarchy by predicting a relationship between the student's college major and the sum of his score on the Status scale of the VPI and his Math score on the Scholastic Aptitude Test (SAT). It has been empirically found that certain college majors require more intelligence than others (Wolfle, 1954). Ss with the highest level hierarchy scores, based on the above formula, were expected to choose the more demanding majors more often than Ss with lower level hierarchy scores. Each student was classified into one of nine categories: a 1-1 indicated a student whose Status score on the VPI test and SAT Math score both fell into the top third of the sample; a 1-2 indicated a Status score in the top third and a Math score in the middle third, and so on. After all the students were so classified, the college major of each student in each category was classified into

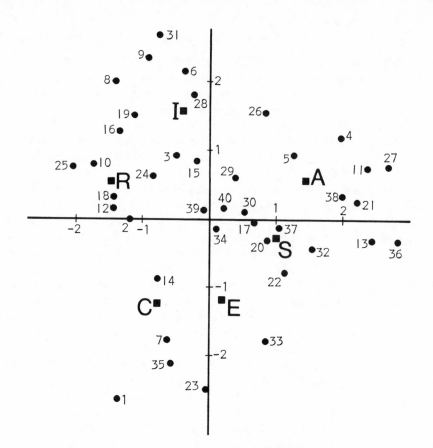

| 1. | Accounting (279) | 21. | Journalism* (62) |
| 2. | Agricultural Science (166) | 22. | Law (288) |
| 3. | Architecture (83) | 23. | Marketing (45) |
| 4. | Art (45) | 24. | Mathematics, Statistics (80) |
| 5. | Art* (179) | 25. | Mechanical Engineering (152) |
| 6. | Biology (55) | 26. | Medicine (354) |
| 7. | Business Management (360) | 27. | Music (41) |
| 8. | Chemical Engineering (94) | 28. | Natural Science Education (86) |
| 9. | Chemistry (87) | 29. | Photography* (100) |
| 10. | Civil Engineering (185) | 30. | Physical Education, Rec., Health (272) |
| 11. | Clinical Psychology (42) | 31. | Physics (61) |
| 12. | Construction* (103) | 32. | Political Science (76) |
| 13. | Counseling and Guidance (36) | 33. | Public Relations, Advertising (40) |
| 14. | Data Processing* (502) | 34. | Radio, TV* (157) |
| 15. | Dentistry (120) | 35. | Sales (64) |
| 16. | Electrical Engineering (259) | 36. | Speech and Drama* (40) |
| 17. | Elementary Education (117) | 37. | Teaching* (739) |
| 18. | Farming (61) | 38. | Theology (77) |
| 19. | Forestry (105) | 39. | Undecided* (824) |
| 20. | History (57) | 40. | Undecided (451) |

FIGURE 2.1 A spatial configuration of occupations based on Vocational Preference Inventory responses of males entering two-year(*) and four-year colleges (N in parentheses). Reprinted from Nancy S. Cole, D. R. Whitney, and J. L. Holland. A spatial configuration of occupations. *Journal of Vocational Behavior*, 1971, *1*, 1-9. Reproduced with permission of the authors and the publisher, Academic Press.

"high" or "low," indicating whether or not the major required more than "average" intelligence. The general trend of the data supports the hypothesis, though much more clearly for girls than for boys. The data for the boys suggest that the Math score is more significant in influencing the level of the choice than the Status score, while the two seem to operate more equally in influencing the choices the girls make.

### Evaluation

Holland's investigations based on his theory are impressively extensive. In addition to devising ways to test specific hypotheses growing out of his position, he has generated additional information as a result of the many aspects of vocational behavior that were studied incidental to tests of his theory. There is considerable evidence from Holland's research that the personal orientations exist much as he described them in his original theoretical formulation, and furthermore that the types are reasonably stable. The occupational environments as postulated also seem to exist. Most of the predicted characteristics of the types were found to hold, plus a large number of other characteristics and traits that further serve to differentiate them from one another. Given a student's high point code, an investigator stands a good chance of predicting the student's vocational choice, some of his personal characteristics, the stability of his vocational choice, and some information about his parents' values and attitudes. He also has a good basis for drawing inferences about the student's motives.

The data strongly indicate that the personal orientations are related to familial patterns, particularly parental behaviors, beliefs, ambitions, and goals for their offspring. The data in this sphere are a source of insight into the development of the personal orientations, though large gaps remain, and Holland draws few, if any, conclusions about the direct causal basis underlying developmental hierarchies. The personal orientations have a strong relationship to the vocational choices the students make and they relate closely, in combination with other variables, to the stability of the vocational choices the students make. However, the data are not always as clear for girls as for boys in this regard.

Holland has been sensitive to the data resulting from his investigations and has suggested several modifications of his theory or, at least, pointed to certain weaknesses in it. In two recent monographs the theory has been revised and updated (Holland, 1966a; 1973), though it remains fundamentally unchanged. As originally presented, Holland's theory was a theory of vocational choice. Proposed were six personal types and six corresponding occupational environments. Following the considerable research he has conducted, Holland chose to broaden the scope of his theory and change it from the relatively narrow context of vocational choice to behavior in general. Thus, the six personal types became not merely vocational orientations but styles of life in general, only one facet being vocational. To quote Holland (1962), he has developed "a theory of personal dispositions and their outcomes." Like Roe, he started with a miniature theory to explain vocational choice and shortly arrived at a larger theory of personality.

More specifically, Holland points to several shortcomings in his theory. In particular, he writes that certain portions of the theory are too ambiguous to be adequately tested and that the personal orientations, as originally stated, were not specific enough. Some of the data concerning the characteristics of the personality types offset this latter defect. He also feels that the applicability of the theory to women is limited and that the theory must be revised to account more adequately for the vocational development of women, whose development and vocational tasks and goals differ significantly enough from those of men to require some different formulations. He does not, however, specify the particular direction these modifications for women in his theory should take. Finally, he concluded, largely on the results of his 1962 study, that the concept of the level hierarchy in his theory is, at best, oversimplified and at worst, unnecessary. Instead, he suggests that level of aspiration is the result of the highly complex interaction of several variables and is not likely to be linearly related to intelligence. As it stood in his original theory, however, the level hierarchy was not likely to be a valid concept. In the rewritten version (Holland, 1966a) the level of career choice is a more intimate part of the personality types and patterns.

## Other Relevant Research

Using the criterion of stimulating research to evaluate a theory, Holland's work stands up extremely well. Beginning in the middle 1960s the tempo of research investigating his theory by independent investigators began to accelerate, reaching very active levels by the early 1970s. The strong interest in testing aspects of Holland's theory partly stems from its simplicity, the available instrumentation, and the attempts Holland himself has made to relate his work to other systems in vocational development such as the *Dictionary of Occupational Titles* and the Strong Vocational Interest Blank.

## Level Hierarchy

One of the first studies testing Holland's theory to be reported was by Schutz and Blocher (1961). They sought to test Holland's assumption that the Occupational Level score of the SVIB is a valid index of the self-evaluation concept used as one of the two factors constituting the level hierarchy. Schutz and Blocher constructed a self-attitude instrument which described the similarity between a person's self-description and ideal self-description. The resulting score was called a self-satisfaction score. Their hypothesis, based on Holland's theory, was that a positive relationship exists between Occupational Level scores and the index of self-satisfaction. Using as a sample 135 male high school seniors from a school more typical of the college-bound population than Holland's National Merit Scholars, Schutz and Blocher first administered the SVIB and then the self- and ideal self-description instruments. After applying statistical transformations to make the data conform to the assumptions of normal statistical analyses, they found a significant product-moment correlation of 0.34 between the Occupational Level and self-satisfaction scores. They concluded, with some caution, that SVIB OL scores may be used to indicate the self-evaluation portion of the level hierarchy in Holland's theory.

Stockin (1964) also investigated an aspect of the level hierarchy in Holland's theory. He studied the correlation between Ss' intelligence and self-evaluation and level of occupational choices. For intelligence data, he used IQ scores available from school files. To obtain self-evaluation scores, he used three separate scales: the Sims Social Status Scale, the Attitude Toward Education Scale (ATE) of Hieronymus (1951), and the Socioeconomic Expectation Scale (SEE), also by Hieronymus (1951). Sums of scores on these three scales resulted in Stockin's self-evaluation index. Then, the self-evaluation scores of the subjects were placed into quartiles and combined with the subjects' ranks on the intelligence test. The index from which occupational level could be predicted developed out of these combined scores. The vocational choices of the subjects had already been assigned to a level based on Roe's occupational classification system (1954). The accuracy of Stockin's predictions about vocational choice was then easy to assess by directly comparing predicted preferences with actual preferences.

The findings indicated that a systematic relationship existed between the predictions and the actual choices, and furthermore, that where the predictions were wrong, a large proportion of the careers chosen were in the level adjacent to the actual choice. Stockin also reports that the accuracy of predicting the level of choice is considerably increased by adding self-evaluation to intellectual measures. The author is quick to point out two cautions necessary in evaluating the results of the study. First, predictions were not really made; at best, postdictions were made about career preferences. Second, the classification of occupational hierarchies into the four levels which Stockin used is likely to be an oversimplification of American occupational structure. Despite the cautions that Stockin (1964) and Schutz and Blocher (1961) suggest, the two investigations of different aspects of the level hierarchy, conducted by independent researchers, found results consistent with the theory. However, a study by Fortner (1970) of the level hierarchy does not entirely support the notion. Using IQ scores, the Sims Occupational Rating Scale as a measure of self-evaluation, and Wage Earners Occupational Level to predict levels of occupational choices in 400 junior and senior girls in high school, she found a combination of all the instruments were related to level of occupations chosen, but that IQ score alone predicted as well as all three together. However, it should be kept in mind that these results concerned females, whose career development is different from and less well understood than males.

*Occupational stereotypes.* It should be recalled that a basic assumption underlying Holland's theory is that occupational preferences are based on occupational stereotypes. A number of investigators have chosen to examine occupational stereotypes in terms of Holland's theory. Hollander and Parker (1969) wrote descriptions of six occupations, each representing one of Holland's six types (auto mechanic, scientist, teacher, bank teller, business executive, and artist) in terms of the need scales of the Adjective Check List. The resulting descriptions were made available to 54 high school sophomores who were then asked to respond to the Adjective Check List as if they were a member of each one of the six occupational groups. With the exception of auto mechanic and teacher, needs emerged matching the Holland types. Banducci (1970) tested differences in knowledge about careers of 600 high school boys as a function of their membership in one of the six Holland types. The boys' knowledge was tested in terms of the accuracy of the occupational stereotypes they held. Realistic, Investigative, and Enterprising students held more accurate occupational stereotypes than Social, Conventional, and Artistic. Unfortunately, it is difficult to interpret these results. Do they mean the three high groups are more in tune with the world of work, that occupations suitable to their types are easier to stereotype than those of other types, or something else?

Still another study by Hollander and Parker (1972) tested three hypotheses: that adolescent self-concept and stereotypic description of most preferred occupation are positively related, that adolescent self-concept and stereotypic description of the least preferred occupation are not positively related, and that adolescent most and least preferred occupational choices represent different occupational environments. The Adjective Check List and an Occupational Preference List were administered to 54 high school boys. The results supported all three hypotheses. Hollander and Parker conclude that these results support Holland's theory since the results suggest that individuals "search for situations which satisfy their hierarchy of adjustive orientations."

*Indecision, persistence, and change.* Holland's theory has been used extensively to orient research concerning career indecision, persistence, change, and adjustment in college students. A comprehensive test of several aspects of Holland's theory was conducted by Osipow, Ashby, and Wall (1966). They proposed to test several hypotheses derived from the theory, many of which replicated Holland's own work, but extended it in that the research was based on college students in general rather than on a selected sample of unusually talented students. Specifically, the theory was tested by four predictions. The first prediction was that subjects would express occupational preferences consistent with their major personal orientation. Second, it was predicted that subjects in the Social category would express greater uncertainty about their vocational preference than would other types of students. Third, it was suggested that subjects expressing a high degree of certainty about their choice would show greater consistency between their first and second choices (the second choice would more likely be in the same occupational environment as the first choice) than Ss whose occupational preferences were tentative; finally, they predicted that the same would hold true for the consistency between major personality orientation and second occupational choice (decided Ss would show greater consistency in this regard than would undecided Ss).

A sample of college freshmen were required to rank six personality descriptions they thought matched their behavior. These descriptions were based upon the six personal orientations described by Holland. As part of the ranking procedure, the Ss were required to rate the degree to which each description fit them, so a measure of the order of the Ss' identification with each type, plus the strength of that identification, was obtained. Information about the occupational preferences of each student was available; each occupational preference was coded into the appropriate occupational environment according to guide lines set down by Holland in several papers (1962; 1963; 1963-1964). It was thus possible to test the first prediction, that Ss' occupational preferences are consistent with the major personal orientation, by comparing the frequency with which students' occupational preferences were in occupational environments consistent with the major personal orientation. The results concerning this hypothesis supported Holland's theory. Some inversions were observed in the data, but to no greater degree than in Holland's own work.

The second hypothesis concerning the greater uncertainty of Social Ss was tested by simply comparing the degree of certainty expressed by the Ss in the six orientations on a four-point scale. The results of this analysis did not support Holland's data; Social Ss were no different from other subjects in their occupational certainty.

The Ss in the study had been classified according to the degree to which they were certain of their educational-vocational plans along the dimension of what college they had entered within a large university. (A college for undecided students was available in addition to the traditional academic colleges.) The prediction concerning the greater consistency between the first and second occupational preferences for students certain of their choice as opposed to those uncertain of it was tested by comparing the category of the choices of students in these two kinds of programs. It was found that Ss with a higher degree of certainty about their plans (as defined by program choice) did show greater consistency in the category of their first and second vocational preferences than did Ss less clear about their plans, thus supporting the prediction.

The final hypothesis was that Ss more certain of their plans, again defined in terms of their college program as described above, would have second occupational preferences consistent with their major personal orientation, while Ss less clear about their plans would not. This prediction did not receive support. In fact, the second preferences for both groups were not consistently related to their major personality orientation.

Comparisons of the subjects by major personality orientation and SVIB group scores revealed consistency between the SVIB scores and assignment to personality categories. For example, Ss in the Realistic category earned their highest scores, and higher scores than any other personality group, on SVIB groups II and III (science-engineering and practical, respectively), which is exactly what the theoretical statements would lead one to expect. In terms of the degree to which the vocational preferences, when assigned to categories equivalent to those of Holland's theory, fell into appropriate SVIB groups, the evidence is even stronger. From the results, it would appear that considerable construct validity exists between the personal orientations, SVIB group scores, and occupational preferences (Wall, Osipow, and Ashby, 1967).

In another study, the same authors (Ashby, Wall, and Osipow, 1966) examined the differences of three groups of college freshmen, varying in their degree of educational-vocational certainty, on a number of variables. Among these were the personality rankings of their earlier study based on Holland's personal orientations. In this study it was found that the most highly certain group of subjects ranked themselves significantly higher on the Investigative and Artistic types than the other two groups of less certain subjects.

With respect to testing the theory, the limitations of these three studies assume the quality of strengths. That is, the personality measures were crude, and the sample was composed of a large proportion of students who were considerably uncertain about educational-vocational plans, from which one might infer conflicted personality orientations. That the results were consistent with the theory in so many respects despite these limitations further adds to the support of the theory.

Baird (1969) has raised the question of how different the undecided student is from other students in a somewhat different way than Osipow, Ashby, and Wall. Baird administered a wide variety of questionnaires (the VPI, Preconscious Activity Scale, Interpersonal Competency Scale, the Range of Experience Scale, the Indecision Scale, the Dogmatism Scale, and many others) to more than 6000 male and 6000 female college students. The scores and responses of those students who expressed educational and vocational commitment were compared with those who were undecided about their plans. Male "decideds" rated themselves higher than "undecideds" on the vocational and academic types, exhibited more achievement drive, expressed more interest in making a scientific contribution, had more scientific potential, and showed more technical competency than "undecideds." For females, the "decideds" were more likely than the "undecideds" to have a goal involving religious activity, and rated themselves higher in homemaking and interpersonal competencies than "undecideds." In another study, reported in the same article by Baird, a comparison of 13,000 undecided students with 43,000 decided students on academic abilities revealed no differences.

Elton and Rose have performed several studies of the differences in career and academic development of decided and undecided students. In one study (Elton and Rose, 1970) they tested the hypothesis that immigrants to a major field should show personality characteristics similar to persisters at the time of graduation. The sample consisted of 530 graduating male students for whom freshmen test data (Omnibus Personality Inventory and the American College Testing Program Battery) were available. The results indicated that senior choice is predictable on the basis of personality and aptitude, but is even more accurately predicted by the freshman's expressed choice. This finding is similar to Holland's (1968a) observations of predictors of college major 8 to 12 months after entrance into college. Elton and Rose found that most undecided freshmen ended their studies in social or enterprising areas. The results of the Elton and Rose (1970) study tend to support the new hexagon model created by Holland, since transfers to fields remote (on the hexagon) from their original choice should have different characteristics than those transferring to adjacent categories, and such was often found to be the situation.

In another study dealing with the question of whether immigrants to a field might conceal the differences between students who changed from one Holland category to another over time, Elton and Rose (1971) examined the Omnibus Personality Inventory scores of 137 college seniors who were originally vocationally undecided at college entrance as compared to seniors persisting in or changing to a major represented by one of the Holland scales. No differences were found, indicating, apparently, that no personality factors differentiate decided from undecided students. In another investigation with a similar purpose, Rose and Elton (1971) compared 85 freshmen undecided students who persisted to graduation with 88 randomly selected undecided freshmen who left by the fourth quarter. Those who stayed to graduation were less conforming and more masculine on the Omnibus Personality Inventory and had higher ACT scores than those who left. Even though the mean ACT scores of those who left were higher than the mean of the freshman class on the ACT, 72 percent of those students who left prematurely were not in good standing at the time of departure.

The result of studies on differences between decided and undecided students are mixed. Essentially, however, the data reveal few systematic and reliable personality or ability factors involved in decision-indecision status. The Rose and Elton results (1971), along with the Ashby, Wall, and Osipow (1966) data, suggest that being decided might have something to do with achievement and performance patterns, but the data do not suggest the nature of this influence. It should be kept in mind, however, that the Baird (1969) study, based on a much larger sample than either the Rose and Elton or Ashby et al. studies, did not reveal any ability differences between undecided and decided students.

*Congruence.* In terms of Holland's theory, congruence has been defined as the degree of consistency between an individual's high point code and the occupational environment of his preferred or planned field. Several studies have examined both the theoretical and applied implications of congruence in student populations. Morrow (1971), using Holland's theory as a basis for hypothesizing about student satisfaction with college major, predicted that congruent students would express more satisfaction with their college major than incongruent students. To test his prediction, he assigned 86 male and 61 female mathematics majors and 54 male and 122 female sociology majors to personality high point code types on the basis of their Vocational Preference Inventory scores and administered a questionnaire concerning satisfaction with college major. Morrow, assuming that a high score on the Investigative scale was congruent for mathematics majors and all other high point codes incongruent for that group, found support for the congruence-satisfaction prediction. For sociology majors, a high VPI score on Social was considered to be congruent and all others incongruent. The prediction was not supported by the results for the sociology majors.

Southworth and Morningstar (1970) divided 102 freshmen engineering students into three groups according to their status during the junior year, i.e., those still majoring in engineering (N = 43), those who had left engineering studies but were still enrolled in the university (N = 33), and those who had left the university (N = 26). The VPI had been administered to the engineering students during their freshman year. Interesting differences in VPI scores were found to occur according to the status of the students' enrollment during their junior year. The "changers" were found to be higher on the Social and Artistic scales than the engineering "persisters," and those who left the university seemed to have lower scores on the Investigative scale than those students who stayed till their junior year. There was also some evidence to indicate that those students who left the university had fewer overall interests. The implication appears to be that students leave engineering to pursue other interests that are not satisfied in engineering, that students who leave university studies entirely do so because of the lack of a scholarly inclination, and that academic persistence in college may require some minimum development of openness of interest. Taken in combination with Morrow's results (1971), it might be speculated that the mathematics majors were satisfied with their major because there were no other important interests *uninvolved* in their studies, while the sociology majors' satisfaction was not predictable because the Social environment did not necessarily include all their major activity needs.

Walsh and his students have investigated several other aspects of congruence and career development, always using the VPI and self-reported college major to establish congruence. In one study, Walsh and Russel (1969) found that "congruent" students exhibit better personal adjustment (defined in terms of the Mooney Problem Check List) than do incongruent students. Walsh and Barrow (1971) studied 30 male and 30 female congruent students' and 30 male and 30 female incongruent students' personality characteristics on the California Personality Inventory. No major systematic personality differences were found as a function of congruence-incongruence. Finally, Walsh and Lewis (1972), on the basis of the Omnibus Personality Inventory, found that congruent male students exhibit more satisfaction with their academic programs, more personal stability, and more stable college choices, than do incongruent students. The results of these three studies might suggest that while congruent and incongruent students do not differ in a systematic personal way to begin with, the different effects of studying a field that "fits" one to varying degrees may have an important impact on one's adjustment as time goes on. Little is known about the factors that enhance the development of congruent choices, though Bodden (1970) reported that cognitive complexity is positively related to expressing a congruent vocational choice.

*Holland's theory applied to other settings.* One of the early criticisms of

Holland's work was that the data were too dependent, first, on highly talented groups, and second, on student populations in higher education (Osipow, 1968). Since those earlier observations of the theory were made, a number of investigators have extended the Holland theory downward in age and level of talent, outward in terms of moving away from student groups, and upward in terms of applications to older populations. In one of the early studies of high school students, Rezler (1967a) administered the Kuder Preference Record, the VPI, and the California Test of Mental Maturity to two groups of high school junior and senior girls, 33 representing pioneer fields, or those girls who wanted to study medicine, mathematics, or natural science, and 33 representing the traditional careers in nursing or elementary school teaching. The results indicated that the Pioneers scored higher on Computational, Scientific, and Social Service interests on the Kuder, higher on Investigative and Masculinity, and lower on Social, Self-control, and Status than Traditionals. The Pioneers also scored higher on CTMM, IQ, and PSAT Mathematics and Verbal scales. Within the Pioneers the premedical students scored higher on Scientific and Social Service interests than the mathematics and science students, and also higher on the Investigative and Social scales of the VPI. The traditionalist nurses scored higher on Kuder Outdoor and Scientific scales, and lower on the Computational, Literary, and Clerical scales than prospective elementary teachers, while the future nurses were higher on Investigative than the future elementary teachers.

In a study comparing the work roles and preferred work roles of a 2½ percent sample of clergymen in one state association, Osipow (1970) found that most of the respondents were Social types but reported working in Conventional roles more than in Social environments. A student sample, classified by VPI results primarily into the Social category, anticipated Social work roles. Though the VPI results of both the students and professionals apparently confirms that the clergyman is a Social type, there is apparently an important discrepancy between the preferred and anticipated role of the clergyman and what he later finds himself doing.

Lacey (1971) attempted to extend Holland's theory to a sample of employed men representing each of the six types described by the theory. Except for those individuals classified as Realistic, the VPI and the occupational activity engaged in by these men were consistent with the theory. Hughes (1972) has also attempted to extend Holland's theory to an employed sample. He tested the hypotheses that individuals are employed in jobs appropriate to their type, that individual occupational level can be predicted on the basis of intelligence and self-evaluation, that individuals give self-ratings consistent with their personal orientation, that individuals with consistent personality patterns change their work less often than those with inconsistent patterns, and that those with consistent patterns are more satisfied with their work than those with inconsistent patterns. Hughes administered the VPI, SVIB, 16 PF, a self-rating personality scale, the Quick Word Intelligence Test, the Sims Occupational Rating Scale, and a personal information sheet to 400 employed men ranging in age from 25 to 35.

The results did not support the hypothesis that people work at jobs appropriate to their personality orientation. The level hierarchy prediction, however, was supported in that it was found that intelligence and self-evaluation predicted occupational level. No evidence was found that self-ratings were consistent with personality attributes. No evidence was found that consistent patterns resulted in fewer job changes over time. Finally, no evidence was found to support the hypothesis that occupational satisfaction is related to personality type consistency. Hughes' study is one of the few whose major findings are completely at odds with Holland's theory.

Williams (1972) applied Holland's theory to a graduate student population. She administered the VPI, Allport-Vernon-Lindzey Study of Values, Miller Occupational Values Indicator, and the 16 PF to 145 graduate students representing 18 departments. She concluded that discriminant analysis revealed that the VPI assigned students to their field fairly well, though the Realistic and Enterprising types were marginal, the AVL similarly assigned accurately though the Realistic and Enterprising were not assigned satisfactorily, the Miller OVI assigned adequately only the Social type, and the 16 PF was adequate for all types. Overall, the Investigative and Conventional were most clearly discriminated, Enterprising and Realistic most poorly. Most field selections were congruent with personality type, thus Williams concluded that the theory was supported. In another study in a graduate school setting, Frantz and Walsh (1972), however, found an overriding Investigative orientation in the students which obscured other differences that might have been expected as a function of field differences. It is difficult to know whether this result reflects the impact of environmental press or a flaw in Holland's theory.

Two other investigators (Folsom, 1969; Osipow, 1969) report studies in which students in baccalaureate or associate degree programs describe themselves in terms generally consistent with the Holland characteristics for their field.

The results of the studies of samples drawn from outside the highly talented undergraduate student group generally indicate support for the general outlines of Holland's theory. Only the Hughes (1972) study stands out as an exception, and it must be seriously considered because of the size of the sample he observed. Obviously, before the question of how well Holland's theory fits the world of the employed worker can be answered, more data are necessary.

*The relation of the VPI to other instruments.* Considerable interest has been shown in relating the VPI to other interest measures, probably because of the value in relating the empirically strong interest inventories to one based on a theory of career development. One approach has been the application of canonical correlation analysis to some combination of interest measures. Navran and Kendall (1971) did a canonical correlational analysis of the VPI, SVIB, and the EPPS based on data from 277 freshmen in a military college. They concluded that the SVIB and VPI are related more to each other than to the EPPS, but that enough differences exist between the two interest inventories to make the use of both worthwhile. Salomone and Muthard (1972) used canonical correlation to relate the Minnesota Importance Questionnaire (a measure of vocational needs) to the VPI, basing their data on 333 counselors. In this study, no significant relation was found between the two instruments, suggesting a need to differentiate between vocational needs and vocational interests. Haase (1971) performed a canonical correlation between the VPI and the SVIB based on 176 male college students and found six common factors. Cole and Hanson (1971) attempted to assess the structural relationships between the SVIB, the Kuder Occupational Interest Survey, the VPI, the Minnesota Vocational Interest Inventory, and the ACT Vocational Interest Profile. All these instruments were found to be similar, and some evidence was noted supporting the circular configuration of interests along the lines Roe and Holland each suggest.

Rezler (1967b) compared the Kuder Preference Record and the VPI using interest data based on the responses of 250 junior and 265 senior girls in high school. Performance on the Realistic scale was found to be positively correlated with Kuder Outdoor and Mechanical, and negatively with Kuder Persuasive and Literary; Investigative positively correlated with Kuder Science and Outdoor and negatively with Persuasive and Clerical; Social positively correlated with Kuder Social Service and Persuasive and negatively with Outdoor, Mechanical, Computational, and Artistic; Conventional positively correlated with Computational and Clerical, negatively with Outdoor, Literary, and Musical; Enterprising positively correlated with Persuasive, and negatively with Outdoor and Scientific; and Artistic positively correlated with Kuder Artistic, Literary, and Musical, and negatively with Computational and Clerical.[1]

Some deliberate efforts have been made to relate the SVIB and the VPI. Recent work on the SVIB has resulted in the development of Holland scales on the SVIB. Forerunners of this work are studies by Cockriel (1972), Blakeney, Matteson, and Holland (1972), Eggenberger and Herman (1972), and Lee and Hedahl (1973). The major study is one reported by Campbell and Holland (1972), who describe the procedures followed which provide the basis for the development of each of the Holland scales based on SVIB responses. The results of these attempts clearly indicate that the two systems, Holland's and Strong's, can be usefully and logically related to one another. As Campbell and Holland point out in their paper, three levels of classification exist – general categories, such as the Holland types; underlying dimensions, such as the basic interest scales of the Strong; and empirical scales, such as the occupational scales of the Strong. Each may provide a useful and distinctive function. The Hansen and Johansson (1972) paper does the same thing for the women's Strong and the VPI as the Campbell and Holland (1972) paper does for the men's version.

One other study is of some interest in connection with the relation between

---

[1] Since Rezler's (1967) findings are based on girls, they are of particular interest since most investigators have either ignored studying women with the VPI or have had difficulty in interpreting findings for women since their scores are constricted, the Realistic category being rarely used. Osipow and Ashby (1968) found that two-digit codes for men were far more varied than for women, the latter sex having profiles dominated by a social aspect.

the Holland system and others. Griffith and Trogden (1969), applying Shaw's (1966) theory, have studied differences in self-expressive styles in female nursing and music students. Shaw has postulated four styles: humanistic, interpretive, promotional, and technological. The Preference Association Survey, developed to measure these styles, was administered to the nursing and music students. Griffith and Trogden predicted that nurses would score higher than music students on the humanistic and lower on the promotional scales, while music students would score higher on interpretive and lower on technological scales than nursing students. They also predicted that nurses, compared within their group, would score highest on humanistic and lowest on promotional scales, while the music students, compared to themselves only, would score highest on interpretive and lowest on technological scales. The Shaw system and the Griffith and Trogden study are of interest in that in some ways their approach seems similar to Holland's (though the Shaw system has four types rather than six) and has similar implications. Further research relating Holland's and Shaw's work might be of interest.

*Environmental aspects of Holland's theory.* In his early work, Holland had little to say about how a person became a particular type, or about the events that enhance or influence membership in a type. However, Holland has had much to say about environmental events and their importance in maintaining or shaping type membership once established. A number of investigators have followed the line of research suggested by Holland's emphasis on environment's role in vocational preference and persistence.

Barclay, Stilwell, and Barclay (1972) have taken an interesting approach to the study of environmental aspects in the development of personality types. Barclay studied the effect of father's occupation on, among other things, children's vocational awareness. The Barclay Classroom Climate Inventory was administered to 1386 elementary school children. The occupations of the fathers of these children were also obtained and classified into Holland categories. The results of the BCCI allowed Barclay to make generalizations about the behaviors associated with being the child of a father classified as a particular Holland type, as inferred from the father's occupation. The many generalizations are too extensive to be covered here. An example is: having a father as a teacher enhances the child's (both girls and boys) Social, Artistic, and Investigative areas; having a father as a physician or lawyer seems to result in the child's possession of Social and Conventional skills (as perceived and reported by peers). The large amount of data generated from this study as well as the method and instrumentation introduced offer some promise to fill the gap in Holland's theory dealing with the development of personality.

Elton (1971) examined the effects of environment on personality development in the context of Holland's theory by giving the Omnibus Personality Inventory to three samples of 50 males continuously enrolled in college for four semesters. One of the three samples had moved from an engineering to an arts and science program during the period of enrollment. Scores were "factor change" scores between two administrations of the Omnibus Personality Inventory. Some interesting changes were observed: the nonauthoritarianism score of the transfers to arts and science changed more than the engineering persisters; in addition, the transfers to arts and science were more realistic, nonjudgmental, intellectually liberal, and religiously skeptical. These results certainly generate the impression of a changing, open, liberal student moving from engineering to arts and science, and of a conservative, stable, traditional student remaining in engineering, but some limitations should be noted. First, there is really no way to know whether the personality changes seen in those leaving engineering were the result of interaction with the different academic environment or whether they precipitated the change from engineering. In addition, these results must be viewed tentatively because of the small sample and lack of cross validation.

Several studies have examined the impact of environment in terms of student achievement. Barclay (1967), by testing students exemplifying successful performance in certain academic fields, successfully describes both the environmental press enhancing achievement in various fields as well as the personal characteristics required for success according to field. Astin and Panos (1969) report findings which support the idea that, at least in technical and teachers colleges, there is a pressure to conform to the popular majors – students seem unlikely to switch to unpopular majors and highly likely to change to the popular ones. As Holland himself found in another study (1968a), Astin and Panos found that the best predictor of a student's final major is his initial choice of major field. Posthuma and Navran (1970), on the basis of the SVIB, EPPS, and VPI scores of 110 students and 44 faculty, found some crude evidence to indicate that congruence between the students and their faculty, especially on the SVIB and the VPI, enhances student academic achievement.

Finally, there is a series of studies by Walsh and his students dealing with the impact of collegiate academic environment on the individual student's perceptions of personal change over time. Walsh and Lacey (1969) examined the hypothesis that college students enrolled in a major perceived themselves as changing in a direction congruent with that personal orientation over the period of their college years. One hundred fifty-one college male seniors, representing each of the six occupational environments described by Holland, were studied by means of the Perceived Change Inventory. Engineering, chemistry, and fine arts students (representing Realistic, Investigative, and Artistic types) report changes consistent with the typical personality orientation for their field. Psychology, political science, and economics students (representing Social, Enterprising, and Conventional types) did not report consistent changes. In another study, Walsh and Lacey (1970) extended their approach to college women, with generally similar results. Women in Investigative, Artistic, and Conventional fields reported seeing themselves as having changed in direction consistent with their field's modal personality type. Walsh, Vaudrin, and Hummel (1972) examined the question of whether college students changed in the direction of their existing personality orientation over time. Based on the responses of 154 and 165 third-quarter male and female students to the Perceived Change Inventory, some evidence was produced indicating that a modest degree of accentuation of existing personality attributes results from exposure to an environment (defined as a college major in this study). The longer a student was in an environment, the greater the development of appropriate traits.

Overall, these studies of environmental aspects of personality orientation suggest at least two important influences: family and school. In addition, the results of the Walsh studies, and possibly the Elton study, suggest that at least to some extent, "work" environment can play an important role in changing or maintaining personality characteristics associated with vocational matters.

# STATUS

**The Implications for Counseling Practice**

As is the case with most theorists of vocational choice, Holland did not at first attempt to devise a model for counseling young people and adults with regard to their vocational decisions. However, based on Holland's early writings, inferences which apply to counseling settings may be drawn from the content of the theory and the resulting empirical data testing it. For example, a point that may easily be overlooked is that Holland's theoretical statement denotes a classification of occupations which may be of use to counselors in helping their clientele become oriented to the world of work. Within the context of that occupational classification system the counselor might apply one of the various techniques to identify the major personal style of the individual (the techniques used so far are the VPI, selected SVIB scores, first occupational preferences, and ranking of descriptions based on the characteristics of the six personal orientations), to identify the particular occupational environment that is relevant, and to help his client locate the level in that hierarchy which is suitable to him. This approach is much like the traditional trait-factor approach used for generations in vocational counseling and is best exemplified today in the use counselors make of the SVIB and various ability measures in their practice. The advantage Holland's system possesses over the empirical systems (nontheoretically derived, such as the SVIB) is that the occupational environments may offer a greater potential from which to choose a career field than SVIB categories, which are not always internally consistent.

Of significance, too, is the potential that the theory holds for identifying institutional characteristics in terms of the six potential environments of the theory. It will be recalled that some evidence was found indicating that students in schools where the major orientation was congruent with their own major personal orientation were less likely to change fields than those in schools where differences existed between the individual and institutional orientations. It was also found that institutional orientations tend to influence the behavior of their constituents in subtle ways. If counselors were to become sophisticated with respect to the identification of modal institutional environments, they could help students to recognize the psychological characteristics of the schools they considered attending and to add to their decision some evaluation of this subtle dimension.

The potential of institutional evaluation along the lines of psychological characteristics does not end with unversities. There is nothing to prevent professional counselors from systematically studying the psychological characteristics of industries, particular business organizations, hospitals, government agencies, and so on. Such data might well be useful for people advanced in their careers, if they are considering changes in their mature years or when they are considering the organization in which to begin their career. It has been suggested that effective organizations play a major role in generating effective careers for individuals, and therefore it is likely that the psychological context an organization provides is a major factor in career satisfaction, progress, and effectiveness. It is a well-known fact that two positions with the same title but in different organizations are likely to be very different because of environmental differences the organizations produce for the person holding the position.

There are other uses the counselor may find for Holland's theory. Because of the considerable data that Holland has collected about the features of people possessing different personal orientations, a counselor has a considerable body of information about a client simply by knowing his major personal orientation to life. The counselor may make some educated guesses about the client's background, his parents' behaviors toward him and their ambitions for him, his goals, values, social relations, motivators, distractors, and so on.

In one paper Holland (1964b) made some explicit statements about limitations of current practices in vocational counseling and some suggestions about the direction vocational counseling should take in its future development. He is particularly critical about the rigidity of vocational counselors in using interviews with students as the main vehicle to effect change. Holland maintains that few people can be reached in that way, and furthermore, that even those who are reached are only minimally influenced by the things their counselors say to them. Holland proposes as an alternative the use of "environmental programmers and specialists," whose functions are not clearly defined in his mind, but who would generally be concerned with devising techniques through which students could be exposed to real and meaningful occupational experiences. Work-study programs such as exist at Antioch and Northeastern represent meaningful work experiences. Though his theory has undoubtedly influenced his thinking in this matter, the proposals Holland makes along these lines are neither specific enough to be implemented nor seem to bear any direct relation to his theoretical constructs. Holland's theory possesses some general utility for counselors in their conceptualization of occupational selection for their clientele, but it offers little in the way of suggestions about specific procedures and techniques that the counselors may use in their face-to-face work with their clients. For example, until some questions concerning the antecedents of the personal types are answered, counselors will find it difficult to develop interview procedures based on Holland's theory beyond an empirical trait-factor approach such as is represented by SVIB. That is, counselors might be able to say, "You are a realistic type of person and your intellectual apparatus and personal evaluations place you at a moderate level; thus you might find work as an electronics technician, welder, or draftsman suitable."

As the research effort of a variety of investigators has grown, an impressive amount of data regarding the characteristics and background of members of the various personal types have been accumulating, overcoming, at least in part, some early deficiencies in understanding how people become a member of a type, and what events influence their continuing membership. Early shortcomings regarding the narrowness of the data base, i.e., National Merit Scholars, have, to a large degree, been eliminated because data have been collected extensively on college students in general, high school and junior high school students, employed men, and adult women (Harvey and Whinfield, 1973). Despite the growth in data about how the personal types develop, there still is no clear statement summarizing this issue.

The theory is much more applicable to counseling now than in its earlier stages. Holland has become more directly concerned with applications of the theory, and in this regard has developed the Self-Directed Search (Holland, 1971), an instrument which combines the VPI with questions about self-estimates of competency. The goal of this instrument is the stimulation of self-inquiry which produces a summary statement combining the individual's perception of his abilities and preferences. Holland claims that about half the people who take this instrument find it is all they need to begin the process of vocational selection, while for the other half it sensitizes them to a need for further counseling. The instrument is too new for evaluation and little data are yet available regarding its validity, but it does seem to offer considerable potential value to the counselor and researcher. The occupational classification booklet, listing over 400 occupations, that accompanies the SDS is a useful career exploration adjunct in itself.

Other developments which make the theory more applicable are the publication of VPI norms (Holland, 1968b), the developing relation between the theory and the SVIB, and recent applications to the *Dictionary of Occupational Titles* system of classification. Frantz (1972) has shown how Holland's theory can be applied to the problem of counseling an individual with regard to an undifferentiated SVIB profile. Viernstein (1972) has developed procedures designed to extend Holland's occupational classification system to the *Dictionary of Occupational Titles* in terms of the data-people-things relationships described in the DOT. Her data indicate that these data-people-things relationships hold in theoretically predicted ways: e.g., involvement with things is higher for Realistic types than for others; Social and Enterprising types are higher on "people" involvement than Realistic, Investigative, and Conventional; and only the high

Artistic involvement with people seems inconsistent theoretically.

Thus the nature of the theory is such that imaginative counselors might find it possible to generate counseling procedures based on Holland's theory. Some idea about how difficulties in the choice process develop is given in the theory. For example, problems in the realm of the level of choice are likely to be the result of an inconsistent self-evaluation. Circumstances leading to an ambiguous developmental hierarchy presumably lead to choice conflicts. Ambiguous developmental hierarchies, in their turn, may develop because of a vagueness about the real world. In such a manner Holland's theory would explicitly account for misdirected vocational behavior or problems in vocational choice. As a result, the theory could be useful to a counselor in diagnosing the underlying factors contributing to vocational indecision.

### Evaluation

With respect to the research testing it, the record of Holland's theory is extremely good. The research program has been broad, varied, and comprehensive. Early shortcomings in the breadth of samples studied have been overcome.

Holland's theory seems to suffer from the problems that are inherent in trait-factor approaches to vocational choice. For example, it is possible for people to change their environments and themselves. The environmental and individual traits that the trait-factor approach tries to match are not only variable but are subject to change by one of the portions of the equation, that is, the individual. Consequently, when a young man discovers that his job as a salesman is not what he thought it would be, he may, and frequently does, exert his efforts at changing his definition and emphasis of his job without changing its title.

Some problems seem evident in the formulations about the level hierarchy, despite the empirical support for the notion found by Stockin (1964) and Schutz and Blocher (1961). A formulation about occupational level is a crucial feature of a theory about vocational behavior, yet Holland's concept of the level hierarchy as a function of self-evaluation and intelligence seems to ignore the likelihood of a high positive correlation between self-evaluation and the implications of such a correlation for the selection of level. Holland goes to great pains in his original formulation to point out that the level hierarchy is a function of the *sum* of intelligence and self-evaluation. No evidence seems to exist to support the notion that the relationship is additive as opposed to multiplicative. In fact, it would seem that other factors must be introduced to account adequately for the aspiration level of an individual, and these factors are not made explicit by Holland, though they can be guessed; for example, social status, economic status in interaction with personal orientation, and so on. What is evident, however, is that any attempt to derive a mathematical formula predicting occupational level at this stage of development is likely to be premature and may be deceptive as to the level of sophistication of the theory. To be sure, the counselor's aspiration might well be to develop a formula to account for and weigh the relevant variables in vocational preference and attainment, but this appears to be in the future.

A final serious limitation is that the theory, as stated, explains little about the process of personality development and its role in vocational selection. This is a serious deficiency since an understanding of personality development is crucial to understanding career development in this theory. It is one thing to state that people with Investigative orientations are looking for an environment in which they can express their major personality orientation, but it is quite another thing to explain how or why they developed their Investigative orientation to begin with. The data Holland has reported concerning the familial characteristics of people holding the various orientations are suggestive of causal factors, but only very tenuous inferences can be drawn. It is in the area of the growth of these developmental hierarchies that much valuable empirical work can be done with respect to Holland's theory. The effect of these orientations in vocational behavior in later life is also an important area for further study. Indeed, the question as to whether these models of personal styles hold validity for older people is open at present.

As for the overall status, how does Holland's theory rate according to the specific criteria outlined in the first chapter? Certainly, the proposal is comprehensive, covering not only vocational choices, but life style in the broadest sense. Tests of the theory indicate its validity in broad outline. Certain aspects are open to rigorous test, while others must of necessity be tested indirectly, or worse, crudely. The theory does not describe the development of the personality types, but does indicate the process of normal choice and misdirected choice from the point of an established personal orientation and beyond. Unfortunately, few suggestions are made for the treatment of problems in career choice, and for identifying relevant vocational counseling goals. The theory does logically and parsimoniously account for a good deal of vocational behavior, but falls down somewhat in respect to explanation of why people develop in various types.

It is to be expected that other investigators will continue to evaluate the adequacy of the theory and a continually broadening base of data will develop on which to judge Holland's contribution. Thus, one might well expect that investigators will continue to study the personal orientations and their correlates in noncollege groups, older workers at less than the professional level, and extend the empirical base with respect to the vocational development of women.

It is also to be expected that investigators might try to show how early experiences in childhood and adolescence are related to the development of one of the six major personal orientations (e.g., Barclay, Stilwell, and Barclay, 1972). Such data will be highly useful to both counselors and researchers in developmental psychology. In a later chapter, an example of how personality and career are intermeshed illustrates how research may uncover the ways personal orientations such as Holland describes evolve (Robert White's *Lives in Progress*, 1952). The number of unanswered and answered questions that remain with respect to

Holland's theory, however, suggest that the theory will exert an influence on research in careers for some time, and begin to have a growing impact on counseling itself.

# REFERENCES

Ashby, J. D., Wall, H. W., and Osipow, S. H. Vocational certainty and indecision in college freshmen. *Personnel and Guidance Journal*, 1966, *44*, 1037-1041.

Astin, A. W., and Panos, R. J. *The educational and vocational development of college students.* Washington, D. C.: American Council on Education, 1969.

Baird, L. L. The undecided student — how different is he? *Personnel and Guidance Journal*, 1969, *47*, 429-434.

Banducci, R. Accuracy of occupational stereotypes of grade-twelve boys. *Journal of Counseling Psychology*, 1970, *17*, 534-539.

Barclay, J. R. Approach to the measurement of teacher "press" in the secondary curriculum. *Journal of Counseling Psychology*. 1967, *14*, 550-567.

Barclay, J. R., Stilwell, W. E., III, and Barclay, Lisa K. The influence of paternal occupation on social interaction measures in elementary school children. *Journal of Vocational Behavior*, 1972, *2*, 433-446.

Blakeney, R. N., Matteson, M. T., and Holland, T. A. A research note on the new SVIB scales. *Journal of Vocational Behavior*, 1972, *2*, 239-243.

Bodden, J. L. Cognitive complexity as a factor in appropriate vocational choice. *Journal of Counseling Psychology*, 1970, *17*, 364-368.

Campbell, D. P., and Holland, J. L. A merger in vocational interest research: applying Holland's theory to Strong's data. *Journal of Vocational Behavior*, 1972, *2*, 353-376.

Cockriel, I. W. Some data concerning the VPI scales and the SVIB. *Journal of Vocational Behavior*, 1972, *2*, 251-254.

Cole, Nancy S., and Hanson, G. R. An analysis of the structure of vocational interests. *Journal of Counseling Psychology*, 1971, *18*, 478-486.

Cole, Nancy S., Whitney, D. R., and Holland, J. L. A spatial configuration of occupations. *Journal of Vocational Behavior*, 1971, *1*, 1-9.

Eggenberger, J., and Herman, A. The Strong Inventory and Holland's theory. *Journal of Vocational Behavior*, 1972, *2*, 447-456.

Elton, C. F. Interaction of environment and personality: a test of Holland's theory. *Journal of Applied Psychology*, 1971, *55*, 114-118.

Elton, C. F., and Rose, Harriet A. A longitudinal study of the vocationally undecided student. *Journal of Vocational Behavior*, 1971, *1*, 75-92.

Elton, C. F., and Rose, Harriet A. Male occupational constancy and change: its prediction according to Holland's theory. *Journal of Counseling Psychology*, 1970, *17*, part 2, 1-19.

Folsom, C. H., Jr. An investigation of Holland's theory of vocational choice. *Journal of Counseling Psychology*, 1969, *16*, 260-266.

Fortner, Mildred L. Vocational choices of high school girls: can they be predicted? *Vocational Guidance Quarterly*, 1970, *18*, 203-206.

Frantz, T. T. Reinterpretation of flat SVIB profiles. *Journal of Vocational Behavior*, 1972, *2*, 201-207.

Frantz, T. T., and Walsh, E. P. Exploration of Holland's theory of vocational choice in graduate school environments. *Journal of Vocational Behavior*, 1972, *2*, 223-232.

Griffith, A. V., and Trogden, K. P. Self-expressive styles among college students preparing for careers in nursing and music. *Journal of Counseling Psychology*, 1969, *16*, 275-277.

Haase, R. F. Canonical analysis of the Vocational Preference Inventory and the Strong Vocational Interest Blank. *Journal of Counseling Psychology*, 1971, *18*, 182-183.

Hansen, Ida-Jo, and Johansson, C. B. The application of Holland's vocational model to the Strong Vocational Interest Blank for women. *Journal of Vocational Behavior*, 1972, *2*, 479-493.

Harvey, D. W., and Whinfield, R. W. Extending Holland's theory to adult women. *Journal of Vocational Behavior*, 1973, *3*, 115-127.

Hieronymus, A. N. A study of social class motivations: relationship between anxiety for education and certain socio-economic and intellectual variables. *Journal of Educational Psychology*, 1951, *42*, 193-203.

Holland, J. L. A personality inventory employing occupational titles. *Journal of Applied Psychology*, 1958, *42*, 336-342.

Holland, J. L. A theory of vocational choice. *Journal of Counseling Psychology*, 1959, *6*, 35-45.

Holland, J. L. The relation of the Vocational Preference Inventory to the Sixteen Personality Factor Questionnaire. *Journal of Applied Psychology*, 1960, *44*, 291-296.

Holland, J. L. Some explorations with occupational titles. *Journal of Counseling Psychology*, 1961, *8*, 82-87.

Holland, J. L. Some explorations of a theory of vocational choice: I. One- and two-year longitudinal studies. *Psychological Monographs*, 1962, *76*, No. 26 (Whole No. 545).

Holland, J. L. Explorations of a theory of vocational choice and achievement: II. A four-year prediction study. *Psychological Reports*, 1963, *12*, 547-594.

Holland, J. L. Explorations of a theory of vocational choice: IV. Vocational preferences and their relation to occupational images, daydreams and personality. *Vocational Guidance Quarterly*, 1963, *11*, 232-239; 1963, *12*, 17-24; 1964, *12*, 93-97.

Holland, J. L. Explorations of a theory of vocational choice: V. A one-year prediction study. *Chronicle Guidance Professional Service*, 1964. (a)

Holland, J. L. Some new directions for vocational counseling. Paper read at American Educational Research Association Meetings, Chicago, February, 1964. (b)

Holland, J. L. *The psychology of vocational choice.* Waltham, Mass: Blaisdell, 1966. (a)

Holland, J. L. A psychological classification scheme for vocations and major fields. *Journal of Counseling Psychology*, 1966, *13*, 278-288. (b)

Holland, J. L. Explorations of a theory of vocational choice: VI. A longitudinal study using a sample of typical college students. *Journal of Applied Psychology, Monograph Supplement*, 1968, *52*, 37 pages. (a)

Holland, J. L. ACT Guidance profile manual. Iowa City, Iowa: The American College Testing Program, 1968. (b)

Holland, J. L. A theory-ridden, computerless, impersonal, vocational guidance system. *Journal of Vocational Behavior*, 1971, *1*, 167-176.

Holland, J. L. *Making vocational choices: a theory of careers.* Englewood Cliffs, New Jersey: Prentice-Hall, 1973.

Holland, J. L., and Nichols, R. C. Explorations of a theory of vocational choice: III. A longitudinal study of change in major field of study. *Personnel and Guidance Journal*, 1964, *43*, 235-242.

Holland, J. L., and Whitney, D. R. Changes in the vocational plans of college students: orderly or random? ACT Research Report, No. 25, Iowa City, Iowa, 1968.

Holland, J. L., Whitney, D. R., Cole, Nancy S., and Richards, J. M., Jr. An empirical occupational classification derived from a theory of personality and intended for practice and research. ACT Research Report, No. 29, Iowa City, Iowa, 1969.

Hollander, M. A., and Parker, H. J. Occupational stereotypes and needs: their relationship to vocational choice. *Vocational Guidance Quarterly*, 1969, *18*, 91-98.

Hollander, M. A., and Parker, H. J. Occupational stereotypes and self-descriptions: their relationship to vocational choice. *Journal of Vocational Behavior*, 1972, *2*, 57-65.

Hughes, H. M., Jr. Vocational choice, level, and consistency: an investigation of Holland's theory on an employed sample. *Journal of Vocational Behavior*, 1972, *2*, 377-388.

Lacey, D. W. Holland's vocational models: a study of work groups and need satisfaction. *Journal of Vocational Behavior*, 1971, *1*, 105-122.

Lee, D. L., and Hedahl, Beulah. Holland's personality types applied to the SVIB basic interest scales. *Journal of Vocational Behavior*, 1973, *3*, 61-68.

Morrow, J. M., Jr. A test of Holland's theory of vocational choice. *Journal of Counseling Psychology*, 1971, *18*, 422-425.

Navran, L., and Kendall, L. M. A canonical correlational analysis of the SVIB, the Holland VPI, and the EPPS. *Journal of Counseling Psychology*, 1971, *18*, 514-519.

Osipow, S. H. *Theories of career development* (1st ed.). New York: Appleton-Century-Crofts, 1968.

Osipow, S. H. Cognitive styles and vocational-educational preference and selection. *Journal of Counseling Psychology*, 1969, *16*, 534-546.

Osipow, S. H. Interaction between occupational environments and personality types. In Bartlett, W. (Ed.), *Evolving religious careers*. Washington, D.C.: CARA, 1970.

Osipow, S. H., and Ashby, J. D. Vocational Preference Inventory high point codes and educational preferences. *Personnel and Guidance Journal*, 1968, *47*, 126-129.

Osipow, S. H., Ashby, J. D., and Wall, H. W. Personality types and vocational choice: a test of Holland's theory. *Personnel and Guidance Journal*, 1966, *45*, 37-42.

Posthuma, A. B., and Navran, L. Relation of congruence in student-faculty interests to achievement in college. *Journal of Counseling Psychology*, 1970, *17*, 252-256.

Rezler, Agnes G. Characteristics of high school girls choosing traditional or pioneer vocations. *Personnel and Guidance Journal*, 1967, *45*, 659-665. (a)

Rezler, Agnes G. The joint use of the KPR and the Holland VPI in the vocational assessment of high school girls. *Psychology in the Schools*, 1967, *4*, 82-84. (b)

Roe, Anne. A new classification of occupations. *Journal of Counseling Psychology*, 1954, *1*, 215-220.

Roe, Anne. Early determinants of vocational choice. *Journal of Counseling Psychology*, 1957, *4*, 212-217.

Roe, Anne, and Siegelman, M. The origin of interests. *APGA Inquiry Studies* No. 1, Washington, D. C.: American Personnel and Guidance Association, 1964.

Rose, Harriet A., and Elton, C. F. Attrition and the vocationally undecided student. *Journal of Vocational Behavior*, 1971, *1*, 99-103.

Salomone, P. R., and Muthard, J. E. Canonical correlation of vocational needs and vocational style. *Journal of Vocational Behavior*, 1972, *2*, 163-171.

Schaefer, E. S., and Bell, R. Q. Development of a parental attitude research instrument. *Child Development*, 1958, *29*, 339-361.

Schutz, R. A., and Blocher, D. H. Self-satisfaction and level of occupational choice. *Personnel and Guidance Journal*, 1961, *40*, 595-598.

Shaw, F. J. *Reconciliation: a theory of man transcending.* Princeton, New Jersey: Van Nostrand, 1966.

Southworth, J. A., and Morningstar, Mona E. Persistence of occupational choice and personality congruence. *Journal of Counseling Psychology*, 1970, *17*, 409-412.

Stockin, B. S. A test of Holland's occupational level formulations. *Personnel and Guidance Journal*, 1964, *42*, 599-602.

Wall, H. W., Osipow, S. H., and Ashby, J. D. SVIB scores, occupational choices, and Holland's personality types. *Vocational Guidance Quarterly*, 1967, *15*, 201-205.

Walsh, W. B., and Barrow, Cynthia A. Consistent and inconsistent career preferences and personality. *Journal of Vocational Behavior*, 1971, *1*, 271-278.

Walsh, W. B., and Lacey, D. W. Perceived change and Holland's theory. *Journal of Counseling Psychology*, 1969, *16*, 348-352.

Walsh, W. B., and Lacey, D. W. Further exploration of perceived change and Holland's theory. *Journal of Counseling Psychology*, 1970, *17*, 189-190.

Walsh, W. B., and Lewis, R. O. Consistent, inconsistent, and undecided career preferences and personality. *Journal of Vocational Behavior*, 1972, *2*, 309-316.

Walsh, W. B., and Russel, J. H. College major choice and personal adjustment. *Personnel and Guidance Journal*, 1969, *47*, 685-688.

Walsh, W. B., Vaudrin, Donna M., and Hummel, Ruth A. The accentuation effect and Holland's theory. *Journal of Vocational Behavior*, 1972, *2*, 77-85.

White, R. W. *Lives in progress.* New York: Dryden Press, 1952.

Williams, Constance M. Occupational choice of male graduate students as related to values and personality: a test of Holland's theory. *Journal of Vocational Behavior*, 1972, *2*, 39-46.

Wolfle, D. *America's resources of specialized talent.* New York: Harper & Row, 1954.

Viernstein, Mary Cowan. The extension of Holland's occupational classification to all occupations in the *Dictionary of Occupational Titles. Journal of Vocational Behavior*, 1972, *2*, 107-121.

# 3

# The Ginzberg, Ginsburg, Axelrad, and Herma Theory

An economist, a psychiatrist, a sociologist, and a psychologist collaborated to produce a rationale describing vocational choice which exerted a most profound influence on vocational psychology during the decade following its publication in 1951. The work was the result of an empirical investigation into the character of events influencing vocational selection. The theoretical formulation was a direct reaction to the absence of elaborate and comprehensive theoretical constructs in vocational psychology. It was the plan of these four investigators to construct a theoretical approach to the matter of vocational choice.

The empirical findings of their own earlier studies and those of other investigators influenced the approach they took to the problem. Ginzberg's group concluded, on the basis of earlier research, that at least four significant variables were involved in vocational choice. The first of the four was identified as the reality factor, which causes an individual to respond to the pressures of his environment in making decisions with vocational impact. Then, the influence of the educational process is felt, since the amount and kind of education a person has had will limit or facilitate the flexibility and type of vocational choices he makes. Third, emotional factors involved in the individual's responses to his environment are important since it seemed, on an intuitive basis, that personality and emotional factors should have vocational concomitants. Finally, individual values were deemed to be important in vocational choice, since they should influence the quality of the choices made by virtue of the differing values in various careers.

## THE THEORY

Simply stated, Ginzberg, Ginsburg, Axelrad, and Herma (1951) concluded that vocational choice is an irreversible process, occurring in reasonably clearly marked periods, which is characterized by a series of compromises the individual makes between his wishes and his possibilities. The three major periods of the process have been entitled the Fantasy, Tentative, and Realistic periods. Probably less is known about the Fantasy period than the other two. Ginzberg and his associates suggest that the chief feature of the Fantasy period is the arbitrary nature of the child's choices and the lack of reality orientation reflected in the occupational preferences expressed during that period.

The Tentative period has been further subdivided into four stages: Interest, Capacity, Value, and Transition. Thus, children begin their vocational considerations by asking themselves what they are interested in and what they like to do. Soon, however, they become aware that there are some things they do more skillfully than others, and thus they temper their unrestrained desires with the notion of abilities. As they grow older, they recognize that certain activities have more intrinsic or extrinsic value than other activities, and they introduce this recognition as a third element in their vocational deliberations. At this point, they are beginning to integrate the four stages of the Transition stage and move into the final period, that of Realistic choice.

The Realistic period, too, has several stages. The first has been called the Exploration stage. Having reached the point of integrating his likes and dislikes with his capabilities and tempering these two variables with society's and his own values, the young adult begins to devise ways to implement the still tentative choices. This stage is distinct from the Tentative period in that the individual evaluates the feedback of his vocational behaviors in a highly realistic context, such as an entry job or early years in college. The results of these evaluations gradually blend into the Crystallization stage. Crystallization is characterized by the emergence of some clear vocational pattern based on the success and failures the individual experienced during the Exploration stage. Once this crystallization is complete it leads to the final stage, entitled Specification. The individual chooses a position or a professional specialty. At this point, the process is complete, having occurred over perhaps as much as a 15-year period in the life of the individual.

How is the 10- to 15-year period distributed with regard to the three periods and substages within the periods? Ginzberg and his collaborators take pains to caution their readers that individual variations of timing and degree may be very large. Certain general patterns of timing are evident, however, and are suggested as part of the theory. The Fantasy period seems to terminate at about age 10 or 12. The specific age is partly a function of the rate of emotional and intellectual development of the child. Generally, by age 12 most children have entered the Interest stage of the Tentative period. The three remaining stages of the Tentative period are likely to be concluded by age 17 or 18, though once again, considerable variability is likely. Lower income children are likely to enter the Realistic period at an earlier age than more affluent adolescents who may go to college, mainly because the poorer children are faced with the task of earning a living sooner and partly because the cultural values they are exposed to encourage an earlier assumption of an adult role than the cultural values of upper and middle class groups. The latter groups tend to prolong the period of adolescent dependency upon parents. The crystallization stage of the Realistic period is likely to have a very broad range, though Ginzberg and his associates suggest that for most young people Crystallization occurs between the ages of 19 and 21.

The theory is heavily dependent on general concepts found in developmental psychology. Beyond these basic concepts, however, the work is subtly influenced by the Freudian model of personality development. The theorists assume that the vocational choice process occurs primarily during the adolescent period and is closely linked with the physical changes that occur during adolescence. The authors of the theory further assume that adolescence is a period of "storm and stress" in general, and that the storminess of the period influences the pattern of the process of vocational development.

The eventual shape of the theory was heavily influenced by the nature of the students observed. A particular effort was made to select students who represented a population which is relatively unhampered by reality constraints in vocational choice; these constraints being the limits that personal or environmental situations place on the choices one can implement. The assumption made was that such a group would reflect the "purest" features of the vocational choice process. To accomplish this, a sample of white boys of Anglo-Saxon descent of upper and middle class Protestant or Catholic background was selected. The mean family income in the late 1940s was between $10,000 and $12,000. Both parents were alive and living together. Furthermore, the boys were generally emotionally stable, considerably above average intellectually, and were all ostensibly college bound. Eight subjects at each two-year interval between age 11 through about age 23 or 24 were chosen for intensive study. At the college level, freshmen at Columbia College (the male undergraduate school of Columbia University) who had completed a semester and a half of college work were chosen on the assumption that they had experienced enough of college to evaluate its influence on their career development. At the graduate level, several subjects at the master's degree level were chosen, and several doctoral candidates were also included. No students in professional schools such as medicine and law were included, and special pains were taken to distribute the sample evenly with respect to scientific and nonscientific fields.

## The Fantasy Period

The primary task the child accomplishes during the first period of vocational development is part of the general maturational process of changing from a "play-orientation" to a "work-orientation." According to Ginzberg and his associates, children state clear vocational preferences and their play reflects what they call "function pleasure" as a motive. As a child grows older and approaches the terminal point of the Fantasy period, a gradual reorientation occurs, reflecting a preference for vocational activity which leads to accomplishments which will result in abstract satisfactions, such as pleasing a parent. The "function pleasure" principle refers to the observation that very young children delight in activities for the sheer sake of the characteristics intrinsic in the activity. Making mudpies is fun because of the feel of the mud. Later, as the children grow more socialized, they seek out activities that possess potential for extrinsic rewards, such as parental approval, success and its rewards, money to buy toys with, and so on.

Coupled with the developmental change described above is the hypothesis that children are frustrated by a sense of inadequacy and impotency which results from their small size and their relative ineffectiveness as compared to adults. One way that children can attempt to relieve the sense of frustration their size instills is by identifying with and emulating the adults around them. Adult roles are most clearly manifest in work; thus children "play at" working and assuming make-believe identities in the work roles they pretend to hold. In so doing they try out a variety of adult situations. At this same time they relieve the frustration generated by their feelings of inadequacy and internalize the values of the adult world. During the Fantasy period the children ignore reality, their abilities and potentials, and the time perspective, three of the very important ingredients in the vocational choice process, according to the Ginzberg group.

## The Tentative Period

These play activities, nevertheless, help to propel the child to the next period in his vocational selection, the Tentative period. This occurs between the ages of approximately 11 and 18 and is divided into three stages which differ in their vocational developmental tasks. The *Interest stage* is the time, around ages 11 and 12, when the child is beginning to recognize the need to identify a career direction. At this stage, the need is reflected in a growing concern for the identification of activities liked and disliked. Choices are considered in terms of the potential they hold for intrinsic enjoyment. Often these choices reflect a strong identification with the father, but the identification shows signs of ambivalence. The children recognize their instability, a function of the anticipation of physical and emotional changes in adolescence, and accept the need and possibility of deferring final selections until they are older. Nevertheless, they begin circumscribing their arena of choice during the Interest stage. The *Capacity stage*, ages 12 to 14, logically follows the Interest stage. Here, students begin to introduce the notion of ability into their vocational considerations. They begin to evaluate their ability to perform well in areas of interest. There appears to be a decrease in the degree of father identification as an influence in vocational choices and a corresponding increase in the influence of other, more distant models.

In the *Value stage*, next to follow during the 15th and 16th years, students undergo a very marked change in their approach to vocational choice. Of special note is the introduction of the idea of service to society. They seem to become aware that work offers more than the potential for satisfying their own needs, and for the first time show signs of choosing careers such as medicine for humanitarian reasons, rather than because of its status or intrinsic work activities. Clearer conceptions of differing life styles offered by occupations also emerge during the Value stage. It becomes more evident to boys that a salesman leads a different kind of life than an accountant. It is during the Value stage that the students become more cognizant of the uses to which they may put their special abilities. For example, those skilled interpersonally will begin looking for ways to use that skill in work.

Finally, two significant developments concerning time awareness take place during the Value stage. First, the students begin to develop a broader time perspective than they formerly held. They begin thinking of a career in terms of day-in and day-out activities for years which will eventually become a life pattern. At the same time, as their time perspective broadens, they become more sensitive to the imminence of vocational commitment. Clearly, by age 16 only a few more years remain before they are almost irrevocably committed to a life pattern, and their recognition of this introduces a sense of urgency in their planning which is frustrated by their continued dependence on their parents.

The *Transition stage* closes the Tentative period. Occurring at about age 17 or 18, this stage is characteristically calmer than preceding stages of the Tentative period. It is during this stage that the individual begins to face the necessity to make immediate, concrete, and realistic decisions about his vocational future, and furthermore, to assume the responsibility for the consequences of the decisions. This stage differs from the Value stage which preceded it in that during the Transition stage the young person has considerably more independence of action than he formerly possessed. The increased freedom leads to a seeking of new surroundings in which to try out skills and talents. A heightened awareness of the externals of work occurs. The amount and kind of preparation necessary for various careers is studied, recognition of varying financial rewards is keener, and the awareness of the different life-circumstances of careers is sharpened. It is during this stage, too, that increasing sexual impulses and the desire for early marriage run headlong into the necessity for delaying marriage in order to pursue the required career training.

### The Realistic Period

The Realistic period follows the final stage of the Tentative period and takes place from approximately 18 to 22, or even as late as age 24. This period is more variable in its timing than many of the others, partly because of the different training patterns various careers require. While biological maturation and processes exert a strong influence on the rate with which a student progresses through the Tentative period, such physical factors have little to do with the

Realistic period. The rate of biological change slows markedly by age 18 or 19, when the Realistic period begins.

The first stage of the Realistic period is the *Exploration stage*. Starting at college entrance, it is marked by narrowed goals in contrast with the broader goals of earlier periods, but maintains a good deal of vocational flexibility. Having moved into a college environment, the students experience much more freedom than they had before, but at the expense of considerable ambiguity. The general indecisiveness continues, partly because their interests are still changing and partly because the reality of the situation does not yet require a specific decision to be made. The principal task during this stage is typically the selection of a path to follow from among two or three strongly held interests. In the face of the selection, the students are fearful of choosing what will eventually be an unsatisfying occupation and are still relatively naive about the specific financial rewards to be expected in certain occupations. They especially feel the pressures of time acutely, since job or graduate school applications will need to be made at a specified time in the predictable future.

The *Crystallization stage* occurs next. By this time the students have become more or less deeply involved in a specific major field. They definitely have a clear idea of what occupational tasks they wish to avoid. In the face of definite and impending deadlines, by which time decisions must be made, their decisions become firm and the degree of commitment to a choice grows strong. Although most students have reached the Crystallization stage by the time of college graduation, Ginzberg and his colleagues point out that by no means do all students reach Crystallization so early. For some, there is a stage of pseudo-crystallization, where the student thinks and acts as if he has crystallized his decision, but later events indicate otherwise. This is not to say that truly crystal-lized choices are not subject to change as a function of new experiences or the reappraisal of old experiences. Ginzberg and his associates do not clearly indicate how one is to tell pseudocrystallization and revised crystallization apart. The concept of pseudocrystallization becomes a loophole to explain the behavior of a certain (unspecified) class of students who make late and unpredicted changes in their plans.

The final stage of the Realistic period is the *Specification stage*. For some, this stage never genuinely arrives. It is the final point of career development. The individual here elaborates upon his choice by selecting a specific job or graduate school subspeciality. Once again, however, Ginzberg and his associates suggest the possibility of a pseudospecification, but do not distinguish the pseudoevent from the real one.

### Variations in the Pattern

Although the authors of the theory visualize the career choice process as occur-ring within the framework just described, they recognize that individual varia-tions in the patterns will occur for biological, psychological, and environmental reasons. Such variations will occur in two possible behavioral realms. Individuals will vary with regard to the range of choices they express over time. Some people will select one occupation early in life and never vary significantly from it, while others will make a series of widely diverse occupational choices over the years before eventually implementing one. Ginzberg and his associates suggest that the specific nature of an individual's abilities will partly influence the range of his choices. Thus, if a person possesses a highly developed skill with specific occupational implications and if that skill emerges early in his life, it is very likely that he will exhibit a very narrow range in his choice pattern.

The other dimension of variability is with respect to the timing of the Crystallization stage. Some people make crystallized vocational choices toward the end of the Tentative period, and at the other extreme, crystallization may occur well into the twenties. In addition to normal variability of patterns of career development, Ginzberg and his collaborators describe certain conditions which differ from normal variations. They consider these conditions to be deviant patterns. The general principle in identifying deviant occupational patterns is that the individual does not conform to his age mates in some significant aspect of his vocational development. Thus, he might pursue an unrealistic choice far beyond the time when his age mates have discarded their earlier and ill-founded choices, or he may approach the end of the Realistic period but be chronically unable to achieve a crystallized choice. Reasons for deviant patterns may be highly variable, but might include severe emotional disorder or unusual personal financial circumstances, such as excessive affluence.

*Exceptional groups.* It will be recalled that Ginzberg and his associates developed their theory in concert with an empirical investigation of the vocational development of a group of highly privileged boys. They did so in order to identify the process that occurs in people subject to a minimum of environmental constraints. Thus, the theory described above is oriented toward the college-trained youth. In order to establish the generality with which their formulation holds, Ginzberg and his group studied two other groups of subjects.

*Underprivileged boys.* The sample of boys facing considerable environmental limitations was structured in a manner similar to the highly endowed boys. Boys in the eighth through twelfth grades were studied, with the heaviest weighting in ninth and tenth grades. The boys were all Catholic or Protestant white sons of semiskilled or unskilled fathers (a few fathers fell into higher categories) whose income in 1947 was in the general range of $2500-$3000 and who were all reasonably well adjusted emotionally. A total of 17 such boys were studied intensely and compared to the privileged boys.

It was possible to make several general observations on the basis of the interviews. The behavior of the lower income boys during the Tentative period was similar to that of the higher status boys during the same period. True, their choices differed, and their educational goals were lower, but the level of abstraction, the developmental tasks, and their timing were roughly equivalent. In particular, the problems and solutions of the Interest and Capacity stages were very similar for the two groups of boys. During the Transition stage the similarity was not as clear, but was still evident. The Realistic period might have some tendency to occur earlier for the lower economic group as a function of environmental circumstances, but this did not necessarily mean the Crystallization and Specification periods occurred earlier.

Ginzberg and his associates observed one very marked difference between the patterns of the two groups of boys which overshadows many of the similarities, however. The lower class boys generally seemed to be more buffeted by experience and more passive in their approach to vocational choice than did the higher economic sample. The lower class boys were evidently equally concerned about and interested in their eventual careers and the implications such careers had for their style of life in the future, but they seemed to take little initiative in influencing its direction in comparison to the upper class boys. Though there were obvious exceptions to this, the general passive pattern of career selection was pervasive in the lower economic group of boys.

*Women.* In addition to the group of underprivileged boys that were studied, Ginzberg's group chose to interview a small group of women to assess the similarities and differences between the male and female vocational choice process. This sample consisted of seven Barnard College sophomores and three Barnard College seniors, generally a socially privileged and intelligent group. These ten women were interviewed intensively in a manner similar to the interviews with both male groups. Because of the nature of the sample, however, certain differences in the data necessarily occurred. Thus, since no girls were included in the ages 11-17 category, data about the Tentative period were entirely based on retrospect.

The recollections of the girls about the nature of their vocational behavior during the early stages of the Tentative period correspond closely to the behavior observed in the interviews with boys 11 to 15. The girls reported early choices (around 11 years or so) that were almost entirely based on their interest. Later, again like the boys, they became concerned with their abilities and special talents. Following the Capacity stage, however, the sexes apparently begin to deviate in their vocational tasks. By the Transition stage, the girls are heavily oriented toward marriage and all its implications, while the boys are moving toward vocations. Transition, in a sense, occurs for both sexes, but the object of the transition is apparently different.

The focus on marriage that girls begin to develop at about age 17 underlies a major problem females encounter in their career planning. While boys may formulate vocational plans on the basis of their impressions of themselves and their observations of the world around them and exert a reasonable degree of control over their future, girls' careers are entirely tentative depending upon their marital future. Girls cannot realistically plan on a career as they do not know if they will marry or not, since if they do marry, the individuals they marry and their characteristics are highly important to the vocational plans of the girls. Financial status and attitudes toward the wife working are two of many important characteristics of the husband affecting women's career plans. The age of a woman at marriage is also an important but unpredictable factor, as is the number and timing of children. Many other factors beyond the control of the female increase the difficulty of her planning soundly for her vocational future. This greater uncertainity in planning is probably the major difference between male and female career development. Men can make their plans with a higher probability of accuracy than women because they have a sounder data base than women do.

Of course, there are other differences between the sexes in career development. Some of these differences are related to the greater vocational uncertainty of women, while others are not. Perhaps one difference related to female vocational uncertainty is that girls are clearly not as work-oriented in general as men are. Work outside the home is not as central a concept to women as to men, and their status is less dependent on whether or not they have a career. Ginzberg and his co-investigators classified their female sample into three work types, namely, work-oriented, marriage-oriented, and an orientation combining work and marriage. Only one girl was placed in the work-oriented category, and even she, at the extreme for women, was significantly different from men in her vocational plans. For example, she was less concerned about the kind of work she would do in the future than about the fact that she would work, married or not. Such an attitude is markedly different from that of college men.

Other sex differences were noted. The girls seemed much more verbal about their plans than the boys and were clearly more naive about careers and their future plans than the males, the latter probably because they had been more protected than the boys. Curiously, the girls seemed to have been much more influenced in their educational and vocational plans, such as they existed, by their fathers than by their mothers. The only exception to this seemed to be in a negative way — girls often were influenced in their vocational behaviors by a desire to avoid what they considered to be their mothers' mistakes.

### Recent Developments

Ginzberg (1972), responding to some of the criticisms that have been raised concerning the theory over the years, has suggested three conceptual changes in his theory. First, he would modify his assertion that occupational decisions are a life-span phenomenon, not simply a short-term event restricted to the adolescent and early adult years. Second, the notion of irreversibility has been toned down, and is now viewed in terms of the expenditure of time and resources. That is, careers may be redirected in major ways, though there are costs involved, and these costs operate in some ways to make the process irreversible for some people at some times. Finally, the concept of compromise has been changed to one of optimization; that is, Ginzberg proposes that there is a continuing search on the part of the individual for the best fit between the career avenues he prefers and the opportunities open to him. These three changes considerably improve the theory, though the basic style of the conception remains unchanged.

## Some General Concepts of the Theory

Ginzberg and his associates place a heavy emphasis on the role that emotional factors play in career development, though their research has not been notably successful in identifying the specific role played by emotional factors in career choice. In designing their investigations, they went to special lengths to exclude subjects who seemed to be emotionally unstable. Despite the screening, several subjects presented evidence of emotional problems upon intensive interviewing. The observations made of the few emotionally disturbed subjects in the sample led the investigators to conclude that emotional problems were important factors in the deviant vocational choice patterns that they occasionally observed.

The authors of the theory conclude that four important ingredients contributed to the adequacy of an individual's occupational choice process during adolescence. These are reality testing, the development of a suitable time perspective, the ability to defer gratifications, and the ability to accept and implement compromises in their vocational plans. Should too many of these ingredients fail to develop properly, a deviant vocational pattern is likely to emerge. It further seems reasonable that should these four traits fail to develop adequately, the youth's overall emotional adjustment is not likely to be effective. Thus, a tie between emotional stability and vocational deviancy seems to exist, but whether of a causal or correlate nature is not clear.

Another critical feature in the career development process is the child's ability to identify with suitable models at appropriate times. During the Fantasy period, children identify with all adults, and play games reflecting these many identifications. As they enter the Interest stage of the Tentative period, however, they narrow their models down, so that many boys vocationally identify with their fathers at about ages 11 or 12. A vague awareness seems to exist that there may be some things about their fathers' work not suitable for them, and this apparently is involved in the gradual shift in identification from the fathers' field to other, and perhaps more suitable, adult vocational models, such as a teacher or an admired young adult. This latter identification is usually complete by about ages 16 to 18. The identification with emulated adults that occurs during the various stages gives some direction for the vocational planning of the boy and actively involves him in the task of vocational selection. It is much easier to emulate a specific model than a vague abstraction.

One more important concept about people and work exists in the proposal of the Ginzberg group. They suggest that two basic personality types exist with respect to work, the work-oriented person and the pleasure-oriented one. This does not imply that an individual is in either one category or the other, but merely that one mode characterizes each individual's approach to life. The work-oriented individual can be identified by his ability to defer gratification and to be relatively impervious to deflection from his work or occupational goals. On the other hand, the pleasure-oriented person is not likely to defer gratifications for work and he is easily distracted from his vocational course by alternatives that seem reasonably desirable. In combination with the work-versus-pleasure orientation, people seem to be either active or passive problem solvers. The active people attack their problems and attempt to solve them, whereas the passive individuals seem to be reactive. Events "happen" to them which elicit responses from them; rarely do they emit problem-solving responses as do the active people.

The interaction of these two variables exerts an influence on the style with which the young person approaches the developmental task of occupational choice. Active, work-oriented boys are likely to behave differently than passive, pleasure-oriented boys during the various periods of career development. The particular style, then, influences to some extent the kind of vocational pattern that the individual has during his adolescent period.

## Variations on the System

Tiedeman and O'Hara (1963) have built upon the somewhat simple concepts described by Ginzberg and his associates, creating a more complex and, thus, probably a more realistic system. Their approach stresses the role of the self-concept in negotiating the developmental stages and includes a complicated and sophisticated set of developmental notions. Briefly stated, Tiedeman and O'Hara view career development as a function of the developing self becoming increasingly differentiated and comprehensive. The critical ingredients of this emerging self include situational and social factors as well as biological. The self is seen as an entity that is always either expanding or contracting and for whom crucial decisions occur at points of discontinuity with the past, i.e., graduation from high school, college, marriage, taking one's first full-time position, etc. The decision-making process involves anticipation, implementation, and adjustment. The system describes anticipation in terms of the following sequence of events: exploration, crystallization, choice, clarification, induction, reformation, and integration. The entire sequence is characterized by somewhat disorganized thinking about occupational fields at first, followed by the development of clearer distinctions among fields accompanied by judgments about their advantages and disadvantages and relative values. On the basis of this evaluative process, some preliminary decision-making occurs, followed by a refractory period in which the individual has an opportunity to experience his doubts regarding the choice, and further elaborate the decision. Following this, the individual is "inducted" into a group during which time he identifies closely with the purposes of his new group, later beginning to question those same purposes (the reformation period) where he may try to change the group somewhat. The final stage, integration, involves the process by which the individual resolves his individuality and the group's demands and integrates the two in some way.

Kroll, Dinklage, Lee, Morley, and Wilson (1970) have taken the Tiedeman and O'Hara position and added some further points of emphasis. First, they emphasize the notion that career development represents a balance between changing the environment to fit oneself and changing oneself to fit the environment. Considerable weight is given to the importance of self-evaluation in the learning of one's areas of competence and incompetence; descriptions of this learning process during childhood and adolescence are provided, largely stemming from the framework of Piaget and Erikson.

The work of Tiedeman and O'Hara (1963), along with that of Kroll et al. (1970), in some ways stands as a bridge between the early developmental formulations of Ginzberg and his group and the work of Super (which is described in Chapter 5). These writers share the view that career development is an aspect of general development, in that self-concepts interact with career decision-making. In addition, it appears to be assumed that individuals with inaccurate self-evaluations are more prone to make inappropriate or inadequate career decisions than those with accurate self-evaluations. Finally, all (Ginzberg et al., O'Hara and Tiedeman, Kroll et al., and Super) seem to assume that the ability and motivation to evaluate oneself realistically can be enhanced through education and counseling.

## Summary

Ginzberg and his associates have thus developed a conception of career development which construes the vocational choice process as a specific behavior (one of many) based on the adolescent development pattern. They further have proposed that a systematic and predictable series of tasks face young people as a function of the changes that occur during adolescence. These tasks culminate, during the early twenties, in a specific vocational choice, the adequacy of which is related to the adequacy of the accomplishment of the various tasks along the way.

# RESEARCH

Probably the most elaborate study concerning the Ginzberg conception of career choice is the one conducted by O'Hara and Tiedeman (1959). They sought to explore the implications of the developmental approach of the Ginzberg group for the self-concept approach to behavior. O'Hara and Tiedeman were interested in studying the relationship between aptitude, interest, social class, and values in the Ginzberg model and the development of a vocational self-concept. For this study, over a thousand students of a private Catholic day school in Boston were tested on the verbal reasoning, numerical ability, mechanical reasoning, space relations, and abstract reasoning sub-tests of the Differential Aptitude Test and the Kuder Preference Record. Further, the social class of these students was estimated by means of the Home Index developed by Gough (1949), their general values assessed by the Allport-Vernon-Lindzey Study of Values (1951), and their work values measured by means of Super's Work Values Inventory (1955). Finally, each student was required to complete a self-estimate questionnaire devised by O'Hara and Tiedeman which forced the subject to reveal his concept of himself with respect to his interests, aptitudes, and values. The sample included 160 students in the senior year in high school, 264 in the junior year, 276 sophomores, and 321 freshmen.

The design thus permitted data about aptitudes, interests, and values to be compared with the self-estimates of these attributes by a group of subjects representing the age range of the last half of the Tentative period. Only the variable of social class failed to show an increasing relationship between self-estimates and tested findings over the four-year age period represented in the sample. Social class was fairly constant and students probably become aware of their own class when relatively young. Thus, it is not unreasonable to infer that no change occurred over time in the ability of the students to estimate their social class. Correlations among the other variables (aptitudes, interests, general values, and work values) and self-estimates, however, reflected increasing congruence through high school. By inferring that increasing vocational clarification is reflected in the increasing congruence of tested attributes and relevant self-estimates, O'Hara and Tiedeman concluded that a view of vocational clarification as a developmental process is very likely.

O'Hara and Tiedeman also attempted to discover if the stages in the development of vocational choices, such as those described by Ginzberg, do indeed exist. Examining the correlations between the self-estimates and the test estimates, they were able to infer the termination of a period of development. For example, the correlations between the self-estimates and tested estimates of interest were 0.70, 0.81, 0.79, and 0.83 for the freshman through senior years, respectively. The period of greatest increase occurred between the freshman and sophomore years, when the correlation increased from 0.70 to 0.81. O'Hara and Tiedeman inferred from these data that the interest period ended in their sample after the tenth grade. Applying the same reasoning to the other variables, they concluded that aptitudes and general values continuously increased in congruence; thus no real aptitude or general values period seems to exist (within the age range they studied). They also observed an increase of the growth in work values occurring between eleventh and twelfth grades. Although O'Hara and Tiedeman did not attempt to compare directly the timing of the stages of development, they found a degree of agreement with those predicted by the Ginzberg theory. More significantly, however, O'Hara and Tiedeman suggest that while boys may *talk* about their vocational plans in a manner which suggests they are concerned with one sphere or development, the *quality* of their estimates of their progress in these spheres is erratic.

In a pilot study, O'Hara (1959) examined the age at which values begin to serve as a focus for vocational preferences. Studying a sample of 15 boys, three boys in each of the first, third, fifth, seventh, and ninth grades, chosen to represent superior, average, and below average intelligence, he inquired into the development of the boys' interests, their self-descriptions, their current and past occupational preferences, and their reasons for making and for subsequently discarding the choices. His findings suggest that boys engage in reality testing at an earlier age than the theory of Ginzberg and his associates predicts. Thus, he found boys talking about the possibility of implementing their plans as early as the third grade. Compromise, according to the theory, should occur around ages 16 or 17. In this study, O'Hara observed that boys were planning compromises as early as 12 or 13 years of age. He found evidence that the Tentative period, which theoretically should begin about age 11, may occur as early as age 9, since many of the "fantasy" choices made by boys during the third grade and later actually have a rational basis. Finally, he observed that while interests are a major basis for preferences in these younger boys, values and aptitudes are significant forces in the formation of these preferences at much earlier ages than Ginzberg's group suspected. O'Hara observed that values are involved in preferences as early as fifth or sixth grade instead of tenth or eleventh as the theory suggests, and that capacity assumes importance even to third or fourth graders instead of the lower limit of eighth or ninth grade as the theory proposed.

The results of O'Hara's study are useful in evaluating the theory. In one respect, they contradict the theory, since the periods of development all seem to occur much earlier than expected; yet, in another respect, they support the theory, for the periods as predicted do actually seem to occur — and in the order expected — at least insofar as they might occur in the age range O'Hara studied.

Davis, Hagan, and Strouf (1962) compared the frequency of occupational preferences stemming from fantasy motives with the frequency of choices having Tentative antecedents in sixth grade students. The sample consisted of 116 boys and girls, whose ages ranged from 11 to 16 years, with a mean age of 12. The students were instructed to write a paragraph describing what they wanted to do as adults and the reasons for this choice. Two judges classified the responses as representing either the Fantasy or Tentative period.

The results indicated that sixth grade girls are likely to express more choices representative of a Tentative period than boys and that intelligence and stage of vocational development seem to be correlated. The more intelligent the student, the more likely he is to express a vocational preference which seems to reflect more advanced thinking about his career. In this study then, intelligent girls were most advanced in their vocational thinking while boys of below average intelligence were least developed. The authors of the study concluded that since the Ginzberg theory assumes that age 11 will mark the onset of the Tentative period, and most of their subjects reported plans which were consistent with the Tentative period of development, their results supported the theory of Ginzberg and his associates. It would seem, however, that generalizations must of necessity be limited, since the sample was fairly small and confined to a relatively narrow age range. Had the study included younger Ss, they might have found evidence that the Tentative period starts even younger than 11.

Another study related to ages when vocational decisions are made in the framework of the Ginzberg theory was conducted by Tucci (1963). He divided college freshmen into three groups of students: those who were definitely decided about their careers, those who were tentatively decided, and those who were undecided. His sample consisted of 163 male freshmen at Wayne State University. He asked these students how long they had held their current vocational choice. He found that 34 percent of his sample reported themselves to be definite about their vocational plans, another 48 percent said they were tentative, and 18 percent said they were undecided. Of those who said they were definitely sure of their vocational goal, the mean age at which they had made that choice was 14.63 years. The tentative subjects had decided at a mean age of 15.38 years. These ages of decision conflict somewhat with the Ginzberg theory, since the theory suggests that boys' vocational decisions would not really become resolved until considerably later. Two possible explanations for this occur: the verbal reports of the subjects may not correspond with reality; that is, while they may report themselves to be definite, many changes might occur in the future, or changes occurring in the past may have been forgotten. It is also possible that a boy may have first thought of becoming an engineer at age 14, and succeeding years might have strengthened that decision. In terms of the theory, however, his original thoughts might well be considered tentative, with the crystallized decision occurring later.

Small (1953), while observing a variety of personality factors which influence vocational choice (which will be described in detail in a later chapter), touched on several aspects of the career development process that are pertinent to Ginzberg's theory. His data allowed him to assess the hypothesis that reality factors exert an increasing influence in the vocational preferences boys express from age 11 on. No evidence indicating that such an increase occurred was found. This is interestingly similar to O'Hara's observation that the Ginzberg periods may actually be set at age levels higher than they should. Thus, it is possible that reality factors increase in influence prior to age 11 and there reach an asymptote. Small also noted that evidence in support of the compromise aspect of the theory existed. That is, boys included the reality factors in their choices which led them to make relevant modifications in the preferences they expressed.

Harren developed a Q-sort designed to assess Tiedeman and O'Hara's (1963) formulation of the stages of vocational choice, based on the notion that choice is a cognitive process of differentiation and integration. On this basis he predicted that a difference would be discernible between the decisions individuals made regarding choice of college major and those involving an occupation. The responses of 86 male undergraduate liberal arts students indicated that most saw the two as the same, and that those who did not equate educational and vocational choice either treated the two as separate problems or failed to see the two as pieces of the same chain of events. One might guess that the use of more vocationally oriented groups of students, perhaps enrolled in engineering, would even enhance these findings. However, some question could be raised regarding logical development of Harren's prediction from the constructs of differentiation and integration described by Tiedeman and O'Hara.

In a cross-sectional study of more than 4600 students in grades six through twelve, Hollender (1967) found that career choices do indeed become more realistic with age (using the individual's intellectual adequacy for his occupational preference as the criterion of realism), thus supporting the Ginzberg group's notion that choices move from fantasy to reality with age.

Finally, as part of a major longitudinal investigation of career development, Gribbons and Lohnes (1968) report finding evidence that the role of values in early vocational decision-making predates the timetable suggested by Ginzberg et al.

### Evaluation

The empirical evidence in support of the theory is mixed. A thread of data consistent with the major tenets of the theory has been found by several investigators. There does seem to be evidence suggesting that boys emphasize different kinds of experiences in their vocational development at various age levels. There also appears to be reason to believe that boys must compromise their career preferences in deference to the reality of the world they observe. The evidence is mixed, however, with respect to specifically what the stages are, when they occur, and the order in which they occur.

## STATUS

Ginzberg and his associates have proposed a neat, cohesive, systematic theoretical statement to describe the process of vocational choice. The theory has the significant virtue of being closely related with the broader theoretical structure of developmental psychology. There are, however, some points where the description becomes somewhat diffuse and perhaps excessively broad. Several questions also come to mind with reference to the sample studied. It is difficult to see how the theory was developed from the data base they report in their book. Trends of behavior imputed from interviews with various people can only reasonably be recognized from an already established framework, which causes a reader to suspect that previous reading and research was more influential on the development of the theory than the empirical study reported. The study is more likely to have served to confirm and refine some theoretical expectations than to have shaped them in the first place.

In view of the very serious limitations of the research sample, perhaps it is just as well that the theory seems to have preceded the research. It seems unlikely that such a comprehensive theory could have been developed from the inadequate data base observed. For example, the sample was too small to permit generalizations to be drawn with confidence. In particular, the lower income male and college female samples were extremely small. No statistical analysis was reported, so that the generalizations were apparently based on the interpretations of the investigators, leaving the readers no basis for independent evaluation.

No older people were studied, only adolescents and a few young adults. Since the major portion of vocational behavior occurs after the adolescent period, ignoring adult career processes is as detrimental to the development of a theory of vocational choice as it would be to the development of a theory of marital adjustment on the basis of the dating behavior of adolescents. However, such a criticism can be made about all the current vocational choice theories. In fact, though the theory is concerned with vocational choice, the actual data, with the possible exception of a few of the advanced graduate students and older lower income boys in the sample, are based on educational decisions rather than vocational ones. Even though the theory provides a significant amount of information about the vocational preferences expressed by the subjects, it fails to state the differences between preference, choice, and attainment, thus reducing the clarity of the theory.

Another shortcoming lies in the complete absence of test data. Despite the concern the authors of the theory express about the role of personal and emotional factors in career choice, no tests of any kind were reported to have been used, not even measures of intellectual ability. A study of career development should at least use one inventory of interest measurement, such as the Strong Vocational Interest Blank.

Some of the assumptions about the principles of adolescent development are crucial to the adequacy of the theory. The position of Ginzberg and his colleagues is that adolescent behavior is characterized by stress, and that the conflicts, having a physiological basis, significantly permeate the adolescent approach to vocational choice. That the adolescent period is more stressful than other periods of life for the majority of young people is not a universally held opinion (e.g., Kuhlen, 1952). By itself, such a criticism is not crucial, since the authors of a theory are entitled to make certain assumptions upon which to base their position. However, after stating that physical changes are a key part of the adolescent developmental process and that the process in general affects vocational choice, the Ginzberg group says little more about physiological antecedents to vocational problems. The only physiological development they discuss is sexual, and that only with reference to the problems older adolescents face in controlling their sexual impulses while accomplishing the training necessary to implement their career plans. The approach taken by Hulslander (1958) represents the kind of correlation between specific physical development and occupational processes that might be of relevance to this theory.

The concept of the irreversibility of the career development process is stated strongly, perhaps too strongly in the original theory. Obviously, career decisions and early experiences can neither be undone nor erased, yet the direction of the vocational process may be diverted by the sequence of continuing events. In witness of that fact are the many people who change careers in maturity, and the many college students who change majors (often as many as half of the freshmen change their college major by college graduation). A study at Kansas State University (Cross, 1960) indicated that about half of its graduates were working in positions with no direct relevance to their college major. Clearly, some aspects of the career development process are irreversible, but the process is not as inflexible and deterministic as the Ginzberg theory would lead one to expect.

Ginzberg's failure to differentiate clearly between occupational preference, selection, and attainment leads to difficulties in empirically evaluating the theory. At age 12, a boy is willing to express occupational preferences very readily, since few responsibilities are assumed or consequences incurred as a result. At 18, when entering college, the situation is different, since selections must occur, with real and permanent consequences. The student who selects engineering as a field of study in college to some degree commits himself to a career pattern different from that of a young man selecting journalism. Furthermore, immediate consequences in terms of specific course work and associates result. Considering these differences in the meaning of "occupational choice" at ages 12 and 18, how does an investigator rigorously investigate occupational development and yet stay within the framework of the theory? This consideration becomes a difficult problem, indeed.

### Implications for Counseling Practice

It seems that the theory is too vague to suggest techniques for counselors beyond a general notion that experiences should be arranged for young people that will facilitate their progress through whatever stage they happen to be in (see Katz, 1959, for an illustration of such an approach). If the theory has any accuracy and validity, it can be used to highlight developmental tasks and bring them to the attention of counselors, teachers, and parents. The theory might also be useful in helping a counselor to anticipate problems that might be encountered by students at predicted stages of development. This anticipation would allow the counselor to develop preventive procedures to deal with the expected problems. An example of this might be the tendency of children in the Capacity stage to overemphasize a course grade, a test score, or the opinion of some significant person in evaluating their skills or potentials. Were children alerted to this tendency and to the possibility of evaluating themselves in a variety of ways, some problems might be avoided.

It should also be noted that Tiedeman (1968) has devoted considerable energy toward the development of an information system to foster career development in terms of information gained through exploration. It does seem reasonable that a system such as Ginzberg's could serve as the framework for the practical development of such a computer-based career information-exploration system as Tiedeman proposes.

## Evaluation

The absence of data based on older students is a serious limitation. The authors of the theory state that some veterans had been included in a pilot group of subjects, and the interviews with them revealed that little had occurred during the few additional years of military life to accelerate the vocational developmental process. Contrary to this is the observation of many counselors that periods of employment or military service in the middle of college years may facilitate growth in the maturity of the individual's attempts at educational and vocational decision-making. Within the limits of the theory, it would seem logical that despite minimal connections between the job or military activities and the eventual career of the individual, maturity would be facilitated through more extensive periods of reality testing, a greater tendency for an appropriate time perspective to emerge, an increase in the interpersonal experience bank of the individual, the decrease in the rate of physical changes that occur as the youth matures, and the resolution of sexual problems by marriage and a gradual reduction in the intensity of sexual impulses.

Does the theory contain the general features attributed to a good theory of vocational counseling? Certainly, the theory seems to rate well on its comprehensiveness and its relationship to what is known about human development. The process of normal vocational development is clearly evident in the theory, and to a lesser extent, patterns of deviant vocational behaviors are also described. Thus, it is possible for a counselor to have expectations about the development of an individual along vocational lines from the theoretical statement. The theory also permits a counselor to develop some expectations of the problems in career development when he is confronted by an individual with a deviant vocational pattern.

In another paper, Ginzberg (1952) explicitly discusses some of the implications the theory has for vocational counseling. First, he suggests that the theory provides a counselor with normative information about vocational process, so that he can identify children who do not appear to be developing according to usual patterns of maturation. Thus, a counselor can identify those students who perhaps need extra or special kinds of attention to facilitate their growth in the career development area. Ginzberg also states that the theory suggests a particular type of counseling for the student. A student stalled in the Interest phase of development would need counseling with respect to his interests, not information about his aptitudes. Similarly, questions about values might be appropriately discussed with a young man obviously in the Value stage who is not progressing toward a career goal as expected.

The theory does not, however, suggest corrective measures when deviant patterns are observed, nor does it give any specific techniques for counseling to facilitate occupational development, but some possibilities may be inferred from the nature of the theory, primarily with respect to the developmental stages. As a corollary to the absence of counseling techniques, no counseling goals are suggested beyond that of facilitating the individual's growth in the four basic features of major vocational growth: the reality testing, adequate time perspective, the deferment of gratification, and the ability to compromise.

It would seem that certain specific features of the theory are open to testing, in that certain behaviors should distinguish students in one stage from those in another and should appear approximately at predictable times. One limiting feature in the testability is the problem presented by the pseudocrystallization and pseudospecification stages which the authors allow themselves, but these do not affect the stages that come earlier in the process which could be tested independent of the validity of the advanced periods.

Perhaps the most useful purpose the theory has served for vocational psychology is its stimulation of interest in the development of theoretical foundations for the study of career development. While the Ginzberg group may not have developed the first attempt to formulate a system of understanding vocational choice, the attempt was timely, widely circulated, and stimulated considerable thought about career development. Certainly, the theory has heuristic value (the stages seem valid in a general way and correspond to a view of reality in adolescent development) and has exerted its influence on later theorists in vocational psychology. It is likely that as such, its purpose has been served, and its general concepts will be modified many times by other approaches that attempt to explain and describe vocational choice processes.

# REFERENCES

Allport, G. W., Vernon, P. E., and Lindzey, G. A. *A study of values* (rev. ed.). Boston: Houghton Mifflin, 1951.

Cross, K. D. *Comprehensive occupational survey of 1947 and 1952 Kansas State University graduates.* Manhattan, Kansas: Kansas State University Placement Center, 1960.

Davis, D. A., Hagan, Nellie, and Strouf, Judie. Occupational choice of twelve-year-olds. *Personnel and Guidance Journal,* 1962, *40,* 628-629.

Ginzberg, E. Toward a theory of occupational choice. *Occupations,* 1952, *30,* 491-494.

Ginzberg, E. Toward a theory of occupational choice: a restatement. *Vocational Guidance Quarterly,* 1972, *20,* 169-176.

Ginzberg, E., Ginsburg, S. W., Axelrad, S., and Herma, J. L. *Occupational choice: an approach to a general theory.* New York: Columbia University Press, 1951.

Gough, H. C. A short social status inventory. *Journal of Educational Psychology,* 1949, *40,* 52-56.

Gribbons, W. D., and Lohnes, P. R. *Emerging careers.* New York: Teachers College Press, Columbia University, 1968.

Harren, V. A. The vocational decision-making process among college males. *Journal of Counseling Psychology,* 1966, *13,* 271-277.

Hollender, J. Development of a realistic vocational choice. *Journal of Counseling Psychology,* 1967, *14,* 314-318.

Hulslander, S. C. Aspects of physical growth and evolution of occupational interests. *Personnel and Guidance Journal,* 1958, *36,* 610-615.

Katz, M. R. *You: today and tomorrow.* Princeton, New Jersey: Cooperative Test Division, Educational Testing Service, 1959.

Kroll, A. M., Dinklage, Lillian B., Lee, Jennifer, Morley, Eileen D., and Wilson, E. H. *Career development: growth and crisis.* New York: Wiley, 1970.

Kuhlen, R. G. *The psychology of adolescent development.* New York: Harper & Row, 1952.

O'Hara, R. P. Talks about self – the results of a pilot series of interviews in relation to Ginzberg's theory of occupational choice. *Harvard Studies in Career Development,* No. 14, Center for Research in Careers, Harvard Graduate School of Education, Cambridge, Mass., October, 1959.

O'Hara, R. P., and Tiedeman, D. V. Vocational self-concept in adolescence. *Journal of Counseling Psychology,* 1959, *6,* 292-301.

Small, L. Personality determinants of vocational choice. *Psychological Monographs,* 1953, *67,* No. 1 (Whole No. 351).

Super, D. E. *Notes on career pattern study tests.* New York: Columbia University, February, 1955 (mineographed).

Tiedeman, D. V. Information system for vocational decisions. Project Report No. 12, Cambridge, Mass.: Harvard Graduate School of Education, 1968.

Tiedeman, D. V., and O'Hara, R. P. *Career development: choice and adjustment.* New York: College Entrance Examination Board, 1963.

Tucci, M. A. College freshmen and vocational choice. *Vocational Guidance Quarterly,* 1963, *12,* 27-29.

# Psychoanalytic Conceptions of Career Choice

According to Erik Erikson (1950), Freud once stated that the most significant indication of a psychologically normal being was the ability "to love and to work" effectively. Elaboration upon the first half of the statement, love, is not relevant here. The second aspect, however, illustrates the implicit role that work has in the psychoanalytic conception of personality and psychopathology. Basic in the system of psychoanalysis is the mechanism of sublimation. It provides an acceptable way for an individual to release portions of his psychic energies that would be unacceptable in society if expressed directly. Work is ideally suited to provide outlets for sublimated wishes and impulses. Considering the general role that work plays in psychoanalytic theory and the general pervasiveness of psychoanalytic concepts in psychology as a whole, it is not surprising that some attempts have been made to conceptualize the process of vocational development within the framework of psychoanalysis.

## GENERAL PSYCHOANALYTIC THEORY AND CAREER CHOICE

Several analytic writers have indicated their concern, at least indirectly, with matters of vocational choice. Perhaps Brill, of all the analysts, devoted the most attention to career choice. He elaborated upon the notion that vocational selection is one realm of behavior in which society permits an individual to combine the pleasure and reality principles (1949). The pleasure principle drives an individual to behave in a manner that is immediately gratifying, forgetful of the future consequences of his actions, while the reality principle focuses attention on eventual and long-term gratification at the expense of immediate ones. In choosing a vocation, an individual presumably is able to compromise between the two principles. Ideally, he gets some immediate satisfaction as a consequence of his choice while at the same time he lays the foundation for future success. For example, the selection of law as a career goal provides the law student with some prestige, status, and vicarious satisfaction in addition to the potential stability of eventual entry into the profession.

Brill further elaborated on the theme that sublimation is intimately bound up in vocational choice. He proposed that the particular vocation an individual chooses is not the result of an accidental arrangement of events. Rather, an individual's personality and impulses lead him to choose a career in which he may satisfy, through sublimation, his basic life impulses. According to Brill, unconscious motives underlie all behavior, including vocational selection. Brill documents his position by reporting several cases in which he personally observed the role that occupation plays in the gratification of impulses. To illustrate the role of psychopathological tendencies in career selection, Brill suggests that sadistic impulses may be satisfied in such diverse activities as those of butchers, surgeons, and murderers. Jones (1923) describes a patient who successfully transformed his childhood fascination with the process of urination and bodies of water in general into a successful career as an engineer constructing bridges and canals. Zilboorg (1934) discusses a patient whose father, a successful toilet fixtures businessman, was extremely concerned with his son's bowel functions.

Among Brill's ideas about vocational choice is the interesting notion that vacations represent "neurotic fads" for which well-adjusted individuals have neither need nor desire. According to Brill, the well-adjusted person works because he enjoys work and because it includes activities which permit him to engage successfully in otherwise tabooed behaviors. In support of this assumption Brill points out that men who retire lose interest in life and die earlier than those who do not retire. (Of course, other explanations of this difference in longevity can be made. For example, men who retire earlier may do so because of physical illnesses or less vigor, which may cause earlier death; then, too, the loss of identity as a worker could be a factor producing apathy, rather than an inability to satisfy unacceptable impulses.)

Brill concluded that physical and mental abilities alone play only a partial role in the kind of career a man chooses, since sublimation is the key ingredient. Accordingly, vocational counseling based on abilities and interests is likely to be of little value, although Brill conceded that such counseling might be of temporary value for certain individuals whose personality organization is insufficient to permit them to sublimate their impulses effectively. In general, however, vocational counseling is ineffective, according to Brill, and the few attempts he made to advise patients about vocational matters invariably had undesirable outcomes. He concluded that psychoanalytic techniques would not, in passing, facilitate the selection of a satisfactory vocational choice. That is, when basic problems of psychopathology are resolved, issues in daily life, the selection of a mate or a vocation, for example, will proceed smoothly and without the need for outside consultation.

While not taking as extreme a position as Brill, other psychoanalytic writers have illustrated how psychopathology viewed in psychoanalytic terms may account for vocational problems. By the case method, Bell (1960) illustrates the manner in which irrational vocational choices may persist in the service of ego integrity. Forer (1953), in depicting the role that personality variables play in vocational selection, chose to stress the importance unconscious motivation has on the selection of a career in relation to libidinal needs. Dragsow (1957) reported the results of a survey involving the reasons people had for selecting the vocation they chose. His results indicated that nearly every person in his very large sample expressed more than one reason for their choice. Such findings, he concludes, suggest that Freud's principle of overdetermination operates in vocational choice in that no one factor alone influences a career decision, but the interaction of many factors.

Writing from the point of view that the pleasure and reality principles are not sufficient to account for much of human behavior, Hendrick (1943) proposed a "work principle." In contrast to the behaviors derived from the reality principle, presumably based on libidinal energy, those dependent on the work principle are based on the instinct to master one's environment. The "mastery instinct," in its turn has a biological foundation, which is a function of man's attempt to control or change some portion of his environment through the combined use of his intellectual and neurological processes. The mastery instinct requires an individual to integrate his behavior and develop skill in performing certain tasks. Thus, Hendrick concludes, work pleasure represents gratification of the mastery instinct. Work satisfaction, then, is clearly an ego function since it is not sublimated sexual pleasure.

Several writers have tried to demonstrate how some aspects of career development can be explained in terms of psychoanalytic theory. Using case studies, Galinsky and Fast (1966) attempted to show how the identity problems often seen in young people may frequently be defined in terms of difficulty with vocational decision-making and vocational indecision. In a similar way, Malnig (1967) has developed a psychoanalytic interpretation of the failure to achieve well in school and work; this explanation postulates the notion that competition with one's father, coupled with the possibility that one's achievements might surpass those of his father, is frightening to some people, since parental reprisal might result. Neff (1968) has written a major study of vocational development and behavior with a distinctive psychoanalytic flavor. In his work, Neff describes how psychoanalytically oriented writers have logically shown how adult behavior, including work behavior, is a function of early experience. According to Neff, psychoanalytic viewpoints regarding work have in common a strong emphasis on the role instincts play in motivating behavior, a common opinion that adult difficulties with work are primarily the result of early shaping of affective processes through the vehicle of early parent-child interaction (a statement reminiscent of Roe), and an underemphasis of the role that culture plays in individual development.

The interests of the work and the reality principles often overlap despite the fact that the reality principle is libido-based while the work principle is based on the mastery instinct. During adolescence the satisfactions derived from work are more dependent on libidinal energy whereas at maturity, work mastery (satisfaction of the mastery instinct) is more important as a source of gratification. In terms of human development, adolescence is a time when attention centers on sexual growth, whereas at maturity, with sexual needs reduced and competency demonstrated, growth and accomplishment offer a primary source of gratification. Vocational success serves as a likely vehicle for the demonstration of mastery.

The very important psychoanalytic concept of identification also receives emphasis in the vocational choice process. Many writers and a number of investigations have attempted to isolate important ingredients in the process of identification that have relevance for vocational choice. Such questions as whom the individual identifies with assume much significance when assessing the impact of identification on vocational choice. Sommers (1956) analyzed the histories of three therapy cases with respect to the role that conflict in identification assumed in their vocational choices. The cases Sommers reports are so well developed that they deserve some elaboration here. In the first case, a woman suffering from a postpartum depression was shown to be in conflict about her identification with her despised and feared mother. As a child, in response to shame over her economic poverty and to accommodate her feelings toward her overcontrolling mother, the patient developed the technique of high academic accomplishment as a means of trying to reduce her self-hatred. Consequently, she habitually took a logical and intellectual approach to problem solving of all sorts and eventually selected mathematics as a career. After her marriage and the birth of a child, she found her logical approach to be ineffective in resolving her emotional feelings toward her baby. Her anxiety could not be explained intellectually. In the course of therapy, the patient became aware of her similarity to her mother and developed a more positive attitude toward her feminine attributes. She was more able to accept the role of mother and needed less to live the role of mathematician, which had served to masculinize her life. In this case a career was chosen as a rejection of the feminine role and as a means of facilitating a detachment from the emotional demands of life, both of which developed from the patient's ambivalence toward the female model available to her for identification during her childhood and adolescent years.

A second case concerned a Japanese-American youth who rejected the Oriental values of his father. As a consequence, the youth came into conflict with his father, adopting rebellious attitudes toward him. Guilt feelings about the rebellion and consequent self-punishment resulted in depression, suicidal tendencies, fear of insanity, sleeplessness, and ulcers. His background at home had been heavily permeated with Oriental culture. He spoke Japanese and his father practiced Buddhism. In his rebellion against his father and Oriental beliefs and customs, the patient rejected his father's wish that he become an engineer (like the father) and instead became an English teacher. The goal of the treatment seemed to be helping the patient to realize his similarity to his father and to accept the ambivalent feelings about these similarities, which had partly caused his rebellion. He was eventually able to continue his professional work in English but without the rebellious and spiteful component toward his father.

The third case is perhaps most striking of all. A young man was seeking relief of symptoms of insomnia, irritability, and tension. Though the patient's current occupation was a policeman, the therapist was impressed by his timidity and shyness. The patient revealed that his experiences on the police force had made him doubt whether he was aggressive enough to succeed as a policeman. His occupational history included varied jobs in which he was consistently ineffective. He had been unsuccessful as an insurance salesman, a truck driver, a hospital attendant, and a laborer. He concluded that he had never been properly fit for any job he held and, furthermore, he had no idea about what he would like to do.

Interviews with the man revealed that he had been raised by his grandparents. After his prostitute mother died, his bad-tempered father could not handle the responsibility of the child and turned him over to the grandparents. When he misbehaved during childhood he was told he would turn out like his father. The threat was made so frequently that the patient eventually believed the prediction himself. A series of unfortunate experiences in life further convinced him of his unworthiness, and he began to believe more firmly than ever that he was destined to become like his father, to be bad-tempered, aggressive, and "crazy." In all his anxiety and tension was the germ of a fear of homosexuality, the impulses of which his superego would not permit him to accept. Becoming a policeman was the culmination of his efforts to fight off his homosexual fears and to reassure himself of his courage and masculinity. A policeman is a masterful, virile being, and in the act of becoming a policeman himself, the patient denied his homosexual fears. Although the case had an undesirable end, it does illustrate how one man desperately tried to cope with unconscious fears acquired by identifying with a psychopathic father by means of an occupational choice.

The three cases summarized by Sommers give some suggestion of the subtle ways that personality can be woven into occupational events within the psychoanalytic approach to behavior. They also illustrate the complexity of vocational choice within such a framework, point out one way in which such choices can go awry, and suggest some steps that might be taken to correct difficulties in vocational life which are a reflection of basic personality disturbances and which exacerbate the disturbances at the same time that they are symptoms. Oberndorf (1951) suggests another example of the role that work may play in psychopathology. Work, requiring deprivation in the form of delayed gratification, stands in marked contrast to play, which permits prompt gratification of "autoerotic" instincts. In psychopathology, then, one might see "laziness" as the prolongation of infantile behaviors, or overwork as an attempt to control infantile libidinal wishes through denial.

### The Bordin, Nachmann, Segal Framework for Vocational Development

The most ambitious scheme to define the process of career development entirely within the psychoanalytic framework and with the appropriate language was proposed by Bordin, Nachmann, and Segal (1963). These three investigators tried to develop the framework of a system based on a few occupations to illustrate the generalizations and the general methods that might be developed for a wide variety of occupations. The framework is summarized in Table 4.1. The three occupations used to illustrate the system were accounting, social work, and plumbing. A number of psychic dimensions or body zones with potential for gratification were assessed for their degree of involvement in each of the three occupations. For example, under the *dimensions* of nurturance were classified "feeding" and "fostering." Only social workers were involved to any extent in feeding, and since they frequently distribute food to their clientele, social workers get a high rating on "feeding" (three on a one-to-three scale). Accountants and plumbers, not involved in feeding their clientele at all, get zero on the "feeding" subdivision of the Nurturance dimension. The *objects* toward which the social workers' feeding activities are directed are the "needs of the clients"; the *Sexual Mode* is feminine, and the social workers' typical defense mechanism is reaction formation. The next subdivision of the Nurturance dimension is "fostering," which the accountants do to some extent (worth a score of one on the involvement scale) in financially advising their clientele, and the social workers do to a considerable degree (earning a rating of three) in encouraging and protecting their clients. The objects fostered by the accountants are the client's financial affairs, and for the social workers, the client's growth and health. The accountants' activity is in a masculine Sexual Mode, the social workers' a feminine one. The preferred way of handling affect for the accountants is to experience it, while the social workers either experience it or engage in reaction formation.

In the Genital dimension there are subdivisions of Erection, Penetration, Impregnation, and Producing. Only the plumbers have any degree of involvement in the Erection subdivision, and that is only to a slight degree with respect to the use of their hands and tools (mode) for fixing faucets and fixtures (objects). The Sexual Mode is masculine, and the typical defense is isolation. In Penetration, again, the plumbers, by virtue of their reaming and coupling (mode) of pipes and joints (objects) are slightly involved and, again, the Sexual Mode is masculine and the defense is isolation. Impregnation involves only the social workers, and then only slightly. The mode is through the prevention or encouragement of family planning (object). It is feminine and usual defenses are isolation and/or reaction formation. Producing, too, involves only the social workers, with their giving or withholding (mode) of babies for adoption (object) and, once again, the Sexual Mode is feminine and the defense is isolation. More examples of the system are presented in Table 4.1 Selected dimensions with the occupations, manner of involvement, and so on can be used to represent the system further.

The virtue of the system is that, when and if it is elaborated to extend to a wide variety of occupations, an individual can more accurately identify the significance of a particular area of impulse gratification for a given occupation and the likelihood of his ability to satisfy such impulses within that field. Furthermore, inferences may be drawn concerning the sex mode of the field, the occupation's potential for reducing anxiety, and the typical defenses available in the occupational setting.

The analytic conceptualization of career choice emphasizes the techniques of impulse gratification and anxiety reduction which a field offers rather than the interests and abilities a career requires. Assuming then, that a counselor should wish to base his vocational counseling on this framework, he would use a trait-factor approach, but client modes of impulse gratification, psychosexual development, and anxiety level would take the place of interests and abilities. The counselor would try to find the occupation which offered the maximum potential for fitting his client's psychological style. Presumably, psychoanalytic interview methods would underlie the assessment of the individual.

## Summary

We have seen that a number of psychoanalytic concepts have implications for vocational psychology and that a few attempts have been made to apply these concepts directly to career development.[1] Generally speaking, the attempts employ the usual analytic methods of the assessment of individuals, such as interviews aimed at assessing the status of psychosexual development and patients' sources of impulse gratification. Career choice is typically construed as a by-product of personality development and, consequently, is not considered to be worth attention in and of itself. Career development deserves attention only because unusual difficulty in career choice is a symptom of more basic psychological disturbance, or as the choice process itself represents the general status of the individual's psychological development. Aptitudes and interests are of minimal importance in vocational selection (though such writers as Brill give a nod in the direction of aptitudes when they suggest that a man may become a surgeon or a butcher in order to satisfy sadistic impulses, depending upon his abilities and the state of the individual's psychosexual development and his source of impulse gratification).

Some particular aspects of psychoanalytic theory are more relevant to vocational choice and have been given more attention. For example, the process of identification, with whom the individual identifies, to what extent, and whether there are conflicts in the individual with respect to the person he identifies with, is very important in vocational behavior. Another mechanism of significance in vocational development is ego strength, the role the ego plays in influencing the

---

[1] Writers such as Roe (1957) and Ginzberg et al. (1951) use some psychoanalytic concepts in their theories, but their theories seem broader than the psychoanalytic position and so are described in other chapters.

**TABLE 4.1. The Matrix of Basic Need Gratifying Activities for Three Occupations: Accounting, Social Work, and Plumbing**

| I | II | III | IV | V | VI | VII |
|---|---|---|---|---|---|---|
| Dimension | Occupation | Degree of Involvement | Instrumental Mode | Objects | Sexual Mode | Affect |
| **Nurturant** |  |  |  |  |  |  |
| Feeding | A | 0 |  |  |  |  |
|  | S | 3 | material and psychological supplies | needs of clients | F | R |
|  | P | 0 |  |  |  |  |
| Fostering | A | 1 | financial advice and safeguards | client's financial affairs | M | A |
|  | S | 3 | encouragement and protection | client's growth and health | F | R–A |
|  | P | 0 |  |  |  |  |
| **Oral Aggressive** |  |  |  |  |  |  |
| Cutting | A | 0 |  |  |  |  |
|  | S | 1 | words | client's resistance | F | I |
|  | P | 1 | lathes, gouges, clippers | pipes | M | I |
| **Biting** |  |  |  |  |  |  |
| Devouring | A | 0 |  |  |  |  |
|  | S | 0 |  |  |  |  |
|  | P | 1 | wrenches, pliers | pipes | M | I |
| **Manipulative** |  |  |  |  |  |  |
| Physical | A | 0 |  |  |  |  |
|  | S | 0 |  |  |  |  |
|  | P | 2 | pipes, valves | steam, water pressure | M | A |
| Interpersonal | A | 3 | advice, recommendation | business and government policy | M | A |
|  | S | 2 | provocation, influence, seduction | feelings and attitudes of client | F | I |
|  | P | 0 |  |  |  |  |
| **Sensual** |  |  |  |  |  |  |
| Sight | A | 0 |  |  |  |  |
|  | S | 0 |  |  |  |  |
|  | P | 0 |  |  |  |  |
| Sound | A | 0 |  |  |  |  |
|  | S | 0 |  |  |  |  |
|  | P | 0 |  |  |  |  |
| Touch | A | 0 |  |  |  |  |
|  | S | 0 |  |  |  |  |
|  | P | 1 | hands-smoothing-sculpting | joints | M | A |
| **Anal** |  |  |  |  |  |  |
| Acquiring | A | 2 | recommendations reinvestment | fortunes of clients | O | A |
|  | S | 1 | efforts to equalize distribution | wealth of society | F | R |
|  | P | 0 |  |  |  |  |
| Timing-ordering | A | 3 | systems, audits | financial policy | O | A |
|  | S | 1 | records, budgets | own work, lives of clients | O | A |
|  | P | 0–1 | calculating costs, estimating | materials | M | A |

| Mode | | Degree | Activity | Object / Focus | Sexual mode | Affect |
|---|---|---|---|---|---|---|
| Hoarding | A | 2 | prevent waste, encourage saving | money of client | O | I |
| | S | 0 | prevention of blockage-expulsion systems to combat disorder | waste—actual anal products | O | R |
| | P | 2 | | financial affairs of business | O | R |
| Smearing | A | 0 | | | | |
| | S | 2 | hands, trowels | pastes, greases | O | A |
| | P | 0 | | | | |
| Genital Erection | A | 0 | | | | |
| | S | 0 | hands—tools | faucets—fixtures | M | I |
| | P | 0–1 | | | | |
| Penetration | A | 0 | | | | |
| | S | 0 | reaming, coupling | pipes, joints | M | I |
| | P | 1 | | | | |
| Impregnation | A | 1 | prevention or encouragement | family planning, marital counseling | F | I–R |
| | S | 1 | | | | |
| | P | 0 | | | | |
| Producing | A | 1 | giving or withholding | babies for adoption | F | I |
| | S | 0 | | | | |
| | P | 1 | | | | |
| Exploratory Sight | A | 2 | audits to detect fraud | financial behavior of others | O | A |
| | S | 2–1 | visual investigation | homes of clients | O | A |
| | P | 2 | detecting leaks and blockage | in pipes and water systems | O | A |
| Touch | A | 0 | hands to determine shapes | where can't see | O | A |
| | S | 1 | | | | |
| | P | 1 | | | | |
| Sound | A | 1 | questioning | financial statement of clients | O | A |
| | S | 2 | questioning | private life of clients | O | I |
| | P | 1 | detecting leaks and disturbances | sound of running water | O | I |
| Flowing quenching | A | 0 | | | | |
| | S | 0 | | | | |
| | P | 3 | | | | |
| Exhibiting | A | 0 | arranging of pipes, valves | flow of fluids, waste products | M | I |
| | S | 0 | | | | |
| | P | 0 | | | | |
| Rhythmic Movement | A | 0 | | | | |
| | S | 0 | hands, tools, physical movement | pipes | O | I |
| | P | 1 | | | | |

NOTE: Degree of involvement: 0 = no significant involvement, 1 = peripheral importance, 2 = secondary importance, 3 = primary importance. Sexual mode: M = masculine, F = feminine, O = not sex linked. Affect: A = affect experienced, R = reaction formation, I = isolation.

Source: E. S. Bordin, Barbara Nachmann, and S. Segal. An articulated framework for vocational development, *Journal of Counseling Psychology*, 10, 1963, Copyright 1963 by the American Psychological Association, and reproduced by permission.

field chosen, the persistence of the choice, and the degree to which its strength plays a role in the successful implementation of a choice.

As far as describing the process of vocational development in the normally developing individual, the analytic approach is not detailed. If a person is developing normally in general, presumably his vocational life will also proceed according to schedule. If his psychological development is not healthy, then one can expect to see some effects of his difficulties in his work life. Treatment would presumably follow the general analytic method (or one of the derivatives) and would not focus on the career life but on the general development of the individual, based on the assumption that once the developmental pattern is corrected, vocational life would automatically fall into line. Of course, probably no analyst would treat an individual primarily complaining of vocational difficulty, nor is it likely that a person would seek an analyst for such difficulties alone.

# RESEARCH

## General Personality Development and Vocational Choice

Several attempts to test hypotheses about vocational choice derived from psychoanalytic theory have been made in the general context of the Bordin, Nachmann, and Segal framework. Most of the research antedates the actual publication of the proposal. One of the first was an ingenious study by Segal (1961) in which students of creative writing and accounting were compared with respect to personality development. Several hypotheses about differences in the personality development of writers and accountants were derived from the general principles of psychoanalytic theory. Segal's study was based on the presumption that the personality development of accountants and creative writers differs, that each group has chosen its occupation on the basis of different stereotypes embodied in the careers they prefer, and that the writers' and accountants' choices, based on these occupational stereotypes, are consistent with the developmental history of their personality up to the time of their choice.

The hypothetical personality development of the accountant is similar to the following. As a child, he quickly learns that parental approval may be gained by means of conformity to parental wishes. Conformity to parental demands in exchange for approval is epitomized by the toilet-training period of child development. During this period the child learns to control one segment of his impulses in return for parental praise and love. It is in exchanges such as these that the superego of the accountant develops and thrives. The child's identification with his parents becomes strong, thus serving to reduce the child's fear of the loss of parental love. As a result, a typical compulsive pattern develops, bolstering the child's defense against the anxiety of loss of parental esteem. The compulsive mechanisms to be seen are isolation, reaction formation, and intellectualization. Eventually the child, now growing toward adulthood, generalizes his attitudes toward his parents to all authority figures. When the necessity for vocational decision-making occurs, in view of the need to conform in exchange for the approval of authority and the use of compulsive behaviors practical in maintaining conforming behavior, it is natural for the young man to select accounting as a career. The stereotype of accounting suggests that the career offers clear and obvious guidelines to behavior.

The background of the creative writer, of course, is very different. As a child the writer learns to rebel rather than conform to the demands of authority, his parents. The resulting parentally induced frustrations cause the child to identify less with his parents, and consequently, the child develops a weaker superego and less acceptance of social norms. As he grows older, the individual attempts to resolve his poorly defined identity and to change the social order; given the appropriate abilities, a writing career is a natural way to implement such personality needs. The defenses such a person would erect are likely to be projection, repression, and denial.

Based on this theory, Segal developed several specific hypotheses about personality and behavior, which he tested. His subjects were 15 advanced undergraduate accounting students and 15 advanced and successful creative writing students. Care was taken not to confound the two groups by assuring that SVIB scores for accountants were not high on literary, and similarly, that for the creative writers the accounting scores on the SVIB were not high. Furthermore, the general background of each group of subjects was similar, that is, their ages, intellectual levels, and so on, were similar. They were administered the Rorschach Inkblot Test and the Bender-Gestalt and were required to write a one-page vocational autobiography.

First, Segal predicted that the general level of adjustment of the two groups would not be different, and the results bore him out. No differences in general adjustment were found. On the basis of his formulations about personality development, Segal then predicted that the accountants would accept social norms to a greater degree than the writers and also that the accountants would attempt to control their emotions more than the writers. On the other hand, the writers would be more sensitive to emotional situations than the accountants. The results concerning this prediction are mixed. On the basis of the observation that accountants chose their career at an earlier age than the writers and that their Rorschach protocols reflected less spontaneity than those of the writers, Segel inferred that the accountants are more concerned with social norms than the writers, who chose careers later than the accountants and whose Rorschach responses suggest concern with "integrating and theorizing" and "less concern with social expectation." The strength of the findings in support of the hypothesis is reduced by the finding that some Rorschach responses that should have differentiated the two groups did not; in fact, no Rorschach differences were found between the groups in the number of popular responses and the percentage of animal response. Differences in age at the time of vocational choice can also be explained in other terms than sensitivity to social expectations. For example, accounting is a more visible occupation than writing, which is likely to result in an earlier age of choice. The Rorschach indicated that the accountants are more emotionally controlled than the writers and the writers more sensitive than the accountants, but the Bender-Gestalt did not support that expectation.

Segal made several predictions about other behavioral differences between writers and accountants. He predicted that accountants would have more compulsive defenses than writers, that writers would show more hostile responses on the tests than accountants, that writers would be able to tolerate ambiguity better than accountants, that the writers would be more skillful in handling complex emotional situations than the accountants, and that the test protocols of the accountants would reflect a rigid, fearful identification while that of the writers would reflect an attempt to "complete multiple identifications." With reference to these hypotheses, the Rorschach results indicated that the writers were more hostile than the accountants and handled emotional and ambiguous situations more adequately than the accountants. Also, there was some evidence for the notion that accountants have a rigid, fearful identification. This was inferred from the autobiographies, which revealed that the most significant occupational influence was some adult figure. It had been expected that the writers would have had a larger number of different occupational choices than the accountants as a reflection of their attempts to implement their "multiple identifications." However, no such differences were found; probably, Segal suggests, because the vacillation of career choice throughout the adolescent population in general obscured the differences between accountants and writers.

Segal concluded that the results in general were consistent with the psychoanalytic model of vocational choice he devised. However, some questions can be raised about the data from which Segal drew his inferences and even about some of the inferences themselves. As mentioned earlier, the assumption that the degree of social concern of an individual is reflected in his age at the time of career choice seems questionable. Using the Rorschach to validate hypotheses about personality development is also questionable, with respect to the reliability and validity of the instrument in such research as well as with regard to the pathological basis of the Rorschach as opposed to the relatively normal process of choosing a vocation. Finally, using students for the sample was undoubtedly convenient, but being a student is a career in itself in some respects, and the strength of the results probably would have been increased had practicing accountants and writers been used as a sample. This last criticism, however, suggests that what differences Segal was able to find between writing and accounting students were minimal. Finally, the very basic question of why the people who eventually become accountants should, as children, strive to please their parents while the writers rebel is never really resolved, or even raised.

In another study, Segal and Szabo (1964) retested the hypothesis that accounting students have a rigid and fearful identification and that writing students, in contrast, attempt to complete multiple identifications in their professional choice. Again, 15 students in accounting and 15 creative writing students were used as subjects. They were required to take a Sentence Completion Test which included 16 items particularly relevant to the hypothesis under test. It was predicted that accounting students would have more positive attitudes toward their parents in contrast to the negative attitudes held by the creative writing students. It was also predicted that accounting students would express more favorable attitudes toward people in general than would the creative writing students. The responses to the 16 relevant completion items supported both predictions. This finding has a more valid behavioral base than Rorschach data, but is also fairly distant from psychoanalytic theory and the basic hypothesis about the differences between the identifications of accounting and creative writing students.

Another investigator (White, 1963) studied the behavior of clerical bank personnel with reference to Segal's general hypothesis that analytic principles of personality are related to vocational choice. Studying three groups of subjects — two groups of experienced clerical personnal in banks and a control group of job applicants at banks (apparently not necessarily for clerical jobs) — White asked two questions: "What would you most like to be if you were not a human being? Why?" and "What would you least like to be if you were not a human being? Why?" The results indicated that the experienced bank clerical workers overwhelmingly disliked the idea of things that were "dirty, sloppy, repulsive, slimy, infectious, and filthy," whereas the control group chose objects on a dimension not necessarily relevant to cleanliness. White concluded that the cleanliness attribute was highly important to clerical workers, a finding consistent with the psychoanalytically based idea that bank clerks are compulsive.

In another study of the relationship between personality and career based on analytic theory, Weinstein (1953) predicted that lawyers, engineers, and social workers would differ in a systematic manner in oral and anal characteristics. He hypothesized that engineers are more anally retentive than lawyers and social workers, that lawyers are more orally aggressive than engineers and social workers, that social workers are more orally receptive than engineers and lawyers, and that lawyers and engineers are more anally expulsive than social workers. Using the Q-technique, the subjects were required to make judgments on 40 anal items and 40 oral items as to the relevance of their ideal self and also to their actual self. The items were based on Weinstein's (1953) classification of descriptions of behavior in the psychological literature. The subjects were 20 law students, 20 social work students, and 20 senior engineering students; the samples were not matched but were heterogeneous with respect to age and socioeconomic background.

Weinstein concluded from the Q-sorts that most of his expectations about the personality characteristics under study were supported. He inferred that anal and oral traits are motivating factors in career selection, though no evidence was presented to show how or under what circumstances these traits were developed. Other explanations for the differences in Q-sorts of engineers, lawyers, and social workers might be proposed which would not be invalidated by the results of his study.

Reasoning that because various occupations require different work activities offering diverse potential for needs and satisfactions and that childhood experiences influence the development of needs, Nachmann (1960), using an analytic framework, assessed the question of personality differences between lawyers, dentists, and social workers. One aspect of behavior that should in particular differentiate those three occupational groups is their attitude toward aggressive behavior. In their work lawyers must be verbally aggressive, whereas social workers are not permitted to express their hostility and aggression in their jobs. Dentists, on the other hand, are very aggressive physically in the grinding, drilling, cutting, and inflicting of pain that is inherent in their work. The relationship of these three professionals to privacy is another differentiating feature. Lawyers are permitted a "privileged curiosity" into certain aspects of their clients' lives. The social worker is allowed unlimited access to the most private parts of a client's life, even more than a lawyer, but at the price of passivity. The dentist is openly permitted to peer into the mouth, ordinarily a private segment of the body. Such are examples of occupational differences, in analytical terms, that led Nachmann to expect significant differences between the childhood experiences of the three occupational groups.

A number of hypotheses about early experiences were tested by means of data obtained through interviews with 20 graduate students representing each of the three occupations. Most of the hypotheses were supported. Nachmann found aggressive impulses were more accepted in the families of lawyers and social workers and repressed in the families of dentists. She also discovered that in the families of lawyers and dentists, the fathers were more dominant and masculine and the discipline more masculine, fairness being emphasized in the lawyers' and obedience to authority in the dentists', in contrast to the families of social workers in which the mother was stronger and more dominant, the father either weak or absent, and the discipline less masculine. The fathers of lawyers were more remote physically and emotionally than the fathers of dentists, and a strong male figure maintained more importance in the childhood of lawyers than in that of either dentists or social workers. The home atmosphere of lawyers was warmer and stimulated preschool verbal skills, curiosity, and intellectual development most in contrast to that of dentists in which propriety and conventionality were most dominant and warmth least, preschool verbal skills, intellectual development, and curiosity least encouraged, physical mastery being more rewarded than in the families of lawyers or social workers. The early experiences of social workers included a severe traumatic deprivation prior to age two and emphasis on concern for the feelings and suffering of others; lawyers experienced a less severe trauma at a later age and little emphasis on concern for others, while dentists had no trauma, little emphasis on concern for others, and they experienced an event focusing attention to the inside of their bodies which lawyers and social workers did not. The only hypothesis that was not supported, that sexual curiosity was not satisfied in any group, was most re-buffed for the dentists; this question may have been confounded by the fact that few people of the generation studied had adequate sexual education. From these results, it is evident that Nachmann's findings are impressive support for the utility of psychoanalytic concepts in explaining the personality differences through childhood experiences of at least the three occupational groups she studied. Nevertheless, as with all retrosepctive studies, the answers of the subjects might have been influenced more by the current events of their lives than by the childhood events influencing current behavior.

**Identification**

Identification is an important psychoanalytic concept and is consequently important to analytically based vocational choice theory. Crites (1962) has combined the analytic and vocational streams of thought in a recent study which investigated the relationship between occupational interest development and parental identification. Reasoning that since identification results in the embodiment of one individual's values and attitudes in another, Crites hypothesized that the degree of parental identification will be reflected in the interest patterns of the offspring. Furthermore, since certain interest areas are masculine and others feminine, the sex of the parent predominantly identified with should be reflected in the student's interest profile. For a mixed-sex identification, Crites suggests that careers in social work, for example, provide suitable outlets since social work embodies both masculine and feminine attributes. Finally, a combination of both the sex of the parent and the degree of identification should produce the particular interest pattern which will reflect the relevant interaction of masculine-feminine interest for that individual.

Using as subjects 350 males, further divided into three groups (100 vocational-educational clients at a university counseling center, 100 more vocational-educational clients as a replication group, and 150 nonclients as a generalization group), Crites assessed the kind, degree, and pattern of parental identification by means of the subjects' responses to semantic differential ratings of "self," "father," and "mother" on nine scales. The scales represented the potency, activity, and evaluative dimensions of meaning. Interest patterns were analyzed by Stephenson's (1961) pattern analysis technique applied to the Strong Vocational Interest Blank (1943).

The results indicated that the degree of identification with fathers is correlated with the interest pattern on the SVIB, but not so for identification with mothers. Sons identifying strongly with their fathers scored high in business detail, sons with slight father identification had high interest scores in the literary area, while sons moderately identifying with their fathers scored high in groups including physical and social sciences. Interestingly, it was observed that as long as some identification with parents existed, predictable interest patterns emerged. Thus, males with male identifications had interests in the business detail area and males with mixed identifications had interests in technical and verbal areas. The findings relevant to the third hypothesis are also as expected: patterns of interests were consistent with the degree and kind of parental identification.

Steimel and Suziedelis (1963) tested the hypothesis that the predominance of perceived parental influence of one parent will be related to Strong Vocational Interest Blank scores. The expectation was based on a model which suggests that the role of identification with parents in the development of interests is pronounced. They predicted that father-influenced male college students will have different interest patterns on the SVIB than will mother-influenced students. To test this prediction they administered a perceived parental influence instrument to 198 college freshmen and sophomores and selected 84 subjects whose responses placed them at the extremes in terms of perceived parental influence. The SVIB scores (43 occupational scales and 3 nonoccupational scales) of both groups were compared. The father-influenced boys were significantly higher than the mother-influenced boys on a number of occupational scales and two nonoccupational scales (specifically, engineering, chemist, production manager, aviator, math-science teacher, forest service, YMCA director, personnel director, public administrator, senior CPA, accountant, interest maturity, and masculinity), while the mother-influenced boys were higher on the occupational scales for real estate salesman, advertising manager, and lawyer. While Steimel and Suziedelis did not predict directions in which differences would occur for specific scales, they observed that the differences that occurred were consistent with expected sex differences. Father-influenced boys scored higher on masculine occupations and mother-influenced boys were higher on more feminine careers.

Steimel and Suziedelis report several other interesting findings. The father-influenced subjects were more likely to select college majors in the exact sciences, while the mother-influenced subjects leaned toward the liberal arts. More of the fathers of father-influenced subjects were engaged in occupations at the professional level and had more education than fathers in the mother-influenced group. Furthermore, the fathers of father-influenced subjects averaged almost two years more formal education than the mothers of those subjects, whereas the parents of mother-influenced subjects were about equal in their level of educational attainment.

An interesting question may be raised on the basis of these findings. Is father influence related to the status and respect accorded to fathers by their sons because of their professional and educational achievement, or do well-educated fathers assume a greater role in influencing their sons because of their greater sophistication? Though Steimel and Suziedelis cannot answer this question from their data, they did demonstrate that the perception of parental influence is clearly related to vocational interests.

In a study based on Erikson's (1950) hypothesis that the mother in American culture transmits general cultural values to her son, Stewart (1959) tested the hypothesis that the SVIB scores of adolescent males are related to the degree of their identification with their mothers. Reasoning that individuals develop their values by observing respected individuals and that these values would be reflected in interest inventories, Stewart had 97 junior and senior high school boys perform a number of Q-sorts about their self-concept, their ideal self-concept, and their concept of what they thought their mothers would prefer them to be. Fifty-four mothers of the boys in the sample were available to perform Q-sorts on their concept of what their sons were like and how they would like them to be ideally. In addition to the Q-sorts, each student subject took the SVIB and answered a brief questionnaire pertinent to his vocational aspiration.

Stewart found that, in general, the boys were somewhat sensitive to their mothers' ideals for them and that this sensitivity resulted in some behavior pleasing to the mothers. Either the boys were aware of their mothers' values for them and acted to please them, or they were aware of their mothers' values which, in turn, were consistent with their own values and hence, in implementing their own desires they were pleasing their mothers. Stewart also found that Interest Maturity scores on the SVIB were related to the degree to which boys accepted their mothers' ideal as their own. This, Stewart suggests, is because Interest Maturity is correlated with social sensitivity, which presumably boys learn from their mothers. The closer the identification with the mothers' values, the greater the acceptance of socially sensitive behaviors and the higher the Interest Maturity score.

Also consistent with Erikson's theory was the finding that the Masculine-Feminine (MF) scores on the SVIB were related to the boys' awareness of their mothers' ideal sons. In a finding inconsistent with the theory, however, Stewart found that the closer the boy's identification with his mother, the more likely he was to have a SVIB rejection pattern in a masculine area. Thus, boys who most strongly accepted their mothers' ideal of them seemed more likely to reject masculine occupations. In contrast to this finding is Erikson's expectation that the mother would transmit to her sons her masculine ideal, presumably based on her idealized and overdrawn recollections of her own father. Instead, Stewart's findings suggest she passes on her feminine attitudes.

Crites' (1962) and Stewart's (1959) findings are somewhat at variance, since Crites found that fathers were more influential as identification figures with vocational significance for their sons than were mothers, while Stewart found that mothers influenced their sons' choices by means of the identification process. Of course, Stewart did not study fathers in comparison to mothers, so perhaps the strength of the influence is relative, as Crites' findings suggest, or variable, as Steimel and Suziedelis' results indicate.

White (1959) also studied the relationship between the values of parents and their offspring, but she studied daughters rather than sons. She tested the hypothesis that parents transmit their female ideal to their daughter by means of assessing the relationship between the vocational interests, self-concepts, and parental identification of college girls. She required 81 freshman college women to perform Q-sorts of their self-concept, of their ideal self-concept, and their concept of what they thought their parents would like them to be. In addition, each girl took the SVIB and provided some personal information. Thirty-four sets of parents were interviewed, and each set also made Q-sorts of their daughter as she is and as they would like her to be ideally. Thus, the design is the same as Stewart's (1959).

White found that the girls' sorts were more like those of their mothers than their fathers on most of the self, ideal self, and parental ideal descriptions. Thus, it would seem that the girls identify more with their mothers than with their fathers. In addition, high Femininity scores on the SVIB were found for girls who showed more agreement between their self- and ideal self-concepts, who had more agreement between their self- and parental ideal concepts, who showed congruence between their ideal and their parents' ideal, and whose parents were both alive (whether living together or not) as opposed to one parent deceased. This latter point suggests that it is necessary, at least for a girl, to have both parents alive to learn a proper female role. A mother without a husband alive apparently must assume too much of the male role and shows too little of how a female interacts with a male for a daughter to acquire a socially acceptable female identification.

Hershenson (1965) extrapolated Erikson's concept of identity to the question of perception of self in an occupational role. Hershenson administered a questionnaire to 162 Harvard College juniors to measure the degree to which people feel their occupational choice reflects their abilities, interests, and values and to assess their view of the role a career plays in one's life. Among the observations was the finding that occupational prestige plays an important role for students holding an emergent or "other directed" orientation.

In another aspect of the same study, Hershenson (1967) tested the hypothesis that the degree of adolescent identity achieved is positively related to the extent that an individual perceives himself as fitting into an anticipated occupational role. Hershenson also predicted that the sense of identity that is achieved by adolescents is positively related to the degree of enculturation, and that the degree that adolescents feel they fit into their anticipated occupational role is positively related to their degree of enculturation. Though the results supported the three hypotheses, the data were not clear enough to cause Hershenson to feel confident that the hypotheses were supported in the way Erikson's position would predict.

In another study of the identification process and vocational choice, Sostek (1963) found that girls with female occupational choices identified more with their mothers than females who chose masculine occupations. He also found that males who chose female-type occupations identified more with their mothers than did those boys who chose masculine occupations. Finally, he reports that males and females choosing feminine occupations identified more with their mothers than with their fathers, and the males and females who chose masculine occupations identified more with their fathers than with their mothers. Of general significance is his finding that identification is facilitated by parental warmth, regardless of sex. Thus, if a parent wishes to serve as a model for his child, he can increase the likelihood of succeeding by generating a warm, close relationship with his offspring.

Tipton (1966) tested some aspects of the role of identification in occupational selection. He compared the frequency of having parents who are teachers for groups of education and noneducation majors. No differences in frequency were found. When both student groups were compared with respect to the degree of identification with a teacher by means of response to a rating scale, Tipton found that education majors exhibited stronger identification with the teacher model than noneducation majors. Malnig's (1967) hypothesis, that some individuals might avoid competition directly with their parents, discussed earlier, is interesting to consider in the light of Tipton's failure to find offspring of teachers overrepresented in teacher training programs.

Heilbrun (1969) computed an index of perceived similarity between offspring and their same-sex parent over 15 personality dimensions. Since the possible personality styles could be either masculine or feminine, an individual could potentially identify with a masculine or feminine father or a masculine or feminine mother. The results, based on 47 male and 33 female college counseling center clients, indicated that sons' identification with their fathers is correlated with positive vocational interests; sons' identification with a masculine figure (either father or mother) is associated with career interest rejects; and that daughters' identification with feminine models of either sex is associated with a high number of career rejects on the SVIB. Heilbrun concludes that identification with a masculine father enhances the crystallization of positive vocational interests and rejects in sons whereas identification with a feminine mother has the opposite effect. As is so often the situation, however, the results are less conclusive for girls than for boys.

In a similar type of study, Hollender (1972) observed the similarity between SVIB profiles for 31 college and 28 high school male students and those of their parents. Neither group of students showed many high correlations between sons and their parents on the SVIB, in contrast to the findings of many other studies.

The results of these studies seem to imply the conclusion that identification with a parent or adult model is indirectly important in the vocational choice process, but no direct relationships have been demonstrated, and the findings of the studies are not entirely consistent with one another. Unfortunately, the measures of identification are not powerful, and they have nearly always been related to interest inventory scores rather than other behaviors, such as vocational selection or attainment. Even statements of vocational preference might be more revealing in clarifying the relationship between identification and vocational choice than scores on interest inventories.

Small (1953), exploring personality variables influential in vocational choice, proposed that certain aspects of career decisions are based on ego functioning. He hypothesized that a healthy ego, since it is in close contact with reality, will be able to delay gratification to a much greater extent than a weak ego, which is more distantly removed from reality. Since adjustment is partially a function of ego strength, and according to his reasoning, vocational choice is partly a function of ego strength, reality factors in vocational choice are related to ego functioning. Thus, he predicted that adolescent males who are well adjusted will express realistic first occupational preferences and unrealistic second preferences, while the reverse should hold for poorly adjusted boys.

To test this prediction, he studied the job preferences and reasons for their selection of 50 pairs of 15- to 19- year-old boys, matched on all significant background features except adjustment. The results supported the hypothesis; the choices of the better-adjusted boys reflected participation in their environments, while the choices of the maladjusted boys reflected detachment from their environments, a tendency to act out their impulses and to have feelings of self-deprecation. These findings led Small to conclude that vocational counseling is most effective with people who have strong egos because they are reality oriented and that those with weak egos need psychotherapy before they can profit from vocational counseling or make realistic vocational plans. Small concluded with the provocative hypothesis that vocationally undecided people are unable to commit themselves vocationally because they have retentive fantasies and do not care to give up any of their career alternatives.

Very and Zannini (1969), testing the Adlerian hypothesis that birth order affects behavior, predicted that a significant number of beauticians would be second born because of the similarity between the personality attributes of the second born (i.e., easygoing, harmony-seeking, and casual, according to Adler) and those of the successful beautician. A significant number of the 210 beauticians Very and Zannini observed were, in fact, found to be second born.

A final study of relevance to the psychoanalytic point of view of vocational choice is Crites' (1960) investigation of the relationship between ego strength and vocational choice. In particular, he was concerned with the correlation between ego strength and occupational interest level and between ego strength and the degree to which interests are patterned. Crites assumed that a strong ego would result in a clearer pattern of vocational interests at a more professional level than would a weak ego. He also predicted that older students, having a stronger ego as a function of more advanced age, would have clearer interest patterns. Using the SVIB occupational level (OL) scale and the number of A and B+ scores on the SVIB as measures of level and patterning, respectively, and the ES scale of the MMPI as an ego strength measure (Barron, 1953), Crites tested his hypotheses on a sample of 100 male college students who had come to a college counseling center for educational-vocational counseling.

The results failed to support the hypothesis that higher occupational levels are related to strong egos, but the data did support the second hypothesis, that interest patterning is related to ego strength in older students but not in younger ones. Unfortunately for analytic theory, other conceptions of maturity might account for greater interest patterning in older adolescents than in younger ones, especially using the Strong Vocational Interest Blank, since the SVIB was developed using mature men as standardization groups. Older adolescents might have clearer interest patterns than younger ones simply because they are more like the criterion groups.

Crites made several suggestions for counseling students who have unpatterned interests. He proposed that vocational-educational counseling for such students be preceded by personal counseling which has as its goal the development of a more adequately functioning ego. To accomplish this task the interviews would apply procedures based on a combination of learning theory and psychoanalysis, similar to the suggestion of the Dollard and Miller formulation (1950).

### Evaluation

Considering the general antagonism professionals holding the psychoanalytic point of view have toward vocational counseling, there have been a large number of attempts to test empirically hypotheses about vocational choice stemming from analytic thought. No investigators have attempted to integrate vocational behavior into analytic theory in a complete way; rather, attempts have been made to integrate analytic theory into vocational psychology. The concepts of ego strength, identification, and personality development in general have been especially scrutinized by reasearchers. Of these processes, ego strength seems to have been studied most carefully and with the greatest success, identification least carefully and with results of a contradictory nature, and personality development within the analytic framework studied too generally to allow it to acquire its potential use in counseling.

The research methods typically have involved the use of Q-sorts to describe some features of the subjects and/or their parents in combination with Strong Vocational Interest Blank patterns of scores. It seems likely that more meaningful results might have been obtained through the use of statements of vocational preference, vocational selection, and possibly vocational attainment rather than through the exclusive use of SVIB scores. The difficulties involved in requiring subjects to do large amounts of Q-sorting are rarely discussed, but it is likely that subjects become careless as they are doing the third sort of 75 or 100 items describing their behavior or someone else's evaluation of their behavior. While most of the investigators report positive findings in studies based on Q-sorts, consideration of the actual meaningfulness of the research tasks for the subjects must be taken in evaluating results of studies.

In nearly all the studies, with the possible exception of Crities' work, the size of the samples used was relatively small, in some cases as low as 15 subjects per group. While that in itself is no error and often larger samples are difficult to obtain, the generalizations to be drawn from such research are of necessity limited. Such limitations are serious since replication of research in vocational development is difficult to accomplish, and consequently, very unusual. Furthermore, the samples themselves are often not typical of groups of individuals with whom counselors are concerned. It is hard to generalize about mature populations from data based exclusively on student samples. At the same time, the student samples in many cases are not representative of any population outside the particular sample studied, not even other students. College students, especially advanced ones, are not typical of high school youths not planning to enter college.

# STATUS

## Implications for Counseling

The psychoanalytic view does not suggest any special techniques for vocational psychology other than those used in psychoanalysis in general. The view is presented that career choice is one of several important decisions individuals must make during their lifetime. The normally functioning individual is presumably capable of identifying vocational factors important to him which will lead him to make vocational decisions and he will be able to develop the resources to implement his decisions. Indeed, it will be recalled that one-half of Freud's definition of a well-ordered person is the ability to work effectively.

In the disordered person vocational choice may be disrupted along with other major behavioral responsibilities. For such unfortunate individuals the purely psychoanalytic position suggests no shortcuts for intensive analysis designed to identify the snag in development, unravel it, and accelerate the process to the point of maturity. Less orthodox psychologists of an analytic persuasion suggest that analytic concepts may be of use in understanding the motives and developmental history behind the choice of a career. The Bordin, Nachmann, Segal (1963) proposal, for example, might be useful as both an occupational information tool in identifying the potential for satisfying various motives in occupations and as a diagnostic device providing a framework for conducting interviews to appraise vocational suitability.

Perhaps a proposal Crites offers (1962) is suggestive of the kind of potential analytic concepts have for vocational counseling. With reference to the question of ego strength and its relation to vocational choice problems, Crites questions the feasibility of trying to help a client develop an appropriate masculine identification in two or three interview hours of vocational counseling. If ego strength is, in fact, a crucial variable in the development of inappropriate vocational behaviors, Crites' suggestion is that vocational counseling must devote its attention to the strengthening of the ego through the use of personal counseling methods rather than in emphasizing occupational information and the techniques of the trait-factor approach.

## Evaluation

The major strength of the psychoanalytic approach to vocational choice lies in its comprehensiveness and integration with respect to psychological theory in general. To offset this positive attribute, however, several negative ones exist.

First, since psychoanalytic theory essentially concerns psychopathology, the very normal process of vocational choice must be added to the theory as an afterthought, despite the emphasis that Freud placed on the role work plays in a satisfying life. Freud thought work was important, but he did not comment further. Such a limitation is analogous to the criticism made about the Ginzberg theory: the development of vocational choice concepts from a theory of psychopathology is similar to the development of a marital adjustment theory based only on data available on divorced couples.

A very serious limitation of analytically based conceptions of vocational choice is the limited role aptitudes play in psychoanalytic thinking. While it is highly possible that psychology has overemphasized the role of aptitude in vocational theory, it does not seem reasonable to ignore the feedback of experiences people use to guide them in their work selection. If one chooses to use the concept of career attainment as a criterion in career development theory, aptitude would necessarily play a highly important role.

A final problem in the analytical approach to vocational selection is the general failure of psychoanalytic theory to assume a parsimonious position with respect to explanations of behavior and the corollary of this, the difficulty of experimentally validating or refuting analytical concepts. Since the concepts are so intricate, experimental data are often consistent with them, but at the same time can usually be explained by other constructs of a simpler and more direct nature.

To date, the analytical model has played only a minor role in vocational psychology, although some aspects of it are highly integrated into the practice of vocational psychology, much as the psychoanalytic method and constructs are intertwined with psychology (especially clinical psychology) in general. Some aspects of the analytical approach are appealing and enrich the understanding of vocational behavior, but others, especially those of more orthodox analysis, are difficult to apply to vocational counseling. It is likely that analytic theory will continue to exert a peripheral though strong impact on vocational psychology, but it does not seem likely that any new, rigorous, or productive formulations will result from the psychoanalytic quarter.

# REFERENCES

Barron, F. An ego strength scale which predicts response to psychotherapy. *Journal of Consulting Psychology*, 1953, *17*, 327-333.

Bell, H. M. Ego-involvement in vocational decisions. *Personnel and Guidance Journal*, 1960, *38*, 732-736.

Bordin, E. S., Nachmann, Barbara, and Segal S. J. An articulated framework for vocational development. *Journal of Counseling Psychology*, 1963, *10*, 107-116.

Brill, A. A. *Basic principles of psychoanalysis.* Garden City, New York: Doubleday, 1949.

Crites, J. O. Ego strength in relation to vocational interest development. *Journal of Counseling Psychology*, 1960, 7, 137-143.

## 128 / Theories of Career Development

Crites, J. O. Parental identification in relation to vocational interest development. *Journal of Educational Psychology*, 1962, *53*, 262-270.

Dollard, J., and Miller, N. E. *Personality and psychotherapy*. New York: McGraw-Hill, 1950.

Drasgow, J. Occupational choice and Freud's overdetermiñism. *Vocational Guidance Quarterly*, 1957, *6*, 67-68.

Erikson, E. *Childhood and society*. New York: Norton, 1950.

Forer, B. R. Personality factors in occupational choice. *Educational and Psychological Measurement*, 1953, *13*, 361-366.

Galinsky, M. D., and Fast, Irene. Vocational choices as a focus of the identity search. *Journal of Counseling Psychology*, 1966, *13*, 89-92.

Heilbrun, A. B. Jr. Parental identification and the patterning of vocational interests in college males and females. *Journal of Counseling Psychology*, 1969, *16*, 342-347.

Hendrick. I. Work and the pleasure principle. *Psychoanalytic Quarterly*, 1943, *12*, 311-329.

Hershenson, D. B. Some personal and social determinants of occupational role-taking in college students. *Journal of Counseling Psychology*, 1965, *12*, 206-208.

Hershenson, D. B. Sense of identity, occupational fit, and enculturation in adolescence. *Journal of Counseling Psychology*, 1967, *14*, 319-324.

Hollender, J. Differential parental influences on vocational interest development in adolescent males. *Journal of Vocational Behavior*, 1972, *2*, 67-76.

Jones, E. The significance of the sublimating process for education and re-education. In *Psychoanalysis*, New York: Wood, 1923.

Malnig, L. R. Fear of paternal competition: a factor in vocational choice. *Personnel and Guidance Journal*, 1967, *46*, 235-239.

Mowrer, O. H. *Learning theory and personality dynamics*. New York: Ronald, 1950.

Nachmann, Barbara. Childhood experiences and vocational choice in law, dentistry, and social work. *Journal of Counseling Psychology*, 1960, *7*, 243-250.

Neff, W. S. *Work and human behavior*. New York: Atherton, 1968.

Oberndorf, C. P. Psychopathology of work. *Bulletin of the Menninger Clinic*, 1951, *15*, 77-84.

Roe, Anne. Early determinants of vocational choice. *Journal of Counseling Psychology*, 1957, *4*, 212-217.

Segal, S. A psychoanalytic analysis of personality factors in vocational choice. *Journal of Counseling Psychology*, 1961, *8*, 202-210.

Segal, S. J., and Szabo, Ruth. Identification in two vocations: accountants and creative writers. *Personnel and Guidance Journal*, 1964, *43*, 252-255.

Small, L. Personality determinants of vocational choice. *Psychological Monographs*, 1953, *67*, No. 1 (Whole No. 351).

Sommers V. S. Vocational choice as an expression of conflict in identification. *American Journal of Psychotherapy*, 1956, *10*, 520-535.

Sostek, A. B. The relation of identification and parent-child climate to occupational choice. Unpublished doctoral dissertation, Boston University, 1963.

Steimel, R. J., and Suziedelis, A. Perceived parental influence and inventoried interests. *Journal of Counseling Psychology*, 1963, *10*, 289-295.

Stephenson, R. R. A new pattern analysis technique for the SVIB. *Journal of Counseling Psychology*, 1961, *8*, 355-362.

Stewart, L. H. Mother-son identification and vocational interest. *Genetic Psychology Monographs*, 1959, *60*, 31-63.

Strong, E. K. Jr. *Vocational interests of men and women*. Stanford, Calif.: Stanford University Press, 1943.

Tipton, R. M. Vocational identification and academic achievement. *Journal of Counseling Psychology*, 1966, *13*, 425-430.

Very, P. S., and Zannini, J. A. Relation between birth order and being a beautician. *Journal of Applied Psychology*, 1969, *53*, 149-151.

Weinstein, M. S. Personality and vocational choice: a comparison of the self-conceptions and ideal self-conceptions of students in three professional schools. Unpublished doctoral dissertation, Western Reserve University, 1953.

White, B. J. The relationship of self-concept and parental identification to women's vocational interests. *Journal of Counseling Psychology,* 1959, *6,* 202-206.
White, J. C. Cleanliness and successful bank clerical personnel — a brief. *Journal of Counseling Psychology,* 1963, *10,* 192.
Zilboorg, G. The problem of constitution in psychopathology. *Psychoanalytic Quarterly,* 1934, *3,* 339-362.

# 5

# Super's Developmental Self-Concept Theory of Vocational Behavior

In fashioning his theory of career development, Donald Super appears to have been strongly influenced by two themes. The first influence, self-concept theory, may be illustrated by the writings of Carl Rogers (1942; 1951), Carter (1940), and Bordin (1943). These writers have suggested that behavior is a reflection of an individual's attempt to implement his self-descriptive and self-evaluative thought. With particular reference to vocations, Bordin (1943) proposed the notion that responses to vocational interest inventories represent an individual's projection of his self-concept in terms of stereotypes he holds about occupations. A man selects or rejects an occupation because of his belief that the field is or is not consistent with his view of himself.

The other major influence on Super's work is Charlotte Buehler's (1933) writings in developmental psychology. She suggested that life can be viewed as consisting of distinct stages. The first is a growth stage, starting at birth and ending around age 14. Following this is an exploratory stage, occurring between ages 15 and 25. The maintenance stage comes next and covers the next 40 years, ending at about age 65, whereupon the final stage, called decline, begins. According to Buehler, life tasks vary according to the stage. Super's conception of career development is built upon the framework of these life stages and based on the assumption that vocational tasks reflect larger life tasks.

While other writers, for example Beilin (1955), have recognized the applicability of developmental psychology to career behavior and have attempted to formulate principles of vocational behavior taking human development into account, no one has so intricately woven developmental hypotheses into career development as successfully as Super.

131

## THE THEORY

Hints of a theoretical basis were evident in Super's research (e.g., 1940) in the field of career development many years before the publication of his first theoretical statement. Nevertheless, by his own admission, he was impelled into his first formal theoretical statement by the attempts at theorizing of Ginzberg and his colleagues (1951). Super thought the Ginzberg work had serious shortcomings, one of which was the failure to take into account the very significant existing body of information about educational and vocational development.

Super's theoretical writings have been extensive. His initial formulations were stated in an address before the American Psychological Association (1953) and further elaborated in a book (1957), a monograph (Super et al., 1957), and several papers (most significantly 1963a, 1963b, and 1963c). Super proposes the notion that a person strives to implement his self-concept by choosing to enter the occupation he sees as most likely to permit him self-expression. Furthermore, Super suggests that the particular behaviors a person engages in to implement his self-concept vocationally are a function of the individual's stage of life development. As one matures, his self-concept becomes stable. The manner in which it is implemented vocationally, however, is dependent upon conditions external to the individual. Thus, attempts to make vocational decisions during adolescence assume a different form than those made during late middle age. According to Super, diverse vocational behaviors can be understood better by viewing them within the context of the changing demands of the life cycle on the shape of attempts to implement a self-concept.

In the development of his theory, Super strived to implement a specific stream of thought and research in psychology (1953). The attempt to build a theory on the groundwork laid by previous efforts was deliberate, since Super soundly criticized the Ginzberg theory because of the failure of its authors to use the existing data relevant to vocational choice.

### Occupations and Careers

Important to Super's theory is the difference between the psychology of occupations and the psychology of careers. The psychology of occupations is based primarily on differential psychology and on the assumption that once an individual and a career are matched they will "live happily ever after." The psychology of careers, on the other hand, stemming from developmental psychology, rests on the assumption that career development conforms with the general principles of human development, which is fundamentally evolutionary in nature. Vocational psychology is the term Super chose to represent the field of study resulting from the fusion of the two streams of thought. Since the methods and tools of vocational counseling are currently more suitable to the study of the psychology of occupations than the psychology of careers, Super asserts that the latter has been neglected in favor of the former (Super, 1961a; 1964a). He would correct the neglected condition of the psychology of careers by means of his theoretical formulations.

## The Antecedents of the Theory

Super's theoretical framework is based on three psychological areas. The first is the field of differential psychology. The stream of research related to differential psychology is mature and has contributed much to vocational psychology. On the basis of existing data, Super drew the assumption that any given man possesses the potential for success and satisfaction in a variety of occupational settings. He elaborated on the trait-factor notions that people are differentially qualified for occupations by suggesting that interests and abilities are likely to fall into patterns more consistent with some occupations than others and that people are likely to be more satisfied if they are in an occupation that requires a pattern of interests and abilities closely corresponding to their own characteristics.

A second psychological influence on Super's theory stems from self-concept theory. Super proposed that vocational self-concepts develop on the basis of children's observations of and identifications with adults involved in work. Third, Super relied heavily on principles of developmental psychology. The concept of life stages suggested by Buehler (1933) led Super to propose that a person's mode of adjustment at one period of his life is likely to be predictive of his techniques of adjustment at a later period.

Developmental concepts also led Super to the idea of career patterns. From the work of Miller and Form (1951) and Davidson and Anderson (1937) Super expanded the concept of career patterns. The career behavior of people follows general patterns which may be recognized as regular and predictable after study and examination of the individual. These patterns are the result of many psychological, physical, situational, and societal factors which, when accumulated, make up an individual's life. Among the various career patterns are the *stable* pattern, where a career such as medicine is entered into relatively early and permanently; the *conventional* pattern, where several jobs are tried, one of which leads to a stable job; the *unstable* pattern, characterized by a series of trial jobs which lead to temporary stability which is soon disrupted; and finally the *multiple trial* pattern, in which an individual moves from one stable entry level job to another, such as may be observed in domestic service careers (Super et al., 1957).

The career pattern concept suggests that the life cycle imposes different vocational tasks on people at various times of their lives. Attention to career choice as a one-shot decision occurring in adolescence reflects only a segment of significant vocational behavior in the life of an individual. To comprehend fully a person's vocational life, the whole cycle must be observed. Super also notes the different roles that environment and heredity play in maturation, bringing attention to those aspects of environment that may be manipulated to facilitate vocational maturity.

On the basis of principles just described, Super generated ten propositions which should underlie a vocational development theory. These are summarized in the following list.

## A Theory of Vocational Development*

1. People differ in their abilities, interests, and personalities.
2. They are qualified, by virtue of these characteristics, each for a number of occupations.
3. Each of these occupations requires a characteristic pattern of abilities, interests, and personality traits, with tolerances wide enough, however, to allow both some variety of occupations for each individual and some variety of individuals in each occupation.
4. Vocational preferences and competencies, the situations in which people live and work, and hence their self-concepts, change with time and experience (although self-concepts are generally fairly stable from late adolescence until late maturity), making choice and adjustment a continuous process.
5. This process may be summed up in a series of life stages characterized as those of growth, exploration, establishment, maintenance, and decline, and these stages may in turn be subdivided into (a) the fantasy, tentative, and realistic phases of the exploratory stage, and (b) the trial and stable phases of the establishment stage.
6. The nature of the career pattern (that is, the occupational level attained and the sequence, frequency, and duration of trial and stable jobs) is determined by the individual's parental socioeconomic level, mental ability, and personality characteristics, and by the opportunities to which he is exposed.
7. Development through life stages can be guided, partly by facilitating the process of maturation of abilities and interests, and partly by aiding in reality testing and in the development of the self-concept.
8. The process of vocational development is essentially that of developing and implementing a self-concept: it is a compromise process in which the self-concept is a product of the interaction of inherited aptitudes, neural and endocrine makeup, opportunity to play various roles, and evaluations of the extent to which the results of role playing meet with the approval of superiors and fellows.
9. The process of compromise between individual and social factors, between self-concept and reality, is one of role playing, whether the role is played in fantasy, in the counseling interview, or in real life activities such as school classes, clubs, part-time work, and entry jobs.
10. Work satisfactions and life satisfactions depend upon the extent to which

the individual finds adequate outlets for his abilities, interests, personality traits, and values; they depend upon his establishment in a type of work, a role which his growth and exploratory experiences have led him to consider congenial and appropriate.

*From D. E. Super, A theory of vocational development, *American Psychologist*, 1953, *8*, 189-190.

### Revised Theory

Despite the considerable research that resulted from the ten propositions (e.g., the Career Pattern Study), the theory remained relatively general for almost ten years. Then, Super and several of his students published a series of papers which provide a more explicit and detailed set of statements about how vocational development occurs. Super began by making the notion of the self-concept as explicit as possible (1963b). Starting with the awareness of self (as differentiated from the nonself) which an infant perceives at birth, Super described a process which leads first to primary self-percepts and then to more elaborate, or secondary percepts. The primary self-percepts deal with raw sensations such as hunger, pain, and temperature. As the child matures and begins to develop secondary percepts, the sensations begin to become ordered and assume a relationship with one another. As maturation continues, the self-percepts become even more complex and abstract, developing into self-concepts and systems of self-concepts. Among the many systems of self-concepts is the vocational self-concept, the system of major concern to Super.

According to Super (1963a), self-concept formation requires a person to recognize himself as a distinctive individual, yet at the same time to be aware of the similarities between himself and others. The self-concept of a well-integrated individual is a continually developing entity, shifting somewhat through life as experiences indicate that changes are necessary to reflect reality. Presumably, the vocational self-concept develops in a similar way. As an individual matures, he tests himself in many ways, most of which have implications for educational and vocational decisions. The process begins with the self-differentiation that occurs as part of a person's search for identity. A child learns that the hot stove he touched hurts him, not his mother. In adolescence, the differences between self and others are broadened and make one aware that he is fat or tall, shy or poised, athletic or clumsy, good in academic matters or bored in school. These recognitions, in turn, lead to decisions about education and work that are consistent with self-concepts. The athlete makes different decisions than the musically talented youth; the scholar thinks of himself in the future in different terms than the "drop-out."

At the same time that the process of differentiation of self from others occurs, a process of identification goes on, partly facilitating the differentiation and partly facilitated by it. Beginning with their identification with the like-sexed parent, children develop images of themselves and behavior appropriate to culturally approved sexual norms. They progress from identification with general to specific models. Recognizing that his father's life is not ideal, the adolescent may find other adult males with whom to identify. The grocer's son may model himself vocationally after the neighbor who is an engineer, while at the same time identifying with his father's hobbies and personality traits.

Role playing, stimulated by the process of identification, further facilitates the development of the vocational self-concept. The youth who observes a fireman will pretend he is one himself and will play games in which he may act out the role of a fireman. As he grows, his role playing becomes more subtle and sophisticated. The budding physician imagines himself as the great surgeon and observes doctors in order to adopt their mannerisms and values. The prospective lawyer may deliberately seek out extracurricular political activities and become involved in school government, or even real political campaigns.

Hadley and Levy (1962) have suggested that much of the role playing that occurs to facilitate career development takes place in formal and informal groups. The child evaluates potential roles in the world of work from the point of view of his family, which communicates the differential values of various kinds of work. As the child reaches adolescence, his reference group shifts from the family to the peer group, and his vocational role activities, real and vicarious, are evaluated in the context of the teen-age world. In later life, when careers have been embarked upon and established, professional associations and trade unions serve as vocational reference groups. Codes of conduct, modes of behavior, and values are informally or formally set by the vocational group to which a person belongs.

Finally, throughout all of the adolescent period, but actually involved in career development in any life phase prior to decision-making, reality testing must occur. Is the hopeful physician a good student? Is the potential musician successful in his attempts to extend his musical activities? Can the prelaw student earn admission to law school? Can the junior executive perform his duties well? Is the scientist able to publish his research? Are the consequences of these vocational decisions entirely consistent with the aspirations of the individual? These reality factors must of necessity either confirm or negate tentative educational and vocational decisions and cause them to be modified accordingly.

The various processes in the development of vocational self-concepts are likely to occur in more complex ways than the examples given suggest. While it is possible for an adolescent's identification with a person to lead him directly to an educational-vocational decision, it is more likely that the identification will stimulate a chain of events having vocational implications that might not have occurred otherwise. Similarly, the adoption of a role may lead directly to a career, but it is more likely that role playing will have immediate consequences which may eventually influence vocational decisions. Talents explored will often lead to talents in new fields that have not been acknowledged previously. Thus, in playing the role of journalist, a student may join the school newspaper staff and meet a teacher who inspires him to become a writer. This decision, in turn, may lead him to join a literary club, read Sinclair Lewis' *Arrowsmith* (1925), and eventually become a research scientist.

## Vocational Maturity

In a more recent extension of his theory Super (1963c) elaborated upon the concept of vocational maturity (Super et al., 1957; 1960). Vocational maturity allows the observer to assess the rate and level of an individual's development with respect to career matters. It is to be expected that vocationally mature behavior will assume different shapes depending upon the context provided by an individual's life stage. The vocationally mature 14-year-old will be concerned with assessing his interests and abilities to reach the goal of deciding on an educational plan, while the vocationally mature 45-year-old man will be concerned with ways he can maintain his career status in the face of competition from younger men. In view of the fluid nature of vocational maturity, Super defined the concept normatively, in terms of the congruence between an individual's vocational behavior and the expected vocational behavior at that age. The closer the correspondence between the two, the greater the individual's vocational maturity.

## Stages of Development

To specify further the process of vocational development, Super (1963c) extended the analysis of life stages with reference to vocational behavior. He proposed the idea that each of the two major stages in the vocationally significant life periods have several substages. The exploratory stage is composed first of the tentative substage, then the transition substage, and finally the uncommitted trial substage. Following these periods comes the establishment stage, which is composed of the committed trial substage and the advancement substage. These stages, while not precisely the same as those of the Ginzberg theory, show some general correspondence to it. The names of the stages suggest the gradual nature of vocational concerns, starting in late childhood in tentative probes and questions, becoming stronger stirrings in early adolescence as recognition of the importance of these decisions grows, and finally leading to educational, and sometimes preliminary, vocational decisions. These decisions, in turn, are evaluated and either are modified or become crystallized, and lead to the mature stage of elaboration and embellishment of vocational behaviors.

The process occurs by means of five activities, which Super has called vocational developmental tasks. The first of these tasks, crystallization of a vocational preference, requires the individual to formulate ideas about work appropriate for himself. It also requires him to develop occupational and self-concepts that will help him to mediate his tentative vocational choice by means of relevant educational decisions. While the crystallization task can occur at any age, as can all the vocational developmental tasks, it most typically occurs during the 14- to 18-year age range. In the following list the necessary attitudes and behaviors for the successful negotiation of the crystallization of a career pattern are summarized. These prerequisites reflect the necessity for an individual to make his plans explicit, to learn to identify cogent variables and their manner of implementation, to accumulate data appropriate to those important variables, and to translate the data and interpret them so that a plan to reach the next stage of the process can be made, implemented, and evaluated.

### Attitudes and Behaviors Relevant to Vocational Development Tasks*

1. Crystallization (14-18)
   a. awareness of the need to crystallize
   b. use of resources
   c. awareness of factors to consider
   d. awareness of contingencies which may affect goals
   e. differentiation of interests and values
   f. awareness of present-future relationships
   g. formulation of a generalized preference
   h. consistency of preference
   i. possession of information concerning the preferred occupation
   j. planning for the preferred occupation
   k. wisdom of the vocational preference
2. Specification (18-21)
   a. awareness of the need to specify
   b. use of resources in specification
   c. awareness of factors to consider
   d. awareness of contingencies which may affect goals
   e. differentiation of interests and values
   f. awareness of present-future relationships
   g. specification of a vocational preference
   h. consistency of preference
   i. possession of information concerning the preferred occupation
   j. planning for the preferred occupation
   k. wisdom of the vocational preference
   l. confidence in a specific preference
3. Implementation (21-24)
   a. awareness of the need to implement preference
   b. planning to implement preference
   c. executing plans to qualify for entry
   d. obtaining an entry job
4. Stabilization (25-35)
   a. awareness of the need to stabilize
   b. planning for stabilization

   c. becoming qualified for a stable regular job or accepting the inevitability of instability

   d. obtaining a stable regular job or acting on resignation to instability

5. Consolidation (35 plus)

   a. awareness of the need to consolidate and advance

   b. possession of information as to how to consolidate and advance

   c. planning for consolidation and advancement

   d. executing consolidation and advancement plans

*From D. E. Super, Vocational development in adolescence and early childhood: tasks and behaviors, pp. 84, 88, 90, 91. In Super, D. E., Starishevsky, R., Matlin, N., and Jordaan, J. P., *Career development: self-concept theory*, New York: College Entrance Examination Board, 1963. Copyright 1963 by CEEB, reproduced by permission.

The next vocational developmental task is called the specification of a vocational preference. Here, the individual is required to narrow a general career direction into a specific one and take the necessary steps to implement the decision. Thus, the prospective applied physicist enrolls in an electrical engineering program in college, while the young man who likes the outdoors and has a technical bent begins the study of forestry. The specification task is most prominent during the age span of 18 to 21 years. Once again, Super has indicated the attitudes and behaviors that are necessary to the successful accomplishment of the specification vocational task. These are also summarized in the list on page 138. They are similar to behaviors required in the crystallization task, except that they relate to the need for specification rather than crystallization. The third vocational task is the implementation of a vocational preference. This task, well advanced by age 21 and usually complete by age 25, requires the individual to complete some training and enter relevant employment. The necessary attitudes and behaviors for this task are to be seen in the list on page 138 and call for the individual's recognition of the need to plan for the implementation for a preference and the execution of this plan.

Stabilization within a vocation comes fourth in the list of developmental tasks for career development. Occurring approximately between the ages of 25 and 35, this task is represented by behavior which reflects settling down within a field of work and the use of one's talents in such a way as to demonstrate the appropriateness of the career decisions previously made. It is to be expected that an individual changes *positions* during the stabilization period, but rarely his *vocation*. The attitudes and behaviors appropriate to this task are also summarized in the list. The final vocational development task Super mentions is the consolidation of status and advancement, which occurs most clearly during the late 30s and mid-40s. Here, the worker firmly establishes himself, his skills, and his seniority, so that he can generate a secure and comfortable vocational position for himself as his career matures into his 50s and early 60s. The necessary attitudes and behaviors, also summarized in the list on page 139, are highly similar to those of the implementation and stabilization tasks. While Super fails to mention the specific task of readiness for retirement and decline in this list of vocational tasks, he has called attention to this task as a final phase in the life cycle in other writings (Super, 1957).

In summary, the individual moves through life stages, each of which calls for vocational behavior of a different sort. The adolescent finds himself cast in the role of explorer until he finds direction for himself. The young adult must translate the direction he has taken into action for training and job seeking. The more mature adult must find his place within his vocation, and, once he has done so, he must elaborate upon it and secure his position. During each of these phases of vocational development, certain behaviors are more apt to result in growth than others. The degree to which the individual accomplishes the vocational tasks is a function of the adequacy with which he has performed the behaviors appropriate to each phase of his development.

### Exploratory Behavior

Jordaan (1963), one of Super's colleagues, has attempted to make the concept of exploratory vocational behavior explicit enough to study empirically. Jordaan has suggested that while experimental psychologists have studied the phenomenon of exploratory behavior in general, vocational psychologists have failed to recognize the full potential of research in what he calls "vocational exploratory behavior." Jordaan proposes that a complex relationship exists between an individual's exploratory behavior and his knowledge of himself. Logically enough, Jordaan states that exploratory behavior often leads to experiences in which the outcomes provide information that contradicts the beliefs the individual may hold about himself. Where such contradictions occur, the individual often resorts to the inappropriate mechanisms of repression, suppression, or distortion in order to preserve the values and images he holds of himself and his world. Since new information is necessary for growth and since most important behavioral changes must occur in the context of experiences in which results may contradict old beliefs, it is axiomatic that individuals must engage in "undistorted hypothesis testing" in order to grow psychologically. That is to say, people must be psychologically mature enough to tolerate cognitive dissonance and reduce it by resorting to reality rather than by distorting their experiences, if they wish to grow in their ability to cope with the demands life places upon them. While these observations are general in nature, they have a special relevance in vocational psychology.

The exploratory dimensions proposed by Jordaan share the characteristic that vocational exploration is more or less adequate depending upon the degree to which the dimensions are explicit, systematic, overt, and self-initiated. Thus, a person benefits considerably more from his exploratory activities if they are purposeful and have external aspects than if they are random and exist only in mental processes. For example, it is more informative to spend a summer working as a camp counselor than to think about how one might enjoy a career working with young children.

According to Jordaan, certain personal traits and environmental conditions may facilitate exploratory behavior. These traits should serve as goals for counselors to consider in working with individuals in the exploratory stages of career behavior. People are more likely to engage in profitable exploratory acts if they are able to tolerate the ambiguity, uncertainty, tension, and frustration that accompanies the lack of closure and insecurity that one feels prior to making a decision and starting on a course of action. Furthermore, exploration is most useful if defensiveness is minimal, since new information may be threatening to old self-images and values. Parents may facilitate exploratory behaviors by providing an atmosphere which encourages independence and provides emotional support. Society influences the outcome of exploration, too, by virtue of the opportunities it provides for exploratory roles, by the amount of time it makes available for exploration, and by the amount of conflict it places on young people in the exploratory stage of development. Counselors may well direct their efforts toward the task of teaching their students about the fact that exploration requires the ability to tolerate emotional discomfort, toward helping parents understand their role in facilitating exploration, and in helping students develop the ability to keep possibilities open through exploration and implement the best dimensions of the exploratory process.

### Language and Career

In an effort to make explicit the notions of the translation and incorporation of the self-concept into vocational terms, Starishevsky and Matlin (1963) proposed the idea of two vocationally oriented languages. Their proposal was designed to account for the fact that self-concepts vary from one person to another and that people translate their self-concepts to occupations in different ways. The first language is called *psychtalk*. This is the language in which an individual thinks of himself; for all practical purposes, it reflects his self-concept in verbal terms. Examples of psychtalk are: I am short; I am musically talented; I am honest; I always try my utmost; I am lazy. Psychtalk can extend to others, so that one may say "he is fat; you are money hungry; she is unethical." The term *occtalk* has been coined for the second language. Occtalk involves both verbal and behavioral expressions of occupational or educational intent. Thus, "I will be a mechanic," or "I am going to apply to law school," or the actual application to law school are examples of occtalk. The two languages, psychtalk and occtalk, are translatable into each other. One person, when saying "I will apply to medical school" in occtalk, may mean "I am compassionate, responsible, intelligent, and desire status and wealth" in psychtalk. Another person may reflect his ambivalence about himself in psychtalk in his inability to make any clear vocational commitment in occtalk.

The term *incorporation* has been defined to reflect the degree to which the occupational selection an individual makes is congruent with his self-concept. For example, a person who sees himself as intelligent, strong, and humane (psychtalk) may choose law as a career. In his occtalk, lawyers may be described as intelligent, strong, and just. Thus, his choice has a level of incorporation of 66.6 percent, since two of the three ingredients of his psychtalk are included in his occtalk. The level can be represented quantitatively provided all the adjectives descriptive of the individual's self-concept and occupational concepts can be collected and then compared.

The logical extension of the scheme described by Starishevsky and Matlin is for counselors to elicit verbal representations of self-concepts from their clientele and then elicit verbal and behavioral representations of occtalk, hoping to facilitate the client's ability to match his self-concept and occupational possibilities. Presumably, good matches can be achieved either by helping the counselee modify his self-concept where it appears to be inappropriate, or by helping expand or modify his occupational dictionary, where his occupational language appears to be limited or inaccurate.

# RESEARCH

## Vocational Maturity

As might be expected, the most comprehensive research concerning vocational maturity has been conducted by Super and his associates and students. Most of these studies were conducted within the context of Super's programmatic Career Pattern Study (Super and Overstreet, 1960). Super's purpose was to test the concepts of vocational maturity suggested by the theory. To accomplish this, he selected a group of ninth grade boys attending school in Middletown, New York, and set out to follow their vocational development over the 20-year period to follow, or until 1971. The Middletown sample was selected because the community and school systems have characteristics that led Super to conclude that they are representative of a large segment of American culture and thus would allow considerable generalization to be made from the findings. The final number of students actually included in the study of ninth grade boys, however, was small (142).

Five dimensions of vocational maturity were identified for study. Each of these dimensions was examined by means of several indices. The first dimension, entitled orientation to vocational choice, was assessed by examining the degree to which the student showed concern for vocational problems and the effectiveness of his use of the resources available to him in coping with the decision-making task. Both of these factors were examined by means of ratings made on the basis of interviews conducted with each student. Dimension II, information and planning about the preferred occupation, was assessed by studying (1) the specificity of information possessed by the student about his preferred occupation, (2) the degree of specificity of his planning for the occupation of his choice, and (3) the extent to which the student was involved in planning activities of a vocational nature. Once again, these indices were generated on the basis of data obtained in structured interviews with the boys.

Dimension III, consistency of vocational preferences, has three indices, which are the consistency of vocational preferences within fields, within levels, and within families (or fields and levels combined). These indices were based on a modified version of Roe's occupational classification scheme (1956). The student's first two preferences were examined to see the degree to which they were in the same field (Roe's terms), the same level (Roe's terms), and then to see the degree to which the combination of field and level of the first choice agreed with the combination of field and level of the student's second occupational choice. The data, while objectively scored, were based on the semistructured interviews conducted with the students.

Dimension IV, entitled crystallization of traits, has six indices. Two of these, interest maturity and patterning, were derived from Strong Vocational Interest Blank results. Liking for work, concern for work rewards, vocational independence, and acceptance of responsibility for educational-vocational planning were based on data from the interviews. Patterning of work values was based on scores on the Work Values Inventory, an instrument specifically designed by the staff of the Career Pattern Study. The fifth and final dimension, wisdom of vocational preferences, consisting of indices reflecting the agreement between ability and preferences, compared measured interests with preferences, measured interests with fantasy preferences, occupational level of measured interests with the occupational level of preferences, and the socioeconomic accessibility of the preference of the student. The indices were based on a combination of inventories, such as the SVIB and WVI, as well as interview data.

Six of the indices of vocational maturity were found to be intercorrelated to a significant degree (see Table 5.1). The particular arrangement of these results suggested that two major factors are relevant to vocational maturity in ninth grade, namely orientation to choice tasks and the use of resources. While the other indices are not necessarily less important as a result of these findings, the

**TABLE 5.1. Intercorrelations between Adequate and Marginal Measures of Vocational Maturity**

|  | IA | IVF | IIA | IIB | IIC | IB |
|---|---|---|---|---|---|---|
| **Dimension A. Orientation to Choice Tasks** | | | | | | |
| Index IA concern with choice |  | .56 | .40 | .48 | .29 | .23 |
| Index IVF acceptance of responsibility | .56 |  | .47 | .57 | .51 | .24 |
| Index IIA specificity of information | .40 | .47 |  | .37 | .29 | .17 |
| Index IIB specificity of planning | .48 | .57 | .37 |  | .46 | .07 |
| Index IIC extent of planning | .29 | .51 | .29 | .46 |  | .06 |
| **Dimension B. Use of Resources** | | | | | | |
| Index IB use of resources | .23 | .24 | .17 | .07 | .06 |  |

Source: Reprinted with the permission of the publisher from Donald E. Super and Phoebe L. Overstreet, *The Vocational Maturity of Ninth Grade Boys* (New York: Teachers College Press, 1960), p. 60. Copyright 1960, Teachers College, Columbia University.

relationships among them do not appear to have any systematic basis. Thus, such logical-sounding dimensions as the consistency of vocational preferences, the crystallization of interests and attitudes toward work, vocational independence, and the wisdom of vocational preferences in terms of the consistency between preferences, talents, and socioeconomic factors do not seem to be related to vocational maturity in the ninth grade.

Among the variables important to the development of a useful orientation to vocational choice were those which resulted in behaviors reflecting recognition of the need to make educational decisions that have vocational implications. Also important was the acceptance of the responsibility to plan for these decisions, to collect relevant data toward that end, and actually to make and implement decisions with vocational implications. These behaviors include the effective use of pertinent local resources, such as talking to and observing workers and professionals, reading about vocations, part-time work, and so on.

Super and Overstreet also studied variables that might be associated with vocational maturity. These were classified into several groups:

The first were *biosocial* factors. Taking the vocational maturity index total consisting of factors such as concern with choice, specificity of information and planning, and acceptance of responsibility for choice and planning, or in other words, the "orientation to choice tasks" dimension, and correlating it with such biosocial factors as age and intelligence, Super and Overstreet concluded that vocational maturity is related to intelligence and that age is of less importance in vocational maturity, at least at the ninth grade stage of development. Of course, grade placement reflects greater homogeneity of experience than does age, since school experiences are structured, and consequently, grade placement implies a commonality of experience not necessarily present as a function of chronological age. The difference seems to be primarily a reflection of differences in specificity of planning, which suggests that "bright" youngsters are able to plan more effectively in general than less "bright" ones.

*Environmental factors* were also associated with vocational maturity. The vocational maturity index correlated positively with parental occupational level, school curriculum (college preparatory versus noncollege preparatory programs), amount of cultural stimulation, and family cohesiveness, and negatively with urban background and Protestantism. Most of these relationships are intuitively reasonable, since more enriched family backgrounds are likely to result in greater concern for and skill in planning for a career. The rural boys seemed to be more vocationally mature than the urban ones, possible because the rural boys had work experience on farms and were likely to follow family farming patterns which were already clear to them. The negative finding with respect to Protestantism, however, is difficult to explain.

The third group consisted of *vocational factors*. The vocational maturity index correlated significantly with vocational aspirations and also with the degree of agreement between aspiration and expectation.

*Personality characteristics* constituted the fourth group. Vocational maturity was not significantly correlated with any of the personality adjustment or characteristic variables as measured by such devices as the Thematic Apperception Test, Incomplete Sentence Blanks, and a father identification inventory.

The final group of variables was *adolescent achievement.* Some achievements were related to the vocational maturity index. Grades, achievement versus underachievement, participation in school and out-of-school activities, and independence were all positively correlated with vocational maturity, while peer acceptance was negatively correlated.

In all of these five categories, the second major dimension of vocational activity, use of resources, was related only in a negative way with house rating in environmental factors and with achievement-underachievement in the factor of adolescent achievement. It does not appear to be a highly pervasive dimension in vocational maturity, whereas the dimension of orientation to choice is considerably more related to background factors. Super and Overstreet concluded that vocational maturity in ninth grade boys is related to their degree of intellectual and cultural stimulation, the degree to which they are intellectually able to respond to that stimulation, their aspiration to higher rather than lower socioeconomic levels, and their ability to achieve reasonably well in a variety of activities.

With these results in mind, Super suggested that the school curriculum should "foster planfulness" aimed at helping youngsters become aware of their level of occupational aspiration and the general amount of education required to achieve that level. This self-knowledge could be developed without specifically deciding on an occupational goal, which would be premature in the ninth grade. In fact, rather than restrict occupational possibilities at that age, the school should exert its efforts to broaden the student's occupational perspectives and to teach him to use available resources for exploration effectively.

In another study, Super (1961) explored the significance of wise and consistent vocational choices at the ninth grade level in terms of the long-range adequacy of the choice. Reasonable choices held over a long period and from a relatively early age have long been assumed to indicate that good vocational adjustment was to come. In contrast to that assumption is the observed instability of vocational choice in adolescents of all ages. To test the assumption, Super studied 105 ninth grade boys chosen from his Career Pattern sample. Expressions of vocational preference were obtained by means of taped interviews based on a structured interview schedule. The responses about vocational preferences were then scored with respect to their consistency within fields (that is, the number of different categories, minus one, after statements of vocational preference were coded into Roe's [1956] occupational classification), consistency within levels (the number of different levels, minus one, of vocational preferences expressed, translated into Roe's system), and consistency within families (the sum of both consistency measures stated above).

The wisdom of the vocational choice was defined in several ways. If the agreement between a subject's abilities and preferences was high, the choice was considered to be satisfactory. Thus, if the subject's IQ score was greater than that of the bottom quarter of people in his chosen field, the subject was presumed to possess the required ability to function in the field of his choice.

Of concern was the consistency between stated vocational preferences and SVIB scores. A modified SVIB was scored by means of pattern analysis. When the primary pattern was in the field chosen by the subject he was granted a score of four, a secondary pattern earned three points, and a tertiary pattern earned two points. Agreement between the occupational level of the preferred occupation and the SVIB Occupational Level (OL) score was also considered. If the SVIB OL score was not more than one standard deviation below the mean occupational level score of the chosen occupation (Strong, 1943, Table 50, p. 192), the subject's OL score was considered to be consistent with his choice. Finally, the occupation of the breadwinner of the boy's family was rated by means of an occupational rating scale and compared with the rating of the occupation of the boy's choice. An index of social accessibility was thus computed. The smaller the index, the more accessible, and thus the wiser the boy's choice of vocation.

When Super compared the consistency between fields and levels with the standards of wisdom about vocational choices, he found very slight but statistically significant relationships between the two, but these differences could hardly be considered practical. Such findings indicate that vocational preferences fail to show much "wisdom" or consistency at the ninth grade level. Super suggests that at a later point, such consistency may begin to reflect the wisdom of the vocational choice. To this writer, however, the lack of a close relationship between various early vocational preferences seems most reasonable, since the closer in time a boy grows to the criterion of vocational selection – the implementation of the first clearly defined steps toward a vocational field – the more consistent his vocational behavior is likely to become. Early preferences are almost sure to be imprecise, since as time goes on the subject has an opportunity to evaluate and modify his preferences in the light of experience.

The most recent report of the Career Pattern Study deals with the status of the original sample as it approached age 25 (Super, Kowalski, and Gotkin, 1967). Of most interest in the data resulting from this ten-year follow-up, covering the period of the transition from school to college work, is the finding that about half the sample had engaged in what Super calls floundering behavior, and another one-sixth engaged in some floundering combined with stabilization. By age 25, however, when this follow-up occurred, about 80 percent of the sample was engaged in stabilizing behavior. Super, Kowalski, and Gotkin retrospectively related vocational maturity to a variety of criteria. For example, it was noted that vocational maturity was generally predictive of career satisfaction, self-improvement, and occupational satisfaction, questionable as a predictor of economic self-sufficiency, negatively related to early establishment in a career, and not very effective as a predictor of the ability to get and hold a job. In general, it was found that social status and achievement are effective predictors of vocational behavior. The usual measures found in schools (e.g., intelligence tests, parental occupational level, vocational aspirations, curriculum enrolled in, grade point average, age in grade, and, for seniors in high school, degree of participation in school and out-of-school activities) generally were useful predictors of vocational behaviors. The overall conclusion based on the results of the ten-year follow-up was that vocational maturity, in combination with measures of student status and achievement, is a useful predictor of vocational behavior.

### Vocational Maturity — Other Research

Two investigators, Montesano and Geist (1964) chose to compare the occupational choices made by ninth and twelfth grade boys in terms of Super's position. They tested the hypothesis that vocational decisions occur in a developmental context and that the process of vocational development is "predictable and orderly." Sixty ninth and twelfth grade boys, equated with respect to reading skills and socioeconomic variables, were required to respond to the Geist Picture Interest Inventory (GPII) and to give their reasons for the responses they made to the inventory. The reasons were classified according to attitudes toward occupational choice tasks or toward occupations themselves, in terms of categories called simple affect, identified interest, personal need satisfaction, assessment of abilities, assessment of opportunities, assessment of the particular occupation, social value, and ambiguous or evasive.

Montesano and Geist reasoned that if the developmental theory of career preferences has validity, older boys should be more reflective in their reasons for their interests. The findings supported such a view in a general way. Older boys' responses indicated more concern for vocational opportunities, information about careers, and the social value of given careers than did the responses of the ninth grade boys. The younger boys' responses appeared to show considerable reliance on simple affect ("I would like it") or identified interests.

Gribbons (1964) and Gribbons and Lohnes (1964a; 1964b; 1965) have produced a stream of research directed at demonstrating the criteria which are predictable from Readiness for Vocational Planning scores based on an inventory they developed. Their hope was to devise a standard and reliable technique to be used to identify a person's stage of vocational maturity and then introduce experiences to facilitate the growth of aspects of vocational maturity that are not well developed. Such, too, is the end toward which Crites' (1965) Vocational Development Inventory is aimed.

Gribbons and Lohnes (1968) published the result of an extensive longitudinal study concerning their attempt to develop an index of readiness for vocational planning. The project was designed to test the hypothesis that occupational choice is a sequential, developmental process. In particular, attempts were made to determine sex differences in vocational development, study the role of the self-concept in vocational decision-making in adolescence, and assess the impact of intelligence in the choice, entry, and persistence in an occupation. The results of the Gribbons and Lohnes investigation indicate that although students increased in their awareness of their interests and values in relation to their educational-vocational decisions (during the period from eighth to tenth grade), many educational-vocational decisions continued to be made on the basis of irrelevant information. Also, the results point up the fact that eighth graders can be ahead of tenth graders in their readiness for vocational decisions. The data led Gribbons and Lohnes (1968) to postulate four distinct career processes: the steady pursuit of the first expressed vocational goal (called "constant maturity"); the passage through Super's stages of vocational development (called "emerging maturity"); degeneration, seen as the reduction of aspirations and achievement resulting in individual frustration; and constant immaturity, reflected in a fixation on unrealistic vocational goals. Gribbons and Lohnes (1969) have collapsed the original eight scales into one, which makes it a more convenient way to assess vocational maturity.

Crites (1971) has recently published an integrative review of the work pertaining to the Vocational Development Project. In this project, the Vocational Development Inventory was constructed, validated, and applied to a wide variety of theoretical and applied questions in vocational development and behavior. The VDI consists of two parts, one part dealing with attitudes, the other with competencies. The attitudes part has been complete and operational for some time but the competency part has just been published. The results of most of the research indicate that the competency part of the instrument possesses considerable utility for research in vocational behavior.

A third investigator, Westbrook (Westbrook and Parry-Hill, 1973), has developed still another vocational maturity scale, this one emphasizing cognitive, as opposed to attitudinal, aspects of vocational maturity. Super, Bohn, Forrest, Jordaan, Lindeman, and Thompson (1971) have recently published the Career Questionnaire, which purports to combine the best features of all these scales. However, the Westbrook-Parry-Hill and Super et al. instruments are too new to permit an evaluation of their potential as yet. At this time, however, both Gribbons and Lohnes' Readiness for Vocational Planning Scale, and Crites' Vocational Development Inventory provide the theoretician and researcher with useful instruments to apply to certain aspects of vocational development.

Dilley (1965) has attempted to evaluate vocational maturity in terms of decision-making ability. He constructed an inventory purportedly measuring decision-making ability and reported its relationship to intelligence, achievement in school, and participation in extracurricular activities, using 174 high school seniors as subjects. He found that more subjects made good decisions (as defined by his inventory) than were predictable by chance and that good decision-makers earned higher academic aptitude test scores, higher grades, and were more involved in school activities than poor decision-makers. This positive relationship suggests that a general intelligence factor may be involved in vocational maturity. Wurtz (1969), however, has reanalyzed data in a way that suggests that mental age may be a more appropriate way to assess vocational planning than intelligence. In a way, this finding is similar to Crites' (1965) observation that grade level is more closely related to VDI scores than chronological age, since grade level, in general, is a better reflection of maturity during adolescence than age level.

Bartlett (1971) has reviewed much of the research concerning vocational maturity and reminds us of the two general approaches to its study noted by Crites (1961). The work of Super and Gribbons and Lohnes is called the *absolute or relative* approach, and is couched in terms of stages of development and the mastery of tasks associated with them, while the *degree and rate* approach, characterizing the work of Crites, uses the individual's own peers as a comparison group similar to the manner in which intelligence is measured by the Stanford-Binet or the WAIS. It is interesting to note that both approaches seem to produce valid and useful data, though no direct comparison of the two methods has yet been made. In summary, the research evidence in general indicates that vocational maturity is a reasonable and valid concept, and is likely to be of increasing usefulness to our understanding of vocational development.

### Vocational Crystallization

Two investigators have scrutinized the crystallization stage. Madaus and O'Hara (1967) inferred evidence of a crystallization of vocational choice in high school students as a result of a study in which occupational preferences were elicited from 979 high school boys and the preferences classified into nine groups. The Kuder Preference Record differentiated the nine groups in a way similar to the expressed preferences. These results provide evidence from two vantage points that crystallization of vocational preference occurs during the high school years. Buck (1970) surveyed the career plans and experiences of 120 males entering Stanford as freshmen in 1960 and graduating in 1964. Buck administered the California Psychological Inventory, the SVIB, and the SAT to the students in the fall of 1960. In the spring of 1964, a second administration of the SVIB was executed, along with scales describing the extent and effectiveness of vocational exploration. Although changes in interests reflective of crystallization were observed in the subjects, there was no evidence to suggest that crystallization was enhanced by vocational exploratory behavior. The changes in interest crystallization appear to have been influenced by events other than exploratory ones, such as academic exposure and identification with a popular professor. In addition, crystallization was already under way when the students entered college, and the observed changes in crystallization might well have reflected the continuation of an existing trend.

### Vocational Development during High School

The data from the ninth grade follow-up of the Career Pattern Study (Super and Overstreet, 1960) generally indicate that choices made by boys during their early teen years are neither stable nor well founded. Such a finding naturally poses problems for educators concerned with developing curricula designed to teach vocationally related skills, beginning at about the ninth grade period, since assignment of students to relatively narrow programs of study is thus questionable. The likelihood that a student expressing a preference for auto mechanics or law at age 14 will express the same preference at age 18 is relatively slim.

Research reported by Cooley (1967) and Astin (1967a), based on extensive data collected in the Project Talent Study, is somewhat inconsistent with Super's data, however, and suggests an alternative way of dealing with the dilemma of the timing of curricular decisions. Cooley's data, comparing the educational-vocational interests and choices of ninth and twelfth grade boys, indicate that the stated career plan of ninth grade boys is a relatively good predictor of twelfth grade plans. One basis for the difference between Super's work and Cooley's might lie in the specificity of classification used in the twelfth grade criterion. For example, a student might change his plans from physician to hospital attendant; using a criterion of stability of plans, his choice is likely to be viewed as having changed substantially; using a larger set of categories, however, such as "health science," his choice has remained stable. It might be that these larger categories are relatively stable during the ninth to twelfth grade period, and that these choices may represent a major portion of the type of output measured by standard interest inventories. Such a criterion might permit planners to develop general curricula oriented around large categories of vocational events which permit students to make commitments that will remain relatively stable (in fact, such programs do exist in some systems, e.g., Heilman and Gardner, 1971).

Astin (1967b), further studying the shifts in vocational plans that occur during the ninth grade to post high school period, observed that the shifts tend to move students away from science and technology toward careers in business and education. The most likely explanation offered for this change is that reality factors in terms of chances of success in science and technology careers have increasing impact as the students get older.

## Vocational Development during Middle Life

Strangely, since most vocational activities occur after high school and college years, relatively little conceptual basis and even less empirical data exist to describe career development in mid-life. Mills (1970), focusing on religious careers, has tried to extend the idea of vocational developmental tasks from adolescence through the middle years. Mills suggests three specific tasks for this period: first, the need to set one's own milestones. In the middle years, institutions no longer provide clear guidelines of progress or clear identification of transition points as are provided in earlier years by events such as graduation ceremonies, acquisition of privileges to purchase liquor, voting rights, etc. A second task of mid-life is the need to reassert control over one's self-development. Mills suggests an increased need for taking stock of one's progress and becoming active again in controlling one's future, rather than passively following a course of action set in motion some years before. Finally, Mills points to the problems associated with acceptance of self, particularly in the face of adjustments to growing limitations defined in terms of a decrease in energy level, changing relationships with the family (e.g., children leaving home, becoming grandparents) as well as out of the home, and the fact that time is running out on what one will accomplish.

Some empirical studies do exist touching on these issues. Vroom and Pahl (1971) have demonstrated that age is negatively correlated with risk-taking behavior among managers and in the value placed on such behavior in business. Hirt (1964), studying GATB scores earned by individuals during various decades of life, found that older people tend to score lower. This finding should be viewed cautiously, however, because the study was cross-sectional in nature; there is no reliable way to be sure whether the differences in GATB scores between older and younger workers represent deterioration in older people or changes in culture that differentially effect the older workers.

Sheppard (1971) tried to adapt the Vocational Development Inventory to adults. Applying his modified inventory to a sample of 200 unemployed men, 100 vocational trainees, and 100 graduate students, he predicted that the student group would score highest, followed by the trainees, with the unemployed males lowest. The results confirmed his predictions. These results, combined with his item-analysis and cross-validation data, suggest that this instrument might have some potential usefulness in studying vocational maturity in adults.

While relatively little work has been done to study adult vocational maturity and adjustment in terms of development, there does appear to be increasing interest occurring in career development during maturity. Adult vocational development could well become an area of considerable research activity.

## Work Values

In developing concepts of career development, Super proposed the idea of work values and to that end developed a Work Values Inventory (WVI) designed to reflect a preference variable in vocational choice somewhat different from and perhaps more general than the concept of interests (Super, 1957). The work values concept has itself been subjected to considerable research. Hendrix and Super (1968) factor analyzed the Work Values Inventory and found four factors for males (situational or extrinsic, occupational or intrinsic, self-expression, and autonomy) and three factors for females (situational job factors, intrinsic job factors, and occupational self-expression).

O'Connor and Kinnane (1961) also factor analyzed the WVI. The analysis, based on the responses of 191 college men, suggested six factors: Security-economic-material (I), Social-artistic (II), Work conditions and associates (III), Heuristic-creative (IV), Achievement-prestige (V), and Independence-variety (VI). Kinnane and Pable (1962) tried to determine the relationship between family background factors and work value orientation. They tested several hypotheses concerning the relationship between the factors reported by O'Connor and Kinnane (1961) and familial factors. The predictions were that students scoring highest on a given factor would report a family background consistent with that factor.

A biographical inventory developed by Super and Overstreet (1960) for use in the Career Pattern Study was used to measure cultural stimulation, family cohesiveness, social mobility, and adolescent independence. A scale for the measurement of materialistic atmosphere in the home was developed to assess the family background relevant to Factor I. These inventories, plus a modified WVI, were administered to 121 eleventh grade boys between the ages of 16 and 18 years. The results supported many of the predictions that Kinnane and Pable made. Factor I was found to be positively related to the degree of materialistic atmosphere in the home as predicted; Factor II, also as predicted, was significantly correlated with the amount of cultural stimulation in the home, but not with family cohesiveness. Factor III was significantly related to family cohesiveness as predicted and also with materialism in the home, a relationship that had not been predicted. Factor IV was found to be significantly correlated with cultural stimulation in the home, again in line with prediction, and also with family cohesiveness, not expected. Factor V, expected to be related to the upward social strivings of the family, was not found to be significantly correlated with any of the family background variables. Finally, Factor VI reflected the predicted relationship with independence fostered by the family. Thus, five of the six predictions of the relationship between work values and family background were supported, and two additional but unexpected relationships were suggested. These relationships serve to disclose some of the experiential factors involved in the work values aspect of vocational development and to increase the understanding of environmental variables that must be controlled or manipulated if vocational maturity is to be fostered.

In another study, Kinnane and Gaubinger (1963) studied the relationship between life and work values. They predicted that the theoretical score of the Allport-Vernon-Lindzey Inventory of Values (AVL) is highly correlated with Factor IV of the WVI, that the AVL economic score is related to Factor I, that AVL social score is related to WVI Factor II, AVL aesthetic and WVI Factor VI are related, and that AVL religious scores are correlated with WVI Factor II. The AVL and WVI were administered to 143 male college freshmen, generally representative of all college major fields. All the predicted correlations were found to exist at a statistically significant level.

Kinnane and Gaubinger made the interesting observation that when subjects were required to respond to the AVL they did so in an isolated abstracted manner, considering only their values. But when responding to the WVI, other elements entered into their judgments. For example, the theoretical man on the AVL appeared to be exclusively concerned with theory, but in the context of work, suggested by his responses to the WVI, he valued achievement along with theoretical matters. Thus, what appeared to be important to him was the opportunity to work toward and solve problems his theoretical orientation led him to contemplate.

Pallone, Rickard, Hurley, and Tirman (1970), studying a sample of more than 500 lower middle class black and white high school students, found negative correlations between self-meaning and work values using the Work Values Inventory. The investigators concluded that for the sample they studied work may enhance an already existing negative view of self. For those students with a positive self-view, work is apparently not seen as a means to enhance prestige or independence.

Kuldau and Hollis (1971) examined attitudes toward work in elementary school children. The development of work attitudes during early childhood years is of obvious importance to the understanding of work values in older groups. Kuldau and Hollis studied children in "inner city and working blue collar" schools. The results suggested six factors: money, working conditions, status and prestige, self-expression, leadership, and independence on the job. Some overlap between the Kuldau-Hollis factors and those found by Hendrix and Super (1968) exists (working conditions, money, and possibly status and prestige would correspond to situational factors, self-expression is present in both sets of results, and leadership and independence might correspond to autonomy). Kuldau and Hollis also report that attitudes toward work were well developed in the students they studied by the beginning of fourth grade.

### Self-Concept Implementation through a Career

To many psychologists, the vital part of Super's theory lies in the formulations made about self-concept implementation by means of vocational activities. Consequently, it is not surprising that a number of studies inquiring into the relationship between self-concept and career choice have been conducted.

Norrell and Grater (1960) tested the hypothesis that subjects who can accurately predict their interests, defined in terms of SVIB scores, are more aware of themselves, awareness of self defined in terms of scores on selected scales of the Edwards Personal Preference Schedule (EPPS). Fifty-three male college sophomores expressing a variety of vocational preferences were given the SVIB and the EPPS. Those Ss who were able to predict accurately one-half or more of their interests on the SVIB were assigned to a "high awareness of self" group. Twelve of the EPPS scales were judged to possess relevance to self-awareness. These were needs achievement, autonomy, affiliation, intraception, dominance, nurturance, change, and heterosexuality; for low self-awareness, needs deference, order, succorance, and abasement were identified. Subjects in the high awareness group were expected to score higher in the appropriate EPPS categories than Ss in the low self-awareness group. The results were all in the expected *direction*, but only two, order and succorance, were significant beyond the 0.05 level of confidence. Norrell and Grater concluded that the results support the predictions; however, the failure of the relationships to reach the customary level of significance suggests that some caution should be used before reaching such a conclusion. This caution is not mitigated by Brown and Pool's (1966) replication of the study. Of the four EPPS scales that Norrell and Grater concluded to be significantly different for the high and low self-awareness groups (two at the 0.05 level and two at the 0.10 level), three were found to correlate significantly with interest awareness as reflected on the SVIB, but one was in the opposite direction. The two scales that remained significantly related to self-awareness on replication were again needs order and succorance, the only two that reached the conventional level of significance in the Norrell and Grater study.

Englander (1960) studied the relationship between the degree of agreement between self-perception and perception of people and situations relevant to one's chosen occupation. Englander predicted that prospective elementary teachers would see the personal characteristics of elementary teachers in a fashion more congruent with their own personal characteristics than would Ss choosing other occupations, that they would see the features of elementary teaching as more desirable than would Ss choosing other occupations, and that they would perceive their families and friends as holding more positive attitudes toward teaching than would Ss choosing other occupations.

To test these hypotheses, Englander required 126 female subjects, some elementary education students, some education majors in other areas, and some noneducation majors, to perform one Q-sort describing themselves and another, using the same items, describing teaching. The agreement between these Q-sorts was then assessed to test the predictions. The results supported the first prediction, that prospective elementary teachers do indeed see a closer relationship between their personal characteristics and those of elementary teachers than do Ss choosing other occupations. The second prediction, that elementary teachers see elementary teaching as more desirable than Ss choosing other fields, must be amended to include secondary teachers as well. Apparently teaching in general holds no differential appeal to elementary and secondary teachers, at least as far as Englander's sample is concerned. The third hypothesis, too, must be amended to include secondary as well as elementary teachers. Teaching majors as a total group appear to have some consistency in their vocational perceptions and impressions of others' values of teaching which differentiates them from students not in the education area.

A study by Stephenson (1961) examined the occupational self-concept of the premedical student. Stephenson explored the timing of the crystallization of the occupational self-concept of the premedical student with respect to the timing of his application to medical school. The subjects were selected from the rejected applicants to the University of Minnesota medical school emanating from the University of Minnesota undergraduate College of Science, Literature, and Arts for the fall classes of 1947 through 1951, a total of 368 students. Presumably, these rejected applicants had conceptions of themselves as physicians which were fairly well developed or they would not have applied to medical school. Since they were denied admission, at least to one medical college, the strength of the development of their medical self-concept should be reflected in the persistence they showed in trying to gain admission to medical or medically related occupations. A questionnaire asking current job title and job duties was sent to these applicants. The titles and duties were rated on a medically related continuum, with medical doctor as one anchor point, leading through medically related professions, medical services, and related areas, to nonmedically related professions as the negative anchor point. Ninety-three percent of the sample responded to the questionnaire.

The results indicate that almost two-thirds of the sample were in medical or medically related occupations, while somewhat more than one-third were in nonmedically related fields. Approximately two-thirds of the subjects who originally applied to the University of Minnesota medical school between the years 1947-1951 were actually admitted to some medical school. Since most of the subjects were in medical or related occupations, Stephenson concluded that the Ss had crystallized their occupational self-concept prior to application to medical school and that they had passed through Super's Exploratory phase and were in the Trial-Establishment substage prior to their application to medical school. Though that is clearly possible, even likely, it is also possible that a large number of rejected medical school applicants entered medically related fields by virtue of the relevance of their college training to the new field. They could have been merely trying to salvage as much as possible out of a misdirected education.

Kibrick and Tiedeman (1961) investigated the role of self-concept in the selection of nursing careers by means of comparing the images of nursing held by nursing supervisors and student nurses. Specifically, they predicted that persistence in nurse's training is a function of the agreement between supervisor and trainee with respect to the image of nursing. Five hundred thirty-eight nursing students from seven different schools plus three or four supervising nurses from each of the schools were used as subjects. They were administered a questionnaire concerning the information they had about the nursing program, the activities of the student nurse, the personality characteristics of the ideal nurse, their own personality characteristics, and the rights and obligations of nurses with respect to superiors, peers, and patients. The results indicated a tenuous relationship between the congruence of student and supervisor images of nursing and persistence in training. Probably reducing the relationship is the absence of controls for ability for nursing training. The findings suggest to Kibrick and Tiedeman that "self-concept and learning through role playing may still determine the goal elected when choice is necessary."

Blocher and Schutz (1961), studying the relationship between self-descriptions, occupational stereotypes, and vocational preferences, predicted that a person's vocational self-description and ideal self-concept are similar to his stereotype of a member of an occupation in which he is interested. They administered a descriptive checklist surveying self, ideal self, and occupational stereotypes to 135 twelfth grade boys. The boys also rated 45 occupations represented on the SVIB in order of interest to them. Using the $d^2$ procedure for profile analysis, Blocher and Schutz observed that the resulting self-, ideal self-, and vocational self-concepts were similar, as had been predicted.

In a similar study, Warren (1961) predicted that changes in a college major field are likely to occur when a discrepancy exists between a person's self-concept and the occupational role he expects his college major to prepare him for. He measured the self-concept of 525 male National Merit Scholars during the summer prior to their entrance into college by means of the Omnibus Personality Inventory (OPI), mailed to all Merit Scholars. During the spring of their freshman year, he measured the students' expected occupational roles by having them rate the appeal 13 possible sources of job satisfaction held for them. A measure called self-role discrepancy was based on the agreement between 95 pairs of self-concept and expected role statements. Finally, changes in field were tabulated in several ways. Prior to starting college each subject stated his proposed field of study. During the freshman and sophomore year each student reported his actual major field. The student's field was considered to have been changed if any two of the three expressions of preference were not the same, unless the precollege and sophomore fields were alike. The changes were coded "no change," "minor change," and "major change." For example, a change from physics to geology was rated as no change, from engineering to physics as a minor change, and movement from engineering to music was rated a major change.

The major hypothesis, that changes in major occur more frequently when discrepancies between self-concepts and occupational role expectancies exist, was not supported. A secondary hypothesis, however, did receive support. Warren noted that movement from an extremely inappropriate choice to an appropriate one, in terms of self-concept and job role expectancies, is likely to be difficult to accomplish all in one effort, so he predicted that students who had made two changes would have higher discrepancy scores than those who had made only one change. Warren also found that grade point average is significantly correlated with change in major while scores on a thinking-introversion scale were correlated with persistence in a field. Thus, one would expect that an academic level of performance that was unsatisfactory to a student might impel him to consider changing his field. It could be that these variables interact, so that a student who might be impelled to make a major change on the basis of his grades might have that impulse moderated by the tendency toward thinking and not acting reflected by a high thinking-introversion score. Such possibilities might have obscured the main effects of Warren's predictions. The use of National Merit Scholars also makes inferences to more typical college students more difficult to draw and makes inferences to noncollege populations almost impossible. Though one might speculate about the impact of performance on changes in academic field, actual observations available from a sample of Merit Scholars are minimal, and thus it is impossible to know if performance overshadows all other variables in bringing about changes in educational and vocational plans.

Morrison (1962) tested the adequacy of the use of Q-sorts in the measurement of self- and occupational concepts. He administered Q-sort tasks to 44 second-semester nursing students and 43 sixth-quarter education students, all females. The nursing students were to sort on their self-concept, their concept of a nurse, and their concept of a teacher. Similar procedures were followed for the sample of education students. Morrison predicted that nursing students would be more likely to report self-perceptions similar to those of nurses than teachers, while the education students would be likely to report self-perceptions more similar to those of teachers than nurses. The results supported the predictions.

As part of an attempt to develop and test a "theory" of general satisfaction based on the degree of agreement between self- and role percepts, Brophy (1959) developed several vocationally relevant hypotheses. He proposed a relationship between general satisfaction level and discrepancies between self-concept and ideal self-concept, self-concept and life role, and ideal self-concept and life role. With specific reference to careers, he hypothesized that occupational satisfaction is inversely related to the discrepancy between self-concept and occupational role, ideal occupational concept and occupational role, and self-concept and ideal occupational role concept.

To test these predictions, Brophy used a variety of instruments, most of which he devised. First, the subjects were given a General Satisfaction Scale, on which they were required to rate their general happiness for the past two months, their degree of happiness relative to others of their own age and sex, and their frequency of feeling happy. A Vocational Satisfaction Scale required the subjects to make the same judgments with respect to their jobs. The Bills Index of Adjustment and Values, consisting of 49 trait adjectives rated on a five-point scale, was directed toward eliciting information about self-concept, level of self-acceptance, and ideal self-concept. An Occupational Role Scale, using the same 49 trait adjectives of the Bills Index, was aimed at eliciting data about perceptions of occupational role, level of occupational role acceptance, and ideal occupational role in terms of a specific position. Finally, a Life Role Scale, modifying the 49 Bills Index adjectives in a manner related to life roles, was administered to the Ss. The subjects were 81 female nurses, most of them young, but ranging in age from 20 to 49 years and in professional experience from less than one year to 27 years. Seventy-seven percent of the sample returned usable questionnaires.

Nearly all of Brophy's predictions were supported. The correlations between the scores on the instruments indicated that vocational satisfaction is inversely related to the discrepancy between self-concept and occupational role, ideal occupational concept and occupational role, and self-concept and ideal occupational role concept. The only major prediction that was not supported was between general and vocational satisfaction. Surprisingly, the correlation between those two variables was not significant.

Oppenheimer (1966) studied the hypothesis that a positive relationship exists between an occupational preference hierarchy based on predictions made from the degree of agreement between self- and occupational concepts and the occupational preference hierarchy directly expressed by a subject. He required his subjects, 81 male liberal arts students below the senior year, to rank 70 occupations in order of their preference for them. A modified Repertory Test was administered to permit the subjects to use their own personal constructs to express their self- and occupational ratings. By comparing the occupational rankings with the responses to the Repertory Test, Oppenheimer found support for his prediction that the occupational preferences expressed by people are consistent with their self-concepts.

Another study of relevance to the implementation of the self-concept through vocational choice is reported by Anderson and Olsen (1965). They predicted a positive relationship between the degree of congruence of self- and ideal self-concepts and the ability to make realistic choices of occupational goals. They collected information on first and second occupational choices from 96 high school seniors (51 males and 45 females). In addition, the Flanagan Aptitude Classification Test (FACT) relative to the realism of the choice in terms of four-year versus two-year college plans was administered, and a Q-sort between congruence of self- and ideal self-concept in terms of both positive and negative items was performed. Student choices, then, were classified as to their adequacy in terms of the probability of the student's completion of the academic training necessary for his preferred field, two-year or four-year college programs. Anderson and Olsen predicted that students whose self- and ideal self-concepts were similar would make choices more in line with their potential for training then would students whose self- and ideal self-concepts were divergent. The results, however, failed to support such a prediction. There was no systematic difference in the realism of choices made by students of varying degrees of congruence between self- and ideal self-concepts.

James (1965), testing a Super-based hypothesis that a lack of congruence between self- and the occupational concept will create cognitive dissonance that will result in the individual becoming more congruent with the occupation, found that future teachers who most preferred their anticipated profession changed their ideas about teachers along with their self-expectations when a discrepancy was made known to them. For engineering students, however, such changes in ideas about teachers were not observed to occur. These findings support the idea that self-concept implementation is important to career choice, at least for education students.

O'Hara (1966) had 308 ninth grade and 152 twelfth grade boys rate themselves on the Kuder Preference Record, the Work Values Inventory, the Allport-Vernon-Lindzey Study of Values, and subtests of the Differential Aptitude Test. Following these self-ratings, the students took the tests and inventories. Four months later, achievement data were gathered in the form of final year grades in several academic subjects. O'Hara concluded that self-ratings seemed generally related to scholastic achievement, leading to the speculation that achievement might be influenced by self-concept, in which case self-knowledge and the self-concept become an even more important factor in vocational development.

Pallone and Hosinski (1967) administered a Q-sort of self, ideal self, and occupational self to 168 nursing students. The students represented seven levels of training in nursing, ranging from basic to graduate. The results yielded significant, predicted relationships among the statements for the graduate-level students but not for the others. These results indicate, once again, that investigations of students are likely to underestimate the true relationship between self-concept implementation and vocational preferences, since by the time students get to the graduate level considerable screening has occurred. The presence of non-screened students in the lower level samples reduces the clarity of the role the self-concept plays in career preference.

The "level of incorporation" concept was tested by Healy (1968). Paid volunteers, students in medicine, accounting, and engineering, were assessed with respect to general personality traits by means of a modified Kelly Role Concept Repertory Test and some particularly relevant occupations by means of semantic differential ratings on 25 bipolar traits. The SVIB was also administered. The incorporation score was the sum of the differences between the self- and the occupational ratings subtracted from 100. The results indicate appropriate differences in the incorporation scores according to curricular group as well as a correlation between level of incorporation and SVIB scores. Healy also (1973) studied the relationship between social class membership, self-esteem, and level of incorporation in accounting and nonaccounting majors, and found that high and low self-esteem accounting students had a higher level of incorporation scores on accounting than other business students, and that the high self-esteem accounting majors' incorporation scores were higher than those of the low self-esteem accounting majors. Lower social class accounting students had higher incorporation scores than middle class accounting students. In another related study, Healy, Bailey, and Anderson (1973) found that high self-esteem veterans exhibit a greater range of incorporation (that is, their self-concept overlapped a greater number of occupations) than low self-esteem veterans.

In a more straightforward test of self-concept implementation in career, Wheeler and Carnes (1968) investigated the similarity between self-concept, ideal self-concept, and ideal and probable occupational stereotypes. One hundred thirty-four college freshmen enrolled in elementary psychology, health education, and general orientation programs responded to a descriptive checklist regarding self- and occupational concepts. The results indicate that self-concept and occupational stereotypes of probable occupation correlate more highly with each other than do self-ideal concepts and occupational stereotypes. In addition, ideal self- and ideal occupational concepts were found to correlate more highly than ideal self- and probable occupational concepts.

Marks and Webb (1969) were concerned with the effects of experience on the accuracy of occupational images. Such accuracy is important to assess since self-concept implementation through career requires adequate knowledge of careers that offer promise for self-expression. In the Marks and Webb study two groups of freshmen, two groups of seniors, and two groups of professionals in industrial management and electrical engineering (along with a sample of freshmen from another university responding in terms of social desirability of the scale) responded to a 95-item trait-description covering numerous behaviors and characteristics of occupational importance. All together, including the social desirability sample, 824 individuals served as subjects. In general, the results indicate that the amount of professional experience one has in a field has little effect on the image one holds of the incumbents of that occupation. However, Marks and Webb did note that college freshmen in engineering and industrial management do describe themselves differently, and in ways that correlate appropriately with the images they hold of their respective future occupational peers. This finding would seem to support Super's hypothesis of self-concept implementation through career choice. However, as Marks and Webb point out, it is necessary to be cautious in drawing conclusions about the implications of this study, since little dissatisfaction with a vocational choice would be expected if it allows self-concept implementation, yet it is well known that college majors are frequently changed. It might have been interesting had Marks and Webb pursued the matter of stability in their sample according to congruence between self and occupational field as measured during the freshman year.

Another study testing self-concept implementation through vocational choice was conducted by Ziegler (1970). Ziegler was concerned with the criticism that much of the early research dealing with self-concept implementation and vocational choice was limited to samples of education and nursing students, and thus of limited generality. Ziegler, studying 428 male college students representing 39 future occupational areas, compared the students' most and least preferred occupational fields against self-concept and most and least preferred occupational characteristics on the Adjective Check List. The results indicate greater congruence between self and most preferred occupational group. In addition, some distinctive and intuitively predictable differences in self-concept characteristics by field were observed.

Greenhaus (1971) attempted to isolate and examine a variable associated with self-concept implementation in career. He predicted that career salience would be positively related to self- and occupational congruence. A career salience questionnaire consisting of 28 items tapping the areas of attitudes toward work, vocational planning, and the importance of work, was administered to 104 male and 273 female college freshmen and sophomores. The results support the hypothesis that salience and congruence are related in the male subjects, but not for female subjects. It is easy to speculate about some important differences in sex role that might affect the impact of career salience on career choice as a function of sex.

Finally, a study by Schuh (1966) raises some significant questions about the basic logic of hypotheses regarding self-concept implementation and career choice. Schuh, using the semantic differential to measure congruence between self-concept and career, predicted that self- and job ratings would be congruent.

In general, based on the responses of 89 graduating college seniors, such congruence is not apparent. Schuh criticizes Super's theory in that it assumes congruence equals satisfaction without dealing with the question of how congruence between undesirable aspects of self should contribute to satisfaction. Logically, a "bad" self-concept congruent with a "bad" occupational concept should produce satisfaction, yet such relations are not found, and, on the surface, would seem foolish to predict. It would seem that self-concept occupational congruence provides a meaningful way to predict occupational preference when both are positive, but not when either is negative.

Overall, considerable convincing research data exist to support the notion that self-concept plays an important role in occupational preference. What appears needed now are additional conceptual links relating the two.

### Self-esteem and Career Preferences

One conceptual link that offers some promise as a way of relating self- and occupational concepts is self-esteem. Korman began a series of investigations studying the role of self-esteem in career preferences and vocational development. In one study, Korman (1966) found that high self-esteem individuals are more likely to implement their self-concept through occupational choice than are low self-esteem individuals (a finding that is a logical outgrowth of Schuh's [1966] criticism). In a more complicated study, Korman (1967) tested the hypothesis that self-esteem is related to the perception of the "difficulty" of an occupation, and, as a result, serves as a moderator of occupational choice. One hundred twenty-six college students were administered the Ghiselli Self Description Inventory as a measure of self-esteem along with a questionnaire to measure perceptions of occupationally required abilities and one designed to measure personal abilities. Vocational choice was also obtained. A discrepancy score between the two highest level occupations (in terms of required abilities) and self-perception was computed. A similar computation was calculated comparing the two lowest occupations and self-perception. The results strongly indicated that individuals with high self-esteem seek high ability demand situations in their work. A "balancing" effect is suggested by Korman; that is, the person who sees himself as competent will seek and enter competence-demanding situations, and vice versa. Korman calls this a closed-loop situation, suggesting that feedback enhances an already existing tendency to accept or reject challenging situations, which feeds back on self-esteem, which then effects the tendency to accept challenge, and so on.

In still another study, Korman (1968) tested the idea that individuals display cognitive consistency in their vocational behavior. In this study, Korman found that task success and task satisfaction are positively related for people with high self-esteem but not for low self-esteem individuals. The former individuals use their own internal frame of reference to determine the value they place on a task and its performance, but the latter look to other individuals to set their standards. Finally, Korman (1969) examined and found support for the hypothesis that self-esteem serves as a moderator variable in that high self-esteem individuals are more likely to seek self-fulfillment in their work than low self-esteem individuals.

Ryan (1969) reports a study in which reinforcement procedures were applied in an attempt to manipulate and enhance the self-concept as an adjunct to improving vocational decision-making. Results of several procedures applied to 333 disadvantaged college students indicated that the group with the best scores on self-concept following treatment scored best in terms of the criteria on educational-vocational behavior. This study is one of the few that at least tenuously establishes a relationship between self-esteem and vocational decision-making.

Not all the research dealing with self-esteem and vocational choice has produced clear results. Resnick, Fauble, and Osipow (1970) postulated that high and low self-esteem college students (self-esteem defined in terms of scores on the self-esteem scale of the Tennessee Self Concept Scale) would differ in vocational crystallization defined in terms of the differentiation of the Kuder Preference Record profiles and self-reported certainty of vocational plans. No differences were found on the Kuder, though the high self-esteem students expressed greater certainty about their plans than did the low self-esteem students. In another study, Greenhaus (1971), testing the hypothesis that self-esteem is positively related to self- and occupational congruence, did not find results to support his hypothesis.

Korman (1970) has suggested a "balance" approach to explaining the complex relationship between self-esteem and vocational behavior. Korman presents the idea that the self-concept of the individual at the moment is the result of the goals he seeks and the outcomes that will satisfy him. In other words, people will find maximally satisfying those behaviors which permit them to feel they are behaving consistently. Applied to self-esteem, then, "to the extent that an individual has a self-cognition of himself as a competent, need-satisfying individual, then, to that extent, he will choose and find most satisfying those situations which are in balance with these self-perceptions." In two experiments designed to test the balance hypothesis, Korman found support for the conclusion that self-perceived competence facilitates task performance and social evaluation of competence seems to become internalized and enhances performance.

### Evaluation

The research and data relevant to the concept of vocational development seem to indicate a steady and reasonably predictable increase in both the amount of attention and the sophistication of that attenton given to vocational choice tasks through the adolescent years. The attention culminates, for well-oriented people, in commitment to a position which is then carried on throughout life, though in varying degrees. It also seems clear that the scholastic aspects of vocational development are closely tied to the educational system. Vocational development exhibits more evidence for the generalization that behavior is a function of the situation in which it occurs. Students seem to make decisions at times that are imposed on them by the structure of the educational system. It is interesting to speculate on the effects of vocational development under the English system of secondary education, in which choice points are imposed at different age levels.

Most of the findings of research support the idea that occupational choice represents the implementation of the self-concept. The results of the research provide an impressive amount of empirical support for the general aspects of the theory proposed by Super. In view of the continuing efforts of Super and his associates to make the theory more explicit (Super, Starishevsky, Matlin, and Jordaan, 1963), even more adequate tests of the theory are apt to be forthcoming.

## STATUS

### Implications for Counseling

One characteristic of Super's theory that distinguishes it from many others is Super's concern for the application of his formulations to counseling on vocational and personal matters. In an early paper published before the theory was clearly formulated, Super (1951) described the role that self-concept development plays in career development. Super reasoned that although the self-concept is likely to be a function of genetic influences on physical factors, such as glandular structure, and psychological factors, such as aptitudes, it operates in combination with environmental variables, such as social and economic conditions. Thus, a certain portion of the self-concept is open to outside intervention. Such intervention is likely to be most effective in shaping the self-concept during early adolescence, since the concept grows more stable during later adolescence and maturity. Counselors, thus, have access to youngsters during the years of greatest development of the self-concept.

Since vocational decisions require a person to state explicitly his conception of himself, people with accurate information about themselves and the world are most likely to make sound vocational decisions. In other words, Super subscribes to the trait-factor approach to vocational choice. The difference is that Super adds several new ideas to the old ones. Since the data about vocational maturity in ninth grade boys reflect considerable instability in vocational preferences, Super suggests that counselors should not take expressed vocational aspirations too seriously. More effort and attention should be directed toward the development of vocationally relevant tasks.

In counseling with vocationally mature boys, attention should be directed toward the collection and understanding of vocationally and personally relevant information which will serve as a basis for the decisions the boys will be required to make. Counseling with vocationally immature boys, a more common task, differs in that the vocationally immature boy knows little about the choices he must make, has difficulty framing vocationally relevant questions, and consequently is not in a position to make sound vocational and educational decisions. Counselors, thus, must work to orient such a student to the tasks required by his life stage before working on the specifics of the stage itself. The goal of counseling in such situations is to develop a sense of planfulness in the student which will facilitate his readiness for choice. To do this the counselor must specifically work on the student's understanding of the relevant factors in vocational choice to increase his effective use of resources for choice and to develop an understanding of the occupational field which most interests the student. When those goals have been accomplished, the student can apply the techniques learned in counseling the assessing this field to investigations of other occupations that he will wish to undertake as he grows older.

In counseling with a vocationally uncertain individual, the counselor should respond to the client's feeling, in this case to the emotions surrounding his uncertainty. Hopefully, by so doing, attention will be brought to bear on the antecedents of the indecision. In the normal course of the well-conducted interview, data become available about the client's cultural, social, and biological background, which the counselor can help the client to integrate into his decision.

In his early papers, Super reveals his steady interest in using theoretical formulations to guide practice. As he was developing his ideas about career patterns, Super (1954) called for, in general terms, the use of the concept of career patterns in vocational counseling. In another article (Super, 1955) he suggested the close relationship that exists between emotional and vocational adjustment and counseling procedures. This relationship has long been recognized; however, Super's treatment of the question of counseling people seriously disturbed emotionally and dysfunctional vocationally is new. Is a desirable sequence with which to approach these problems known? Traditionally, it has been assumed that if emotional concerns are resolved, other concerns, such as vocational, marital, and so on, will all fall into place. Experienced counselors, however, know that such is not always the case. Consequently, Super's suggestion that resolutions of career dysfunctions may be instrumental in resolving more general psychological disorders is appealing.

Attempting to clarify the role that career patterns play in helping counselors to identify the nature of student problems, Super states (1960) that the task at hand for a counselor working with ninth grade boys is to aid them to ascertain career alternatives to be explored and to help them implement exploratory activities. For the older adolescent other assessments must be made, and different counseling techniques might be more appropriate. Super (1964) describes some categories of student concern that might be helpful in identifying relevant counseling techniques.

Operationally, the counseling tasks relevant to the late adolescent period of life are either the facilitation of exploration or of preparation (Super, 1964b). Exploration, either occupationally oriented or nonoccupationally oriented, is aimed at continuing to broaden one's experiences. Preparation, on the other hand, is the result of successful completion of the crystallization stage and the entrance into the specification stage. Thus, counseling the college-bound student in the exploratory stage should include instruction on how to use the facilities of the liberal arts college or general education program, a feat rarely performed.

The student interested in advanced education or training, on the other hand, needs information about which colleges offer programs of study compatible with his plans. Thus, the sophisticated counselor will learn to suggest application to one kind of university to the student who needs great academic flexibility, a second type of school to another student because of its emphasis on theory, and still a third university to a highly professionally oriented student and a two-year technical school to a fourth type. According to Super, much of the counselor's work done in the context of the theory must involve the identification of the differential rates of student development, the ability to appraise students with respect to these rates, and knowledge of the alternatives of higher education which fit such varying students. This poses the task of codifying the programs available in institutions of higher education and passing them on to counselors.

Some attempts have been made to apply Super's principles in connection with a computer-based information and exploration system (Minor, Myers, and Super, 1969). In this approach, an attempt has been made to program information regarding career choices and development in sequences built on the stages of vocational development defined in the theory. Such attempts continue to remain rudimentary and are far from application.

The growing sophistication and refinement in the procedures to measure vocational maturity represent another area in which Super's theory can be applied. The various scales of vocational maturity can be applied as criteria to evaluate career exploration programs (e.g., Osipow and Alderfer, 1968) or counseling for career development, or simply to assess a student's progress through the various stages of growth to determine his current needs.

Other information for the counselor growing from the theory involves differential possibilities for the "early emerger" as opposed to the "late bloomer" (Super, 1964b). The "early emerger" is generally closely identified with the adult world. The counselor should review the important figures in the counselee's life to learn the antecedents of the interests of such a person. The "late bloomer," on the other hand, probably has not identified with the adult world to a sufficient degree and consequently needs an accepting relationship with an adult who is willing to serve as a model and from whom the student can learn acceptable adult outlets for his interests and talents.

Other problems are posed by the multitalented and the untalented. Both groups tend to be generalists, but for very different reasons. The multitalented individual has many interests and possibilities and ordinarily moves from one field to another in search of bigger and better opportunities. In maturity, they are the people who succeed in a profession, then move into executive or administrative positions, and frequently end their careers in government, politics, or policy-making activities. When young, such people must be helped to chart a course satisfying to themselves, since often they express no special vocational interests such as are ordinarily demanded of young people. The untalented, too, often express no special vocational preferences. They usually drift from one job to another with little system. Their jobs have little continuity; so one may work as a bread salesman, a laborer, a clerk, and an assembly-line worker in succession. These people need to learn to harness the talents they do possess through some training so they are not completely open to the changing conditions of their local economic situation.

Super also attends to the problem of retirement (1956). He suggests problems facing retirees and differing alternative solutions to these problems, depending upon the career field. Super's description of counseling procedures to be followed with special groups, late bloomers, and talented and untalented students indicate his emphasis on approaches for counselors.

Others have suggested applications of Super's theory. Hummel (1954) suggested that the theory highlights the differences inherent in counseling people at different stages of development, the early adolescent as opposed to the young adult, for example. What must be done is to identify the differential techniques that must be applied for maximum effectiveness to the problems of each stage. These remain to be worked out in detail, though they are further along in development than they were at the time Hummel wrote.

LoCascio (1964) suggested that special attention be paid to misdirected vocational development in the context of Super's theory. Since career development is a continuous process in which a person is successively faced with some vocational developmental task, the outcome of the person's efforts to deal with that task influences not only the context of his later tasks, but also the subsequent approaches to deal with vocational problems which he has at his disposal. Consequently, a well-functioning person faced with a vocational developmental task applies relevant behavior and learns additional vocationally relevant behaviors as a result. These behaviors are added to his knowledge of vocational behavior, and he uses this additional learning in dealing with later vocational tasks. At the other extreme is the individual, who, when faced with a vocational task, does not apply relevant behavior, learns little as a result, and whose vocational behavior is not only ineffective but who chronically shows little growth. These latter people present special counseling problems and need special approaches. The following illustrates the sequence: a well-ordered individual might need to select a college to attend. From his past experiences he knows that he should look for a school which offers the courses he wants (for example, engineering); he finds several such schools, applies to them for admission, is accepted by some of them, chooses one to attend, and enrolls. The sequence reflects his having learned to have several alternatives if possible. He may also have several alternative plans available to him should he encounter difficulty in engineering studies, such as changing to another program or another school, acquiring better study skills, and so on. On the other hand, a poorly functioning person might decide to study engineering, apply to a large, highly competitive institution because of its reputation, irrelevant to his purposes, and also to a small, local liberal arts college with lenient admission requirements as a "safety valve." If he is rejected by the large school and, as a consequence, is forced to enroll in the small school, he may discover his college fails to provide the course of study he wants. Such a person might well continue in the liberal arts school simply because he has already enrolled, without looking for ways to move to a university with programs more relevant to his interests.

Super's theory, particularly the developmental component but also the self-concept idea, seems to be especially compatible with the creation of the career education curriculum. In fact, Super's ideas have so permeated the field of occupational development that it is likely that the architects of career education were both implicitly and explicitly influenced by Super's theory. The career education movement's emphasis on the graded exposure to concepts of self and concepts of work throughout the entire curriculum represents precisely the basic ideas of career development and vocational maturation described by Super. It would seem that curriculum development in the area of career education should lean heavily on the vocational developmental tasks described by Super and also that vocational maturity, as measured variously by Super's Career Questionnaire, Crites' Vocational Development Inventory, and Westbrook's Cognitive Vocational Maturity Test, have the potential to serve as one aspect of the criterion for the evaluation of career education programs. Of course, the instruments do not lend themselves directly to use with the very young or those over the adolescent age range, and new instruments extending the range of use need to be developed. It does seem clear, however, that Super's theory emphasizes self-awareness and occupational exploration continuously, and these seem to be cardinal elements in career education. The goal of career education, it would seem, is to provide students with information about themselves and the educational-vocational world continuously so that it may become an integral part of them. Thus, at the time that decisions need to be made, such as the choice of type of high school program, the student has the personal resources to make an intelligent response, rather than casting about for a week or two for information and opinions and, very likely, making an ill-founded and impulsive choice that will prove to be unsatisfactory as time goes on.

The Super position seems to present some moderately specific guidelines for the practice of counseling. A counselor operating within this framework would try to appraise the life stage of his client in order to define relevant counseling goals. He would also try to help his client to clarify his self-concept, and within the context of his life stage, expose him to events, both in and out of the counseling situation, which would permit him to move toward the implementation of that concept. While Super fails to make explicit statements about particular counseling procedures to accomplish these ends, he does indicate that procedures should be broader than nondirective counseling methods. Among his suggestions are the use of the concept of vocational appraisal, encouragement of the use of experiences out of the counseling office, the use of community resources other than the counselor, and the codification of occupations and colleges to help individuals recognize potentially appropriate steps to take in the decision-making sequence. In some recent work (Super et al., 1963) there is the implication that recommended counseling procedures will grow more specific as the theory matures.

## Evaluation

The theory is a well-ordered, highly systematic representation of the process of vocational maturation. It has the virtue of building upon aspects of the mainstream of developmental psychology and personality theory and demonstrating how those two streams can come together to clarify behavior in one major realm of human activity. The original version of the theory was too general to be of much practical value, and even its conceptual value was limited by its sweeping style. Later versions, however, are much more detailed, as Super and his associates have attempted to indicate the parameters of the theory in more specific terms. Consequently, in its current state, it has considerable utility for both practice and research in vocational psychology.

Most of the research reported on Super's theory generally supports his model. The developmental aspects of the theory are well documented, though certain details have been modified as a result of empirical findings, such as the specific timing of developmental tasks. The proliferation of names for the various phases and stages makes for some apparent inconsistency in the results and certainly for some confusion, but no serious flaws in the developmental hierarchy of the theory seem to exist.

The data with respect to the formulations about the role of the self-concept generally agree with the theory. The samples studied in this respect have generally been broadened with respect to career orientation, and the measures of the self-concept are closer to real life and real work situations than before. As additional instruments to measure self- and career concepts are devised, better research designs will result.

With the increasing emphasis on specificity in the theory, Super's concern for applications, and the generally wide empirical support, the future prospects for this approach to career psychology continue to be promising. However, in order to be comprehensive, Super still must devise a way to include economic and social factors which may influence career decisions in a more direct way than the events described by the theory currently do, as well as to continue the development of specific and rigorous formulations about aspects of career decisions and ways to bring about appropriate behavioral changes which will facilitate vocational maturity.

# REFERENCES

Anderson, T. B., and Olsen, L. C. Congruence of self and ideal-self and occupational choices. *Personnel and Guidance Journal*, 1965, *44*, 171-176.

Astin, Helen S. Career development during the high school years. *Journal of Counseling Psychology*, 1967, *14*, 94-98. (a)

Astin, Helen S. Patterns of career choices over time. *Personnel and Guidance Journal*, 1967, *45*, 541-546. (b)

Bartlett, W. E. Vocational maturity: its past, present, and future development. *Journal of Vocational Behavior*, 1971, *1*, 217-229.

Beilin, H. The application of general developmental principles to the vocational area. *Journal of Counseling Psychology*, 1955, *2*, 53-57.

Blocher, D. H., and Schutz, R. A. Relationships among self-descriptions, occupational stereotypes, and vocational preferences. *Journal of Counseling Psychology*, 1961, *8*, 314-317.

Bordin, E. S. A theory of interests as dynamic phenomena. *Educational and Psychological Measurement*, 1943, *3*, 49-66.

Brophy, A. L. Self, role, and satisfaction. *Genetic Psychology Monographs*, 1959, *54*, 263-308.

Brown, R. A., and Pool, D. A. Psychological needs and self awareness. *Journal of Counseling Psychology*, 1966, *13*, 85-88.

Buck, C. W. Crystallization of vocational interests as a function of vocational exploration in college. *Journal of Counseling Psychology*, 1970, *17*, 347-351.

Buehler, Charlotte. *Der menschliche Lebenslauf als psychologiches Problem*. Leipzig: Hirzel, 1933.

Carter, H. D. The development of vocational attitudes. *Journal of Consulting Psychology*, 1940, *4*, 185-191.

Cooley, W. W. Interactions among interests, abilities, and career plans. *Journal of Applied Psychology Monograph*, 1967, *51*.

Crites, J. O. A model for the measurement of vocational maturity. *Journal of Counseling Psychology*, 1961, *8*, 255-259.

Crites, J. O. Measurement of vocational maturity in adolescence. I. Attitude test of the vocational development inventory. *Psychological Monographs*, 1965, *79*, No. 2 (Whole No. 595).

Crites, J. O. The maturity of vocational attitudes in adolescence. *APGA Inquiry Series*, No. 2. Washington, D. C.: American Personnel and Guidance Association, 1971.

Davidson, P. E., and Anderson, H. D. *Occupational mobility in an American community*. Stanford, California: Stanford University Press, 1937.

Dilley, J. S. Decision-making ability and vocational maturity. *Personnel and Guidance Journal*, 1965, *44*, 423-427.

Englander, Meryl E. A psychological analysis of a vocational choice: teaching. *Journal of Counseling Psychology*, 1960, *7*, 257-264.

Ginzberg, E., Ginsburg, S. W., Axelrad, S., and Herma, J. L. *Occupational choice: an approach to a general theory*. New York: Columbia University Press, 1951.

Greenhaus, J. H. Self-esteem as an influence on occupational choice and occupational satisfaction. *Journal of Vocational Behavior*, 1971, *1*, 75-83.

Greenhaus, J. H. An investigation of the role of career salience in vocational behavior. *Journal of Vocational Behavior*, 1971, *1*, 209-216.

Gribbons, W. D. Changes in readiness for vocational planning from 8th to 10th grade. *Personnel and Guidance Journal*, 1964, *42*, 908-913.

Gribbons, W. D., and Lohnes, P. R. Relationships among measures of readiness for vocational planning. *Journal of Counseling Psychology*, 1964, *11*, 13-19. (a)

Gribbons, W. D., and Lohnes, P. R. Validation of vocational planning interview scales. *Journal of Counseling Psychology*, 1964, *11*, 20-25. (b)

Gribbons, W. D., and Lohnes, P. R. Predicting 5 years of development in adolescents from readiness for vocational planning scales. *Journal of Educational Psychology*, 1965, *56*, 244-253.

Gribbons, W. D., and Lohnes, P. R. *Emerging careers*. New York: Teachers College Press, Columbia University, 1968.

Gribbons, W. D., and Lohnes, P. R. Eighth-grade vocational maturity in relation to nine-year career patterns. *Journal of Counseling Psychology*, 1969, *16*, 557-562.

Hadley, R. G., and Levy, W. V. Vocational development and reference groups. *Journal of Counseling Psychology*, 1962, *9*, 110-114.

Healy, C. C. Relation of occupational choice to the similarity between self-ratings and occupational ratings. *Journal of Counseling Psychology*, 1968, *15*, 317-323.

Healy, C. C. The relation of esteem and social class to self-occupational congruence. *Journal of Vocational Behavior*, 1973, *3*, 43-51.

Healy, C. C., Bailey, Mary L., and Anderson, E. C. The relation of esteem and vocational counseling to range of incorporation scores. *Journal of Vocational Behavior*, 1973, *3*, 69-74.

Heilman, C. F., and Gardner, R. E. Exploration in Careers Education. School of Education, University of Oregon, Corvallis, 1971.

Hendrix, V. L., and Super, D. E. Factor dimensions and reliability of the Work Values Inventory. *Vocational Guidance Quarterly*, 1968, *16*, 269-274.

Hirt, M. L. Aptitude changes as a function of age. *Personnel and Guidance Journal*, 1964, *43*, 174-177.

Hummel, R. Vocational development theory and guidance practice. *Journal of the National Association of Women Deans and Counselors*, 1954, *18*, 13-18.

James. F., III. Occupational choice and attitude change. *Journal of Counseling Psychology*, 1965, *12*, 311-315.

Jordaan, J. P. Exploratory behavior: the formulation of self and occupational concepts. In Super, D. E., et al., *Career development: self-concept theory*. New York: CEEB Research Monograph No. 4, 1963.

Kibrick, Anne K., and Tiedeman, D. V. Conception of self and perception of role in schools of nursing. *Journal of Counseling Psychology*, 1961, *8*, 62-69.

Kinnane, J. F., and Gaubinger, J. R. Life values and work values. *Journal of Counseling Psychology*, 1963, *10*, 362-366.

Kinnane, J. F., and Pable, M. W. Family background and work value orientation. *Journal of Counseling Psychology*, 1962, *9*, 320-325.

Korman, A. K. Self-esteem variable in vocational choice. *Journal of Applied Psychology*, 1966, *50*, 479-486.

Korman, A. K. Self-esteem as a moderator of the relationships between self-perceived abilities and vocational choice. *Journal of Applied Psychology*, 1967, *51*, 65-67.

Korman, A. K. Task success, task popularity, and self-esteem as influences on task liking. *Journal of Applied Psychology*, 1968, *52*, 484-490.

Korman, A. K. Self-esteem as a moderator in vocational choice: replications and extensions. *Journal of Applied Psychology*, 1969, *53*, 188-192.

Korman, A. K. Toward a hypothesis of work behavior. *Journal of Applied Psychology*, 1970, *54*, 31-41.

Kuldau, Janice E., and Hollis, J. W. The development of attitudes toward work among upper elementary school age children. *Journal of Vocational Behavior*, 1971, *1*, 387-398.

Lewis, S. *Arrowsmith*. New York: Harcourt, Brace, 1925.

LoCascio, R. Delayed and impaired vocational development: a neglected aspect of vocational development theory. *Personnel and Guidance Journal*, 1964, *42*, 885-887.

Madaus, G. F., and O'Hara, R. P. Vocational interest patterns of high school boys: a multivariate approach. *Journal of Counseling Psychology*, 1967, *14*, 106-112.

Marks, E., and Webb, S. C. Vocational choice and professional experience as factors in occupational image. *Journal of Applied Psychology*, 1969, *53*, 292-300.

Miller, D. C., and Form, W. H. *Industrial Sociology*. New York: Harper & Row, 1951.

Mills, E. W. Career development in middle life. In Bartlett, W. E. (Ed.), *Evolving religious careers*. Washington, D.C.: CARA, 1970.

Minor, F. T., Myers, R. A., and Super, D. E. An experimental computer-based educational and career exploration system. *Personnel and Guidance Journal,* 1969, *47,* 564-569.

Montesano, N., and Geist, H. Differences in occupational choice between ninth and twelfth grade boys. *Personnel and Guidance Journal,* 1964, *43,* 150-154.

Morrison, R. L. Self-concept implementation in occupational choices. *Journal of Counseling Psychology,* 1962, *9,* 255-260.

Norrell, Gwen, and Grater, H. Interest awareness as an aspect of self-awareness. *Journal of Counseling Psychology,* 1960, *7,* 289-292.

O'Connor, J. P., and Kinnane, J. F. A factor analysis of work values. *Journal of Counseling Psychology,* 1961, *8,* 263-267.

O'Hara, R. P. Vocational self-concepts and high school achievement. *Vocational Guidance Quarterly,* 1966, *15,* 106-112.

Oppenheimer, E. A. The relationship between certain self construct and occupational preferences. *Journal of Counseling Psychology,* 1966, *13,* 191-197.

Osipow, S. H., and Alderfer, R. D. The effects of a vocationally oriented speech course on the vocational planning behavior of high school students. *Personnel and Guidance Journal,* 1968, *47,* 244-248.

Pallone, N. J., and Hosinki, Marion. Reality-testing a vocational choice: congruence between self-, ideal, and occupational percepts among student nurses. *Personnel and Guidance Journal,* 1967, *45,* 666-670.

Pallone, N. J., Rickard, F. S., Hurley, R. B., and Tirman, R. J. Work values and self-meaning. *Journal of Counseling Psychology,* 1970, *17,* 376-377.

Resnick, H., Fauble, Marianne Leeson, and Osipow, S. H. Vocational crystallization and self-esteem in college students. *Journal of Counseling Psychology,* 1970, *17,* 465-467.

Roe, Anne. *The psychology of occupations.* New York: Wiley, 1956.

Rogers, C. R. *Counseling and psychotherapy.* Boston: Houghton Mifflin, 1942.

Rogers, C. R. *Client-centered therapy.* Boston: Houghton Mifflin, 1951.

Ryan, T. Antoinette. Reinforcement techniques and simulation materials for counseling clients with decision-making problems. *Proceedings,* 1969 American Psychological Association.

Schuh, A. J. Use of the semantic differential in a test of Super's vocational adjustment theory. *Journal of Applied Psychology,* 1966, *50,* 516-522.

Sheppard, D. I. The measurement of vocational maturity in adults. *Journal of Vocational Behavior,* 1971, *1,* 399-406.

Starishevsky, R., and Matlin, N. A model for the translation of self-concept into vocational terms. In Super, D. E. et al., *Career development: self-concept theory.* New York: CEEB Research Monograph No. 4, 1963.

Stephenson, R. R. Occupational choice as a crystallized self-concept. *Journal of Counseling Psychology,* 1961, *8,* 211-216.

Strong, E. K., Jr. *Vocational interests of men and women.* Stanford, California: Stanford University Press, 1943.

Super, D. E. *Avocational interest patterns.* Stanford, California: Stanford University Press, 1940.

Super, D. E. Vocational adjustment: implementing a self-concept. *Occupations,* 1951, *30,* 1-5.

Super, D. E. A theory of vocational development. *American Psychologist,* 1953, *8,* 185-190.

Super, D. E. Career patterns as a basis for vocational counseling. *Journal of Counseling Psychology,* 1954, *1,* 12-20.

Super, D. E. Personality integration through vocational counseling. *Journal of Counseling Psychology,* 1955, *2,* 217-226.

Super, D. E. Getting out of an occupation. *Personnel and Guidance Journal,* 1956, *34,* 491-493.

Super, D. E. *The psychology of careers.* New York: Harper & Row, 1957.

Super, D. E. The critical ninth grade: vocational choice or vocational exploration. *Personnel and Guidance Journal,* 1960, *39,* 106-109.

Super, D. E. Some unresolved issues in vocational development research. *Personnel and Guidance Journal,* 1961, *40,* 11-14. (a)

Super, D. E. Consistency and wisdom of vocational preference as indices of vocational maturity in the ninth grade. *Journal of Educational Psychology*, 1961, *52*, 35-43. (b)

Super, D. E. Self-concepts in vocational development. In Super, D. E., et al., *Career development: self-concept theory*. New York: CEEB Research Monograph No. 4, 1963. (a)

Super, D. E. Toward making self-concept theory operational. In Super, D. E., et al., *Career development: self-concept theory*. New York: CEEB Research Monograph No. 4, 1963. (b)

Super, D. E. Vocational development in adolescence and early adulthood: tasks and behaviors. In Super, D. E., et al., *Career development: self-concept theory*. New York: CEEB Research Monograph No. 4, 1963. (c)

Super, D. E. A developmental approach to vocational guidance. *Vocational Guidance Quarterly*, 1964, *13*, 1-10. (a)

Super, D. E. Goal specificity in the vocational counseling of future college students. *Personnel and Guidance Journal*, 1964, *43*, 127-134. (b)

Super, D. E., Bohn, M. J., Jr., Forrest, D. J., Jordaan, J. P., Lindeman, R. L., and Thompson, A. S. Career Questionnaire, Form IV. New York: Teachers College, Columbia University, 1971.

Super, D. E., Crites, J., Hummel, R., Moser, Helen, Overstreet, Phoebe, and Warnath, C. *Vocational development: a framework for research*. New York: Bureau of Research, Teachers College, Columbia University, 1957.

Super, D. E., Kowalski, Ruth S., and Gotkin, Elizabeth H. *Floundering and trial after high school.* Cooperative Research Project No. 1393. New York: Teachers College, Columbia University, 1967.

Super, D. E., and Overstreet, Phoebe, L. *The vocational maturity of ninth grade boys.* New York: Bureau of Publications, Teachers College, Columbia University, 1960.

Super, D. E., Starishevsky, R., Matlin, N., and Jordaan, J. P. *Career development: self-concept theory*. New York: CEEB Research Monograph No. 4, 1963.

Vroom, V. H., and Pahl, B. The relationship between age and risk-taking among managers. *Journal of Applied Psychology*, 1971, *55*, 399-405.

Warren, J. R. Self-concept, occupational role expectation, and change in college major. *Journal of Counseling Psychology*, 1961, *8*, 164-169.

Westbrook, B. W., and Parry-Hill, J. W., Jr. The measurement of cognitive vocational maturity. *Journal of Vocational Behavior*, 1973, *3*, in press.

Wheeler, C. L., and Carnes, E. F. Relationships among self-concepts, ideal self-concepts, and stereotypes of probable and ideal vocational choices. *Journal of Counseling Psychology*, 1968, *15*, 530-535.

Wurtz, R. E. Developmental intelligence and vocational development. *Journal of Counseling Psychology*, 1969, *16*, 584-586.

Ziegler, D. J. Self-concept, occupational member concept, and occupational interest area relationships in male college students. *Journal of Counseling Psychology*, 1970, *17*, 133-136.

# 6

# Personality and Career

All theories of career choice are in some sense related to personality development. However, the theories reviewed so far either have a particular orientation to personality or have generated distinctive personality-related research. Many other studies of personality and career, conducted by a variety of investigators, were not devised to test a general theory but nevertheless may be viewed as having certain commonalities. It is the purpose of this chapter to organize and analyze these studies to make more explicit the additional personality-based approaches to career development these studies represent.

Out of the melange of thought concerning personality and career, several distinctive patterns may be detected. The trait-factor view has made substantial efforts to match men and jobs with respect to a great many variables. Among those variables personality traits assume a prominent position. By asking questions such as what are the personality traits of engineers, or lawyers, or doctors, trait-factor researchers have generated a very large body of data about personality and career. A second stream of thought has grown out of psychological needs theory. Beginning with the assumption that psychological needs serve as principal motivators of behavior, this theory views all behavior as related to several fundamental needs. Accordingly, many investigators have tried to postulate and test the relationships between career aspiration or membership and the manifestation of particular psychological needs.

Related to the needs approach, but somewhat different, stands the role of values in determining career development. Values are assumed to be different from needs, yet they influence behavior in similar ways. The primary difference between needs and values seems to lie in their origins: needs seem to be fundamentally intrinsic to individuals, though they have some social aspect, whereas values are predominantly social though they are built upon one's fundamental personality structure. Also similar to needs, but affecting career behavior in a slightly different way, is what has been labeled in this chapter as personality style. This view of career behavior is that needs and personality in general lead to patterns of behavior that characterize the individual in all the settings in which it operates. Thus, if the basic style of an individual is observed, better predictions may be made about his occupational behavior. Finally, although it does not represent a distinctive view of personality and career in the developmental sense, the relation between psychopathology and career has been included in this chapter. This section has surveyed several studies which have investigated the possible connection between mental disorder and career membership or preference.

## PSYCHOLOGICAL NEEDS AND CAREER

The concept of the psychological need has a long and distinguished history in psychology. Perhaps the most complex characterization of the operation of needs has been presented by Henry Murray (1938). Since Murray's theory has been elaborately described (Hall and Lindzey, 1957), there is no need for a detailed explication here. Briefly, Murray proposed an extensive list of psychological needs involved in a wide variety of human functioning. These needs, in combination with environmental "press," permit the construction of hypotheses to explain individual behavior. Individuals are motivated to behave because of tension states. These may be reduced by need satisfaction. In time, the organism is assumed to associate tension reduction with particular objects and behaviors. Because of these associations when certain recognizable tensions are perceived, the individual knows what behavior will reduce the tension and satisfy the motivating need. Thus, tension reduction comes under individual control through the identification of needs and relevant behavior. One group of investigators applied Murray's thinking to the study of motivation for a career in teaching (Stern, Masling, Denton, Henderson, and Levin, 1960).

A psychological needs conception, along with the idea of tension reduction through needs satisfaction, is, in many ways, ideally suited to explain many aspects of career behavior, both selection and maintenance. Thus, it is not surprising that some years ago, Darley and Hagenah (1955), reviewing the research concerning the relationships between vocational interests, occupational preferences and selections, and personality characteristics, concluded that interest patterns represent the various ways that individuals see as potentially meeting their personal needs in careers.

Hoppock (1957) expanded the needs approach to career development. He suggested a theory of occupational choice that was based mainly on the use of occupational information built upon personal needs. The rationale stemmed from the assumption that occupational activities are related to basic needs and that the adequacy of occupational choice improves as people are better able to identify their own needs and the potential need satisfaction offered by a particular occupation. Thus, Hoppock reasoned that "satisfactions can result from a job which meets our needs today, or from a job which promises to meet them in the future." According to the needs reduction approach to career development, a hungry man will take any job he can get to obtain enough to eat. Once the need for food has been reduced, he will look for a new job which offers the potential of satisfying other physical and psychological needs. To the degree that he is able to find and enter jobs relevant to his higher order needs, the more or less satisfied he will be with his work.

A number of studies have taken an approach which has explored the role that psychological needs play in determining occupational decisions and membership. Suziedelis and Steimel (1963) compared inventoried needs measured by the Edwards Personal Preference Schedule with inventoried interests measured by the Strong Vocational Interest Blank to test the hypothesis that certain needs are characteristically found in people who enter particular occupations. A sample of college freshmen and sophomores was tested with the EPPS and then subdivided so that for each of the Edwards needs a group of Ss earned high scores and another group low ones. The frequency of A and B+ scores on each of the SVIB occupational groups was tabulated for each group of subjects. These procedures allowed the identification of interest areas that are systematically related to the Edwards needs.

Some of the resulting correlations are intuitively reasonable. For example, high interest scores in the biological and physical sciences and literary occupations might well be expected to be related to achievement needs, as was indeed found to be the case. Order needs seemed to be negatively related to similarity of interests to men in social service and literary occupations. Curious, however, is the failure to find a relationship between order needs and business detail interests and the low correlation between affiliation needs and similarity of interest to men in business contact occupations.

Though data such as those reported by Suziedelis and Steimel are interesting, little more is understood about personality and career as a result. The correlation between responses on two inventories seems to be too far removed from the real world of both personality and occupational interest to reflect meaningful behavior. At best, the results must be subject to highly cautious interpretation.

In another study of a similar kind, Bohn (1966) related needs inferred from responses to an adjective checklist to Holland personality types. In contrast to Suziedelis and Steimel's findings, some of the resulting matches do *not* seem intuitively correct. For example, the Realistic personality type was found to be high on abasement need and low on dominance and heterosexual needs. Others, however, are more in line with expectation: Conventional people were high on achievement, order, affiliation, dominance, endurance, and defensiveness needs and Enterprising subjects were high on achievement, exhibition, affiliation, dominance, and heterosexual needs.

Blum (1961) predicted that a positive relationship between desires for security and choices of highly secure occupations exists. Blum also examined the relationship between personality (defined in terms of EPPS scores) and the background factors of Ss emphasizing security in their vocational choices. To accomplish these ends he administered the EPPS, a biographical information questionnaire, and a homemade security needs inventory to 513 Ss, which resulted in 346 usable protocols. Blum found that the Ss with the highest score on security desires chose occupations involving a secure setting such as civil service jobs, for example, or teaching, while avoiding relatively unstable but high payoff careers such as law.

Some unusual findings occurred, however. For example, business careers were highly sought by the security seekers. Do these latter choices reflect attempts to gain the security of large organizational membership? Security desires were significantly correlated with EPPS needs deference, order, succorance, abasement, and nurturance and negatively related to needs achievement, autonomy, dominance, and change. These correlations seem to be subject to the same criticism as those of the Suziedelis and Steimel (1963) study. That is, what do response-response correlations between two sets of inventory scores mean in a larger behavioral sense?

Dipboye and Anderson (1961) studied the relationship between occupational stereotypes and needs on the assumption that the stereotypes reflect, to some degree, projections of needs relevant to occupational membership. An instrument descriptive of 14 needs based on EPPS items was devised and administered to male and female high school seniors with instructions to rate each of several occupations on the degree of the accuracy of the descriptions. The resulting stereotypes reflected cultural estimates of the occupations. For example, scientists were seen as having high needs for endurance, achievement, and change, while high school teachers were perceived as high on needs order and intraception. Boys saw engineers as high on achievement and order needs and physicians as high on nurturance, intraception, and achievement needs. Girls perceived nurses as having high nurturance, intraception, order, and endurance needs. The findings are suggestive about the nature of needs related to occupational selection and membership. Some relevant data will be discussed later in this chapter revealing needs scores of people in occupations such as nursing and engineering, at which time judgments can be made about the accuracy with which Dipboye and Anderson's subjects made their ratings.

Hall and Nougaim (1968) have studied needs and career development in the context of organizational characteristics. Their observations led them to conclude that the needs individuals exhibit in connection with their career are not unchanging. Over a five-year period, Hall and Nougaim found that as managers advance, their affiliation, achievement, esteem, and self-actualization needs increase, and their safety needs decrease (these results are consistent with Maslow's theory). In another study, Bradshaw (1970) found similar results for professional men. These results indicate, though tentatively, that opportunities for higher order needs satisfaction in work increase as one moves up the vocational hierarchy.

## Needs and Job Satisfaction

It seems reasonable to expect, if one postulates needs as a factor in occupational selection, that needs satisfaction is directly related to job satisfaction. Schaffer (1953) devised a questionnaire designed to measure the strength of each of 12 needs, the degree to which each need is being satisfied in one's job, and overall job satisfaction and administered it to 113 subjects in various industries, department stores, and government agencies. Though the questionnaire was distributed through administrators in those agencies, participation was voluntary, and the questionnaire was completed during the subject's personal time. As a result, only 32 of the 113 questionnaires were completed and returned, raising serious questions about the generality of the findings. Generally, the strongest needs expressed were for creativity and challenge, followed by needs for mastery, achievement, and social welfare. The lowest needs were socioeconomic rewards and the expression of dependency. Examination of the correlations between an individual's needs and the degree to which they are satisfied in his job revealed significant relationships for the three highest needs. More important, the correlation of 0.58 between the mean satisfaction of the subjects' two strongest needs in the job and overall job satisfaction was highly significant.

A study similar in objective was conducted by Walsh (1959). He tested the hypothesis that subjects like or dislike job duties which are consistent or inconsistent, respectively, with their needs. To test the hypothesis, he devised a Job Description Questionnaire (JDQ) containing 24 job descriptions with eight duties each to which Ss were to respond in terms of the appeal the duties had for them. In addition, the Ss, 96 college males in an introductory psychology course, took the EPPS and were asked to recommend two features of each job which should be emphasized and two which should be deemphasized in a recruiting campaign. Correlations were then computed between the EPPS scores and the needs reflected in the duties the Ss selected to be emphasized or deemphasized. Of the 24 correlations that were computed, 17 are significant, lending considerable support to Walsh's hypothesis.

Wolf (1970) has gone so far as to propose a "theory" of job motivation on the basis of the Herzberg, Mausner, and Snyderman (1959) and Maslow (1954) theories combined. According to Wolf, the level of need gratification as defined by Maslow is important to satisfaction-dissatisfaction; the *content* of the activity is involved in the gratification of active needs by means of job-related behaviors, but *context* factors are not so involved.

## Summary and Evaluation

Psychological needs have been presumed to relate to an individual's desire to enter certain careers in which he expects his particular needs structure to be especially well satisfied. To the degree that he identifies his needs and the needs satisfaction potential of the occupation he enters, he will be content with his occupational decision. The research concerning the needs satisfaction hypothesis of career choice generally substantiates the hypothesis that different kinds of needs satisfaction potential are perceived in occupations. However, the research leans very heavily on paper-and-pencil personality and interest inventories, which introduces some serious limitations in the degree of confidence with which the hypothesis can be viewed. In order truly to function as a theory, relationships between needs and career decisions, behavior, and satisfaction must be identified.

## OCCUPATIONAL VALUES AND CAREERS

Human beings postulate a variety of concepts around which to orient their lives. Some operate within the context of these orientations explicitly, others implicitly, but most people adhere to some anchor points in maintaining the direction of their life. These anchor points, which typically include religious beliefs, the place of material goods in life, and how interpersonal relations should be conducted, have been formalized by a number of psychologists. Most notably, the ideal types of men, described by Spranger (1928), have served to combine several fundamental views toward living into one representation.

It has seemed reasonable enough to many people to suppose that these personal values underlie occupational choice and attainment. Surely, it has been reasoned that a man whose main value in life is spiritual will choose different careers and behave differently in them than another whose primary value is economic. Complicating the issue is the fact that values are least stable during the post high school years when many crucial decisions are being made about careers.

It is likely that personal values play a major role in determining human behavior. As a person matures, his culture and perceptions influence the shape of the values he will eventually hold. These values, in turn, will affect his interactions with others, and his hopes and interests will influence his choice of a mate, and play a large role in determining his occupational choice and attainment. Implicit in the above is the notion that values are not static; they change as they develop. Consequently, the study of the behavioral correlates of values and the forces that shape them, both during early years and maturity, have importance for the study of career development.

Some writers have speculated about the role that values and their satisfaction play in job satisfaction. Locke (1970) has presented a formulation of job satisfaction that relates it to work outcomes in terms of the degree to which these outcomes permit the individual to attain and satisfy important job values. In other words, Locke hypothesizes that performance is related to (or "causes") job satisfaction if good performance is seen as significantly involved in the individual's reaching important job values. Mobley and Locke (1970) further examined the relationship between values and job satisfaction-dissatisfaction for important but not for unimportant values. The results of Mobley and Locke's experiment supported the hypothesis. These results led Mobley and Locke to point out that one major difficulty in studying the impact of values on job satisfaction lies in the way the question is asked; if an individual is asked what is wrong with his job, in terms of values satisfaction, he will tell us, but possibly ignore important values that are currently being satisfied. Thus, it is necessary to know what people value highly, how these values operate in their jobs, and how well the values are being satisfied in work in order to establish clearly the relationship between values and job satisfaction.

## College Student Occupational Values

Among the most extensive studies of occupational values is one reported by Rosenberg (1957). Using several thousand Cornell University students enrolled during the early 1950s as his basic sample, he asked questions about the fundamental reasons for their selection of an educational objective. He found that three basic values were expressed: working with people in a helping manner; earning large amounts of money, social status, and prestige; and having the opportunity to be creative and use special talents. These values seemed to be continuous, ranging from the desire to express creativity and originality on one end of the scale to the desire for a stable and secure future on the other.

Rosenberg found that the expression of values of students in different fields varied systematically. For example, architecture, journalism, drama, and art students valued self-expression more than other groups, while students in sales fields, hotel and food studies, real estate, and finance valued self-expression the least. Social work majors, premedical students, and education majors were highest in the desire to help and work with people, while engineering, natural science, and agriculture students were lowest in this value. The real estate, finance, hotel and food, and sales students scored highest on extrinsic reward values, while the social work, teaching, and natural science students scored lowest on this scale.

Rosenberg studied the reliability of occupational values over time. As might be expected, he found that a number of changes in both values and occupational preferences occurred over a two-year period. Where subjects' values and occupational choices changed, the changes generally reduced the disparity between choices and values. In examining the differences of the occupational values of men and women, Rosenberg observed that both sexes desire to use their special talents, but that women seem more inclined to value "working with people" whereas men lean more toward seeking security in their work. Career-oriented women, significantly enough, were found to express values more similar to those of career-oriented men than women oriented to marriage and family.

Astin and Nichols (1964) mailed questionnaires concerning life goals to National Merit finalists and Commendation winners and received 5495 usable responses in return (3830 males and 1665 females). A factor analysis of the responses revealed seven factors, subsequently entitled self-esteem, personal comfort, artistic motivation, scholarship, science-technology, prestige, and altruism. With the exception of prospective clergymen, who scored high only on altruistic values, most of the students were high on altruistic and personal comfort factors, regardless of their orientation. This finding does little to clarify occupational motivation and very likely reflects the tenor of the times during which the study was conducted (the mid-1960s) in the same way that the Rosenberg data reflected their time. The instability of values, in combination with the fact that the Astin and Nichols sample consists of unusually talented students, imposes serious limitations on the generalizations to be drawn from the Astin and Nichols study.

Another study (Miller, 1956) oriented toward objectives similar to the Astin and Nichols survey compared the vocational values of 60 students classified in each of three vocational categories: those with no vocational choice, those with a tentative choice, and those with a definite choice. The results indicated that the highest single value held by the "no choice" group was security, whereas among the subjects with a definite choice, career satisfaction was the highest value category. In other studies of the occupational values of college students, Hammond (1956) and Simpson and Simpson (1960) observed, as expected, that business students valued economic activities, were materialistic, and comfort-oriented, whereas education majors and other transmitters of the culture were high on humanitarian values.

Wagman (1968) examined the similarities in occupational values of students and their parents by means of Centers' Job Values and Desires Questionnaire. The subjects, 123 male and 138 female psychology undergraduate students, first responded to the instrument for themselves, then as they believed their fathers, then their mothers, would. Numerous similarities were noted, especially within sex groups (that is, sons were like their fathers, daughters like their mothers).

Fretz (1972) studied the responses to an occupational values questionnaire of 120 preprofessional students heading for law, medicine, engineering, business, and education. The preprofessional groups were distinguishable on the values; it should be noted that such differences are probably underestimates since professional attainment will not parallel choice.

In general, studies of values of college students enrolled in different programs reveal stable value differences associated with vocational objectives.

## Occupational Values of Secondary Students

A number of studies have examined the occupational values of junior high and high school students. Dipboye and Anderson (1959) administered a questionnaire concerning the plans and values of high school students in terms of security, prestige, salary, interest, advancement, working conditions, relations with others, independence, and benefits. At the ninth grade level, girls highly valued matters such as prestige, interest in work, working conditions, and relations with others, while the ninth grade boys valued independence, salary, and advancement opportunities. Twelfth graders were very similar: the older girls valued the same things as the younger ones with the exception of the stress on interesting work, while the older boys held similar values to the younger ones except that their regard for advancement dropped. Looking at the sample as a whole, however, interesting work and prospects for advancement seemed more important to twelfth graders than to ninth graders. It may be that younger boys and girls are less concerned with the need for interesting work than older students because work is not so imminent for them.

In another paper based on data from the same sample and questionnaire, Anderson and Dipboye (1959) report the results of a comparison between the occupational values of high school students who have expressed a vocational preference as opposed to those without a preference. Occupational values of those students who had made post high school educational or vocational plans were further compared. No differences in the values of vocationally decided and undecided twelfth grade students were found. For the total sample of ninth and twelfth graders, those expressing a vocational preference were found to value prestige more and salary and advancement less highly than the undecided students. At the ninth grade level, undecided students rated salary and advancement more highly than did the decided students. In a later study, Anderson and Bosworth (1971) found that ninth grade students in 1970 were somewhat different than their 1958 counterparts concerning occupational values; in 1970, the ninth graders valued high pay and enjoyable work instead of the stable, enjoyable work their elders had desired.

In a study along similar lines, Perrone (1965) administered a value orientation instrument to a sample of junior high school girls and found that intelligent and high achieving girls sought careers offering intrinsic satisfaction whereas lower achieving, less intelligent girls sought educational objectives inconsistent with their abilities and talents. However, since education is highly valued in the American culture and thus something for which many individuals strive, people in lower intelligence levels may be instilled with inappropriate educational goals by the culture itself.

In one of the few studies comparing the occupational values of black and white students, Dole and Passons (1972) found black students to be higher than white students in altruism. Sex differences were also noted: males held material and altruistic values in higher regard than females.

### Changes in Occupational Values with Age

Mention of the effect of maturation on the development of values leads to the consideration of several studies devoted to identifying the changes in occupational values occurring over time. In an attempt to answer the question of what changes in occupational values occur in individuals as they grow older, Miller (1954) administered the Occupational Values Indicator to 196 male college students, whose ages ranged from 17 through 30. No differences by age groups were found, though individual values were observed to vary considerably but unsystematically as far as age groupings were concerned. In general, career satisfaction seemed to be the most highly valued occupational attribute and prestige the least. This study would have been more conclusive if the younger men had been college students and the older ones in business or professional life instead of all the subjects being students. The homogeneity of college life may have reduced differences in values that ordinarily occur as men grow older and assume mature responsibilities.

Another study concerning the values of people at different stages of development overcomes the shortcomings of the Miller study to some extent. Wagman (1966) compared the values of groups of high school and university students on Centers' Job Values and Desires Scale. The results of Centers' studies (1949) also provided an adult comparison group, but it must be remembered that the Centers' adult group represents values expressed in an earlier decade. Attending only to the high school and college student samples, a number of differences were evident. The high school students preferred jobs which offer security and independence while the college sample valued interesting work most highly. The difference could be an outgrowth of socioeconomic differences between high school and college students. The former probably have lower socioeconomic backgrounds more commonly than the college students, which, in turn, might lead to greater concerns for security. The age differences between the college and high school samples might also be related to the finding that the younger group was more concerned with matters of independence. High school students are probably still fighting an independence battle with their parents to a greater extent than college students.

Gordon and Mensh (1962) explored the changes in values of medical students as they progressed through their professional training. Gordon's Survey of Interpersonal Values was administered to all students in the first through fourth year of medical training in a large midwestern school. Examining the data obtained from male students only, Gordon and Mensh found that the desire for support from others rose significantly, desire for recognition and independence increased, and leadership remained unchanged. Although it is easy to infer that medical training influenced these changes, other factors can easily be identified that might have been involved. For example, maturation might result in similar value changes over the same four-year period out of the context of medical school.

A final study noting age changes in values was conducted by Gribbons and Lohnes (1965). They elicited adolescent vocational values by means of interviews with a group of students starting in 1958, conducted again in 1961 and in 1963. Satisfaction with and interest in work consistently headed the list of occupational values over the five-year period. Generally, the correlations, ranging from a low of 0.46 between eighth and twelfth grade girls and a high of 0.95 for eighth and tenth grade girls, reflected considerable stability of values over the junior high and high school years.

## Summary and Evaluation

The basic procedures followed in the study of values and occupations involve interviewing or administering questionnaires to subjects concerning their goals and objectives vis-a-vis careers. Typically, the samples are large, the research is conducted in a school setting, and the responses to the questionnaire are subjected to factor analysis. Some factors recur in most of the studies, though with somewhat different names: interest in work, satisfaction, and self-expression are three commonly occurring values that appear variously named.

The results of studies of changes in occupational values over time suggest that the values are generally stable for individuals, though subject to some change over time. As a result of cultural influences, the relationship of any particular value to any one occupational group is open to question insofar as significant differences are concerned. For the most part, the values reflect those that are widely held by middle class American society, and thus, cut across occupations. Nevertheless, statistical, if not necessarily meaningful, differences between some occupations on certain values have been reported.

The "values" approach to occupational behavior seems to explain little about career motives or behavior. Other concepts are likely to be more useful in understanding career behavior. The studies of occupational values seem to find answers framed in the language of the questions asked to an extent that limits the resulting information. In counseling, discussions about values with students may be useful in generating self-understanding, but the approach seems limited to the role of an interviewing device and is certainly limited conceptually.

## The Relationship Between Interests, Needs, and Values

Because of the character of the measurement approach taken to study interests, values, and needs, some argument has arisen over the distinctiveness of these three concepts. One view asserts that the overlap among the three is so great that no useful purpose is served by trying to distinguish each from the other, while the opposing view asserts that although some commonalities among the three concepts exist, there are several important distinctions that are useful to maintain.

Among those who take the position that interests, needs, and values essentially tap the same pool of questionnaire and behavioral events are Thorndike, Weiss, and Dawis (1968a; 1968b). These investigators used a canonical correlation technique to study the relationship between interests as measured by the SVIB and Minnesota Vocational Interest Inventory along with needs as measured by the Minnesota Importance Questionnaire. The results of the investigations of Thorndike et al., revealing high correlations between the interest and need measures, convinced them that interests and needs are highly related constructs, possibly indistinguishable. Along the same lines, Siess and Jackson (1970), using a multimethod factor analysis which focused on "between" rather than "within" correlations, found seven factors which provided evidence that the Personality Research Form and the SVIB jointly define the needs and interests events described by the two instruments. Finally, Kohlan (1968) correlated the results of the SVIB, EPPS, and Minnesota Importance Questionnaire and found many high correlations on the scales of the three instruments.

Arguing from the opposite perspective, however, is Katz (1969), who took issue with Thorndike, Weiss, and Dawis (1968a; 1968b). Katz concludes that although needs and interests are similar, the similarity is the result of the impurity of the SVIB. Baird (1970) performed a canonical correlation of over 20,000 college student responses to the Vocational Preference Inventory and self-ratings of ability, personality, and life goals. Baird concludes that although the relationships among the variables are significant, the results are complex and are not sufficient to indicate that interest measures can legitimately be substituted for measures of goals, self-concepts, or personal potential. Salomone and Muthard (1972) administered the Minnesota Importance Questionnaire and the Vocational Preference Inventory to 333 counselors and performed a canonical correlation. No significant relationships between the two inventories were found, and the investigators conclude that these two instruments measure needs and vocational style independently.

It is possible that needs and values may be subtly related. For example, Meir and Freidland (1971) found support for the hypothesis that since extrinsic needs are not occupationally specific they do not relate to occupational preferences, but intrinsic needs are occupationally specific and, thus, do appear to be related to occupational preferences.

In general, the question of the independence of interests, needs, and values does not appear to have an answer at this time. The results of research suggest that the instrumentation plays an important role in influencing the degree of relationship to be observed among the three variables. Such results, though they suggest that the item pool may be similar for the three at times, do not necessarily lead to the inference that the concepts are fundamentally the same.


## PERSONALITY STYLE AND VOCATIONAL BEHAVIOR


A recent and very promising approach to the study of occupational psychology is the idea that personality style influences occupational choice and behavior. This approach presumes that individuals engage in modes of behavior which characterize them regardless of the specific nature of the tasks in which they are engaged at the moment. For example, a person whose style leads him to be relatively willing to accept risks is expected by this line of thought to be likely to take risks in many phases of life, in such diverse realms as the physical, emotional, financial, and vocational. The promise of the personality style approach lies in its flexibility, enabling it to encompass the abrupt changes in the occupational market that sometimes occur and at the same time to retain the stability required to remain a useful concept in career development theory. Furthermore, the personality style conception of vocational behavior sensibly relates occupational behavior to behavior in general.

Two kinds of personality variables seem especially suitable for study in regard to career behavior. The first kind are motivational variables, such as might be implied in the study of the achievement motive, motives growing from fear of failure, and mastery motives stemming from desires to subdue one's environment. The other kind of personality variable with promise for understanding career development is response style. Questions are raised about the characteristics of acquiescent or resistive individuals, the personality development of such individuals, and the implications for career behavior.

## Achievement Motive and Fear of Failure

*Risk taking.* No systematic theoretical point of view has generated all the research on the effects of personal style on occupational choice and behavior; rather the research has generated the concept. However, Atkinson's formulations (1957) of the role of the achievement motive in behavior have been very influential. One of the first personal styles whose career implications were studied was risk taking. Atkinson (1957) was concerned with the motivational antecedents of risk taking. He proposed that motivation is a function of a specific motive (or drive), the expectancy of success, and the incentive or attractiveness of a goal. Since risk taking is one aspect of motivation, the manipulations of any of these three variables should result in a modification of one's risk-taking propensities. According to Atkinson, both the achievement motive and the motive to avoid failure operate on human behavior. People with an unusually strong motive to avoid failure will frequently set defensively high or low goals for themselves, while individuals influenced more by the achievement motive are likely to aspire to intermediate and attainable goals. There is little risk of failure involved for a poverty-stricken youth who announces his plans to become a doctor, because he is so unlikely to attain his goal that there would be no personal sense of failure should he fail to become a doctor. Similarly, a bright youngster who decides not to go to college is likely to avoid career situations where some risk of failure might exist. Hence, people striving vigorously to avoid failure (rather than to achieve) are to be expected either to take unusual risks or to go to great lengths to avoid risk taking, whereas achievement-motivated people are likely to engage in moderate risk-taking activities. Occupational achievement is a very obvious vehicle for social advancement and thus is an ideal context in which to study risk taking.

Several experiments grew directly from Atkinson's proposal. Mahone (1960) took the view that since people with a high fear of failure are likely to avoid even the consideration of information that is high in achievement content, they are unlikely to examine seriously achievement-oriented occupational information. If they value achievement themselves, they place themselves in a position where they select occupations that are distantly related to the main gratifications they value and hope to find in their life work, because they avoid collecting relevant information. For similar reasons, the fearful person is not likely to possess accurate information concerning his abilities and their suitability for the occupation he intends to enter. In particular, the lack of realism should occur with respect to discrepancies between ability and judgments about the amount and kind of talent required by a chosen occupation. To test this line of reasoning, the interests and personality attributes of 135 college students were assessed so that judges could estimate the degree to which each subject over- or underaspired occupationally. Mahone found, as expected, that people fearful of failure avoided competitive behavior, and thus, were generally perceived to be over- or underaspiring, while low fear of failure subjects were more moderate in their career expectations.

Tseng and Carter (1970) explored the effects of levels of fear of failure on perceptions of occupational prestige, level of aspiration, and the types of occupations chosen in 228 ninth through twelfth grade boys. As a measure of achievement need the TAT was used; the Mandler-Sarason Test Anxiety Questionnaire was used to measure fear of failure, and the Haller Occupational Aspiration Scale was used to assess aspirations. The results of this study extend Mahone's (1960) findings: high achievement/low fear of failure boys differed from the low achievement/high fear of failure group in that the high achievement/low fear group possessed more accurate occupational prestige perceptions, aspired to higher level occupations, and chose more occupations of high prestige than the low achievement/high fear of failure group.

In another study stemming from Atkinson's formulations about achievement motivation and risk taking, Burnstein (1963) explored the relationship between achievement motive, fear of failure, and aspiration to enter prestigious occupations. Using Thematic Apperception Test scores to measure achievement motivation and test anxiety scores to assess fear of failure, subjects were divided into four groups representing various combinations of high and low fear of failure with high and low achievement need. Questioned about career preferences, avoidances, and attitudes, these Ss revealed that fear of failure was a strong factor in their selection and avoidance of occupational goals, exerting an influence above and beyond that of talents and interests. As fear of failure increased, Ss were more willing to consider entrance into less prestigious occupations.

Isaacson (1964), assuming that test anxiety scores represent the strength of the motive to avoid failure, reasoned that Ss with high test anxiety scores would choose either extremely easy tasks in order to avoid failure or extremely difficult tasks where failure would be relatively less painful, since so many others would also be failing. In contrast, Ss high in achievement need were expected to make choices of intermediate difficulty. The prediction that high test anxiety scores are related to the choice of either extremely easy or extremely difficult fields was supported for male students.[1] In a similar vein, Morris (1966) found that students high in achievement motivation seemed to be making occupational choices that reflected a greater willingness to assume an intermediate degree of risk than Ss low in achievement motivation. Other studies (Minor and Neel, 1958; Meyer, Walker, and Litwin, 1961) reported results supporting the view that high achievement motivation is related to strivings for membership in prestigious occupations and/or competitive situations.

*Risk-taking situations.* In an attempt to simulate real conditions of decision-making in order to study the role of risk taking in occupational membership and behavior, a number of investigators have contrived situations requiring Ss to make choices possessing somewhat realistic consequences in a controlled situation. A good example of these studies is one devised by Phelan (1962). He used a decision-making game to study risk-taking propensities in business students. The game required the students to make decisions about purchasing, processing, and selling of raw materials, making loans, and buying capital improvements. Since all teams began the game with the same amount of property, differences in property value at the end of the game determined the winners and losers. According to the lore of the game, if a team won a bid by underbidding unrealistically, it made little profit or even took a loss. If it bid too high, it might not sell any services that month and hence make no profit. Phelan, reasoning that bidding should be related to cautiousness, had classified his subjects according to their tendency toward cautiousness (reflected by the cautiousness scale of the Gordon Personality Inventory) and arranged the teams so that each was composed of either cautious, impulsive, or "neutral" members. The results supported Phelan's predictions: the teams composed of cautious members bid lower than those composed of neutral or impulsive individuals in seven out of eight games.

The effects of the contrived nature of risk-taking experiments have been explicitly discussed by Williams (1965). First, in such experiments, an assumption seems to be made that risk-taking is a pervasive characteristic, that is, some people are risk-takers while others are not. As an alternative to this, Williams suggests the possibility that people might assume risks partly as a function of a general tendency within themselves to do so, but also partly as a function of the specifics of the risk-taking situation and the other variables contributing to motivation suggested by Atkinson (1957), motive, expectancy, and incentive. Furthermore, Williams points out that the contrived risk-taking experiments are

---

[1] Isaacson explained the failure to find the expected results for women in terms of questions about the validity of the use of TAT measures in studying women. An alternative explanation that seems more likely is that women do not concern themselves with academic failure as much as men do since the arena of success for women does not lie primarily in the educational-vocational realm. The situation is further complicated by the fact that women college students tend generally to earn better grades than males, probably for a variety of reasons not relevant to this discussion.

more often constructed around gambling-like situations rather than truly chance activities (e.g., Hancock and Teevan, 1964). Chance situations in their natural setting have a capriciousness which the individual recognizes and which probably influences his behavior in a way different from gambling situations where a calculated risk is taken. Vocationally, a tendency to take risks and a lack of concern for job security as inferred by an observer might reflect high self-esteem and a self-confidence to manage his work demands. As a result, such behavior has different implications and takes different shapes than risks taken in chance situations for minimal stakes, such as gambling in a poker game. A man may behave differently on his job because of confidence in his vocational skill than in his Tuesday night poker game with his friends. These speculations lead to the expectation that vocational risk-taking should be related to positive self-evaluations, intelligence (or relevant aptitude), and the utility the risk has for one's self-concept, the converse of the predictions made by Mahone (1960).

Ziller (1957) conducted a risk-taking study that seems to minimize the problems outlined by Williams. Ziller reasoned that although the choice of a specific vocation is largely dictated by such things as interests, abilities, economics, and information, the remaining variance is a function of the individual's judgment of his chances for success and the price he must pay to accept these chances. Ziller devised a study to test the hypothesis that differences in risk-taking exist between college students majoring in different fields. Using college sophomores enrolled in the ROTC program as subjects, he administered an instrument devised to measure the risk-taking propensity of the students. The content of the test was relevant to problems encountered in ROTC studies, but the ability to answer the questions required information which the Ss did not actually possess. As a result they were not able to respond with certainty since they did not have sufficient information to do so. Consequently, utility for risk was inferred from the degree to which Ss were willing to make guesses.

The results of this study reflected significant differences in guessing as a function of the college enrollment and occupational plans. Students interested in sales occupations had the highest scores, followed by those of mechanical engineering students, education, business administration, chemical engineering, electrical engineering, civil engineering, and undecided students. While there may be no particular reason to expect the groups in the middle of the distribution to be different from one another in risk-taking propensities, the groups at either extreme are coincident with expectations. One intuitively expects sales people to be risk-takers, while one also assumes that people unable to make decisions find themselves in that predicament at least partly because they cannot take even the minimal risks involved in committing themselves to a course of action. Unfortunately, these fairly clear results were not duplicated (Stone, 1962) in a study partially replicating Ziller's. Slakter and Cramer (1969) also replicated and extended the Ziller study by administering a Ziller-type risk-taking questionnaire (one characterized by a need to answer questions based on insufficient information) to more than 1000 male and 700 female students entering college. Relationships observed between risk-taking scores and vocational preferences were low and often illogical. This result, in combination with Stone's (1962) findings, suggests that Ziller's method may not be as promising as it first appeared.

That risk-taking has relevance to vocational behavior if not vocational preference seems highly likely. Williams (1965) reports that subjects who score high on a job risk-taking scale express a high degree of concern for promotions, a preference for doing work for which they are most skilled, and express relatively little concern for steady employment. Subjects scoring low on the scale report opposite concerns. He also found that when people who are high risk-takers are in jobs with a low probability for promotion, they express more dissatisfaction with their work than low risk-takers.

The constructs proposed to explain certain kinds of occupational choices and predict behavior in work settings seem to have a relationship to career events, even though much of the research has a contrived flavor. General personality characteristics related to achievement motivation, fear of failure, and a willingness to accept risks seem to provide a useful personality framework on which to make predictions about the course of vocational events in an individual's life.

### Other Personality Characteristics

*Mastery.* To contrast the role of risk-taking in occupational behavior with other personality variables, a study conducted by Liberty, Burnstein, and Moulton (1966) must be considered. They were interested in the relationship between the degree of competency required to function in an occupation as opposed to the prestige of an occupation in determining the attractiveness of the occupation to the individual. Male college students were required to rate occupations in terms of prestige and the competency required for success in them. Though the resulting correlation between the two ratings was high, those occupations whose prestige was considerably higher than required competency, and vice versa, were selected to become part of two occupational scales that Ss rated on attractiveness. Subjects were also given the Strodtbeck scale to measure the value the individual places on competence, mastery, and autonomy (example: "planning only makes a person unhappy since your plans hardly ever work out anyway"), and the deCharms scale purporting to measure the same thing but differing in that it reflects the degree to which a person feels achievement orientation is important.

The occupational preferences that resulted from the ratings Ss made on the occupational scales constructed from prestigious versus mastery occupations were related to the scores Ss earned on the mastery indices. The results indicated that in general Ss who preferred occupations higher on competency requirements than prestige earned higher scores on the mastery index than Ss who preferred occupations that are lower on competency requirements than prestige. The authors speculated that for some people, mastery is a more potent occupational motivator than power and prestige. Obviously, such a possibility should be included in individual counseling in terms of individual assessment and the degree to which occupations vary in their demand for competency. Furthermore, other personality correlates of mastery needs are of interest, as well as the ramifications of differences in mastery concerns in job performance and satisfaction.

*Response style.* Couch and Keniston (1960) have proposed the interesting hypothesis that response set, that is, a person's tendency to respond in a particular manner regardless of the specific stimulus complex presented, is based on a personality factor which results in acquiescent or resistant behavior. They coined the terms "yeasayers" and "naysayers" to represent these two types of response set. From their studies, they concluded that the yeasayers are "id-dominated," that is to say, these people express their impulses freely, are adventurous, rarely delay impulse gratification, seem to value change, novelty, and adventure, and see the world as a "stage where the main theme is an acting out of libidinal desires." In general, they are highly responsive to stimuli. The naysayers, on the other hand, seem to see impulses as something to be controlled and as a threat to personal stability. They are characteristically stimulus rejecting. The yeasayers, in more negative terms, seem to have "weak ego control," are externally oriented, and are highly responsive to group demands. The naysayers, more positively, are internally oriented, introverted, and possess greater capacity to inhibit impulses.

The characteristics of the yeasayers and naysayers strongly resemble those of the several styles of behavior reported by Heath (1959). He analyzed the behavior of college students respective to vocational activity and concluded that four styles exist: the "reasonable adventurer," who is an ideal type, well integrated, wholesome, competent, involved in life and full of zest and tolerance; the "noncommitted," manifesting a fearful noninvolvement; the "hustler," upward striving and busy defending himself against threats to his strivings; and the "plunger," whose behavior reflects a fearful impulsiveness.

That such differing types of response style should not be reflected in vocational choices and behaviors is hardly imaginable. Some peripheral indication that acquiescent versus resistant response sets are related to vocational behavior is offered by Lindgren (1962). Postulating a general characteristic of negativism as an indicator of emotional disturbance, Lindgren presented two questionnaires to college students. One questionnaire was a list of 25 male and 26 female jobs, all of a tedious, lowly, and unpleasant nature, the other a list of 39 foods. The Ss were "to indicate which foods they disliked so much they wouldn't eat them and which jobs (appropriate to sex) they would not do under any circumstance." The findings indicated that younger (under age 21) males and females expressed significantly more food and occupational aversions than older subjects. Furthermore, the correlations between the two lists of aversions reflected a tendency for people expressing many aversions in one realm to express many in the other. These observations apparently confirm Couch and Keniston's general hypothesis that two basic response styles exist and further indicate that these styles have implications for vocational decision-making.

The vocational implications may be seen more vividly in a study by Armatas and Collister (1962), who proposed the notion that response sets influence people taking the SVIB to respond in terms of like, indifferent, or dislike responses, according to their personal style and over and above the content of the item. Since the response set may influence the nature of responses when other factors in the item do not exert a strong influence, they can be highly important in determining the resulting interest patterns. Armatas and Collister predicted that the "like" person is socially oriented, impulsive, spontaneous, and flexible, in other words, much like the yeasayer of Couch and Keniston (1960). The "dislike" person is impersonal, object oriented, rigid, suspicious, conforming, passive, and insensitive, like the naysayer, and the "indifferent" responder is unable to cope with the various stimuli he finds in the world, is indecisive, passive, ambivalent, and tends to procrastinate. A total of 98 Ss exhibiting a marked response set on the SVIB were given the EPPS and the Cattell 16 PF. The results showed that compared to with the I and D subjects, the like subjects scored high on social service and business contact occupations on the SVIB, low on physical science scales, high EPPS needs of heterosexuality, dominance, and aggression, low on succorance and exhibition, and earned scores on the 16 PF test indicating a general tendency to be outgoing.

The dislike subjects were high on SVIB scales of physical science and business contact and low on social service, high on EPPS needs of aggression, succorance, and deference, and low on heterosexuality and dominance. They generally appeared to be apprehensive on the 16 PF. Finally, the indifferent respondants, in contrast with the others, were high on social service and physical science occupations on the SVIB and low on business detail careers. They were also low on EPPS needs for aggression, dominance, and deference, and may be characterized as aloof, submissive, timid, unconcerned, and silent on the 16 Pf. These results in general are suggestive of types of people whose characteritics are very similar to those predicted by Armatas and Collister.

Haakenstad and Apostal (1971) compared the nonoccupational interests of high and low acquiescent individuals. High acquiescent individuals revealed a greater diversity of interests on the SVIB than low acquiescent individuals. These results seem related to those reported by Armatas and Collister (1962) and Berdie (1943) indicating that acquiescent individuals are more open to stimuli than resistant individuals. Berdie (1943) described the relationship between personality test scores and the frequency of like and dislike responses on the SVIB. The greater the number of like responses, the higher the scores on morality, social adjustment, and emotionality, while the greater the frequency of dislike responses on the SVIB, the lower the personality scores on those three variables. Also of interest are the kinds of SVIB patterns generated by responding to a Strong blank exclusively in terms of like, indifferent, or dislike. Dislike responses produce interest patterns high in verbal and language oriented occupations and low in technical and social welfare fields; like protocols result in reject patterns in biological and physical sciences and moderately high scores on the social welfare occupations.

Another study along the same lines is reported by Stewart (1960). He administered the SVIB, the Allport-Vernon-Lindzey Study of Values (AVL), and the Omnibus Personality Inventory (OPI) to a sample of National Merit Scholars (N = 593 males and 238 females). He then correlated the number of like, indifferent, and dislike responses made on the SVIB with the scores on the AVL and OPI. He found that men who might be characterized as likes scored lower on theoretical and economic and higher on social and religious scales on the AVL than other men. Their personality scores reflected enthusiastic warmth and interest in other people, independence of judgment, freedom of expression, and a preference for complexity. Women likes were very similar to the men. The indifferent males scored low on political values on the AVL and appeared to be "conservative, compliant, rigid, responsible, cautious, ready to accept authority and tradition," and had "a low degree of self-confidence and a liking for overt action." Except for the indifferent women's higher score on theoretical values and their greater tendency to be flexible and permissive in interpersonal relationships, their scores were highly similar to those of the indifferent males. Finally, the male dislikes had high AVL scores on theoretical, aesthetic, and political values and low scores on social and religious ones. They seemed to have little interest in people and might be characterized in general as inner directed, unsociable, and suspicious of others. Women dislikes differed from likes in that they had high AVL scores only on the aesthetic scale and low scores on the religious scale, and the size of the correlations obtained between response set and personality value scales were smaller than those observed in the men. While the correlations underlying these findings are small, Stewart is satisfied that the results cannot be explained away in terms of socially desirable response sets. Instead, he suggests that these findings imply that the differentiation of interests begins through one's awareness of his dislikes, as Tyler (1951) has suggested.

All of these studies are in general agreement with one another to an extent which demands the serious consideration of the hypothesis that acquiescent versus resistive personal style is a major determinant of career interests. A more general conception of the role of personality style in occupational behavior was proposed by Gough and Woodworth (1960), who suggested that within the scientific community several specific research styles exist which are intimately related to personality. They devised a Q-sort task describing a variety of ways to pursue research as a career, administered it to 45 professional research scientists, and factor analyzed the results. Eight styles of behavior were identified. These types were very descriptively named the Zealot, the Initiator, the Diagnostician, the Scholar, the Artificer, the Aesthetician, the Methodologist, and the Independent.

Kassarjian and Kassarjian (1965) studied still another aspect of personal style and occupational selection. They reasoned that people choose careers in a manner that is related to the degree to which the people and the careers are inner or other directed (Riesman, 1950). The investigators deliberately distinguished between occupational *entry* and *preference*, since they correctly assumed that there are factors other than personality attributes involved in occupational entry. Twenty-five male and 25 female students earning the most extreme scores on a scale of inner and other directedness were selected for study and tested with the Allport-Vernon-Lindzey Study of Values and the SVIB.

The findings generally concurred with the intuitive predictions about the relationship between values and interests and social character. Inner directed males scored higher than other directed males on SVIB scales such as artist, psychologist, architect, physician, dentist, mathematician, physicist, engineer, and chemist, while the other directed males scored higher on scales such as senior CPA, accountant, office worker, mortician, pharmacist, sales manager, and real estate and life insurance salesman. For women, most of the differences between the two groups were similar to those for men. The exceptions seemed to fall in occupations which, while common and acceptable ones for men and thus attractive to other directed males, are unusual for women to enter and as a consequence seem to attract inner directed women. Law is an example of such a profession; women with interests like those of lawyers were found to be more inner directed than women whose interests are different from lawyers, but no such differences existed between inner and other directed men on the lawyer scale.

*Personality and interest stability.* Dunkleberger and Tyler (1961) studied the personality characteristics of people whose scores on the SVIB remained stable over two testings. For male subjects the only significant differences between the "changers" and "nonchangers" were the higher scores of the changers on the heterosexual scale of the EPPS and on the self-control scale of the CPI. For females, nonchangers had higher nurturance scores on the EPPS, while changers had higher CPI scores on capacity for status, well-being, tolerance, achievement via independence, psychology mindedness, and flexibility.

## Cognitive Style in Career Behavior

The research describing the effects of response style on vocational development and behavior has led to the explicit identification of cognitive styles as a variable of potential importance in career development. It has been suggested (Osipow, 1970) that cognitive style might serve as a high level construct to permit the relation of diverse personality trait variables to vocational preferences and behavior to be more clearly seen. It might be, for example, that a general cognitive style of being "receptive" or "open" to stimuli might cause some individuals to report possessing more interests than others.

Broverman (1960) is among the early investigators of cognitive styles and vocational behaviors. In an early study, Broverman (1964) found that cognitive style is related to distractability in various types of tasks. Such distractability could effect scholastic performance and the resulting feedback to the individual, and in this way influence the self-concept, task preferences, and, eventually, vocational preferences and selection. In another study, Broverman, Broverman, Vogel, and Palmer (1964) found strong and weak "automatizers" (people who vary in their ability to perform tasks without explicit attention) have different physical attributes. Broverman and his associates hypothesized that these physical differences have an endocrine basis, that these biochemical variables might affect the individual's rate of physical maturation, which, in turn, affects the development of performance levels. Thus, at the end of a long sequence of events, the individual will receive variable feedback about his stimulus value related to his vocational self-perceptions.

Levine (1968) attempted to demonstrate differences in constricted-flexible cognitive control by means of the Color-Word Test in three vocational groups (physicians, mathematicians, and creative writers). The rationale for this investigation was simply that cognitive differences should be related to the differential functioning of professionals in the three vocations studied. Differences were found, but none that were adequately explained by the constricted-flexible notions of cognitive style. Levine speculated that Color-Word Test performance is related to "molar adaptive" behaviors such as vocational choice, but not in terms defined by the concept of constricted-flexible control.

In a similar study (Osipow, 1969), a number of cognitive style measures were administered to five groups of college women (nursing, home economics, dental hygiene, special education, and undecided students) and two groups of male college students (pharmacy and fisheries technology students). The cognitive style measures included a measure of associative flexibility (assessing an individual's willingness to see relationships between two stimuli), an object sort (to measure conceptual band width or the tendency to use wide versus narrow notions of similarity between objects in relating to them), a measure of the tendency to respond in extremes, and the Closure Flexibility Test, a measure of field-dependence-independence. The results point up some differences in styles which should be accepted tentatively and interpreted cautiously in view of sampling shortcomings and limitations in the validation of the cognitive style instruments. The nursing students appear to be relatively uncritical, open to stimuli, and moderately field-dependent; the home economics students exhibit a wide equivalence range, are somewhat unresponsive to stimuli, and are field-independent; the dental hygiene students are field-independent; the special education students are field-dependent and display a small conceptual band width; the undecided women students are unreceptive to stimuli and have a wide conceptual band width; the pharmacy students display a narrow conceptual band width; and, finally, the fisheries technology students appear to be uncritical and avoid the tendency to respond in extremes. However, the data did not indicate that cognitive style variables are related to the ease of vocational development and selection, contrary to predictions.

Kish and Donnenwerth (1969) examined the relationship between interests and sensation seeking. They expected to find that people who seek sensation will display their seeking tendency in connection with their inventoried interests. Forty-one rehabilitation clients took the Sensation Seeking Scale and the Kuder Preference Record. Positive correlations between sensation seeking and scientific interest and negative correlations between sensation seeking and clerical interests were found. Thirty-two male college students took the SVIB and the Sensation Seeking Scale. Here, positive correlations were found between psychologist, physician, psychiatrist, social worker, minister, and musician on sensation seeking, and negative correlations observed on accountant, purchasing agent, banker, pharmacist, and mortician and sensation seeking. Finally, 46 female college students took the SVIB and the Sensation Seeking Scale. A positive correlation between sensation seeking and lawyer and negative correlations between sensation seeking and housewife, elementary teacher, home economics teacher, and dietician were found. Overall, the results reported by Kish and Donnenwerth suggest that sensation seeking is associated with occupational interests in relatively unstructured tasks.

Using field-dependence-independence as the cognitive style of interest, Gruenfeld and Weissenberg (1970) predicted that differences in field-dependence would be associated with a tendency toward internal versus external sources of job satisfaction. To test the hypothesis, 96 civil service workers were classified into field-dependent-independent categories by means of the Group Embedded Figures Test. Job satisfaction was measured by means of the Wernimont Job Satisfaction Questionnaire. The results, though not exactly supporting the prediction that levels of field-dependency are differentially associated with sources of job satisfaction, do reveal that field-independent individuals perceive intrinsic and extrinsic job satisfiers distinctively, while field-dependent individuals view these two sources of job satisfaction in a highly correlated manner.

In a study dealing with field-dependence and vocational interests, Zytowski (1969) predicted that psychological differentiation is positively related to SVIB scores on engineering scales, and negatively correlated with scores on business detail, business contact, and social service scales. Zytowski's predictions were based on the supposition that field-dependent individuals obtain their orientation from their environment and other people to a greater degree than field-independent individuals. Though one of the measures used revealed some modest support for the hypothesis, generally, the prediction was not validated by the data.

Some investigators have examined the relation between internal-external locus of control and vocational interests. Zytowski (1967) found that, in men, Rotter external control scores were positively correlated with "feminine" SVIB scores and aesthetic interests. Tseng (1970) found that locus of control is a useful construct with which to differentiate rehabilitation clients with respect to their work behavior and potential for training.

Kelly's (1955) concept of cognitive complexity has also been used to study vocational behavior. Bodden (1970) found that more cognitively complex individuals were more likely to make congruent occupational choices (defined in Holland's terms) than cognitively simple persons. However, Bodden found no evidence to indicate that cognitive complexity leads to better occupational choices with regard to the use of abilities. Dolliver (1967) went so far as to modify the Tyler Vocational Card Sort using Kelly's theory of personal constructs as a means of organizing client thinking about occupational and nonoccupational activities. However, efforts to apply Kelly's theory to vocational behavior remain rudimentary.

In general, while cognitive style has been studied in connection with vocational behavior in a number of ways, the results of these studies are not impressive. Considerable work remains to be done in the definition and measurement of cognitive styles before these behaviors can truly be useful to the study of vocational events.

### Summary and Evaluation

The research and theory dealing with personality style and occupational behavior seems to be the most rigorous, both conceptually and experimentally, of all the personality approaches to occupational behavior. It connects psychological theory in general with occupational behavior in an explicit way which has implications for both the selection of careers and eventual career behavior. The notion that acquiescent or resistent response styles influence both career selection and subsequent behavior seems promising. Some questions do remain, however; the definition of risk-taking, for example, needs clarification, especially since risk-taking behaviors seem to be very relevant to the consideration of occupational behavior. The personality style approach promises to be very helpful to counselors in the conceptualization of their client's choice process, but somewhat limited as to implications for counseling procedure. For example, a counselor may be able to infer from his observations about a client that he is acquiescent and motivated by fear of failure rather than mastery, but these judgments do not in themselves lead to any distinctive counseling procedures.

## PSYCHOPATHOLOGY AND CAREERS

There is a long history of interest in the relationship between psychopathological states and vocational selection and behavior. As was seen in Chapter 4 on the psychoanalytic approach to vocational behavior, careers have been viewed as an outlet for sublimated wishes and neurotic impulses. It is interesting, too, to note that in Europe, where vocational interest inventories are not widely used, the

Szondi Test[2] is frequently used to assess vocational interests. In the folklore about occupations there is much speculation about the possibility that certain occupations attract more than their share of mentally disordered individuals. For example, it has been proposed that housepainters and barbers tend to be alcoholic in larger proportions than the general population, that actors, used car salesmen, and door-to-door canvassers tend to be psychopathic personalities, and that male actors tend to be homosexual. Ordinarily, however, these proposals are without the weight of empirical evidence and can hardly be given serious consideration. That such proposals have been made, however, indicates the interest of the general culture in the connection between psychopathology and occupation. In certain careers, medicine for example, occupational responsibilities make it imperative to ensure that trainees and practitioners within the field are not prone to mental disorder.

Klumbies (1967) found evidence indicating that nearly a quarter of 1500 therapy patients described their work setting as the source of their psychological difficulties. Though the proportion of true work conflict shrank upon closer scrutiny, Klumbies found that work remained a major source of difficulty for 14 percent of the patients. It is, thus, not surprising that a number of investigations into the relationship between occupations and psychopathology have been conducted.

## The Case History Approach

Case studies have been written to illustrate the relationship of mental illness to vocational difficulties. Barahal (1953) described a case emphasizing the significance of differentiating a person whose vocational maladjustment is the result of insufficiencies of skill, training, or interest from one who is psychiatrically distressed and whose vocational ineffectiveness is a consequence rather than a cause. A number of case studies describing the interaction between psychiatric and work failures and the way that work can be used to facilitate psychiatric recovery have been written by Simmons (1965). Simmons' studies suggest that psychiatrically disturbed individuals may be effective vocationally and that the work potential of disturbed people has not been used imaginatively as a treatment possibility.

Simmons writes from a social worker's point of view. Psychologists, however, have been more interested in studying the diagnostic aspects of vocational choice and psychopathology than in the social implications of disturbed workers. Small's study (1953), described in Chapter 4, examined the vocational choices of

---

[2] The Szondi Test consists of photographs of people diagnosed in a variety of psychopathological ways. The logic of the test is that under instructions to select the person they prefer from pairs of pictures, Ss will reveal their implicit pathology by selecting pictures of patients whose pathology matches their own.

disturbed boys versus those of well-adjusted boys. The results indicated that the disturbed group sought the satisfaction of needs peculiar to the individuals in the group, regardless of the real potential of the work situation to gratify those needs. Maladjusted boys made poor first choices about careers but realistic second choices, while the reverse appeared to hold for better adjusted boys. This suggests that at some level, even maladjusted individuals can exercise realistic vocational adjustment.

Relatively few studies of the vocational interests of diagnostically pure disordered groups exist. One such study has been reported by Haselkorn (1956). He compared the vocational interests, as reflected by the SVIB and Kuder Preference Record, of a group of 20 homosexual males under treatment for their homosexuality, 20 nonhomosexual male neuropsychiatric patients, and 20 nonhomosexual nonpsychiatric patients. These Ss were similar in work history, education, and job categories. On the Kuder, the only difference found was between the control group of well-adjusted nonhomosexual Ss on the one hand and the homosexual Ss on the other. The homosexual group's scores were lower on the mechanical interest scale. On the SVIB, the homosexuals were different from both other groups on the author-journalist scale and different only from the normal group on the veterinarian, production manager, aviator, and senior CPA scales.

## Kuder Preference Record Interests and Adjustment

One of the more clearly established relationships between interests and adjustment has been one pointed out by Patterson (1957); maladjusted people tend, in general, to express interests in artistic, literary, and musical careers more often than in scientific or musical careers. This was further elaborated in a review by Gobetz (1964), who summarized the results of studies which have examined the relationship between interests expressed on the KPR and psychopathology. Most of these studies followed the procedure of identifying a psychoneurotic group, administering the Kuder, and comparing the resulting scores with those of a control group or with the test norms. Some have compared the Kuder scores with scores on a personality inventory for a normal sample. Klugman (1950) studied the relationship between the range of Kuder scores and performance on the Bell Adjustment Inventory. He predicted that the better-adjusted Ss would show both a greater spread and more fields of interest than maladjusted Ss. The sample was composed of 108 counseling clients at a VA Regional Office. With a few exceptions the hypotheses were not supported. A correlation between spread of interest and age and education and intelligence was found to exist. Also found was a correlation between high scientific and low artistic interest scores with good personal adjustment scores on the Bell Adjustment Inventory.

In another study Klugman (1960) compared the Kuder profiles of 60 male neuropsychiatric patients and 60 counseling cases. This comparison revealed that the profiles of the two groups were significantly different. The neuropsychiatric group scored higher on literary and lower on mechanical interests than the normal group. Interestingly, in terms of the norms, the NP group's interests are more like those of women than men. Similar findings were reported by Steinberg (1952), who compared the KPR scores of 50 psychoneurotic veterans with those of 100 non-neurotic but physically disabled veterans. The non-neurotic veterans' scores were significantly higher on mechanical and lower on musical and literary interests. The only report inconsistent with the tendency for maladjusted Ss to have high literary and musical and low mechanical interest scores was reported by Melcon (1956), who administered the CTMM and the Occupational Interest Inventory to 324 high school seniors. He found that artistic and personal-social interests were correlated with good personal adjustment while Ss with mechanical interests had poor adjustment scores.

Newman (1955) predicted that high social service scores on the Kuder Preference Record would be positively correlated with poor personal adjustment. The hypothesis was tested by administering the Kuder to 141 tuberculosis patients previously rated as to their degree of personal maladjustment. The results indicated that a significant number of the subjects with social service scores above the 75th percentile had been rated as maladjusted and that over 53 percent of the maladjusted Ss earned their highest interest scores on the social service scale. Unexplained terms of the hypothesis, however, was the finding that a significant number of Ss with high scores on the clerical, musical, and computational scales were also judged to be maladjusted.

Sternberg (1956) correlated scores on the KPR with those on the MMPI of 270 white male students at Queens College in New York. He found a number of moderate correlations of a significant nature between the two inventories which indicate that aesthetic interests (Kuder scales literary, artistic, musical) are positively correlated with an inclination toward personal maladjustment and that scientific and technical interests seem to be negatively correlated with a tendency toward personal maladjustment. It is again important to recall, however, that the mean MMPI scores of both types of subjects were well within the normal range.

Building on the data of Klugman (1952; 1960) and several others, Drasgow and Carkhuff (1964) observed that literary, artistic, and musical interests are correlated with mental disorder. They administered the KPR before and following psychotherapy and found that in cases judged to be "successful," the artistic, musical, and literary scores decreased, adding further evidence to the idea that aesthetic interests are in some way related to emotional disorder.

Examining differences among psychiatric patients of various classifications in work history or Kuder Preference Record patterns, Schaffer (1972) found no major differences.

### Interest-Interest and Interest-Ability Discrepancies

The idea that discrepancies between interests and abilities indicate emotional maladjustment has often been suggested. Nugent (1961) studied two groups of high school boys, one with a marked agreement between their aptitudes and interests, the other exhibiting a marked discrepancy. The Kuder was used to study interests, the Differential Aptitude Test to measure ability, and the California Personality Inventory to measure personality. No differences in personality adjustment, by either personality inventory or judges' ratings, were found between ninth grade boys with high and low discrepancy between interests and aptitudes. However, significant differences in personal adjustment were found to exist at the eleventh grade level. Looking only at the personality scales relevant to personal adequacy and security, however, Nuget inferred that the relationship between discrepant interests and aptitudes and maladjustment holds not only for eleventh graders but also for ninth grade boys.

Approaching the matter of interest discrepancies from another direction, Pool and Brown (1964) postulated a relationship between Kuder and SVIB discrepancies and psychological maladjustment. They administered the SVIB, Kuder, and MMPI to 27 physically handicapped VA male patients who had been referred for vocational counseling. They matched the Kuder and SVIB areas; the mechanical scale on the Kuder was judged to be equivalent to Group IV on the SVIB. Interest scores were classified as either high, medium, or low for each area. Discrepancy points were scored when a subject earned a high score on one test and a medium or low score on the other test in the same area. Degrees of discrepancy were taken into account in terms of the deviation between the scores on the two tests. Thus, a high score on mechanical on the Kuder and a low Strong Group IV score earned two discrepancy points, while a medium score on persuasiveness on the Kuder and a high literary group score on the Strong earned only one point. The results showed a correlation of 0.30 (p<0.06) between the number of interest discrepancy scores and MMPI scores with T scores above 65 (still within the normal range). Discrepancies between the interest inventories in the mechanical, computational, and literary scores appeared to be the most sensitive in reflecting MMPI maladjustment. The study is interesting, but the correlation only approaches what is usually considered to be statistical significance; the sample is small, and the measurements gross. The implications of findings such as were predicted are not entirely clear.

Munday, Braskamp, and Brandt (1968) examined the psychological adjustment of individuals with undifferentiated SVIB profiles using the MMPI. The subjects were 314 male counseling clients who had taken the SVIB as part of educational-vocational counseling and had also taken the MMPI either as part of programmatic freshman testing or as part of their counseling. The results, contrary to common expectation, do not show any significant relationship between flat SVIB profiles and poor intelligence, age, or maladjustment.

## Vocational Conflict and Personal Adjustment

Landis (1963) studied the relationship between emotional maladjustment and interest in particular vocations. Using as an experimental sample 214 male college students who sought help for emotional-personal problems at a college counseling service and 214 randomly selected college males from the same university as a control group, he tested a series of hypotheses predicting that maladjusted students generally are more conflicted about their educational-vocational plans than well-adjusted students. The data were available from the SVIB and a Personal Information Blank, answered by all freshmen, designed to acquire, among other things, information on career choice, certainty, and parental wishes about student career plans. Not one of Landis' seven predictions was supported. Landis observed that maladjusted Ss earn significantly higher SVIB scores than adjusted students on the clinical psychologist, artist, minister, advertising man, author-journalist, and musician scales and significantly lower scores on the farmer, purchasing agent, production manager, and army officer scales. These results are consistent with other findings which reflect a positive correlation between masculine, technical, scientific interests, and good personal adjustment while feminine (for men), aesthetic interests correlate positively with maladjustment. One might speculate about this persistent finding in terms of the fantasy and daydreaming component of maladjustment, but equally possible is the speculation that boys with aesthetic interests come into conflict with their culture more readily than boys with typical interests, and as a consequence, are more prone to become maladjusted.

Carnes (1964) pursued the hypothesis that the vocational interests of psychiatric patients are less varied, less intense, less masculine, less mature, and are at an increasingly lower occupational level as the degree of severity of disorder increases. In a study comparing the interests of psychiatric patients with varying degrees of severity, he found that although some interests do seem to be correlated with some aspects of abnormal personalities in a general way, more often the interests of psychiatric patients are so varied as to obscure systematic differences by diagnostic category. Some evidence was found for the expectation that psychiatrically disordered individuals show less interest patterning and are less vocationally mature than more normal individuals.

A related hypothesis about personal adjustment and career has been suggested by Roe (1963). Growing out of her interest in the lives of scientists, she has speculated about the influence on and interaction that exists between scientific careers and personal problems. She suggested that successful scientists encounter a major cultural difference between their home and the school environments during youth. For such young people, the chances are that their schools promoted conventional thought while their home environment encouraged individual inquiry and independence. In Roe's opinion it becomes important to devise conditions that socially support the young person whose culture pulls him two ways in order to avoid isolating him socially during childhood. The tendency during childhood for scholarly interests to be looked upon as feminine further adds to the difficulties of the bright male youngster in school. Other cultural problems exacerbate the maladjustment of bright youngsters, for example, the "moral" tone of the concepts taught in the early grades. Arithmetic, languages, and social conduct are all taught with a sense of absolutism and a rejection of individual judgment. Thus, creativity is discouraged and deviant behavior in the form of repression, withdrawal, or acting out frequently occurs instead.

As the bright "scientist-to-be" grows older, he experiences conflicting loyalties — organizational and personal (spouse and family) loyalties come into conflict with professional and scholarly interests which can become consuming. Often, interpersonal difficulties arise as a result of professional involvement as reflected by the not uncommon occurrence of divorce among scientists. Finally, there seems to be clinical evidence for the frequent occurrence of a neurotic basis for scientific work. When that exists, apparent solutions to scientific problems are not seen, and work is often carried on well beyond the appropriate time to terminate. Roe's assessment is interesting, for it might well apply to all intelligent youngsters, as well as some ordinary ones, and could serve as a basis for understanding the etiology of maladjustment that sometimes seems to go hand in hand with certain endeavors.

Walsh and Russel (1969), using the simple procedure of asking 124 college undergraduates to respond to the Mooney Problem Check List, found that congruent students (those choosing educational majors consistent with their high point code on the Vocational Preference Inventory of Holland) exhibit better personal adjustment than incongruent students. A more complicated study of vocational and personal adjustment was conducted by Osipow and Gold (1968). In the Osipow and Gold study, the SVIB patterns of 42 male and 23 female personal adjustment counseling cases were compared with the profiles of 53 male and 35 female students selected at random. The male counseling subjects exhibit fewer primary interest patterns, more flat profiles, fewer primary patterns in practical, scientific, and engineering categories, were more likely to reject scientific, engineering, and business detail areas and less likely to reject literary fields than the randomly chosen males. The women counseling clients show fewer flat profiles, fewer primary patterns in the domestic area, and fewer rejects in sales and education areas than the randomly chosen women. Overall, the results for both sexes indicate that the counseling population is more likely to have interest patterns that are mildly atypical for their sex, a finding similar to that of Roe and Siegelman (1964) who observed similar sex role conflicts for male social workers and female engineers. In addition, while the inventoried interests of the subjects in the Osipow and Gold study are different for the counseled versus the randomly chosen individuals but programs enrolled in are similar, it might be inferred that the students receiving personal adjustment counseling are more likely to be enrolled in a program inconsistent with their interests than the randomly selected students.

In another study investigating SVIB profiles and adjustment, Brandt and Hood (1968) observed individuals who sought counseling during a ten-year period (1955-1964) who had taken both the SVIB and the MMPI. The objective of the Brandt and Hood study was to see how well the SVIB predicted vocational choice for men with normal versus deviant MMPI patterns. All told, some 915 such profiles were available. The results indicate that the SVIB is a better predictor of vocational choice for men with "normal" MMPI profiles than for men with deviant profiles. Furthermore, the vocational satisfaction of the "normal" men is greater than that of those classified as deviant. Of course, as in most of the research examining the relationship between personal and vocational adjustment, it is difficult to determine whether vocational maladjustment causes or is caused by, personal maladjustment.

### Summary and Evaluation

Most of the research relating vocational choice and behavior to psychopathology has been conducted at a very simple level. In general, no data exist to suggest a specific relationship between psychopathology and career, though some informed guesses may be made concerning the role occupation may play in exacerbating mental disorder. What does appear to recur in the data is the implication that aesthetic interests in men are associated with personal maladjustment. Whether that observation reflects the attitude of the culture toward men with such interests, or the results of a lifetime of being out of tune with one's contemporaries, or is a manifestation of a rich fantasy life involved in maladjustment remains unclear, but would be a useful area for exploration. The primary implication of the research on psychopathology and career lies in the suggestions it poses for preventive measures along the lines of Roe's (1963) analysis of the personal problems of scientists.

## APTITUDE, INTEREST, PERSONALITY INTERACTIONS IN CAREER

Some interest has been exhibited in the question of which of the three variables, i.e., aptitude, interest, or personality, serves as the best predictor of vocational selection and development, and how the three personal variables interact in terms of a criterion of vocational selection and functioning.

The first question to be raised in examining the issue of aptitude-interest-personality interactions is in connection with the predictive value of interests as a function of the measurement approach that is taken. Super and Crites (1962) have identified four types of interest: manifest, defined in terms of overt behaviors; inventoried, defined in terms of responses to interest inventories such as the Kuder and the SVIB; expressed, defined in terms of activities and vocations people say they like or plan to engage in; and tested, defined in terms of knowledge about specific fields. Dolliver (1969), carefully examining the literature, observes that SVIB interests and expressed interests overlap only modestly. Dolliver notes that although SVIB interests are more reliable than expressed interests, expressed interests have equal or better predictive validity. Such an observation is, at least at first glance, inconsistent, and Dolliver speculates that expressed interests which develop at an early age may be highly predictive of later activities. Overall, Dolliver concludes that there is "no evidence to indicate that inventoried interests are superior to expressed interests." Whitney (1969) goes even further in making a case for the accuracy of expressed interests as predictors of vocational entry. In his review he observes that the "hit" rates for expressed interests are generally as good as inventories, though the criterion categories are necessarily general. It should be noted, however, that while interest inventories may not help the individual who has a clear vocational preference, they do appear to be useful to the individual who isn't sure where he is going and needs some aid to help orient him in his vocational search.

Another potentially confounding aspect of examining the interaction between interests, aptitudes, and personality lies in the limited overlap between educational and vocational interests. Though educational decisions are not identical to vocational decisions, they are frequently treated as if they were the same. A study by Miller and Thomas (1966) indicates that the SVIB scores and scores on an Educational Interest Inventory are highly correlated, but the distinction between the two, small as it is, is important and useful to keep in mind.

*Some studies of performance and personality.* Hansen and Taylor (1970) examined 408 freshman engineering students by means of the ACT, Minnesota Counseling Inventory, Minnesota Scholastic Aptitude Test, and Minnesota Mathematics Test. After one year, the sample was divided into four groups as follows: 56 who withdrew from engineering with better than a C grade point average, 196 who stayed in engineering with better than a C grade point average, 95 who withdrew with less than a C average, and 61 who remained in engineering with less than a C average. A discriminant analysis was performed on the data for each student group, leading to the conclusion that success in engineering is based on ability while continuation is determined by personality attributes. These results are similar to those of Elton and Rose (1967). In sum, the evidence seems to suggest that aptitude determines performance (and possibly success) while personality determines persistence.

Kipnis, Lane, and Berger (1969) studied academic interest, achievement, and impulsiveness in personality style. Kipnis and his associates devised a scale to measure impulsiveness, classified their subjects according to SAT scores, and then assigned the subjects to one of three curricular groups (arts and science, engineering, and business-education-agriculture). All told, 628 subjects were divided into the three curricular groups according to scores on the impulsiveness scale. The results show a relationship between curriculum membership and impulsiveness in high but not low academic ability students. In a second study, 30 business management and 30 mathematics-physics-chemistry students took the impulsiveness scale and the SAT. In this study, the business students were found to be more impulsive than the math-physics-chemistry students; the low impulsive math-physics-chemistry students express more satisfaction with their educational choice than the high impulsive students, an effect which appears to be enhanced by academic aptitude.

In a study designed to investigate the question of whether interest or ability is more important to vocational decision-making in students, Sharf (1970) first required subjects to take a self-ability and self-interest rating inventory which forced the respondents to estimate their ability and interest in 100 occupations. Then the subjects completed a paired comparison task based on the earlier self-estimates, were given feedback regarding their self-ratings, and finally asked to express a preference for one of two occupations. In general, the resulting preferences seemed to reflect interests more than abilities. Sharf suggests these results are consistent with those of Holland and Nichols (1964), Berdie (1955), and Pierson (1962). It should be noted, however, that since there is an important difference between occupational preference and occupational attainment, these results should not be interpreted to imply that in the long run interests are more inportant than abilities in vocational behavior. In fact, Osipow and Scheid (1971) and Osipow (1972) report experimental results indicating that performance feedback of a positive nature in connection with two generally uninteresting tasks influenced preferences for these tasks. At the conclusion of the positive feedback given during the experimental task the originally less preferred of the two tasks became the more preferred.

A number of studies have questioned the relationship between interests and vocational preferences where abilities are marginal. Madaus and O'Hara (1967) concluded that vocational interests differentiate high school occupational preferences better than do personality, aptitude, or value differences. However, Ashby, Wall, and Osipow (1966) found evidence to suggest that aptitude differences affect the *implementation* of preferences more than do interests. Bohn (1968) also found that SAT math scores and high school grades were lower in an undecided group of students than in a group decided about educational-vocational plans, as was interest maturity. Such results could suggest that abilities are taken into account in implementing the decisions that interests might initially encourage. Osipow and Gold (1967) found that second choice occupations seem more inconsistent with first choices when the student is unsure of his ability to implement his first preference: possibly the second choice is based on a different set of abilities than the first as a hedge against failure in the first area of choice.

Overall, viewing the results of research, it is impossible to conclude confidently what the correct proportion of differential impact interests, aptitudes, and personality is upon vocational decisions and implementation. All three seem important; it seems likely that personality may influence the style and persistence of the choice, interests the content, and abilities the attainment.

# PERSONALITY TRAITS AND CAREER

The idea that specific personality traits differentiate people in one occupation from those in another has had appeal for many years and has stimulated considerable research. The rationale underlying the trait-factor approach to the study of personality and career is simple. It is assumed that because of the inherent differences in the roles that occupations require people to play, the ideal personal characteristics of members of various occupational groups vary. At the same time, perhaps recognizing that most people are not rigidly shaped at the time of occupational entry, it is also assumed that exposure to the activities and climate of any given occupation will exert an influence upon an individual's manner of behavior and personality. For example, accountants are often characterized as careful, conservative people, partly because their work requires them to be and partly because careful conservative people are attracted to accounting because of the occupational stereotype. Consequently, the trait-factor approach has as its goal the increasing accuracy of identification of distinctive personality attributes inherent in membership in various careers. The point of view, therefore, is fundamentally research oriented and empirical.

In an early paper, Darley (1941) reviewed the relationship between aptitudes, achievement, personality, and vocational interests. He concluded that business contact interests were correlated with economic conservatism, social aggressiveness, and physical robustness; that technical interests were correlated with immaturity, masculinity, and limited social skill; that men with verbal interests could be construed as feminine, and, relatively speaking, not socially inclined; and that men with welfare interests were mature, socially aggressive, liberal, and slightly feminine. This early study of Darley's was the prototype of research design that has dominated the trait-factor approach to the study of personality and careers for more than 20 years.

The research generally follows one of several formats. A sample, most desirably a vocational one but more frequently composed of students, is tested with respect to interests and personality and is queried about its vocational plans. Statistical comparisons are made between (1) the personality scores of students expressing different vocational preferences or (2) the personality scores of students with differing interest patterns on some interest inventory. Occasionally, an investigator has factor analyzed the resulting data to suggest several dimensions of personality or interest along which subjects expressing interest or preference for various occupations differ.

In effect, the research strategy has been to study all possible variables and their relation to occupational membership or preference in the hope that some connection between occupation and personality traits will become evident. Such an approach is useful in an early stage of investigation about a phenomenon because the research may yield results indicating relationships between variables promising for future study. It has the disadvantage of revealing many spurious relationships by chance and as a result possibly diverting attention from fruitful areas of activity. The "shotgun" approach can retard the theoretical development of a discipline if persisted in too long.

## Trait-Factor Research Methods

With the above caution in mind, we will now turn our attention to the large body of research which has tried to match individual characteristics and occupational possibilities. Four general methods characterize the trait-factor research on personality and career.

*The statistical method* is represented by the prototype of the ultimate of the personality trait approach to career selection and preference, Cattell's studies relating his 16 Personality Factor Questionnaire to occupational membership (Cattell, Day, and Meeland, 1956). Cattell and his associates reported the personality scores earned on the 16 PF by small- to moderate-sized samples of athletes, clerks, cooks, editorial writers, executives, nurses, priests, psychological technicians, salesmen, and teachers. Although the results reflected few occupational differences on individual personality scales, a modified discriminant analysis of the occupational profiles could eventually prove to be useful in identifying the likelihood of any one person's membership in a given occupational group.

More typical of the approach is *the factor analytic method*, exemplified by a study reported by Sternberg (1955). He asked the question: do college students majoring in different fields vary with respect to personality patterns defined in terms of interests, values, and inventories of psychopathology? To answer the question, he administered the Kuder Preference Record, the Allport-Vernon-Lindzey Study of Values, and the MMPI to 270 white, male college students majoring in nine different fields (biochemistry or premedical studies, chemistry, economics, English, history, mathematics, music, political science, and psychology). The subjects were volunteers who had finished two years of general college work and who represented the 60 percent of students, a highly select group, who successfully complete the first two years of college studies. Sternberg factor analyzed the results and identified seven factors, respectively named aesthetic communication versus practical science (I); go-getter versus passive aesthete (II); self-expression through art versus the faith in good works (III); the driven extrovert versus the pure scientist (IV); preoccupation with health (V); quantitative detail versus social welfare (VI); and unnamed, not included in data analysis (VII).

The factors seemed to fall into four academic combinations. The English and music majors scored similarly on factors I, II, III, IV, and VI, reflecting aesthetic preferences, strong tendencies toward emotional maladjustment, interest in idealistic communication with people, and rejection of business and scientific activities and attitudes. The chemistry and mathematics students had scores similar to each other on all the factors, which mirrors interest in scientific, mechanical, and quantitative activities, avoidance of the aesthetic, business contact, and social service activities, and disinterest in interpersonal communication. The biochemical (premedical) and psychology students were similar on factors II, III, and VI, showing strong scientific attitudes in combination with an interest in helping people, plus a fairly strong interest in accumulating power and prestige. Finally, the economics, political science, and history students formed a group similar to each other in some ways. The political science and history majors were similar on factors I and III, while the economics and political science students were similar on factors II and IV. The latter two groups seemed to be responsive to persuasive interests; the economics students were less concerned with social welfare than the political science and history students.

Though Sternberg concluded that significant differences existed in the personality attributes of college students in different majors, the differences were not of a magnitude to permit the prediction of individual personality profiles. In fact, the dimensions he describes are, considering his instruments, very much like the Kuder Preference Record and the Allport-Vernon-Lindzey scores. The SVIB differentiates among students in various college majors in a similar way and can in that sense be construed to be a personality test.

Using *the work setting method*, Miller (1962) took a somewhat different approach to the question of personality traits and career choice. He suggested that the career is best considered in terms of the work setting and work function rather than as a whole unit. Predicting that people in different occupations vary in personality in a way that is relevant to their occupation, he further predicted that the personality differences are more closely related to the differences in work setting than they are to work function and that the differences in personality become more pronounced as one's length of time in the occupation increases. He studied a sample of 50 men in each of three occupations: (1) YMCA business secretaries, (2) YMCA youth workers, and (3) comptrollers. He reasoned that two of these groups are similar to each other in function (the Y secretaries and the comptrollers) and two were similar in setting (the Y secretaries and the Y youth workers). He compared the three groups on 13 selected variables reflecting personal orientation which were drawn from several personality and interest inventories, such as the MMPI, EPPS, SVIB, and so on.

The results reflected significant differences in personality that seemed to be related to the particular occupation of the subject, supporting the first hypothesis. Looking at the way the three groups are paired on responses, Miller found that four variables reflected similarity of personality based on work setting, two variables reflected similarity on work function, one pair reflected similarity on both function and setting, and two pairs reflected no similarity on either function. Thus, the second hypothesis was only partially supported. Comparison of subjects of longer tenure in a field with newcomers indicated no support for the third hypothesis that personality trait differences reflecting occupation become more pronounced as tenure increases.

Finally, a fourth approach to the examination of personality and career, *the clinical method*, is represented in a study by Siegelman and Peck (1960). They proposed to develop and test a theory dealing with the underlying need patterns that exist among diverse vocational groups. The approach was based on several propositions: first, that people possess stable and unique personality need patterns; second, that vocations differ in their job-role requirements; third, that people choose vocations because they believe, consciously or unconsciously, that the job-role requirements of the field they select allow them to satisfy some of their dominant personality needs; and fourth, that the job-role requirements of a vocation best satisfy the dominant personality needs of a certain kind of individual. Finally, Siegelman and Peck assumed that as a consequence of all the previous assumptions, most people in a vocation share a common need pattern which differs from the need patterns characteristic of people in other vocational areas.

The specific hypothesis investigated was that the basic personality need patterns of people in different occupations vary systematically. Sixteen chemistry students (15 doctoral candidates and one senior undergraduate major), 16 career military officers on ROTC duty (eight Army and eight Air Force) who had no less than three years of military experience, and 16 theology students (eleven seniors and five "middlers") comprised the sample. They were administered the following instruments: the Stern Activities Index, which is a needs inventory based on Murray's personality theory and need system; a homemade sentence completion blank about needs; and a biographical data form eliciting information about early life history. In addition, a structured interview was conducted in which the Ss were asked to describe the personality characteristics they considered to be important or unique to members of their occupation.

On the basis of the interview observations, Siegelman and Peck (1960) wrote the following descriptions of each occupational group:

Chemist: curious, imaginative, intellectual, creative, relates to objects, emotionally involved in his work.

Minister: nurturant, personally insecure, feels vocationally inadequate.

Officer: values security, variety in associations and living quarters, is dedicated to his country, accepts responsibility and authority, and is concerned with loyalty and honesty.

On the basis of the data obtained through testing with the Stern Activities Index, the following conclusions were drawn: ministers are high on nurturant, impulsive, and idealistic needs, are introspective, and have a strong vicarious sex interest. Of the three occupational groups they are lowest in practical action and the analysis of natural science interests. The chemists have their highest needs on the analysis of natural and social events, and abstract intelligence, and are lowest in nurturance, impulsiveness, and idealistic action (almost the direct opposite of the ministers). The officers are highest in practical action, compliance, and determination, and lowest in vicarious sex interest, social science analysis, introspection, and abstract intellectualization. Thus, Siegelman and Peck's findings, richer than can be presented here, point suggestively to the coincidence between job roles and personal needs.

## Summary

Four general research approaches to personality and career have been illustrated in this section. One type has tried to identify specific personality traits associated with occupational membership on a purely statistical basis. A second approach uses factor analysis to identify constellations of personality traits that differentiate individuals involved in various educational and vocational activities. The third method rests basically on the study of differences in the work setting, and the fourth approach studies the background and personality attributes of occupational groups in a more clinical way.

## JOB SATISFACTION AND CAREER DEVELOPMENT

Industrial psychologists, and, more recently, vocational psychologists, have shown their interest in assessing job satisfaction in relation to numerous variables (see, for example, the review by Pallone, Hurley, and Rickard, 1971). Notable among the efforts to explain job satisfaction is Herzberg's controversial two-factor theory (Herzberg, Mausner, and Snyderman, 1959; Herzberg, 1966), which postulates that two sources of job satisfaction exist roughly corresponding to intrinsic and extrinsic events. Furthermore, the theory suggests that certain "hygiene" satisfier dimensions exist, whose presence is essential to but not sufficient for job satisfaction. The research concerning Herzberg's theory is too extensive to review here, but some examples of typical findings and their interpretations can be provided. Ewen, Smith, Hulin, and Locke (1966) found that intrinsic satisfaction was more important than extrinsic and seemed to affect extrinsic satisfaction. These findings do not support Herzberg's theory, which would say that if intrinsic satisfiers are present along with extrinsic, the presence of the extrinsic would enhance satisfaction. Hardin (1967) examined job satisfaction and job change from the point of view that job satisfaction is related to the perceived potential rewards of remaining in a job. Hardin also observed how the experiences encountered working toward a goal affect the desire to keep or change jobs, along with the job satisfaction itself. By means of a survey of employees in a medium-sized insurance company, Hardin identified 199 subjects for whom data regarding their desire for change, their job satisfaction, and their readiness for change were available. The results generally, but relatively weakly, support the notion that these two factors (crudely similar though not identical to Herzberg's two factors) are operative in job satisfaction.

Armstrong (1971) tested the Herzberg theory with regard to the importance of context as opposed to the content in combination with occupational level. A comparison of engineers and assemblers revealed that the job content factors are more important to satisfaction than context for members of both occupational levels, another finding inconsistent with Herzberg's formulations. Hulin and Waters (1971) make the point in one study that intrinsic satisfiers seem to predict overall job attitudes effectively and "overall job satisfaction is more predictable than overall job dissatisfaction." Finally, Soliman (1970) has presented a convincing argument showing how the method through which the

Herzberg theory is evaluated will influence whether findings support or contradict the theory. In summary, job satisfaction is an important variable, apparently too complex to study effectively by means of identifying one or two apparently critical dimensions or variables.

## Job Satisfaction and Personal Traits

Lofquist and his associates in the Work Adjustment Project at the University of Minnesota have been developing an approach to the study of job satisfaction and worker adjustment that has implications for career development theory. The approach followed in the program of research directed by Lofquist is a sophisticated trait oriented study, blending needs (these are the traits) together with environmental demands, to predict such career events as satisfaction, effectiveness, and job tenure. Much of the basic thinking and implications of the theory have been summarized in Lofquist and Dawis (1969). In that volume, Lofquist and Dawis present a list of assumptions underlying their approach. These assumptions may be summarized in several sentences. First, people are seen as motivated to fulfill work requirements and have their personal requirements fulfilled by work. The effort of the individual to maintain this "correspondence" is called his "work adjustment," and can systematically be related to job tenure, satisfaction, and effectiveness. The theory concerns itself with defining and explaining the relationships between these various important events. Examples of some of the propositions of the theory are "Satisfaction is a function of the correspondence between the reinforcer system of the work environment and the individual's needs, provided that the individual's abilities correspond with the ability requirements of the work environment," or "Satisfactoriness moderates the functional relationship between satisfaction and need-reinforcer correspondence" (Lofquist and Dawis, 1969, p. 53). A list of nine such propositions is presented, all leading to numerous potential tests of the theory.

The theory is further made operational by the availability of a number of instruments developed in the course of the project. These instruments include the Minnesota Importance Questionnaire, the Minnesota Satisfaction Questionnaire, the Minnesota Satisfactoriness Scales, the Job Description Questionnaire, and a list of occupational reinforcers.

Lofquist and Dawis do not ignore the need to develop applications for their ideas. After all, the theory has grown out of a project that is fundamentally applied in nature. For counseling, the theory would lead to the assessment of client needs, the client's vocational and other problems, his aspirations, personal history, and various ability levels. Taking the information gleaned above into account, a number of potential occupational applications could be generated. The individual would then need to make a series of training or job choices that best conform to his abilities and needs in correspondence with the work environment demands so that work adjustment can be predicted. After job entry, some follow-up is necessary to test the adequacy of the placement. All told, these applications do not sound much different from the tried and true "test them and tell them" approach used by trait-factor counselors for years, except that the blend of ingredients of the Lofquist-Dawis approach includes needs, whereas these have tended to be ignored by most other trait-oriented writers in the past.

Considerable research has been conducted on the instruments and the concepts that have grown from the theory. Here only a sample of some studies and their results can be presented, but these will provide a taste of what has been done and what might be done in the context of this approach.

Tinsley and Weiss (1971) have studied the validity of various methods of measuring job reinforcers. The perceived job reinforcers of 338 supervisors were compared with those of 381 supervisees with the finding that the occupational reinforcer patterns of the two groups are generally similar; some differences were found with regard to extrinsic reinforcers, and less agreement between supervisors and supervisees was found between the two groups regarding reinforcers for lower level jobs.

Betz (1971) predicted that job satisfaction moderates job success expected on the basis of high ability scores. Betz studied 352 assemblers divided into high, middle, and low job satisfaction groups according to sex on the basis of the Minnesota Satisfaction Questionnaire; abilities had been assessed in another context. Job success was determined by production and by supervisor evaluation. The results of her study tend to support the prediction that success is determined by abilities but moderated by job satisfaction. In another study, Betz (1969) tested the hypothesis that job satisfaction can be predicted in terms of agreement between needs and satisfiers. She administered the Minnesota Importance Questionnaire and the Minnesota Job Description Questionnaire to 186 store employees. The hypothesis was supported for some personnel (cashiers and sales clerks) but not for others (checkers and markers).

Gay and Weiss (1970) tested the hypothesis that work experience is related to vocational needs. The subjects were 1620 vocational rehabilitation clients (1180 men and 440 women) who took the Minnesota Importance Questionnaire. Since 12 out of 20 predictions were supported, Gay and Weiss conclude that work experience tends to be associated with specific vocational needs.

### Evaluation

It is too soon to assess thoroughly the adequacy and impact of the work adjustment theory. On the positive side the theory is well instrumented, its propositions are easily open to test, and its concepts relatively straightforward and simple. On the negative side, it is not yet clear whether the approach leads logically to any systematic counseling or program interventions.

# THE PERSONALITY TRAITS OF SPECIAL
# OCCUPATIONAL GROUPS

The trait-oriented approach to career choice and membership is, at least in part, related to Davis' (1965) "birds of a feather" hypothesis, which assumes that mebers of an occupational group exhibit increasingly homogeneous personality traits over time, leading to the possibility that the differentiation of potential occupational persisters versus occupational defectors is technically feasible. The "birds of a feather" hypothesis is controversial, however, as witnessed by Watley and Werts' (1969) data indicating that at least in their study, the hypothesis does not hold. Watley and Werts suggest that one flaw in the hypothesis is that it focuses on one trait at a time whereas in the real world occupational members exhibit a multitude of traits, the combination of which is likely to be significant, not the possession of a single trait.

To give the reader some flavor for the range and content of personality studies of occupational groups, this section is devoted to a summary of a number of studies in which the personality traits of delimited career groups were studied.

### Engineers and Scientists

Table 6.1 summarizes some of the principal findings of several studies of engineers and physical scientists. Generally, the findings, though employing different terms from one study to the next, exhibit a striking degree of agreement in their descriptions of people in engineering or scientific occupations. Most vivid is the preference of technical people to work with impersonal objects and avoid interpersonal conflict and, perhaps as a result, generate the appearance of psychological health.

Three general comments about these studies are in order because they recur in the other studies described later in this section. The use of the MMPI in the Thumin (1951) study carries with it the problem of the relevance of the use of an instrument to assess psychopathology to the study of "normal" individuals. All the scores reported by Thumin, for both groups, were in the normal range. A question is raised on what normal scores on the MMPI reveal about human behavior. Second, comparing engineers with physical scientists, as in the Korn study (1962), is likely to paint a different picture of engineers than a comparison of engineers with advertising men, as in the Thumin (1951) study. Personality attributes may be minimized or maximized, depending upon what comparison group is used. Finally, the use of student groups in this research tends to reduce the clarity of the differences found because an engineering freshman may graduate as a liberal arts prelaw major. Student samples are too unstable to be relied upon.

**TABLE 6.1 Personality Traits of Engineers and Scientists**

| Investigator | Subjects | Method | Findings |
|---|---|---|---|
| Izard (1960) | engineers compared with men in general | EPPS | engineers earned high scores on needs achievement, deference, order, dominance, and endurance, and low scores on needs affiliation, intraception, succorance, abasement, nurturance, and heterosexuality |
| Harrison et al. (1955) | engineers | | emotionally stable, free of psychopathology, uninterested in people, insensitive, unimaginative, and not introspective, goal-oriented, energetic, serious, conscientious, self-sufficient, and straightforward |
| Steiner (1953); Moore and Levy (1951) | engineers | | authoritative, independent, self-directing, orderly, object-oriented, tense, irritable, possessing few friendships, and possessing a positive attitude toward authority |
| Thumin (1951) | engineers vs. advertising men | MMPI | engineers lower on psychopathic deviant, masculinity-femininity, paranoia, psychasthenic, and schizophrenic scales and higher on the social introversion scale. The *shape* of the profiles for the two groups was the same |
| Korn (1962) | engineering vs. physical science students | CPI | physical science students higher on femininity, capacity for status, responsibility, achievement through independence, and flexibility and lower on sociability, social presence, and communality |
| Nadler and Krulee (1961) | engineering students | questionnaire | found to be exoathecting-extraceptive. |
| Roe (1961) | eminent scientists | interviews and tests | oriented to action, independent, self-sufficient, like to bring about order out of disorder, tolerant of ambiguity, have strong egos, not highly compulsive, have strong impulse control, low intensity in interpersonal relations, not gregarious, preoccupied with things rather than people, and take calculated risks with natural, not interpersonal, events |

For a more detailed review of studies of the personality of engineers as well as speculation about their personality development, the reader is referred to Beall and Bordin (1964).

## Health Professions

As might be expected, the personality of people in the health professions has had a major share of attention, since personal characteristics are presumed to be particularly critical to the effectiveness of medical people. Several studies of student nurses, dentists, physicians, and students in other general health professions are summarized in Table 6.2. Once again, the data seem consistent from one study to the next, in those permitting comparison. Nursing students generally seem unsure of themselves and passive, though there is some indication (Healy and Borg, 1951) that as they enter the profession, those with grossly inadequate personality traits are excluded. The others in medicine and related fields generally seem to be well adjusted and healthy.

## Artists

Several studies describing artists are summarized in Table 6.3. Artists are consistently found to be independent, relatively unconcerned with approval and status, creative, and emotionally passive.

## Actors

The results of studies describing the personality organization of actors are summarized in Table 6.4. Drawing mainly from Taft's data (1961), there appear to be very substantial differences between the personality traits of male and female theatrical people. The males seemed more feminine than typical males, whereas the females, though feminine in manner, had many culturally masculine attitudes, such as the desire to control and manipulate others. Generally, the actors and actresses seemed to be impulsive, emotionally unstable, insensitive to others, exhibitionistic, and in the case of males, frequently homosexual or homosexually oriented. In other words, Taft found that the personality of theatrical people conformed to the stereotype in many respects.

## Theological Students

Childers and White (1966) studied 72 male theological seniors and graduate students, looking for personality differences between those who were planning careers as pastors, missionaries, or in religious eduction. The Cattell 16 PF Test, the Marlowe-Crowne Social Desirability Scale, and a Personal Data Sheet were administered. No differences in personality were found among the three groups. Compared with the general norms for the 16 PF Test, some differences did

**TABLE 6.2. Personality Characteristics of People in the Health Professions**

| Investigator | Subjects | Method | Findings |
|---|---|---|---|
| Gynther and Gertz (1962) | nursing students with high school and college girls | EPPS | nursing students were lower on needs exhibition, autonomy, dominance, and change, and higher on needs order and endurance; nurses are timid, see themselves as unfeminine, and have strong guilt feelings |
| Kirk et al. (1963) | dental students, dentists, dental school faculty, and aspiring dental students denied admission | CPI; SVIB | dentists were found to be conforming, conventional, impersonal, insensitive, and unconsciously aggressive |
| Anderson and Barry (1965) | students in occupational therapy, physical therapy, medical technology, or general health professions | MMPI | no differences were found on the MMPI for these groups |
| Cleveland (1961) | student nurses and dietetic interns | TAT | nurses were passive, nonachievement-oriented, emotional, melancholy, depressed, had tense parental relations, and identified with sickness and the underdog; dieticians were status and achievement-oriented, confident, felt superior, and exhibited intellectual curiosity |
| Furst et al. (1962) | nursing students | TAT | in nurses whose needs were fulfilled in the profession, there seemed to be a strong desire to serve others |
| Healy and Borg (1951) | nurses, nursing students, and non-nursing students | Guilford-Martin Personality Inventory | no clear-cut personality pattern for nursing students emerged; graduate nurses were found to be confident, emotionally stable, cheerful, optimistic, agreeable, cooperative, and objective |

| | | | |
|---|---|---|---|
| Schofield (1953a and b) | medical students and general undergraduates | MMPI | profiles of the two groups were similar; medical students showed general reduction of confidence and enthusiasm as they progressed through school |
| McDonald (1962) | medical students | Leary's Interpersonal Check List | medical students described selves as healthy, responsible, and generous |
| Muhlenkamp and Parsons (1972) | nurses in general | literature review | commonly seek helping role, are submissive and dependent, religious, not economically oriented, and conform to female stereotype |
| Hogan (1971a) | nursing students | Adorno F scale Symbolic Test for Authoritarianism, Biographical Questionnaire | compared with other undergraduate females and prison guards, nursing students appear authoritarian |
| Bolton and Seres (1970) | nurses, occupational therapists, social workers, psychologists (female) | behavioral personality via communication in staff relations | nurses lowest in interpersonal contact on 5 of 6 scales |
| Frank and Kirk (1970) | dental hygiene students | California Psychological Inventory | dental hygienists found to be "psychologically strong, well adjusted, outgoing socially" |

**TABLE 6.3. Personality Traits of Artists**

| Investigator | Subject | Method | Findings |
| --- | --- | --- | --- |
| Roe (1946) | outstanding artists | Rorschach | artists were observed to be sensitive, nonaggressive, emotionally passive, hard working, self-disciplined, and of superior intellect |
| Spiaggia (1950) | art and nonart students | MMPI | art students higher on depression, psychopathic deviant, paranoia, psychasthenia, schizophrenia, and hypomania scales (all within normal range) |
| Munsterberg and Mussen (1953) | art and nonart students | TAT; questionnaire | artists had more parental conflict, more guilt feelings, were more introverted, and less willing to conform to parental standards, had less need for personal success and acceptance, and were less overtly aggressive than nonart students |
| Phillips (1963) | art teachers at different levels | Media-preferences Personaltiy Inventory; Teacher Preference Schedule | elementary art teachers described selves as humorous, unselfish, least skilled artistically, least independent, least likely to produce salable art, cynical, hard-headed and demanding, most informal, nurturant, and nondirective in method; junior high art teachers were most independent creatively, highly oriented toward status, and cynical, sarcastic, demanding, self-centered, hard-headed, and least humorous; senior high art teachers were creative and produced considerable salable art; college art teachers were highly formal, nondirective in method, and preferred to work with adults rather than adolescents |
| Irvin (1968) | student artists vs. student architects (all male) | Sentence Completion Test | student artists see selves as more isolated than student architects, have more negative reactions to parents; architecture students have more positive peer relations, are more achievement-oriented, and are more enthusiastic about school than art students |

**TABLE 6.4. Personality Traits of Actors**

| Investigator | Subjects | Method | Findings |
|---|---|---|---|
| Stacey and Goldberg (1953) | actors, active theater students, inactive theater students | Guilford STDCR | active drama students were found to be less socially withdrawn than the other two groups and more extroverted than the inactive art students, who were more extroverted than the professionals; the last mentioned earned higher depression scores than the active students whose depression scores were higher than the inactive students; the active students were most inhibited and controlled, the inactive students least controlled |
| Taft (1961) | dancers, singers, actors, directors, nondrama students | MMPI, intelligence test, biographical inventory, interviews | male actors scored lower on MMPI scales for lying and presenting self in a good light, social responsibility, ego strength, role playing, leadership potential, and higher on validity, depression, femininity, psychasthenia, schizophrenia, manic anxiety, neuroticism, feminine masochism, and self-control; actresses lower on social responsibility and higher on depression, psychopathic deviancy, psychasthenia, and self-control |

emerge, however. The theological students as a whole seemed more persistent, conscientious, serious, introspective, desurgent, sensitive, gentle, and dependent, and showed a higher need for social approval on the Marlowe-Crowne Scale.

Strunk (1959) studied the SVIB scores and the Bell Adjustment Inventory performance of 60 pretheological students, using 50 freshmen enrolled in a business administration program as a control group. The only two characteristics found to be distinctive of preministerial Ss were their greater social aggressiveness and femininity.

Barry and Bordin (1967) collected data about clergymen by means of various tests, surveys, and autobiographies. On the basis of these sources they conclude that the minister is introspective, idealistic, service oriented, and somewhat "feminine" in his orientation. Critical developmental features were seen to be a weak or absent father, a domineering mother, and an exposure to an influential clergyman. Nauss (1968) tested the Barry and Bordin observations more systematically on a sample of 371 graduating clergymen. Nauss found about 75 percent of these men classified as extroverted on the Myers-Briggs. In general, Nauss claims that the results of his study and others do not show clergy to be more intuitive and introspective than others. Byers, Forrest, and Zaccaria (1968) predicted that clergy would differ from a comparison group in their recall of early parent-childhood relationships. In addition, Byers et al. predicted that clergy needs (measured via the EPPS) would differ from those of a comparison group, and that their recall of relations with parents and the adult needs of the clergy would be related (via the Family Relations Inventory of Brunkan and Crites). The results indicate that needs differences on the EPPS from the comparison group do exist, as predicted, and that more recollection of "father avoidance" was noted on the Family Relations Inventory among clergymen than others.

### Businessmen

De Coster and Rhode (1972) found differences on the California Psychological Inventory between younger and older CPA's. The question might legitimately be raised as to whether certain types of people leave occupations as they age because they do not fit in, whether most occupational members change to conform to a model set by their elders, or whether the occupation itself is changing and, thus, the personality of those now attracted to it is different from those who have been engaged in the field for years. The only way to answer this question is to follow up new entering members of an occupation and see who persists and who leaves in terms of personality attributes. It might be noted, however, that the updating of the SVIB has revealed a remarkable stability in at least the interests of individuals attracted to occupations over several decades (Campbell, 1966). De Coster and Rhode have wisely pointed out that it is important to attend to subgroups within a field when considering personality traits, since there may be important differences in the personality characteristics of such groups.

Harrell (1970) administered a variety of personality and interest inventories to seven classes in a graduate school of business. Following up these students five years later (with a response rate of 90 percent), he compared the personality traits of the top versus the bottom third in income. Nine of 55 predictors were found to be significant at the .05 level of confidence. Such a degree of differentiation is not impressive, though one trait (ascendence) was also found to discriminate high versus low earners in big business in another study (Harrell, 1969).

Scott and Day (1972), studying 148 graduate students in business administration with the Adjective Check List, found three factors, i.e., general adjustment, self-assertiveness, and ego control. These factors, in turn, were differentially correlated with the basic interest scales of the SVIB. Self-assertiveness was positively correlated with interests in public speaking, law-politics, business management, sales, merchandising, military activities, technical responsibility, mathematics, mechanical, adventure, and recreational leadership. Ego control was also found to be significantly correlated with a number of basic interests, though the general adjustment scores were not. Two conclusions might be drawn from Scott and Day's results: basic interests in leadership and business types of activities may be significantly related to one of the basic factors of the ACL; second, as Scott and Day pointed out, a wide range of vocations may be potentially appropriate for a given personality type, an observation which occurs repeatedly throughout the literature on personality and career.

## Teachers

The several studies of the personality traits of teachers or education students reveal strikingly similar results. The findings are summarized in Table 6.5. The data indicate that, in general, teachers are not highly motivated toward achievement, but rather that they are steady individuals, people who like stable, predictable lives, and who enjoy identifying with institutions and groups. In addition, they appear to be socially oriented, as is to be expected.

## Some College Student Groups

Trait-oriented research has been conducted along curricular lines similar to that done on vocationally oriented groups. Elton (1967) administered the Omnibus Personality Inventory to students in a variety of majors, performed a discriminant analysis, and found numerous personality differences. For example, he found that the administration, political, and "persuasive" field students were lower on "masculine role" than the engineering, agriculture, and technology students. Business and finance students scored higher on tolerance and autonomy than engineering, scientific, agriculture, technology, and medically oriented students, and lower on tolerance and autonomy than arts and humanities students. Undecided students scored higher on masculine role than arts and humanities students and were higher on social introversion than administration, polit-

TABLE 6.5. Personality Traits of Teachers

| Investigator | Subjects | Method | Findings |
|---|---|---|---|
| Kuhlen (1963) | teachers | EPPS; questionnaires; satisfaction ratings; persistence in job. | female teachers high on need succorance, all teachers high on need endurance |
| Kuhlen and Dipboye (1959) | college upper-classmen in various majors | interest and personality inventories | male education students high on needs nurturance, deference, and abasement, and low on needs achievement, autonomy, and change; female elementary teaching students lower in needs achievement and change and higher in needs order, affiliation and nurturance than female secondary education students |
| Merwin and Di Vesta (1959) | college freshmen | needs scales; perceived instrumentality measure | nonteaching students had higher needs achievement, dominance, and exhibition and education students were higher on need affiliation |
| Martin and Bendig (1961) | college freshmen and sophomores | EPPS | male and female education students were higher on achievement and lower on "obsessive-compulsive needs;" females in education were also higher in social dependency needs |
| Gray (1963) | teachers, accountants, and mechanical engineers | EPPS; Miller Occupational Values Indicator | teachers were higher on needs deference, affiliation, intraception, abasement, and nurturance, and lower on endurance, exhibition, order, dominance, and endurance and higher on achievement, intraception, succorance, and nurturance than the engineers; on the Values Indicator accountants were higher on prestige than engineers, and teachers lower on career satisfaction and prestige and higher on social rewards than both other groups |
| Kuhlen and Dipboye (1959) | college upper-classmen in various majors | interest and personality inventories | education students were lowest of all on manifest anxiety scale and most feminine (both male and female) in their style |

ical, and "persuasive" students. In another study using the Omnibus Personality Inventory, Elton and Rose (1967) compared students who left engineering curricula with those who remained; the findings indicate that those who move to arts and science appear mature and scholarly, those who move to commerce look mature and practical, and those who remain in engineering appear to be relatively immature and were midway between a practical and scholarly orientation. (It should be noted that maturity on the Omnibus Personality Inventory is defined in terms of degree of interpersonal orientation.)

Sherrick administered the flexibility scale of the California Psychological Inventory to 118 seniors in arts and science, and compared the flexibility scores of 73 social science with 45 physical science majors. Social science majors were seen to be more flexible than physical science students. Interestingly, satisfaction with college major is greater for those social science majors who have high flexibility scores but higher for those physical science students who have low flexibility scores. These results suggest the existence of an important interaction between personality and environment in determining suitability for educational (and possibly vocational) programs.

One additional study of interest dealing with college student personality according to major is reported by Goldschmid (1967). Goldschmid developed a means to identify personality traits in various categories of behavior (e.g., Orientation to Life, Mode of Adjustment and Psychological Functioning, Interest Pattern, Behavior in Social Context, and Mode of Cognitive Functioning) descriptive of student functioning according to science enrollment as opposed to humanities.

### Some Miscellaneous Groups

Table 6.6 summarizes the results of other studies investigating the personality traits of a variety of occupational groups. No generalizations may be drawn from these findings beyond pointing out that it is apparently not difficult to find statistical differences between scores on specific scales of personality tests for different occupational group members.

Two additional studies are not included in the table but are of interest. Daniels and Hunter (1949) administered the MMPI to men in 26 different occupations. The data would be extremely interesting were it not for two limitations: no statistical analysis was reported comparing the profiles, and second, some of the occupations studied were represented by samples as small as three or four people, and even the largest samples were not very large. These limitations make generalized personality statements about the men in the 26 careers studied impossible to express.

A study by Rosenberg (1957), described in detail earlier, touched on some personality aspects of career preference. He found that 43 percent of the students who preferred people oriented careers can be considered to be compliant and 24 percent of them as aggressive and detached from others, whereas 32

TABLE 6.6. Personality Traits of Miscellaneous Occupational Groups

| Investigator | Subjects | Method | Findings |
|---|---|---|---|
| Verniaud (1946) | women clerical department store and factory workers | MMPI | clerical workers least hypochondriachal, saleswomen most masculine, and factory workers most hypomanic, paranoid, psychopathic, and psychasthenic |
| Dunnette and Kirchner (1960) | retail and industrial salesmen | EPPS | retail salesmen higher on need order and lower on need affiliation than industrial salesmen |
| Marks et al. (1962) | persisting vs. withdrawing journalism students | Bernreuter Personality Inventory | persistent males were more stable and less self-sufficient than other males; persistent females were more self-sufficient than other females |
| Chambers (1964) | creative and average chemists and psychologists | various inventories | psychologists seen as more Bohemian, introverted, unconventional, imaginative, creative, rebellious, and socially oriented than chemists |
| Winick (1964) | embalmers and butchers | MMPI and Kuder Preference Record | embalmers were higher on validity, hypochondriasis, depression, hysteria, psychopathic deviant, femininity, psychasthenia, and schizophrenia scales and lower on paranoia scale; all scores within normal range |
| Wiener and Simon (1950) | embalmers | MMPI | scores within the normal range |
| Kuhlen and Dipboye (1959) | college upperclassmen in various fields | various inventories | liberal arts women and engineering men were the most masculine; male business students highest on general activity, ascendancy, and sociability while engineering students were lowest on these; elementary education students were highest on sociability, objectivity, friendliness, and personal relations while liberal arts women were lowest for women on these |

| Study | Sample | Instrument | Findings |
|---|---|---|---|
| Gunderson and Nelson (1966) | Navy administrators, technical, mechanical, construction, electrical, and kitchen personnel, all Antarctic volunteers | FIRO-B; AVL; other surveys | administrative and technical personnel were concerned with social participation and career achievement, while other groups were rigid and conforming interpersonally and showed a greated need for support |
| Donnan and Harlan (1968) | counselors vs. administrators | 16 PF | counselors more emotional, unstable, casual, undependable, trusting, adaptable, forthright and natural, and less tough-minded and realistic |
| Walsh and Palmer (1970) | random undergrads, pre-law students, 1st- and 3rd-year law students | EPPS | generally no substantial differences |
| Hogan (1971b) | prison guards | Adorno F scale, attitude and job satisfaction scales | high authoritarianism scores |
| Johansson (1970) | various groups | Occupational extroversion scale of the SVIB | physicists, farmers, astronomers tended toward introversion, while salesmen, governors, and Chamber of Commerce executives tended to be extroverted |

percent of those preferring careers providing extrinsic gratification were aggressive and 20 percent detached and compliant. Thirty percent of those who preferred expressive careers were detached from others and only 14 percent compliant and aggressive. These data clearly lead to the inference that people in each of the three kinds of careers have a characteristic personal style which differentiates them from those in the others.

### Summary and Evaluation

The many studies of personality traits and occupational membership or potential membership typically involve an objectively scored personality inventory or a projective test of personality that is administered to a student sample (occasionally an occupational sample). The scores are then compared to those of either a control group of people who represent no particular occupation, or to those of a group of people representative of another career field, or to test norms. Ordinarily, it is assumed that occupational membership results from personality factors rather than the reverse, though some few investigators have considered the latter possibility.

Several major shortcomings of these procedures come to mind. Reports of replications of trait-factor studies are few. The personality measures employed have serious limitations, and inferences drawn from responses to those inventories may have questionable validity. Most of the instruments have a psychopathological basis which is usually inappropriate and inadequate for the understanding of normal behavior. The sampling represented in these studies is very limited. The results of personality tests based on students who are considering majoring in various academic fields, or correlating personality test scores with interest inventory scores, are procedures very far removed from the observation of personality differences in members of diverse occupational groups, a practice that is extremely rare. In fairness to the investigators, however, the use of student groups is likely to work against the discovery of spurious relationships between personality and career, since the student groups presumably are not as "pure" personality types as would be found in a professional group beyond the screening of the training or education required for vocational entrance.

Super and Bachrach (1957) have pointed out the futility of looking for personality trait differences in members of different occupations because too much overlap exists, and the occupations tolerate a wide range of personality differences among their members. It is likely to be more profitable to look for factors which influence the sequences of career decisions that people make, which seems to be precisely what the personality style approach, discussed earlier, tries to do. Until an extensive effort is made to analyze occupations functionally and to develop highly sophisticated tests of both personality and aptitude, no serious attempt to match people and careers with a simplistic trait-factor method is likely to be highly successful. Most of our psychometric devices are based on groups and are useful in predicting behavior of extreme members of those groups, but fall down sharply in their accuracy when dealing with the majority of individuals who fall in the middle probability ranges. How meaningful is it to tell a young man that he has seven chances in ten to succeed in engineering and five in ten to be a teacher when we do not weigh his desire to be one or the other? It is well to recall that personality tests will frequently fail to generate stable correlations with anything but other personality tests and frequently cannot even perform the task for which they were devised, namely, the differentiation of personally maladjusted people from normals, before we bring them into an arena for which they were never intended (Vernon, 1964).

## SUMMARY

In this chapter five aspects of personality and career have been examined, namely, the role of personal values in career development, psychological needs structure in occupational choice, the interaction between disordered behavior and career choice and functioning, personal style and career behavior, and the personality trait-factor approach to occupational behavior. None of these approaches has been integrated into a cohesive theoretical approach to occupational behavior; rather, each stands for a stream of research or a fragment of an idea concerning some aspect of occupational behavior. A major purpose of this chapter has been to sketch the rationale underlying each of these approaches more clearly in order to facilitate the development of more elaborate theorizing representing these streams of thought.

Each of the streams of thought described in this chapter has flaws. The study of psychopathology and career provides interesting data and is potentially highly valuable in the field of rehabilitation of mentally disordered individuals. Unfortunately, most of the pertinent data do not clearly relate psychopathology with career. The trait-factor approach to personality and career has many problems associated with it. In view of the changing nature of people in various careers, the weaknesses of personality tests, and the similarity of personality traits necessary for success and entry in a variety of careers, there would seem to be little hope that such an approach can lead to fruitful understanding of career behavior. All in all, the trait-factor approach is relative. When musicians are compared with other musicians, subtle differences may be observed, but these differences become academic when musicians are compared with artists. It is hardly meaningful to discuss the personality traits of artists as compared to those of musicians when in fact, the two groups are highly homogeneous when compared with engineers. To further compound the problem, so much overlap exists between the traits observed between members of various careers as to make the individual prediction of membership in a vocational group on the basis of personality variables a highly inaccurate activity. Similar criticisms may be applied to the conception of the role played by values and psychological needs in career selection and behavior.

The personality style approach is the richest conceptually, but supporting data are inconsistent. Currently, it offers few applications to counseling, but ultimately it is likely to lead to more comprehensive understandings of vocational behavior in the context of human development than the other approaches discussed in this chapter.

# REFERENCES

Anderson, H. E., Jr., and Barry, J. R. Occupational choices in selected health professions. *Personnel and Guidance Journal*, 1965, *46*, 177-184.

Anderson, W. F., and Bosworth, D. L. A note on occupational values of ninth grade students of 1958 as compared to 1970. *Journal of Vocational Behavior*, 1971, *1*, 301-303.

Anderson, W. F., and Dipboye, W. J. Occupational values and post-high school plans. *Vocational Guidance Quarterly*, 1959, *8*, 37-40.

Armatas, J. P., and Collister, E. G. Personality correlates of SVIB patterns. *Journal of Counseling Psychology*, 1962, *9*, 149-154.

Armstrong, T. B. Job content and context factors related to satisfaction for different occupational levels. *Journal of Applied Psychology*, 1971, *55*, 57-65.

Ashby, J. D., Wall, H. W., and Osipow, S. H. Vocational certainty and indecision in college freshmen. *Personnel and Guidance Journal*, 1966, *44*, 1037-1041.

Astin, A., and Nichols, R. C. Life goals and vocational choice. *Journal of Applied Psychology*, 1964, *48*, 50-58.

Atkinson, J. W. Motivational determinants of risk-taking behavior. *Psychological Review*, 1957, *64*, 359-372.

Baird, L. L. The relation of vocational interests to life goals, self-ratings of ability and personality traits, and potential for achievement. *Journal of Educational Measurement*, 1970, 7, 233-239.

Barahal, G. D. Personality problems and vocational planning. *Personnel and Guidance Journal*, 1953, *31*, 224-226.

Barry, W. A., and Bordin, E. S. Personality development and the vocational choice of the ministry. *Journal of Counseling Psychology*, 1967, *14*, 395-402.

Beall, L., and Bordin, E. S. The development and personality of engineers. *Personnel and Guidance Journal*, 1964, *43*, 23-32.

Berdie, R. F. Likes, dislikes, and vocational interests. *Journal of Applied Psychology*, 1943, *27*, 180-189.

Berdie, R. F. Aptitude, achievement, interest, and personality tests: a longitudinal comparison. *Journal of Applied Psychology*, 1955, *39*, 103-114.

Betz, Ellen L. Need-reinforcer correspondence as a predictor of job satisfaction. *Personnel and Guidance Journal*, 1969, *47*, 878-883.

Betz, Ellen L. An investigation of job satisfaction as a moderator variable in predicting job success. *Journal of Vocational Behavior*, 1971, *1*, 123-128.

Blum, S. H. The desire for security: an element in the vocational choice of college men. *Journal of Educational Psychology*, 1961, *52*, 317-321.

Bodden, J. L. Cognitive complexity as a factor in appropriate vocational choice. *Journal of Counseling Psychology*, 1970, *17*, 364-368.

Bohn, M. J., Jr. Psychological needs related to personality types. *Journal of Counseling Psychology*, 1966, *13*, 306-309.

Bohn, M. J., Jr. Vocational indecision and interest development in college freshmen. *Journal of College Student Personnel*, 1968, *9*, 393-396.

Bolton, B., and Seres, Margaret. Behavioral-personality differences among occupations: the health related professions. *Experimental Publication System*, Dec., 1970, *9*, Ms. No. 312-6.

Bradshaw, H. H., Jr. Need satisfaction and job level in a professional hierarchy. *Experimental Publication System*, 1970, 7, Ms. No. 264-1.

Brandt, J. E., and Hood, A. B. Effect of personality adjustment on the predictive validity of the Strong Vocational Interest Blank. *Journal of Counseling Psychology*, 1968, *15*, 547-551.

Broverman, D. M. Generality and behavioral correlates of cognitive style. *Journal of Consulting Psychology*, 1964, *28*, 487-500.

Broverman, D. M., Broverman, Inge K., Vogel, W., and Palmer, R. D. The automatization cognitive style and physical development. *Child Development*, 1964, *35*, 1343-1359.

Burnstein, E. Fear of failure, achievement motivation, and aspiring to prestigeful occupations. *Journal of Abnormal and Social Psychology*, 1963, *67*, 189-193.

Byers, A. P., Forrest, G. G., and Zaccaria, J. S. Recalled early parent-child relations, adult needs, and occupational choice. *Journal of Counseling Psychology*, 1968, *15*, 324-328.

Campbell, D. P. *Manual for the Strong Vocational Interest Blank*. Stanford, California: Stanford University Press, 1966.

Carnes, C. D. Vocational interest characteristics of abnormal personalities. *Journal of Counseling Psychology*, 1964, *11*, 272-279.

Cattell, R. B., Day, M., and Meeland, T. Occupational profiles on the 16 Personality Factor Questionnaire. *Occupational Psychology*, 1956, *30*, 10-19.

Centers, R. *The psychology of social class*. Princeton, New Jersey: Princeton University Press, 1949.

Chambers, J. A. Relating personality and biographical factors to scientific creativity. *Psychological Monographs*, 1964, *78*, No. 7 (Whole No. 584).

Childers, R. D., and White, W. F. The personality of select theological students. *Personnel and Guidance Journal*, 1966, *44*, 507-510.

Cleveland, S. Personality patterns associated with the professions of dietician and nurse. *Journal of Health and Human Behavior*, 1961, *2*, 113-124.

Couch, A., and Keniston, K. Yeasayers and naysayers: agreeing response set as a personality variable. *Journal of Abnormal and Social Psychology*, 1960, *60*, 151-174.

Daniels, E. E., and Hunter, W. A. MMPI personality patterns for various occupations. *Journal of Applied Psychology*, 1949, *33*, 559-565.

Darley, J. G. A study of the relationships among the primary mental abilities test, selected achievement measures, personality tests, and tests of vocational interests. In *Studies of higher education*. Minneapolis: University of Minnesota Press, 1941.

Darley, J.G. and Hagenah, Theda. *Vocational interest measurement: theory and practice*. Minneapolis: University of Minnesota Press, 1955.

Davis, J. A. *Great aspirations: volume one. Career decisions and educational plans during college* (Report No. 90). Chicago: National Opinion Research Center, March, 1965.

De Coster, D. T., and Rhode, J. G. Analysis of certified public accounting subgroup and accounting student personality traits using the CPI. *Journal of Vocational Behavior*, 1972, *2*, 155-162.

Dipboye, W. J., and Anderson, W. F. The ordering of occupational values by high school freshmen and seniors. *Personnel and Guidance Journal*, 1959, *38*, 121-124.

Dipboye, W. J., and Anderson, W. F. Occupational stereotypes and manifest needs. *Journal of Counseling Psychology*, 1961, *8*, 296-304.

Dole, A. A., and Passons, W. R. Life goals and plan determinants reported by black and white high school seniors. *Journal of Vocational Behavior*, 1972, *2*, 209-222.

Dolliver, R. H. An adaptation of the Tyler Vocational Card Sort. *Personnel and Guidance Journal*, 1965, *45*, 916-920.

Dolliver, R. H. Strong Vocational Interest Blank versus expressed vocational interests: a review. *Psychological Bulletin*, 1969, *72*, 95-107.

Donnan, H. H., and Harlan, G. Personality of counselors and administrators. *Personnel and Guidance Journal*, 1968, *47*, 228-232.

Drasgow, J., and Carkhuff, R. R. Kuder neuropsychiatric keys before and after psychotherapy. *Journal of Counseling Psychology*, 1964, *11*, 67-69.

Dunkleberger, C. J., and Tyler, Leona E. Interest stability and personality traits. *Journal of Counseling Psychology*, 1961, *8*, 70-74.

Dunnette, M. O., and Kirchner, W. K. Psychological test differences between industrial salesmen and retail salesmen. *Journal of Applied Psychology*, 1960, *44*, 121-125.

Elton, C. F. Male career role and vocational choice: their prediction with personality and aptitude variables. *Journal of Counseling Psychology*, 1967, *14*, 99-105.

Elton, C. F., and Rose, Harriet. Personality of engineering students who transfer out of engineering. *Personnel and Guidance Journal*, 1967, *45*, 911-915.

Ewen, R. B., Smith, Patricia, Hulin, C. L., and Locke, E. A. An empirical test of the Herzberg two-factor theory. *Journal of Applied Psychology*, 1966, *50*, 544-550.

Frank, A. C., and Kirk, Barbara A. Characteristics of dental hygiene students. *Vocational Guidance Quarterly*, 1970, *18*, 207-211.

Fretz, B. R. Occupational values as discriminants of preprofessional student groups. *Journal of Vocational Behavior*, 1972, *2*, 233-237.

Furst, E. J., Raygor, A. W., and Crofoot, A. P. Basic motivation and concept of nursing as chosen profession. *Journal of Psychology*, 1962, *54*, 85-100.

Gay, E. G., and Weiss, D. J. Relationship of work experience and measured vocational needs. *Proceedings, 78th Annual Convention, American Psychological Association*, 1970.

Gobetz, W. Suggested personality implications of Kuder Preference Record (vocational) scores. *Personnel and Guidance Journal*, 1964, *43*, 159-166.

Goldschmid, M. L. Prediction of college majors by personality tests. *Journal of Counseling Psychology*, 1967, *14*, 302-308.

Gordon, L. V., and Mensh, I. N. Values of medical school students at different levels of training. *Journal of Educational Psychology*, 1962, *53*, 48-51.

Gough, H. G., and Woodworth, D. G. Stylistic variations among professional research scientists. *Journal of Psychology*, 1960, *49*, 87-98.

Gray, J. T. Needs and values in three occupations. *Personnel and Guidance Journal*, 1963, *42*, 238-244.

Gribbons, W. D., and Lohnes, P. R. Shifts in adolescents' vocational values. *Personnel and Guidance Journal*, 1965, *44*, 248-252.

Gruenfeld, L. W., and Weissenberg, P. Field independence and articulation of source of job satisfaction. *Journal of Applied Psychology*, 1970, *54*, 424-426.

Gunderson, E. K. E., and Nelson, P. D. Personality differences among Navy occupational groups. *Personnel and Guidance Journal*, 1966, *44*, 956-961.

Gynther, M. D., and Gertz, B. Personality characteristics of student nurses in South Carolina. *Journal of Social Psychology*, 1962, *56*, 277-284.

Haakenstad, K. W., and Apostal, R. A. Acquiescence and nonoccupational interests. *Journal of Counseling Psychology*, 1971, *18*, 501-502.

Hall, C. S., and Lindzey, G. *Theories of personality*. New York: Wiley, 1957.

Hall, D. T., and Nougaim, K. E. An examination of Maslow's need hierarchy in an organizational setting. *Organizational Behavior and Human Performance*, 1968, *3*, 12-35.

Hammond, Marjorie. Motives related to vocational choices of college freshmen. *Journal of Counseling Psychology*, 1956, *3*, 357-261.

Hancock, J. B., and Teevan, R. C. Fear of failure and risk-taking behavior. *Journal of Personality*, 1964, *32*, 200-209.

Hanson, G. R., and Taylor, R. G. Interaction of ability and personality: another look at the drop-out problem in an institute of technology. *Journal of Counseling Psychology*, 1970, *17*, 540-545.

Hardin, E. Job satisfaction and the desire for change. *Journal of Applied Psychology*, 1967, *51*, 20-27.

Harrell, T. W. The personality of high earning MBA's in big business. *Personnel Psychology*, 1969, *22*, 457-463.

Harrell, T. W. The personality of high earning MBA's in small business. *Personnel Psychology*, 1970, *23*, 369-375.

Harrison, R., Tomblen, D., and Jackson, T. A. Profile of the mechanical engineer: personality. *Personnel Psychology*, 1955, *8*, 469-490.

Haselkorn, H. The vocational interests of a group of male homosexuals. *Journal of Counseling Psychology*, 1956, *3*, 8-11.

Healy, Irene, and Borg, W. R. Personality characteristics of nursing school students and graduate nurses. *Journal of Applied Psychology*, 1951, *35*, 275-280.

Heath, R. S. The reasonable adventurer and others – a two-factor model of ego functioning. *Journal of Counseling Psychology*, 1959, *6*, 3-12.

Herzberg, F. *Work and the nature of man.* Cleveland: World, 1966.

Herzberg, F., Mausner, B., and Snyderman, B. B. *The motivation to work* (2nd ed.). New York: Wiley, 1959.

Hogan, H. W. Authoritarianism among nursing students. *Experimental Publication System,* June, 1971, *12*, Ms. No. 399-12. (a)

Hogan, H. W. A social-psychological study of prison guards. *Experimental Publication System,* June, 1971, *12*, Ms. No. 407-256. (b)

Holland, J. L., and Nichols, R. C. Explorations of a theory of vocational choice. III: A longitudinal study of change in major field of study. *Personnel and Guidance Journal,* 1964, *43*, 235-242.

Hoppock, R. *Occupational information.* New York: McGraw-Hill, 1957.

Hulin, C. L., and Waters, L. K. Regression analysis of three variations of the two-factor theory of job satisfaction. *Journal of Applied Psychology,* 1971, *55*, 211-217.

Irvin, F. S. Personality characteristics and vocational identification. *Journal of Counseling Psychology,* 1968, *15*, 329-333.

Isaacson, R. L. Relation between need achievement, test anxiety, and curricular choice. *Journal of Abnormal and Social Psychology,* 1964, *68*, 447-452.

Izard, C. E. Personality characteristics of engineers as measured by the EPPS. *Journal of Applied Psychology,* 1960, *44*, 332-335.

Johansson, C. B. Strong Vocational Interest Blank introversion-extraversion and occupational membership. *Journal of Counseling Psychology,* 1970, *17*, 451-455.

Kassarjian, W. M., and Kassarjian, H. H. Occupational interests, social values, and social character. *Journal of Counseling Psychology,* 1965, *12*, 48-54.

Katz, M. Interests and values. *Journal of Counseling Psychology,* 1969, *16*, 460-462.

Kelly, G. A. *The psychology of personal constructs* (two vols.). New York: Norton, 1955.

Kipnis, D., Lane, G., and Berger, L. Character structure, vocational interest, and achievement. *Journal of Counseling Psychology,* 1969, *16*, 335-341.

Kirk, Barbara, Cummings, R. W., and Hackett, H. R. Personal and vocational characteristics of dental students. *Personnel and Guidance Journal,* 1963, *43*, 522-527.

Kish, G. B., and Donnenwerth, G. V. Interests and stimulus seeking. *Journal of Counseling Psychology,* 1969, *16*, 51-556.

Klugman, S. F. Spread of vocational interest and general adjustment. *Journal of Applied Psychology,* 1950, *34,*108-114.

Klugman, S. F. Comparison of total interest profiles of a psychotic and normal group. *Journal of Counseling Psychology,* 1960, *7,* 283-288.

Klumbies, G. Pathogenic job conflicts. *Psychotherapy and Psychosomatics,* 1967, *15*, 33-34.

Kohlan, R. G. Relationships between inventoried interests and inventoried needs. *Personnel and Guidance Journal,* 1968, *46*, 592-598.

Korn, H. A. Differences between majors in engineering and physical sciences on CPI and SVIB scores. *Journal of Counseling Psychology,* 1962, *9*, 306-312.

Kuhlen, R. G. Needs, perceived need satisfaction opportunities, and satisfaction with occupation. *Journal of Applied Psychology,* 1963, *47*, 56-64.

Kuhlen, R. G., and Dipboye, W. J. Motivational and personality factors in the selection of elementary and secondary school teaching as a career. Technical report, U.S. Office of Education Cooperative Research Program, Washington, D.C., 1959.

Landis, W. A. The vocational interests of emotionally maladjusted male college students. Doctoral dissertation, Pennsylvania State University, 1963.

Levine, F. J. Color-word Test performance and drive regulation in three vocational groups. *Journal of Clinical and Consulting Psychology,* 1968, *32*, 642-647.

Liberty, P. G., Jr., Burnstein, E., and Moulton, R. W. Concerns with mastery and occupational attraction. *Journal of Personality,* 1966, *34*, 105-117.

Lindgren, H. C. Age as a variable in aversion toward food and occupations. *Journal of Consulting Psychology,* 1962, *26*, 101-102.

Locke, E. A. Job satisfaction and job performance: a theoretical analysis. *Organizational Behavior and Human Performance,* 1970, *5*, 484-500.

Lofquist, L. H., and Dawis, René V. *Adjustment to work.* New York: Appleton-Century-Crofts, 1969.

McDonald, R. L. Personality characteristics of freshmen medical students as depicted by the Leary system. *Journal of General Psychology,* 1962, *100,* 313-323.

Madaus, G. F., and O'Hara, R. P. Vocational interest patterns of high school boys: a multivariate approach. *Journal of Counseling Psychology,* 1967, *14,* 106-112.

Mahone, C. H. Fear of failure and unrealistic vocational choice. *Journal of Abnormal and Social Psychology,* 1960, *60,* 253-261.

Marks, E., Vairo, J. D., and Zeigler, M. I. Scholastic aptitude, vocational interests, and personality characteristics of journalism students. *Journal of Educational Research,* 1962, *56,* 37-40.

Martin, Ann M., and Bendig, A. W. Personality needs of college students selecting teaching as a career. *Journal of Psychological Studies,* 1961, *12,* 111-120.

Maslow, A. H. *Motivation and personality.* New York: Harper & Row, 1954.

Meir, E. I., and Friedland, N. The relationship between intrinsic-extrinsic needs and occupational preferences. *Journal of Vocational Behavior,* 1971, *1,* 159-165.

Melton, W.R., Jr. An investigation of the relationship between personality and vocational interest. *Journal of Educational Psychology,* 1956, *47,* 163-174.

Merwin, J. C., and Di Vesta, F. J. A study of need theory and career choice. *Journal of Counseling Psychology,* 1959, *6,* 302-308.

Meyer, H. H., Walker, W. B., and Litwin, G. H. Motive patterns and risk preferences associated with entrepreneurship. *Journal of Abnormal and Social Psychology,* 1961, *63,* 570-574.

Miller, C. D., and Thomas, D. L. Relationships between educational and vocational interests. *Vocational Guidance Quarterly,* 1966, *16,* 113-118.

Miller, C. H. Age differences in occupational values of college men. *Journal of Counseling Psychology,* 1954, *1,* 190-192.

Miller, C. H. Occupational choice and values. *Personnel and Guidance Journal,* 1956, *35,* 244-246.

Miller, S., Jr. Relationship of personality to occupation, setting, and function. *Journal of Counseling Psychology,* 1962, *9,* 115-121.

Minor, C. A., and Neel, R. G. The relationship between achievement motive and occupational preference. *Journal of Counseling Psychology,* 1958, *5,* 39-43.

Mobley, W. H., and Locke, E. A. The relationship of value importance to satisfaction. *Organizational Behavior and Human Performance,* 1970, *5,* 463-483.

Moore, Harriet, B., and Levy, S. J. Artful contrivers: a study of engineers. *Personnel,* 1951, *28,* 148-153.

Morris, J. L. Propensity for risk taking as a determinant of vocational choice. *Journal of Personality and Social Psychology,* 1966, *3,* 328-335.

Muhlenkamp, A. F., and Parsons, Jean L. Characteristics of nurses: an overview of recent research published in a nursing research periodical. *Journal of Vocational Behavior,* 1972, *2,* 261-273.

Munday, L. A., Braskamp, L. A., and Brandt, J. E. The meaning of unpatterned vocational interests. *Personnel and Guidance Journal,* 1968, *47,* 249-256.

Munsterberg, E., and Mussen, P. H. The personality structures of art students. *Journal of Personality,* 1953, *21,* 457-466.

Murray, H. A. *Explorations in personality.* New York: Oxford, 1938.

Nadler, E. B., and Krulee, G. K. Personality factors among science and technology freshmen. *Journal of Educational Psychology,* 1961, *52,* 223-231.

Nauss, A. H. The ministerial personality: on avoiding a stereotype trap. *Journal of Counseling Psychology,* 1968, *15,* 581-582.

Newman, J. The Kuder Preference Record and personal adjustment. *Educational and Psychological Measurement,* 1955, *15,* 274-280.

Nugent, F. The relationship of discrepancies between interests and aptitude scores to other selected personality variables. *Personnel and Guidance Journal,* 1961, *39,* 388-395.

Osipow, S. H. Cognitive styles and educational-vocational preferences and selection. *Journal of Counseling Psychology,* 1969, *16,* 534-546.

Osipow, S. H. Some cognitive aspects of career development. In Evans, E. D. (Ed.), *Adolescents: readings in behavior and development.* Hinsdale, Illinois: Dryden, 1970.

Osipow, S. H. Success and preference: a replication and extension. *Journal of Applied Psychology*, 1972, *56*, 179-180.

Osipow, S. H., and Gold, J. A. Factors related to inconsistent career preferences. *Personnel and Guidance Journal*, 1967, *46*, 346-349.

Osipow, S. H., and Gold, J. A. Personnel adjustment and career development. *Journal of Counseling Psychology*, 1968, *15*, 439-443.

Osipow, S. H., and Scheid, A. B. The effect of manipulated success ratios on task preference. *Journal of Vocational Behavior*, 1971, *1*, 93-98.

Pallone, N. J., Hurley, R. B., and Rickard, F. S. Emphases in job satisfaction research: 1968-1969. *Journal of Vocational Behavior*, 1971, *1*, 11-28.

Patterson, C. H. Interest tests and the emotionally disturbed client. *Educational and Psychological Measurement*, 1957, *17*, 264-280.

Perrone, P. A. Values and occupational preferences of junior high school girls. *Personnel and Guidance Journal*, 1965, *44*, 253-257.

Phelan, J. G. Exploration of personality correlates to business risk-taking behavior. *Journal of Psychology*, 1962, *53*, 281-287.

Phillips, S. K. P. Differences in art media usage, motivational attitudes and personalities of art teachers at four levels of teaching. D. Ed. dissertation, Pennsylvania State University, 1963.

Pierson, R. R. Changes of major by university students. *Personnel and Guidance Journal*, 1962, *40*, 458-461.

Pool, D. A., and Brown, R. A. Kuder-Strong discrepancies and personality adjustment. *Journal of Counseling Psychology*, 1964, *11*, 63-66.

Riesman, D. *The lonely crowd*. New Haven, Connecticut: Yale University Press, 1950.

Roe, Anne. The personality of artists. *Educational and Psychological Measurement*, 1946, *6*, 401-410.

Roe, Anne. The psychology of the scientist. *Science*, 1961, *134*, 456-459.

Roe, Anne. Personal problems and science. In Taylor, C. W., and Barron, F. (Eds.), *Scientific creativity: its recognition and development*. New York: Wiley, 1963.

Roe, Anne, and Siegelman, M. The origin of interests. *APGA Inquiry Series*, No. 1. Washington, D.C.: American Personnel and Guidance Association, 1964.

Rosenberg, M. *Occupations and values*. Glencoe, Illinois: Free Press, 1957.

Salomone, P.R., and Muthard, J. E. Canonical correlation of vocational needs and vocational style. *Journal of Vocational Behavior*, 1972, *2*, 163-171.

Schaffer, Kay F. Vocational interests and emotional maladjustment. Unpublished Doctoral Dissertation, Ohio State University, 1972.

Schaffer, R. H. Job satisfaction as related to need satisfaction in work. *Psychological Monographs*, 1953, *67*, No. 14 (Whole No. 364).

Schofield, W. A study of medical students with the MMPI: I. Scale norms and profile patterns. *Journal of Psychology*, 1953, *36*, 59-65. (a)

Schofield, W. A study of medical students with the MMPI: II. Group and individual changes after two years. *Journal of Psychology*, 1953, *36*, 137-141. (b)

Scott, W. E., Jr., and Day, G. J. Personality dimensions and vocational interests among graduate business students. *Journal of Counseling Psychology*, 1972, *19*, 30-36.

Sharf, R. Relative importance of interest and ability in vocational decision making. *Journal of Counseling Psychology*, 1970, *17*, 258-262.

Sherrick, M. F., Davenport, C. A., and Colina, T. L. Flexibility and satisfaction with college major. *Experimental Publication System*, June, 1971, *12*, Ms. No. 460-6.

Siegelman, M., and Peck, R. F. Personality patterns related to occupational roles. *Genetic Psychology Monographs*, 1960, *61*, 291-349.

Siess, T. F., and Jackson, D. N. Vocational interests and personality: an empirical integration. *Journal of Counseling Psychology*, 1970, *17*, 27-35.

Simmons, O. G. *Work and mental illness*. New York: Wiley, 1965.

Simpson, R. L., and Simpson, Ida Harper. Values, personal influence, and occupational choice. *Social Forces*, 1960, *39*, 116-125.

Slakter, M. J., and Cramer, S. H. Risk taking and vocational or curriculum choice. *Vocational Guidance Quarterly*, 1969, *18*, 127-132.

Small, L. Personality determinants of vocational choice. *Psychological Monographs*, 1953, *67*, No. 1 (Whole No. 351).

Soliman, H. M. Motivation-hygiene theory of job attitudes: an empirical investigation and an attempt to reconcile the one- and two-factor theories of job attitudes. *Journal of Applied Psychology*, 1970, *54*, 452-461.

Spiaggia, M. An investigation of the personality traits of art students. *Educational and Psychological Measurement*, 1950, *10*, 285-293.

Spranger, E. *Types of men*. New York: Stechert, 1928 (translation).

Stacey, C. L., and Goldberg, H. D. A personality study of professional and student actors. *Journal of Applied Psychology*, 1953, *37*, 24-25.

Steinberg, A. The relation of vocational preference to emotional maladjustment. *Educational and Psychological Measurement*, 1952, *12*, 96-104.

Steiner, Mathilda E. The search for occupational personalities: the Rorschach test in industry. *Personnel*, 1953, *29*, 335-343.

Stern, G. G., Masling, J., Denton, B., Henderson, J., and Levin, Rachel. Two scales for the assessment of unconscious motivations for teaching. *Educational and Psychological Measurement*, 1960, *20*, 9-29.

Sternberg, C. Personality trait patterns of college students majoring in different fields. *Psychological Monographs*, 1955, *69*, No. 18 (Whole No. 403).

Sternberg, C. Interests and tendencies toward maladjustment in a normal population. *Personnel and Guidance Journal*, 1956, *35*, 94-99.

Stewart, L. H. Modes of response on the Strong Blank and selected personality variables. *Journal of Counseling Psychology*, 1960, *7*, 127-131.

Stone, L. A. The relationship of utility for risk to college year, sex, and vocational choice. *Journal of Counseling Psychology*, 1962, *9*, 87.

Strunk, O., Jr. Interest and personality patterns of preministerial students. *Psychological Reports*, 1959, *5*, 740.

Super, D. E., and Bachrach, P. B., *Scientific careers and vocational development theory*. New York: Bureau of Publications, Teachers College, Columbia University, 1957.

Super, D. E., and Crites, J. O. *Appraising vocational fitness* (rev. ed.). New York: Harper & Row, 1962.

Suziedelis, A., and Steimel, R. J. The relationship of need hierarchies to inventoried interests. *Personnel and Guidance Journal*, 1963, *42*, 393-396.

Taft, R. A psychological assessment of professional actors and related professions. *Genetic Psychology Monographs*, 1961, *64*, 309-383.

Thorndike, R. M., Weiss, D. J., and Dawis, Rene V. Canonical correlation of vocational interests and vocational needs. *Journal of Counseling Psychology*, 1968, *15*, 101-106. (a)

Thorndike, R. M., Weiss, D. J., and Dawis, René V. Multivariate relationship between a measure of vocational interests and a measure of vocational needs. *Journal of Applied Psychology*, 1968, *52*, 491-495. (b)

Thumin, F. Personality characteristics of diverse occupational groups. *Personnel and Guidance Journal*, 1965, *45*, 468-470.

Tinsley, H. E. A., and Weiss, D. J. A multitrait-multimethod comparison of job reinforcer ratings of supervisors and supervisees. *Journal of Vocational Behavior*, 1971, *I*, 287-299.

Tseng, M. S. Locus of control as a determinant of job proficiency, employability, and training satisfaction of vocational rehabilitation clients. *Journal of Counseling Psychology*, 1970, *17*, 487-491.

Tseng, M. S., and Carter, A. R. Achievement motivation and fear of failure as determinants of vocational choice, vocational aspiration, and perception of vocational prestige. *Journal of Counseling Psychology*, 1970, *17*, 150-156.

Tyler, Leona E. The relationship of interest to attitudes and reputation among first grade children. *Educational and Psychological Measurement*, 1951, *11*, 255-264.

Verniaud, W. M. Occupational differences in the MMPI. *Journal of Applied Psychology*, 1946, *30*, 604-613.

Vernon, P. E. Clinical and psychometric approaches to personality assessment in vocational counseling. Paper read at the XV Int. Cong. Appl. Psychol., Ljubljana, August, 1964.

Wagman, M. Sex and age differences in occupational values. *Personnel and Guidance Journal*, 1965, *44*, 258-262.

Wagman, M. Perceived similarities in occupational value structure. *Vocational Guidance Quarterly*, 1968, *16*, 275-281.

Walsh, R. P. The effect of needs on responses to job duties. *Journal of Counseling Psychology*, 1959, *6*, 194-198.

Walsh, W. B., and Palmer, D. A. Some personality differences between law and nonlaw-oriented students. *Vocational Guidance Quarterly*, 1970, *19*, 11-15.

Walsh, W. B., and Russel, J. H. College major choice and personal adjustment. *Personnel and Guidance Journal*, 1969, *47*, 685-688.

Watley, D. J., and Werts, C. E. Career selection: turnover analysis and the "birds of a feather" theory. *Journal of Counseling Psychology*, 1969, *16*, 254-259.

Whitney, D. R. Predicting from expressed vocational choice: a review. *Personnel and Guidance Journal*, 1969, *48*, 279-286.

Wiener, D. N., and Simon, W. Personality characteristics of embalmer trainees. *Journal of Applied Psychology*, 1950, *34*, 391-393.

Williams, L. K. Some correlates of risk-taking. *Personnel Psychology*, 1965, *18*, 297-310.

Winick, C. Personality characteristics of embalmers. *Personnel and Guidance Journal*, 1964, *43*, 262-266.

Wolf, M. G. Need gratification theory: a theoretical reformulation of job satisfaction/dissatisfaction and job motivation. *Journal of Applied Psychology*, 1970, *54*, 87-94.

Ziller, R. C. Vocational choice and utility for risk. *Journal of Counseling Psychology*, 1957, *4*, 61-64.

Zytowski, D. G. Internal-external control of reinforcement and the Strong Vocational Interest Blank. *Journal of Counseling Psychology*, 1967, *14*, 177-178.

Zytowski, D. G., Mills, D. H., and Paepe, C. Psychological differentiation and the Strong Vocational Interest Blank. *Journal of Counseling Psychology*, 1969, *16*, 41-44.

# 7

# Social Systems and Career Decisions: The Situational Approach

The social systems approach to the consideration of career choice and occupational behavior differs from the other points of view examined in this book primarily in its emphasis. The sociological approach is fundamentally based on the notion that elements beyond the individual's control exert a major influence on the course of his entire life, including his educational and vocational decisions. Supporters of this view suggest that the degree of freedom of occupational choice a person has is far less than might at first be assumed and that a man's self-expectations are not independent of the expectations society has for him. Society, in its turn, is assumed to present occupational opportunities in a manner related to class membership, a matter that has been extensively studied by interested sociologists.

Related to the sociologist's belief that circumstances impose choices on individuals is the proposal that chance plays a major role in occupational decisions. That is to say, being in the "right place at the right time" may have more to do with the vocational decisions people make than systematic planning and vocational counseling. The chance theory of vocational selection is more at home in the social systems chapter than in any other chapter in this book. The psychological theories of career decision-making do not exclude the possibility that chance factors influence decisions, though psychologists do not often discuss the effects of chance factors on careers explicitly. What differentiates the sociological and psychological approaches to the chance issue is a matter of emphasis. To psychologists, the chance variable represents an irritant, hopefully to be minimized, so that better decisions can be made and brought more under the control of the individual. The psychologist strives to understand the nonchance variables better in order to reduce the effect of chance elements in his predictions. The sociologist, on the other hand, is likely to focus his attention on chance (extra-individual) variables themselves and seeks to understand the forces that operate in that dimension in order to introduce some systematic organization of these apparently unsystematic aspects of life. Both disciplines might agree as to the proportion of chance involved in a given decision, but the psychologists are likely to be annoyed with chance variables and ignore them if possible, while the sociologists are more likely to be interested in the phenomenon of chance and study it. Hart, Rayner, and Christensen (1971), although reviewing the career histories of 60 men from the psychologists' point of view, found evidence indicating a clear relationship between occupational level and vocational planning behavior. On the basis of these observations, Hart and his associates urge theorists to take the role of "chance" in thinking about vocational development more seriously than now in that so much of what appears to determine career entry, especially for lower level occupations, is unplanned. The suggestion is reminiscent of Osipow's (1969a) suggestion that a principle of "least resistance" in career development operates and that program planners be mindful of the principle and design training programs that permit easy access and exit.

While impersonal and chance social factors may represent a major portion of the interest of the social system view of career decision-making, the organization of society itself represents another, more systematic, social aspect which influences individual career behavior in a way that is not directly under one's control. So, too, are the influences of the economic opportunities and general situational elements surrounding the individual as a function of his social class and the organization of his society. The social and the organizational environments with their economic implications are the dimensions upon which we shall consider the social systems approach to career choice and subsequent occupational behavior. The ideas and research discussed in this chapter represent several diverse streams of thought. Some of the concepts and data were developed specifically with career development theory in mind, whereas other work was conducted independent of career development theory but has been included here because it has relevance to our study.

# THE SOCIAL ENVIRONMENT

Social organization in America is not without class strata. These social class distinctions, which have grown up over the past two or three hundred years, are continuously changing in order to keep in tune with the expanding economy. Because of the changing nature of the social structure and the geographic mobility open to Americans, the effects on behavior of social class membership have sometimes been overlooked.

Social class membership both influences and is influenced by occupational membership. Hollingshead's study of Elmtown's Youth (1949) is a classic investigation of the role social class plays in human development in general. Although the details reported by Hollingshead may seem somewhat outdated now, his generalizations about the social and ethnic background factors that influence occupational expectation and selection remain true today. Hollingshead reported that, when queried about career goals, 77 percent of Class II adolescents aspired to professional or business careers while only 7 percent of Class V youth had such high aims. About one-quarter of Class V adolescents aspired primarily to service trades while virtually no Class II adolescents had such plans.

Unquestionably, an interaction between personal characteristics, transmitted relatively independently of the culture, and social factors results in occupational choice. Havighurst (1964) described several hypothetical case studies to illustrate the process through which boys in different social milieus mold their life styles. The values in the home, the adult models available and identified with, the differential rewards for work versus play, for enterprise versus academic achievement, all contribute to the production of a given individual and his career pattern.

Some sociological writers have suggested how the world might be if occupational selection were highly subject to social manipulation and selection. In *Brave New World*, Huxley (1946) described a technique of control whereby each individual is trained for his place in society. Young, in *The Rise of the Meritocracy* (1961), produced a fascinating, satirical characterization of life in a culture where people "rise to the top" exclusively on the basis of their talents, with no advantage as a result of family connections, money, or irrelevant personal characteristics. In our own world, it is clear that the idea of complete freedom of occupational choice is exaggerated and that many constraints operate to limit the choice (Cherevenik, 1956-1957). Even the young people making these choices seem to know that complete freedom of choice is lacking, as evidenced by Hollingshead's (1949) data presented above, showing that the occupational aims of most lower class adolescents are consistent with their social class.

Two social anchor points exist to fix a person's occupation (Caplow, 1954). At one extreme is the society in which occupation is hereditary; son follows father, or at least the father's career and life style impose rigid limits on the variety of careers his son may consider. At the other extreme lies the society in which occupational choice is the exclusive result of the individual's personal characteristics. Young's *Meritocracy* (1961), mentioned earlier, represents such a culture. In the Western world, occupational choice lies somewhere in between the two anchor points. At what particular point on the continuum the choice is made is a function of when and where in the culture one chooses to focus his attention.

In American society, the inheritance of occupation is most likely to occur where the older generation has large capital investments to pass along to its offspring. Family-owned businesses, such as retail stores and farms, are good examples of this kind of career heredity. It is interesting to speculate about the role that the production of large families in farming communities has played in the gradual transition in American society from farming to manufacturing. Only the oldest sons could inherit enough farm land to make their efforts profitable.

The others were required to leave the farm and find other means of support, contributing to the urbanization and mechanization of the society, which, cyclically, created opportunities in cities for future farm-born generations.

The inheritance of occupation is also likely to occur where the father's work occurs in a state of relative isolation from other people. Isolation may be either physical, such as in careers in the farming, lumbering, or fishing industries, or psychological, such as in medicine, the military, or religious occupations which set their members apart from the community at large, and in the case of the latter two, frequently add to the psychological isolation by requiring frequent moves from place to place. Counterbalancing these influences toward the inheritance of work in American society is the fact that most parents whose occupational and class status are below Class I hope that their children will exceed their own occupational achievements. Thus, the marginal storekeeper might encourage his son to go to college to become an accountant, or the skilled machinist would hope for his son's success in engineering. Both of these parental careers might have some hereditary characteristics, the first in the real property involved, the second in access to the union, yet parents in subprofessional fields usually hope that their sons will do better than they did through education.

Education is the main element in individual choice and the primary agent of occupational mobility. Educational decisions, though often made rather casually, effectively commit a person to certain courses of action by eliminating other possibilities. Frequently, educational decisions which are made in a school setting but which have occupational implications are based on tenuous assumptions about the world of work. Because the choices are made *for* but not *in* work the students usually find it difficult to make the decisions. Once made, the decisions are far from final (Caplow, 1954). At the Pennsylvania State University, approximately 20 percent of entering freshmen change their college before registering for their first class (Osipow, 1969b). A study conducted at the Kansas State University (Cross, 1960) revealed that relatively few graduates were employed in work directly related to their major field of study in college. To the degree that parents influence the educational decisions of their offspring and to the degree that social class influences parental attitudes toward and capability of providing educational opportunities, social class factors are highly important in educational-vocational decisions.

The scholastic goals of a student are a function of the particular set of experiences to which he has been exposed. His resulting values stem, at least in part, from his parents' beliefs, those of his neighborhood, other children in the neighborhood, and so on (Slater, 1957). One is not likely to find a heavy emphasis on academic training in a low socioeconomic neighborhood where men work hard physically and are admired and respected for their physical skills and strength.

Lipsett (1962) has summarized the role of social variables in vocational development. Social class membership influences the particular choices of career that adolescents make. Sewell and Shah (1968) make a similar point regarding college plans. Although the sequencing of the educational-vocational decisions probably does not differ basically from class to class, the timing is likely to be different. The higher class youth make their decisions when older than their lower class counterparts, and the specific careers they choose are different from those made by the lower classes. The career decisions influence and are influenced by educational decisions and opportunities. Both the home and community stimulate the adolescent. Parents place pressure on students for certain choices and make available or deny certain contingencies accordingly. For example, the availability of the family car may depend upon school grades in one family while in another no such restrictions may exist. While in one community going to college is the normal activity for an 18-year old, in another that may be seen as frivolous, and instead, most parents may insist upon work after high school graduation. All of these factors operate to influence the role the student perceives himself as likely to play when an adult and the degree to which he will strive to fulfill it.

The research strategy most commonly used to study social factors underlying career behavior has been to interview large numbers of students with respect to their occupational preferences and selections and relate these selections to their familial background. Frequently, father's occupation, family income, and parental educational background have been broadly translated into social class terms. Variations of the strategy have included comparisons of fathers' and sons' occupations. Where the latter approach was used, the occupations were usually considered in broad categories, such as the occupational family, much as Roe's classification of occupations would lead to (Roe, 1956), or even more broadly such as occupational level.

In a comprehensive work, Blau and Duncan (1967) have analyzed many sociological factors influential in determining occupational entry and functioning in America. The fundamental question raised by Blau and Duncan is what determines a man's occupation. The answer is, simplistically, his beginning social level, since the lower he is at the beginning, the more likely he is to move up the social-occupational scale. More complexly, however, Blau and Duncan draw conclusions similar to those drawn by Lipsett (1962) and Sewell and Shah (1968), that variables such as race, father's occupation, sex, marital status, family income, place of residence, family status (e.g., broken versus complete) etc., interact with significant variables and affect opportunities as well as training and preparation. According to Blau and Duncan, even more important than family status in determining occupational entry and achievement is one's training and early experience. However, as noted above, training and experience are not independent of familially based factors.

To illustrate the findings of Blau and Duncan, consider the following: men from small families start their careers higher than men from large families; even when differences in the allocation of family resources in large versus small families is taken into account, men from small families are seen to attain more occupationally in the long run than men from large families; the positive effect of small family size on occupational attainment is especially pronounced for "only" children. Furthermore, boys from small families go farther in school than boys from large families, until observations are made at the graduate level, where boys from large families seem to have an advantage for some apparently inexplicable reason.

Rosenberg (1957), whose study was described in detail in Chapter 6, reported some interesting data concerning the relationship between parental class and student career expectations. In particular, father's income seemed to be highly related to the kinds of choices students made. In proportion to their numbers, very few prospective teachers came from families where the earnings exceed $20,000 (in 1950 dollars). On the other hand, families with such incomes produced more than their share of physicians and lawyers, as might be expected in view of their ability to afford the training. Interesting, too, is the finding that the future earnings expected by students correlates very highly with fathers' income level. It is as if students expect to lead a style of life very similar to the one led by their father, while at the same time maintaining generally upward mobile hopes. Family income thus seems to exert a major effect on student expectations of income, opportunities, and specific choices.

Vander Well (1970) used an interesting method of classifying occupational choices into crystallized versus exploratory categories by virtue of the degree of occupational specificity associated with the chosen field. For example, medicine would be considered to be a crystallized choice since it is fairly specific, whereas psychology, which does not specify an occupational activity, is not considered a crystallized choice. The results of Vander Well's study revealed that second year college students qualifying for financial aid reflected a greater degree of crystallization in their educational major and vocational goals than other students.

A study by Hewer and Neubeck (1962) examined the socioeconomic backgrounds of all freshmen entering the University of Minnesota in 1959. As might be expected, the upper socioeconomic levels were overrepresented in the class. More than 14 percent of the freshmen came from professional and technical level families and over 25 percent from families where the main wage earner was a manager or owner, while fewer than 6 percent came from families where the main worker was an "operative" and less than 3 percent from families of laborers. All these figures are disproportionate to the representation of these categories in the general population.

Werts (1968) classified the occupational preferences of more than 70,000 college freshmen into SVIB categories along with the occupations of their fathers and found three general patterns of similarity between sons' and fathers' occupations. First, where fathers were in social sciences, social science fields were overchosen (chosen more often than chance would predict) by the sons (e.g., teachers' sons overchose college professor, clergymen's sons overchose professor, missionary, social worker, etc.). Second, where fathers were engaged in occupations in the physical sciences, the sons overchose physical science fields (e.g., chemists' sons overchose mathematics and physics, biologists' sons overchose architecture, etc.). Third, physicians' sons overchose medical professions (e.g., sons of medical doctors overchose medicine as a career, dentists' sons overchose medicine and dentistry, etc.).

Generally, the results of studies comparing the occupations, or occupational levels, of fathers and sons reveal that children generally follow careers that resemble those of their fathers, within the context of a general upward striving in American society (Samson and Stefflre, 1952; Beilin, 1955; Porter, 1954; Jenson and Kirchner, 1955; Gunderson and Nelson, 1965; Krippner, 1963; Clark, 1967; Hollingshead, 1951; Miller and Form, 1951; Werts, 1968). Thus, some upward movement may be seen, but generally it is slight and is usually statistically offset by the corresponding slight downward social movement, a movement largely ignored by the general public.

The few studies reporting exceptions to this finding deserve some mention. Stewart (1959) studied the relationship between occupational perceptions and socioeconomic background, observing the responses of fifth grade boys to a vocational "guess-who" test comprised of nine pictures of men representative of a variety of occupations: judge, teacher, scientist, mechanic, police sergeant, salesman, laborer, bellboy, and newsboy. The subjects were asked to identify the occupations depicted and then to rank the occupations with respect to earnings, housing, admiration and respect, and education. The resulting rankings were much as might be expected except that the police sergeant was rated somewhat higher and the salesman somewhat lower than predicted. Of most interest was the finding that the rankings revealed little differences as a function of the occupations of the fathers.

Mowsesian (1966) studied and classified the occupational preferences by level of 147 Wisconsin high school students who were participating in a study of the superior student. Information about fathers' occupations was also elicited. The results indicated that most students possessed professional aspirations higher than those of their fathers and that there was a trend away from the fathers' fields.

In a study more self-consciously examining heredity and occupation than most, Vandenberg and Stafford (1967) examined the Minnesota Vocational Interest Inventory scores of 53 pairs of fraternal and 71 pairs of identical twins. The results suggested the presence of a hereditary component in the possession of nonscientific interests, which Vandenberg and Stafford speculate operates on behavior by means of personality variables.

Using Roe's occupational classification system as an index of socioeconomic status, Lunneborg and Lunneborg found that father's occupation enhanced the accuracy of predictions of success in various curricula such as law (if the father was in an organizational career) or architecture (if the father was in business contact it detracted from the probability of the son's success). The Lunneborgs suggest that socioeconomic status relates to a broad array of attributes that are relevant to occupational choice and attainment.

Mulvey (1963), in a study of the career patterns of women over approximately a 25-year period following their graduation from high school, found that although the subjects' own level of education was highly related to the nature of their career patterns, parental socioeconomic status was apparently unrelated to and exerted little influence upon the patterns followed by the women in her sample. Possibly, a woman's career pattern is more significantly affected by her husband's social standing than that of her parents, though it is to be expected that parental status would influence marriage prospects.

Another research approach to the study of social class factors in occupational level is represented in a study of Hewer (1965). She studied the relationship between SVIB scores and the socioeconomic background of the freshman class entering the University of Minnesota in 1959. Socioeconomic class was determined by the assessment of the occupation and education of the students' fathers. The SVIB scores of the students were compared, scale by scale, with nine socioeconomic levels that resulted from the analysis of parental educational and vocational classification. The comparison revealed a relationship between scientific and technical interests on the SVIB and relatively lower socioeconomic social antecedents. It should be kept in mind, however, that Hewer and Neubeck's (1962) findings indicated that most of the freshmen at the University of Minnesota come from the upper half of the social strata.

Hyman (1956), in a similar design, classified high school seniors into social class groups and compared their standing with scores earned on the Kuder Preference Record. When the social class alone was considered, no differences were found in Kuder scores. When intelligence was also included in the analysis (by means of scores on the Otis Self-Administering Test of Mental Ability), upper class students in the "normal" range of intelligence scored higher on the mechanical scale than upper class "superior" intellect students. Middle and lower class "superior" students scored higher than upper "superior" students on the social service scale. It is interesting to speculate about the kind of family experiences that permit a bright lower class youngster to develop a social service interest and compare those experiences with the kind that inhibit the development of the same interests in an upper class adolescent with similar intellectual talents. The bright youngster from a socially prominent family would probably be encouraged to use his talents to maintain his family's status while the lower class youth might develop a sense of mission to help others financially and socially disadvantaged like himself.

A study by Pierce-Jones (1959) correlated scores on the Kuder Preference Record with socioeconomic ratings obtained through the Gough Home Index rating. Based on a sample of eleventh graders, Pierce-Jones found that for boys the home rating was positively correlated with high literary and musical scores and negatively with outdoor interests. For girls, high home ratings were negatively correlated with clerical and mechanical scores. Not surprising is the finding that high socioeconomic status is positively correlated with IQ scores and school grades for both boys and girls. Thus, socioeconomic status may well have an effect not only on the development, nurture, and acceptability of certain interests, but also on the likelihood that the student will achieve well enough academically to keep a wide range of choices open to himself.

Some investigators have examined the differences between social classes in their expectations of work and their approach to it. As Miller and Form (1951) have described the occupational expectations of the various social classes, upper class members come from families where the parents are owners or managers, where much stress is placed on the maintenance of "contacts" designed to uphold the family's high status, and where it is explicitly expected that the son will follow in his father's professional or business footsteps and the daughter marry a man professionally similar to her father.

Middle class youth stem from white collar families. The principal task for these youngsters is to learn to manipulate other people interpersonally. Parents of this class expect their children to work hard and advance in work that pays well and is "clean." The lower class family, largely blue collar or manual, passes on the attitude to its children that they are not going to advance socially to any significant degree. Instead, the main job goals are, realistically, security, respectability, and pleasant and loyal interpersonal associations on the job. The children are taught that as long as one can provide well for his family and enjoy life he can consider himself successful.

Other investigators have observed substantially the same things about occupational expectations. Centers and Bugental (1966) interviewed men and women in a cross section of occupations to investigate various motivations for work. They observed that the motives of white-collar workers are more intrinsically related to their work while the motives of blue-collar workers are more extrinsic. Contrary to this, however, Champagne (1967) found that for underprivileged adults intrinsic job factors were more important to job satisfaction than context factors. Stephenson's (1957) finding that lower class youth are disproportionally represented among students who express no particular vocational choice is probably related to the lower class students' recognition that they have relatively little control over the work they will actually perform. Thus, they are likely to disengage themselves from involvement in any particular work, and instead, remain undecided until specific opportunities present themselves. In contrast to this is Forrest's (1961) finding that National Merit Scholars were less concerned with the practical factors in career choice than most college students. Forrest speculated that the difference may reflect the higher socioeconomic status of Merit scholars and the consequent lesser importance of concern with practical matters.

Friedlander (1966) investigated the importance of work compared to other aspects of life in blue-collar, white-collar, high, and low occupational status groups. He found that work content, context, church, education, and recreation were important, in that order for all groups. Only when the white-collar versus blue-collar status was examined in connection with work status was Friedlander able to isolate any systematic differences in the importance of life activities. Friedlander concludes that work is a major environmental variable that leads to significant sources of satisfaction for most people. Friedlander's conclusion, however, is challenged by the work of Strauss (1963), Dubin (1956), Dubin and Goldman (1972), and Whitehill (1964), who disagree with the often-make assumption that work is a central life interest and that men strive for self-actualization through their work.

A distinctive method of studying one aspect of occupational membership has been reported by Laumann and Guttman (1966). A stratified sample of men was interviewed concerning a number of social and occupational matters. In particular, each subject was asked to state his own occupation, his father's, father-in-law's, those of his three closest friends, and his two neighbors. The relationship between the social status of the subject and those of his associates could then be determined. Through the use of a three-dimensional analysis, variables contributing to associations with others were identified. Laumann and Guttman predicted that occupational prestige alone was overemphasized in other research as a dimension determining interpersonal association. However, the results of Laumann and Guttman's study suggest that of the three major dimensions involved, the most heavily weighted one is highly correlated with occupational prestige.

### Effects of "Minority Group" Membership[1]

It seems clear, based on the work of Blau and Duncan (1967), for example, that variables such as race interact with social class membership in ways that significantly affect occupational membership and attainment.

In many ways, the career development of disadvantaged and minority group members is relevant to the work of Neff (1968) concerning work "psychopathology."[2] Neff has postulated several types of work psychopathology, three of which apply to many minority group members. In type 1, work is perceived in a negative fashion; the individual exhibits little work motivation and finds little or no reinforcing value in work. In type 2, work elicits fear and anxiety, possibly the result of a lack of experience in work and confusion about work roles and rules; in type 3 the individual's response to work is characterized by hostility and aggression; the individual is easily angered and, as a result, frequently comes into confict on the job. This last type is potentially highly relevant to explaining

---

[1] The phrase "minority group" membership does not adequately describe the members of groups whose social-ethnic class membership interferes with their occupational life because of discrimination or poverty. An argument can be made that it is not their minority group status that is most significant (cf. the situation of women, considered a "minority" but actually, of course, in the majority) but rather the poverty and discrimination, along with their consequences, that such groups are exposed to that is important to consider. However, since the usage "minority group" is commonly accepted, it shall be followed in this discussion.

[2] The use of the term "psychopathology" may not be most appropriate here because of the connotation of mental illness which does not seem relevant to this writer. However, Neff uses the term, and the *behaviors* described by the types do appear to be relevant.

the work behavior of some black people who have considerable anger toward the existing social system.

It is, thus, tempting to go on from this point to explain all of the vocational behavior and career development of minority group members in these pathological terms. However, to do so would be inappropriate and oversimplified, because the work behavior of minority group members is complex and differentiated. For example, it would be grossly inaccurate to characterize the career development of minority group members as ineffective. Campbell and Parsons (1972) found that although the vocational maturity (measured by the Vocational Development Inventory) of disadvantaged students in junior high school was not as great as that for nondisadvantaged students, the mean scores on vocational maturity earned by the disadvantaged students were above the norms developed for the VDI.

Gradually, a data base from which to understand the current career development process of minority group members is developing. However, understandings of the situation are rapidly changing, and it is noteworthy to realize that as recently as 1968, Feingold (1968) wrote that work study programs and a wide range of occupational information techniques should be applied to counteract the deprivation of the disadvantaged. Currently (mid-1972), however, the emphasis on minority group membership is less a matter of overcoming disadvantagement (still important, however) than a matter of enabling minority group members to apply the unique aspects of their background to the world at large.

One study of interest, conducted by Pallone, Rickard, and Hurley (1970), asked 161 black and 218 white high school students in grades eleven and twelve what they expected to do (vocationally) and who was the major influence in this choice. For black males, white males, and white females the major influencer was a person who actually held the job chosen. For black females, a job holder was the second most common influence; for black girls, mothers were the most significant influence regarding career, but second most important as an influencer on job choice for white girls. For black males, second most influential were parents; for white males, second place was occupied by father. Least important influencers, except for white females, were neighbors and friends; for white girls, relatives were less often indicated as important influences on careers. What is interesting about this study is the similarity between the races in source of influence in career. It is possible to classify investigations concerning the career development of minority group members into those whose results indicate that few differences exist between minority and "majority" group members versus those studies which indicate that many differences exist.

*Differences between minority and majority members in career development.* Dole and Passons (1972) compared 66 black male and female graduating high school seniors with 276 white graduating high school seniors with respect to post high school plans and goals. (In this study, minority group membership refers to race.) Black students were higher than white students with respect to altruistic values and the influence of school and science on their plans. Clark (1967), using the Vocational Apperception Test, compared 159 male and 139 female elementary students, mostly black inner-city children, with 206 male and 204 female suburban, middle class, mostly white children with respect to vocational preferences and perceptions. The results indicated that middle class boys more often chose professional careers and less often "government" jobs than inner-city boys; middle class girls more often chose business or teaching, and were less often uncertain about jobs than the inner-city girls. Asbury (1968) compared 63 low income Kentucky Appalachia students with 601 Iowa students on the Vocational Development Inventory (measuring vocational maturity) and found the Appalachia students scored lower than the Iowa students. Schmieding and Jensen (1968) compared 39 eleventh and twelfth grade Indian students in a "control" group with 39 eleventh and twelfth grade Indian students in an occupations class and 39 white high school students on the Vocational Development Inventory and the Vocational Tenacity Test. On the VDI the white students scored significantly higher than the Indians, with the Indian students in the occupations class scoring second. No differences among the three groups were found on Vocational Tenacity. Slocum and Strawser (1971) compared black and white CPA's in job attitudes and found significant differences in the sources of needs satisfaction: blacks were less satisfied with respect to social needs, self-esteem, opportunity for independent thought and action, opportunity for growth and development, and financial compensation. The "need importancies" hierarchies for the two groups, however, were very similar. Shappell, Hall, and Tarrier (1971) compared 186 ninth grade males and females from inner-city and suburban neighborhoods on the Hall Occupational Orientation Inventory and found a number of significant differences reflecting social class membership.

*Similarities between minority and majority members in career development.* Ansell and Hansen (1971) examined 375 eighth through twelfth grade boys, representing lower class white, lower class black, and middle class white groups, on the Readiness for Vocational Planning Scales. Differences existed, but seem to be related more to social class membership rather than race. Lower class whites and blacks did not differ, but were different from middle class whites. Unfortunately, these conclusions are somewhat tenuous in the absence of a sample of middle class blacks to compare with the middle class white sample. Maynard and Hansen (1970) compared 180 white, 180 black male students from the inner city with 90 white suburban male students on the VDI. Significant differences were found on Vocational Maturity, but these differences disappeared when controlled for intelligence. Campbell and Parsons (1972) compared 2370 disadvantaged and nondisadvantaged junior high school students from four large, geographically distinct communities with respect to a large number of vocational planning variables. Most of the students, disadvantaged as well as nondisadvantaged, exhibited a readiness for vocational planning, though the nondisadvantaged students scored high on vocational maturity on Crites' VDI. Compared to the VDI norms, however, the mean scores of the disadvantaged students on

Vocational Maturity were above the means for their grade levels. Most of the students from both groups seemed to feel they had some control over their future occupation, most were engaged in some planning behaviors, most aspired to relatively high occupational levels; male and female nondisadvantaged and female disadvantaged students most frequently chose service occupations while male disadvantaged students most often chose technical fields with service occupations second most frequently chosen. One of the most important variables affecting planning and choice was the community variable, which seemed to override sex and advantaged-disadvantged status in influence.

Vriend (1969) developed a vocational maturity rating scale entitled the Vocational Education Survey, based on the following dimensions of vocational maturity: school achievement, relation between aspiration and expectation, educational-vocational planning, vocationally related self-knowledge, general job knowledge, and participation in in-school and out-of-school activities. The survey was administered to 112 college preparatory and 168 inner-city youth, the latter group enrolled in a special two-year program of structured career development. The results indicated that the inner-city students earned higher vocational maturity scores than the college preparatory students. On this basis, Vriend concludes that vocational maturity can be fostered.

*Implications of research on career development of minority group members.* Unfortunately, especially since this is a topic of critical social significance, the information dealing with minority group career development is both confusing and inconsistent. Primarily this appears to stem from a lack of consistency in the definition of minority group membership and an absence of any clear conceptual basis for most of the research. In general, the studies have confounded race, social class, ethnicity, educational levels, and economic variables. This confounding of variables contributes to the confused and conflicting picture that has developed concerning the status and needs of disadvantaged and minority group members with respect to their career development.

## CULTURAL ORGANIZATION AND CAREER

It must be kept in mind that social organizations and culture did not develop independent of a physical context. Geography and climate contributed to the emergence of community structure. The isolated, small family-size farm developed because of the availability of cheap land and the time saved by not commuting to the fields from villages. Hilly lands encouraged dispersed communities; plains encouraged nucleated settlements where farmers commuted from villages to their fields. Similarly, urban centers developed around manufacturing, which is interrelated with market factors, accessibility of labor, power, raw materials, capital, and transportation (Finch et al., 1957). Social organizations often persist long after their reason for being has been modified. Thus, attention to man's ecology is critical if we are to identify which social institutions should be changed, how they may be changed, and what the effects of these changes may be on other aspects of human behavior.

In this section, attention is devoted to the role that the particular setting in which a person finds himself contributes to his subsequent career behavior. Psychological theories about careers and career decisions give little emphasis to matters of situational "accident." Sociological theories, on the other hand, provide some basis for understanding the interplay between the person and his world. Caplow (1954) has suggested that the crystallization of a career choice may occur at any age, the particular timing that is observed usually reflecting one's culture.

Blau and his associates (1956) have devised a complex and comprehensive scheme with which to conceptualize occupational choice in the cultural framework. According to Blau and his group, social structure exerts an influence on vocational choice through both the role it plays in the personality development of the individual and in its influence upon the economic and social conditions that prescribe the choice. The resulting choice made by the individual is the consequence of his estimate of the probability of the attainment of a particular career goal in combination with his evaluation of the career. Blau and his group assumed that people develop a hierarchy of career evaluations, much as Holland (1959) assumes, and estimations of the probabilities of career attainment.

Thus, the occupational decisions people make are a compromise between the two judgments. Accordingly, for the most part, people should select their most highly evaluated career possessing a reasonable probability of attainment. What varies from person to person is the definition of reasonable probability. The evaluations, one might infer from studies of prestige hierarchy, are relatively similar from one person to another. The effectiveness of a view such as Blau and his associates propose is based on the degree to which people are aware of the various career possibilities open to them. Sound occupational information, in the broadest sense, is crucial to good decision-making in this framework.

The Blau group has proposed that a double chain of events determines occupational entry. One chain, based on individual characteristics, includes biological and psychological factors, while the other chain is concerned with conditions affecting the economic opportunities facing the individual, such as geography, social resources, opportunities for mobility, cultural labor conditions, variations in potential rewards, and so on. Both the individual and social chains interact in a manner which shapes the eventual occupational choice. The career development of a young man, well endowed intellectually and highly skilled in physical coordination and strength growing up in New York City, will be different from that of another similar young man living in rural Wyoming. The urban boy is much more likely to rely on his intellectual characteristics than his rural counterpart because of the greater number of educational institutions in the city. At the same time, it is clear that two youngsters with different temperaments and physiques growing to maturity in Pittsburgh will not necessarily both enter the steel mills.

Information about the occupational organizations of American culture is likely to be more effective in bringing occupational information to life than the current methods of disseminating career information. Descriptions of the socio-logical elements of various careers, such as have been written by a few investi-gators and agencies (Danskin, 1955; 1957; U. S. Department of Labor, 1965; the descriptions written by the Research Department of the Vocational Guidance and Rehabilitation Services in Cleveland, Ohio), are more effective in producing the flavor of life involved in a given career than the relatively sterile information about education, income, and necessary special talents such as are often all the information that is available. Samler (1961) has suggested the use of a scheme such as Murray's environmental press and needs theory (1938) to describe career environments.

**Environmental Press**

The ability of the situational context to exert an influence on behavior is well known. Ford and Urban (1965) have shown how significant the modification of student living situations can be in the decision and opportunity to complete a college program. Similarly, Osipow and Grooms (1970) have demonstrated how the analysis of the situational context of a problem may provide suggestions about techniques to modify behavior in desirable ways. Super and Bachrach (1957) have suggested a social systems approach to the study of career develop-ment based on the interaction between the individual and his society. Presum-ably, the society dictates the developmental sequence and timing of vocational behavior and requires the individual to make career decisions within the frame-work of the social system. The social system itself includes the press of the larger culture and its various subcultures, the community, and personal sources of influence such as the home, family, school, and so on. The individual must make a choice which reflects a compromise between himself and the requirements of the social system.

Murray's writings of the 1930s provided the basis for the proposal that the environment exerts a "press" upon the individual which interacts with his per-sonality, affecting the consequent behavior. The experimental prototype of this proposal with an academic context is Pace and Stern's (1958) study of the psychological press of different college environments. Pace and Stern devised an instrument to measure environmental press, administered it to students in five collegiate institutions and were able to write statements illustrative of the en-vironment of each of the schools.

Other investigators have conducted similar studies of academic environments. Thistlethwaite (1960) studied the influence of the college environment on the academic plans of 1500 highly talented students who had completed their junior year. He found that faculty behavior was highly influential in stimulating certain changes in educational plans. A warm and informal faculty seemed to attract students to the social sciences, arts, and humanities, while an enthusiastic and permissive attitude of faculty was conducive to students in the natural and biological sciences.

Astin (1965) also studied the effect of college environment on vocationally related educational decisions but attempted to take into account two other classes of data as well: criterion data, that is, the student's vocational choice at the time of his graduation, and control data, or the student input characteristics of the institution. To do this, he studied the character of National Merit Scholars at 73 institutions and the particular character of the institutions themselves. Considered were institutional variables such as the size of the student body, the mean ability level of the students, and the proportion of students majoring in each of the major personal orientations suggested by Holland (1959; see Chapter 2 of this book). The institutions were also considered with respect to affluence of the student body, the masculinity of tone of the population, and the student homogeneity. The results indicated the students' career choices at the time of their graduation were highly similar to the choices they expressed when they began college. Realistic and Enterprising occupational choices were correlated positively with Realistic and Enterprising college environments and negatively with other environments, suggesting that choices may be reinforced by the atmosphere at a given college. However, the talents of the Merit Scholars introduces a flexibility not likely to exist for more typical students, namely, the ability to exercise their preferences and not be concerned with limitations in ability to any major extent in college. It seems likely that many changes in educational and vocational plans made by students in college reflect achievement problems, not genuine modifications in preference. Preferences may change afterward, possibly to reduce cognitive dissonance.

Herr (1965) applied the environmental press concept to the study of high school students' behavior. He administered a modification of Stern's College Characteristics Index, renamed the High School Characteristics Index, to high school students. Differences were found in student perception of school press associated with academic performance, school grade, public versus parochial elementary school enrollment, IQ score, father's occupation, and parental educational level. These results are suggestive of the interaction between social experiences and consequences of social class attributes and the perception of the environment, which combine to influence behavior.

Most of the emphasis of the environmental approach is based on the recognition that educational and vocational choices reflect a compromise between the individual's basic inclinations and those possibilities that the culture opens to him. Unfortunately, little research has been conducted outside of the educational system concerning the effect of the interaction between the individual and environmental press on career decisions. Systematic research of the effects of environmental press on occupational behavior in industry would be interesting to examine.

*Industrial organization.* Though the effect of environmental press of industrial organizations on career development has not been studied directly, considerable data about organizational effects on behavior are available. One leading writer, Gross (1964; 1967), suggests that it must be recognized that organizations affect career behavior in four general ways. Although there are a great number of small businesses in Western society, large organizations employ more people than do the more numerous small firms because of the large numbers of people employed in a single firm. Consequently, most people adjust to the particular problems of life in large organizations. These problems include learning how to deal with authority, satisfying security needs appropriately, accommodating to work that is routine, resolving the conflict between the need of the organization for creativity and yet its demand for conformity, coping with the distance in interpersonal relations that most large organizations require, and the acceptance of the fact that social mobility in large organizations may be, at retirement, downward rather than upward.

Second, the particular organization in which a worker is employed largely determines the character of the people with whom he may interact. Since interpersonal relations are highly important to vocational success, the character of one's associates may become even more important to a worker than the physical surroundings within which he works. Third, the organization within which one is employed plays a major role in one's job, which in turn influences income, affecting a person's material style of life. A worker's income determines his consumption of goods, a major factor of modern American life. Whether one owns a Chrysler or a Dart, or goes camping on vacation or to a posh resort, depends upon one's income and social expectations, both of which may be largely determined by one's job and institution. The effect of institutional life on noninstitutional behavior has been aptly described by Whyte (1956).

Finally, Gross suggests the notion of his occupational career within organizational structures in that a person needs to learn that he may have a career even though he may change his job several times. Consequently, organizational life requires its workers to avoid becoming too well suited to one job or work setting since their career pattern may require several job changes as their career matures. A promotion may require one to give up old friends; a promising job may necessitate a cross-country move. A personal knowledge of the problems in production acquired in younger days may inhibit an executive's ability to detach himself from the managerial decisions he may be required to make when he has wider responsibilities in a more mature phase of his career.

The four organizational effects imply that people must plan for career cycles which require them to maintain occupational flexibility and ability to adapt to new friends, communities, and ways of life. It also implies that the career decision-making process must be sharpened, and people must strive to identify as many career alternatives as possible at any given point in their career progression, recognizing that they may maximize their chances of choosing wisely but not expecting perfection or finality to result from their decisions. Discussing organizational careers further, Slocum (1965) points out that occupational decisions are not exclusively the province of the chooser, but are subject to the demands of society and the opportunities available. Career choices have many causes such as skills, interest, sex, values, and so on.

Other writers have commented on life in organizations (Miller, 1964) and the way organizations affect work. Wilensky (1964) has pointed out that although men complain about their work to one another, when they are asked in a variety of ways whether they are satisfied with their work, most indicate that they are. Few men say their work is dull and few would choose another line of work if they were able to start again, although the frequency of satisfaction with work decreases as the respondents move from upper to lower class status, and most men say they would continue working even if they suddenly became financially independent of their jobs. Curiously, however, despite the evidence for satisfaction, most men express the hope that their children will do better vocationally than they did.

Related to organizational factors in occupational behavior is occupational sociology. Generally, occupational sociology applies itself to the description of such factors as occupational status and mobility, the relationship between ethnicity and career, occupation and personality, occupational images and stereotypes, occupational culture and ethics, and client-professional relations (Smigel, 1954). It has led to many interesting studies of occupational stereotypes (e.g., Grunes, 1956; O'Dowd and Beardslee, 1960). These investigators showed, by different methods and based on different samples, that vivid occupational images are held by the majority of youth in the process of making entry decisions about careers. Their findings suggest very strongly that these stereotypes provide a large basis for the kinds of occupational decisions that are subsequently made. Although the stereotypes may have considerable validity, as Holland's (1959) theory suggests, for any individual a career decision based on a cultural stereotype of an occupation may prove to be unfortunate.

Another aspect of occupational sociology has been the development of occupational information literature based on sociological data on occupations. True to life descriptions of work and living conditions afforded by membership in certain careers can be very useful to students involved in making entry vocational decisions or educational-vocational decisions (Danskin, 1955; 1957; U. S. Department of Labor, 1965).

*Cross-cultural studies of occupation.* Sociologists and anthropologists have studied various cultures extensively. One aspect, usually not the primary one, of their studies has been the vocational activity that occupies the inhabitants of the culture. The occupational implications of the many different cross-cultural studies that have been conducted deserve a book alone. However, some of these studies and their major implications for vocational behavior may be mentioned briefly here.

Early studies concerning human development across cultures have been reported by Margaret Mead (1930; 1937; 1939), who studied the behavior of islanders in the South Pacific. These studies of the Samoans, Manuans, and New Guineans revealed, as might be expected in primitive cultures, that work was begun at a very early age and was assigned according to the individual's general capability. Although beginning work as young children in these three cultures had its disadvantages, some genuine advantages appeared to exist. Most significant of these was that the work the children did was real and important in marked contrast to the work that children often perform in middle and upper class segments of American society. The artificiality of work for children in American culture may well generate unwholesome attitudes toward work which may interfere with effectiveness later in life. Furthermore, the children who inhabit these primitive cultures had the advantage of relatively easy identification with their like-sex parent, which facilitated the acquisition of work skills and helpful attitudes, once again, a feature missing from the daily experience of most American youth.

Mead's work (1937; 1953) also reveals some interesting aspects of cultural organization on work related behavior. The degree to which a society is based on cooperative versus competitive effort among its members may be highly related to physical characteristics of the land they inhabit, such as the climate, topography, and geography. All of these influence customs about property, which in turn affect the way work is organized, the division of labor among the sexes, and the response to the modification of work procedures from primitive to modern techniques. For example, the difficulty Hindu cultures have in adapting to technical change is predictable from an understanding of Hindu philosophy toward living and working (Mead, 1953).

Other writers, such as Ruth Benedict (1946) and Anne Roe (1956), have extensively discussed work in various cultures. Roe has shown how the complexity of a society influences and in turn is influenced by the variety of work available to the members of the society. Ross and Ross (1957) studied the American Apache Indian to determine some of the background factors in the vocational decisions made by these people. Though the sampling was not representative and thus limits generalizations to be drawn from the results, the findings reveal, much as would be expected, that younger tribe members earned higher IQ test scores than older members and that artistic and clerical interests generally were stronger than scientific ones, a finding not surprising in a culture with a strong artistic tradition and no scientific one.

In this section we have reviewed the idea that the physical and social environment creates institutions whose particular arrangement exerts a significant influence on occupational behavior. It seems likely that a comprehensive approach to career development theory must include the effects of the social organization on the individual's personality characteristics.


## THE CAREER DEVELOPMENT OF WOMEN


It is no longer an idle question to ask whether it is important to consider the special problems of the career development of women. Perhaps the most significant area of concern for advocates of equal rights for women lies in the topic of careers, especially as these rights concern equality of opportunity, treatment, remuneration, and advancement, but also as they concern the general social attitude toward women's careers and marriage and family responsibilities. For many years, questions of career development concerning women were ignored or given cursory treatment, partly out of a lack of general social interest, and partly because the confusing nature of career development in women made the topic difficult to study. That sex affects career development in numerous ways as a function of social organization seems to be generally agreed (Fidell [1970] showed data reflecting how employment opportunities are affected by sex) and thus, the variable of sex becomes a legitimate one to consider in this discussion of social systems and careers.

It seems to be well established that despite the mythology to the contrary, professional women do not surrender their vocational identity lightly. Giuliani and Centra (1968) found that women veterinarians engage in professional practice 78 percent of the total possible years open to them, that 90 percent intend to continue in or return to professional practice, and that 92 percent of the female graduates since 1952 of the veterinary school they studied were in active practice. Studying a sample of women dentists in Israel, Meir, Camon, and Sardi (1967) found that professional goal attainment, in combination with the degree to which dentistry satisfied intrinsic needs, predicted women dentists' persistence in professional practice. Astin (1967) reports that 80 to 90 percent of women doctorates are in the labor force.

## Motivations for Work in Women

Eyde (1968) followed 51 women college graduates of the class of 1953 and 55 more of the class of 1958, five and ten years after graduation, respectively. She required the women to complete "desire to work" and "ranked work" scales. The first instrument measured the relative commitment of the woman to work as compared to other tasks (e.g., childbearing), while the second instrument measured the idea that women, and men, work for a variety of motives (e.g., money, interpersonal development, interest, etc.). The results indicated that mastery-achievement work values do not decline in the period between the fifth and tenth year after graduation (a finding in contrast to Baruch's [1966]). In addition, also contrary to much existing literature, Eyde found that the older alumnae indicated a stronger desire for independence than the younger women, suggesting that the desire for independence in women may have a developmental aspect. Astin (1967) identified the major factors associated with doctoral level women working and found that early commitment to work was a major discriminator relative to working or not. Harmon (1971) asked 1100 college freshwomen to indicate those occupations (from a list of 135) they had at some time considered, along with their age when these were considered. The resulting list was very limited during early years. Altogether, the results indicated that college women are homogeneous in the occupations they express at early ages, and that though this restrictiveness loosens with age, the later choices tend to be primarily in "typical" women's fields, suggesting that one motive operating is the smooth combination of work and marriage.

Of course, in such a rapidly changing area one must be cautious about concluding that these data reflect current thinking among young girls regarding their future careers. Rand and Miller (1972), however, have data which might speak to this point. They conducted a cross-sectional comparison of women at three educational levels in order to assess the differential cultural and developmental effects on career attitudes. There were 20 women each from the junior high, senior high, and collegiate levels. The results indicate that the desire for marriage is present and an important career variable in the junior high girls and by the time they go to college it has become an important aspect of plans. Almost all the girls' plans included combinations of work, marriage, and family responsibilities. Occupational choices were fairly consistent across age levels, with teaching being the most frequently chosen. At all levels, the females seemed to choose stereotyped "women's" occupations. Thus, Harmon's general data are reinforced, and are probably likely to continue to reflect the range of occupations considered by young women for at least the near future.

## Is the Career Development of Women Like That of Men?

Data exist to indicate that the process of career development in women is both similar to and different from the process for men. On the negative side, indicating differences in the process as a function of sex, are the results of numerous studies. Lewis, Wolins, and Yelsma (1967) demonstrated that women have different educational goals and reactions from men; Greenhaus (1971) and Masih (1967) found that careers occupy a more salient position in the lives of men than in the lives of women; Dole and Passons (1972) found more sex differences than racial differences in a study of educational-vocational goals and values; Fortner (1970) found that girls tend to choose more high level occupations than boys; Ace, Graen, and Dawis (1972) found sex to be the most influential variable affecting work attitudes; White (1970) points out the special problem of professional isolation as a result of part-time employment or spaces between employment for women. Lewis (1968), making many generalizations about sex differences in career behavior, asserts that girls make vocational choices earlier than boys; that girls prefer people-oriented rather than object-oriented jobs and service to professional fields; that girls give more consideration to job characteristics than boys do and are less likely to value pay and advancement in their job selection than males, and that girls' choices are more likely to be based on short-term objectives than boys are (possibly a response to the need for women to plan careers in the uncertain context of interweaving marriage and career, a task not demanded of males). Walsh and Barrow (1971) found that females are more concerned with status and prestige in work than males, an observation not entirely consistent with that of Gribbons and Lohnes (1968), who observed that boys ranked salary and prestige high for work values while girls ranked personal contact and social service as important job values.

Evidence indicating that men and women do have essentially the same career development process is provided by several studies. Diamond (1971) found evidence that sex differences in occupational interests are minimal at upper occupational levels though clearly obvious at lower levels. Saleh and Lalljee (1969) found no sex differences in intrinsic versus extrinsic job orientation in samples of university students and public school teachers, and for technical employees only when job level was not controlled. Helson (1967) found that "creative young women" possess personality characteristics similar to those of "creative young men." Osipow and Gold (1968) and Roe and Siegelman (1964) report results indicating that the antecedents and adjustment problems of members of both sexes are similar when they cross into occupational activities stereotyped for the opposite sex.

Rose and Elton (1971) predicted that no interaction would exist between sex and occupational category (in Holland's scheme) as a way of examining the need to develop separate theories for men and women. Rejection of this null hypothesis would lead to the implication that different theories are necessary for each sex. Rose and Elton administered the Omnibus Personality Inventory and classified their sample into five of the Holland categories (78 male and 50 female Investigative types, 47 male and 62 female Artistic types, 48 male and 64 female Social types, 60 male and 40 female Enterprising types, and 42 male and 32 female Conventional types). Sex differences along with occupational category differences on the OPI were found, and, furthermore, these differences interacted, indicating that the differences were not the same for both sexes. Rose and Elton conclude that while the Holland system might be modifiable to include women, it needs revision or otherwise some new theory of career development for women is necessary.

## Toward a Theory for Women

A reading of the similarities and differences between men and women in their career development suggests that while there are some similarities between the sexes in the career process, enough substantial differences exist to warrant attempts to develop distinctive theories for each sex, at least until such time as true sexual equality of career opportunity exists and the results have permeated society at all levels. Efforts to set the stage for the development of such independent theories have already been made. Zytowski (1969) proposed a set of postulates designed to stimulate research and thought in women's career development. These postulates may be summarized by asserting that although most women are homemakers, the frequency and singularity of this role is changing, and that when a careful observation of women's life roles is made they are seen to be orderly and sequential. Zytowski takes the controversial position that the homemaker and career roles for women are mutually exclusive because of their impact on entry and persistence in the labor market, as well as the level of the work the woman engages in while she is employed outside the home. Psathas (1968) makes the point that important elements in women's career development (marriage, timing of children, and spouses' attitudes) are just not considered in theories of career development for men and thus, separate concepts to explain the process in women are essential.

In summary, as Levitt (1971) has pointed out with respect to the vocational development of professional women, several problems exist in our approach. Some questions exist regarding the role of interests. What is the role interests play in predicting career commitment in women? There is lack of agreement among researchers on what constitutes career orientation in women. Finally, how can women who plan to combine marriage and work (or are already doing so) be distinguished from those who plan to engage in either homemaking *or* work as full-time activities. To some extent, the following sections deal with these questions.

### Aptitudes, Interests, and Achievement in the Career Development of Women

Tyler (1964) reports one of the early studies of interest development in females. One small aspect of a longitudinal study of a small number of career and non-career oriented girls, defined in terms of their interest scores on the SVIB, revealed that distinctive interests in females begin to develop prior to age 14, an observation confirmed by Astin's (1968a) Project Talent data. Astin found that ninth grade interests, plans, and aptitudes were good predictors of twelfth grade educational-vocational choices. In an extensive report of the study which examined subsamples of girls included in Project Talent, Astin (1968b) found that girls who change their choice from science, teaching, or some other profes-sional activity generally possess lower aptitude and achievement records than those girls who persist in those choices. Furthermore, those girls who originally planned to be housewives but later changed plans earn higher scores on achieve-ment and aptitude tests than girls who persist in the original choice of house-wife. In addition, girls who change their field of choice are observed to have had lower interest scores in their original field than those who persist. Once again, as for males, choices appear to be substantially influenced by personal abilities, achievement, and possibly interests. However, in a five-year follow up to the original Project Talent study, Astin and Myint (1971) found that events such as marriage, scholastic aptitude, and socioeconomic status proved, retrospectively, to be the best predictors of occupational activity in women.

Harmon (1970a), looking at a group of women 10 to 14 years after college entrance, found similar results. Most of the events that assumed a significant role in distinguishing career and noncareer women from one another seemed to occur after age 18. Variables such as the number of years of college, age at first marriage, number of children, and age when first child was born, were the kind of variables that separated the two groups. Generally, the "career" women had more years of college, married later, had fewer children, and were older when the first one was born than the "noncareer" women.

In another study, Harmon (1972) followed the careers of 72 nursing students, 32 medical technology students, and 56 social work students, all women, over a two-year period. She found that persistence in the original curriculum was related to SVIB consistency with the choice, being firstborn, and having a mother who worked during the child's early years.

The results of the series of studies by Astin and Harmon suggest that social factors, though not the only important variables in women's career development, loom importantly in a way that is distinctive from the way they do for men. This may be demonstrated, for example, in a study reported by Thomas and Stewart (1971). These investigators had school counselors listen to tapes of girls talking about themselves in an interview setting, and then rate the girls on a number of dimensions. The counselors tended to evaluate conforming (traditional career) vocational planning as more positive than "deviant" (pioneer career) vocational talk. Counselors perceived girls with such "deviant" plans as more in need of counseling than girls with conforming plans. As might be expected, female counselors were more accepting of so-called deviant as well as conforming female clients than male counselors. Such evaluations, if widespread, are bound to exert a subtle influence on the career decisions made by women, a factor not likely to be operating on males in the same way. Another study reported by Hawley (1971) tested the hypothesis that "women are influenced in their career development by their perception of what men think is appropriate female behavior." To test this hypothesis, she constructed a career attitude instrument for women yielding five factor analytically derived scales: woman as partner, ingenue, homemaker, competitor, and knower. The scale was administered to 33 homemakers, 30 women in "female" type careers, and 23 women in androgynous or "male" careers. The androgynous women did not see men as possessing ideas about proper career sex roles for women, but the other two groups did. In addition, unmarried women tended to perceive men's attitudes toward women's careers as "separatist" to a greater degree than married women did. Hawley concludes that the "guesses" women make about what men think about careers for women influence female career development substantially. Since such behavior is pervasive and starts early, women's attitudes toward their own careers are likely to be shaped in important ways while the women are still very young girls.

## Problems in Assessing Women's Interests

Special problems have existed in the measurement of women's interests, largely because of the rationale used in most interest measurement. The SVIB, for example, develops occupational scales based on the responses of members of a particular occupation that are different from those of nonmembers. One result of this is that it is difficult to develop scales for occupations in which there are few women. Another problem is the greater difficulty in establishing distinctions between female occupational group members from "women in general" than male occupational group members from "men in general" because of the social-cultural forces that restrict the vocational experiences and ideation of women. Numerous attempts have, and are, being made to correct the deficiencies in measuring women's interests. Farnsworth (1969), for example, has factor analyzed the women's form of the SVIB, and studies by Harmon (1969, 1970b), Nolting (1970), and Stone and Athlestan (1969) have all attempted to improve and test the predictive validity of the SVIB for women. Similarly, the Kuder has been subjected to efforts to improve its usefulness with women. Hornaday and Kuder (1961), for example, investigated the need for independent male and female scoring keys. Comparing the scores of 185 men and 185 women with groups of men and women in general, it was found that at least for a number of occupations, no differences in results were found for women when the men's key was used instead of the women's key. Such a result must be viewed with caution, however, and each occupation must be considered separately on the basis of empirical data. Use of the men's SVIB for women, however, seems inappropriate. In view of the standardization procedure comparing even "career" minded women with the men's key might underestimate and distort their career interests and commitment because of the number of sex-linked items that actually have no theoretical bearing on career interest and satisfaction but have been found to discriminate vocational groups among men.

Cole (1972) has analyzed the relationship between five measures of interest for women (the Strong Occupational Scales, the Strong Basic Interest Scales, the Kuder Occupational Scales, Holland's VPI, and the American College Test's VIP Scales). The results reveal that when women's responses are compared with those of other women, interest factors similar to those for men emerge. Thus, it may be that the methods generally used to measure and predict vocational interests magnify relatively modest interest differences that may exist according to sex.

## Pioneer Versus Traditional Women

Numerous studies have chosen to classify women into one of two groups, pioneer women, or those engaged seriously in career activities, versus traditional women, or those participating full-time in homemaking activities. One of the early studies displaying such an approach was conducted by Hoyt and Kennedy (1958). Hoyt and Kennedy investigated two hypotheses: (1) career-oriented and homemaking women differ on the housewife, stenographer-secretary, office worker, and elementary teacher scales of the SVIB, and (2) personality differences (not specified) exist between homemakers and career women. A total of 407 freshman women at Kansas State College were given the SVIB and EPPS and then queried about their interests. Of the original sample, two groups were formed: a career-oriented group composed of 30 women and a homemaking group, consisting of 71 women, all of whom were highly oriented toward marriage.

The results revealed a great many significant SVIB differences between the two groups of women. The findings, however, seem somewhat circular. Homemaking women, assigned to a homemaking group in the first place by means of inquiries about their plans, have homemaking interests on the SVIB, while career-oriented women, selected because they had career plans, were found to have interests on the SVIB similar to those of career women. In effect, these results validate the SVIB, but add little to our understanding of homemaking versus career-oriented women.

The results of the EPPS comparisons were more meaningful, however. Career women were found to score higher on needs achievement and intraception, while homemakers had higher needs on heterosexuality and endurance. Thus, the career-oriented woman may be viewed as seeking to prove her worth through vocational accomplishments. To some extent she is seen to use her career to avoid the sexual demands that marriage would impose. The homemakers, on the other hand, seemed to be more highly motivated by needs for affection and acceptance, which are more readily available in marriage than in a career.

Wagman (1966) replicated and extended the Hoyt and Kennedy study. His findings substantially duplicated those of the earlier study. The career-oriented women had higher theoretical and lower religious scores on the Allport-Vernon-Lindzey Study of Values than the homemakers. Three interest patterns for the career women on the SVIB were tentatively identified: a verbal-linguistic pattern, including lawyer and social worker; a science-technical pattern represented by physician, nurse, and author; and a combination pattern including psychologist and several other occupations that overlapped the two major patterns. In contrast only one pattern was found for the homemaking women: dietician, housewife, and home economist.

Career versus marriage orientation in women is obviously an important variable to be studied in connection with female career development. Watley and Kaplan (1971), examining the career aspirations of more than 800 female National Merit Scholarship winners, found that most (85 percent) indicated they had plans for a career, but important differences in the fields and the timing of these careers were evident. Nearly half planned on marriage *and* an immediate career, about one-third planned on marriage and a deferred career, and the remaining one-fifth were evenly divided between plans for marriage only, career only, and indecision. Not entirely surprising was the finding that those women planning on immediate careers (or careers only) were more likely to be found in the humanities and arts, while the marriage and deferred career women were commonly found in education fields. Farley (1970) has shown that career women differ from noncareer women in a number of important ways: career women desire fewer children, are more willing to use child-care facilities, are less willing to give priority to their husband's career, and are more likely to intend to work while their children are preschoolers than noncareer women.

Other investigators have reported differences between pioneer and traditional women: Rezler (1967a), defining pioneers as girls who wanted to study medicine, mathematics, and the natural sciences and traditionals as girls who wanted to study nursing or elementary teaching, compared 33 high school juniors and seniors of each type on the Kuder Vocational Preference Record, the Vocational Preference Inventory, and the California Test of Mental Maturity. Pioneers were found to be higher on computational and scientific, and lower on social service interests, higher on the intellectual and masculine and lower on the social, self-control, and status scales of the VPI, and higher on CTMM IQ. Rand (1968), comparing the responses of 828 pioneer and traditional college freshwomen on the American College Survey, found evidence to indicate a "masculine" orientation in career women. Of course, numerous questions have been raised about the meaning of masculinity and femininity as these are usually scaled (e.g., Diamond, 1971), so it is hard to interpret Rand's findings. Along a similar line, Elton and Rose (1967) found two discriminants on the basis of the Omnibus Personality Inventory (OPI) and the American College Test administered to over 600 college women. One dimension was called scholarly-practical, the other masculine-feminine, and these related to curricular choices. Other studies (e.g., Parker, 1966; Gysbers, Johnston, and Gust, 1968) have also demonstrated that psychometric and demographic differences between traditional and homemaking women can be identified. This effort seems to have culminated in an effort by Schissel (1968) to develop a career orientation scale for women based on the SVIB-W. On the basis of comparisons between career-oriented women (defined as those who had worked for five consecutive years) and noncareer women (who did not work within two years of leaving school, before or after marriage), Schissel found that career women do have interests different from noncareer-oriented women. The most discriminating scales were production manager and, once again, masculinity-femininity. The problems with Schissel's scale, however, lie in the lack of cross-validation data and the fact that the career-noncareer definition may not really represent an important distinction.

Several recent studies have approached the study of career versus traditional women by assuming that three, not two types of women exist with respect to vocational development: the homemaker, who exhibits no out-of-home work activity, the traditional career-oriented woman, who works but in a female-dominated or accepted work setting, and the pioneer career woman, who works in a male-dominated field where women are either not commonly found or well accepted or both. Nagely (1971) studied the responses of two groups of 20 women each, all mature, married, and mothers, to a TAT-like instrument, an attitude scale, and a biographical questionnaire. One group of women was working in traditional women's fields, the other in nontraditional fields, but both groups "career-oriented" in the sense that they were committed to out-of-home vocational activity. One particularly interesting difference was found between these two groups. The women in nontraditional careers seemed more career committed than those in traditional careers, yet seemed to have more successfully integrated their working and family roles than the women in the traditional fields.

Working independently, Wolkon (1972) divided women into two groups, pioneer and traditional, on the basis of their responses to two scales: the Desire to Work Scale and the Ranked Work Scale. The resulting data, however, indicated that really three groups exist: homemakers, traditional career women, and pioneer career women. An interesting aspect of the pioneer women was the observation that they were less concerned with economic motives in their work than with the satisfaction of mastery and independence motives.

Finally, Kriger (1972) also compared two groups of career women, calling those in female-dominated occupations "homemakers," and those in male-dominated occupations "career women." Based on the adaptation of Roe's (1957) theory, she predicted that women in female-dominated occupations would report perceptions of their parents' child-rearing attitudes as overprotective, and that women in male-dominated occupations would report perceptions of child-rearing attitudes as accepting and casual. The procedure was for each of three groups of 22 women to take the Parent Attitude Research Instrument and the need achievement scale of the Edwards Personal Preference Schedule. The three groups consisted of the two career groups, plus a group of women exclusively engaged in homemaking activities. The women ranged in age from 28 to 48 years. The results indicated that career orientation is a function of parental practice. The field and level of each woman appeared to be a function of her achievement motivation, which in turn, seemed to be related to her perception of her parents' treatment of her as a child. Kriger presents the interesting idea that instead of using the notion of an orientation toward or not toward people to account for career development (mostly in men) later in life, examination of parental treatment of daughters be used to predict orientation toward homemaking or toward a career for women. Kriger suggests that parental overcontrol leads to a homemaking orientation, while parental casualness leads toward a career orientation.

A significant question that remains, not nearly answered satisfactorily, is what events influence a women's career direction. Baruch, Segal, and Handrick (1968) used a structured projective technique to study career motivations in women and tentatively concluded that married working women identify with male figures while housewives identify with female figures. Matthews and Tiedeman (1964) found data which suggest that girls career-marriage attitudes are a function of their developmental stage. Such observations, however, still seem to raise more questions than they provide answers. And, finally, occasionally a truly puzzling result is encountered. Harmon (1967), comparing the SVIB profiles of women whose lives outside the home had been permanently interrupted by marriage with those of women who had worked outside the home consistently during the same 25-year period, found no differences!

## Summary

The most apt way to summarize current understandings about the career development of women is to make several assertions. First, the study of women's careers is a highly timely endeavor. Second, there are data which indicate that women's careers are not substantially different from men's, and at the same time, data exist suggesting just the opposite conclusion. One hypothesis might be that at the extremes of vocational levels certain similarities exist: the career of the woman functioning vocationally at very high professional levels and the woman at the unskilled level may bear more similarities to their male counterparts than the large mass of women in the middle level careers. Even so, there are likely to be important sex distinctions between men's and women's careers and their perceptions of their careers, as well as in the way they perform their duties in the same positions. It does seem clear that women frequently face obstacles in the pay they receive, promotions, and the accessibility of certain positions as a function of sex, and these discriminations naturally would be expected to exert an influence on female career development not experienced by men. A third and final assertion that might be made about women's careers is that so much social change is now occurring in the area of sex and vocation that any theoretical proposal made now is likely to be premature, as is any generalization about women's career development.

## EVALUATION AND STATUS

Of all the theoretical approaches to career development that have been discussed in this book, the social systems approaches are the most difficult to apply directly to the development of individual counseling techniques for career development. It would be particularly inappropriate to apply the requirement of individual counseling methods to the social systems approach because it is primarily a group-oriented way of thinking about the variables that influence behavior. Applications, thus, are more appropriately thought of in terms of programs rather than procedures. One exception is a scheme for decision-making proposed by Kaldor and Zytowski (1969). They sketched a model of career decision-making based on decision-making in economics. The model takes into account the individual's preferences, resources, and anticipated outcomes. The prediction is thus made that the resulting decision will reflect the individual's guesses about "maximal net gain" in terms of meeting his needs, taking his resources into account. While this model has potential for application, it obviously needs further instrumentation and elaboration before it can be said to be a practical device.

The impact of the social systems approach could be keenly felt in work with culturally disadvantaged people. For example, one of the major problems in trying to help the disadvantaged develop appropriate vocational behaviors is involved in getting them to change their conception of work from a *job* that must be done to the broader conception of work as a *task*, an *occupation*, and a *career* (Fried, 1966). As a task, work provides some rewards based on the personal pride that results from doing a job well. As an occupation, work values become more abstract and include a sense of social participation. As a career, work can begin to satisfy both individual and social needs. Lower class people see themselves permanently limited to working at jobs.

This perspective is not entirely inappropriate, since for many lower class individuals, their own behaviors operate to trap them in their current setting. Contributing to their difficulties and implicit in the many studies of both social class and organizational effects on occupational behavior and expectations are the problems imposed on lower class individuals by their manner of communication. The inability of a lower class boy to express himself in a way that is acceptable and comprehensible to his middle class employer and colleagues, combined with his corresponding inability to receive messages effectively, is likely to be a chronic source of vocational frustration (Osipow and Phillips, 1967). Efforts, thus, should appropriately be directed at dealing with the communication needs of the poor (Friedman and Phillips, 1966). The job interview, the school situation, the work setting, all require particular language and communication skills. The prospective member of the work group finds his chances for success sorely limited if he deviates significantly from the acceptable communication patterns of the group to which he aspires.

Thus, career development applications of social systems theory may be made at a very fundamental level. Some possible applications lie in teaching people to communicate in a manner relevant to the new and desired setting, helping people to understand how they interact with the organizational constraints placed on them, dealing with feelings toward authority that may interfere with work in an institutional setting, and learning to perceive some of the social implications of their work. As to its adherence to the formal aspects of theory, the social systems approach does not fare well. It is loosely structured, very broad in its explanations of behavior compared to older sciences, and difficult to translate into empirical research. Nevertheless, its broad conceptual basis should provide some leavening for the psychologist's thinking about behavior in highly individualized and operational terms.


# SUMMARY


In this chapter, the role social environment and cultural organization play in career development has been examined. Considerable attention has been given to the influence of social class membership on occupational entry and career behavior. Research has demonstrated that social class membership and sex are important situational determinants and affect attitudes toward education and work, the amount and kind of education and training acquired, and the economic resources one has to implement career plans.

More recently, writers have become interested in the effects of man's ecology on his career development. Geographic, climatic, and economic factors contribute importantly to the situational context within which career decisions are made. Environmental press, in the form of institutional variables, is a major source of influence in career decisions. Institutional membership creates problems and structures solutions. The size and character of the industrial organization in which an individual works is a significant source of situational stress. Related to organization are the effects on career development of the extensive geographic and economic mobility enjoyed by workers in twentieth-century America.

The most far-reaching contribution likely to result from the social systems approach to career development is an increasing sophistication in program development as a consequence of a greater understanding of the social forces that affect individual decisions. The approach points to the need for a greater attempt to relate career development to geography, climate, and economics.

# REFERENCES

Ace, M. E., Graen, G. B., and Dawis, René V. Biographic correlates of work attitudes. *Journal of Vocational Behavior*, 1972, *2*, 191-199.

Ansell, E. M., and Hansen, J. C. Patterns in vocational development of urban youth. *Journal of Counseling Psychology*, 1971, *18*, 505-508.

Asbury, F. A. Vocational development of rural disadvantaged eighth grade boys. *Vocational Guidance Quarterly*, 1968, *17*, 109-113.

Astin, A. W. Effects of different college environments on the vocational choices of high aptitude students. *Journal of Counseling Psychology*, 1965, *12*, 28-34.

Astin, Helen S. Factors associated with the participation of women doctorates in the labor force. *Personnel and Guidance Journal*, 1967, *46*, 240-246.

Astin, Helen S. Career development of girls during the high school years. *Journal of Counseling Psychology*, 1968, *15*, 536-540.(a)

Astin, Helen S. Stability and change in the career plans of ninth grade girls. *Personnel and Guidance Journal*, 1968, *46*, 961-966.(b)

Astin, Helen S., and Myint, Thelma. Career development of young women during the post high school years. *Journal of Counseling Psychology Monograph*, 1971, *18*, 369-393.

Baruch, Rhoda. The achievement motive in women: a study of the implications for career development. Unpublished doctoral dissertation, Harvard University, 1966.

Baruch, Rhoda, Segal, S., and Handrick, Fannie A. Constructs of career and family: a statistical analysis of thematic material. *Journal of Counsling Psychology*, 1968, *15*, 308-316.

Beilin, H. The occupational mobility of a rural 1924 high school group. *Personnel and Guidance Journal*, 1955, *34*, 18-20.

Benedict, Ruth. *Patterns of culture*. New York: Mentor, 1946.

Blau, P. M., and Duncan, D. D. *The American occupational structure*. New York: Wiley, 1967.

Blau, P. M., Gustad, J. W., Jessor, R., Parnes, H. S., and Wilcox, R. S. Occupational choice: a conceptual framework. *Industrial Labor Relations Review*, 1956, *9*, 531-543.

Campbell, R. E., and Parsons, Jean L. Readiness for vocational planning in junior high school: a socioeconomic and geographic comparison. *Journal of Vocational Behavior*, 1972, *2*, 401-418.

Caplow, T. *The sociology of work*. New York: McGraw-Hill, 1954.

Centers, R., and Bugental, D. E. Intrinsic and extrinsic job motivations among different segments of the working population. *Journal of Applied Psychology*, 1966, *50*, 193-197.

Champagne, J. E., and King, D. C. Job satisfaction factors among underprivileged workers. *Personnel and Guidance Journal*, 1967, *45*, 429-434.

Cherevenik, E. Who says there is freedom of occupational choice? *Vocational Guidance Quarterly*, 1956-1957, *5*, 57-59.

Clark, E. T. Influence of sex and social class on occupational preference and perception. *Personnel and Guidance Journal*, 1967, *45*, 440-444.

Cole, Nancy S. On measuring the vocational interests of women. *ACT Research Report*, No. 49, Iowa City, Iowa, 1972.

Cross, K. D. Comprehensive occupational survey of 1947 and 1952 Kansas State University graduates, Kansas State University Placement Center, 1960.

Danskin, D. G. Occupational sociology in occupational exploration. *Personnel and Guidance Journal*, 1955, *34*, 134-136.

Danskin, D. G. Studies on the sociological aspects of specific occupations. *Personnel and Guidance Journal*, 1957, *36*, 104-111.

Diamond, Esther E. Occupational interests: male-female or high level-low level dichotomy. *Journal of Vocational Behavior*, 1971, *1*, 305-315.

Dole, A. A., and Passons, W. R. Life goals and plan determinants reported by black and white high school seniors. *Journal of Vocational Behavior*, 1972, *2*, 209-222.

Dubin, R. Industrial workers worlds: a study of the "central life interests" of industrial workers. *Social Problems*, 1956, *3*, 131-142.

Dubin, R., and Goldman, D. R. Central life interests of American middle managers and specialists. *Journal of Vocational Behavior*, 1972, *2*, 133-142.

Elton, C. F., and Rose, H. A. Significance of personality in the vocational choice of college women. *Journal of Counseling Psychology*, 1967, *14*, 293-298.

Eyde, L. D. Work motivation of women college graduates: five year follow-up. *Journal of Counseling Psychology*, 1968, *15*, 199-202.

Farley, Jennie. Graduate women: career aspirations and desired family size. *American Psychologist*, 1970, *25*, 1099-1100.

Farnsworth, K. E. Vocational interests of women: a factor analysis of the women's form of the SVIB. *Journal of Applied Psychology*, 1969, *53*, 353-358.

Feingold, S. N. Presenting educational and occupational information to the disadvantaged. In Amos, W. E., and Grambs, Jean D. (Eds.), *Counseling the disadvantaged youth*. Englewood Cliffs, New Jersey: Prentice-Hall, 1968.

Fidell, L. S. Empirical verification of sex discrimination in hiring practices in psychology. *American Psychologist*, 1970, *25*, 1094-1098.

Finch, V. C., Trewartha, G. T., Robinson, A. H., and Hammond, E. H. *Elements of geography: physical and cultural* (4th ed.). New York: McGraw-Hill, 1957.

Ford, D. H. and Urban, H. B. College dropouts and social strategies. *Educational Record*, 1965, *46*, 77-92.

Forrest, A. L. Persistence of Vocational choice of the Merit Scholarship winners. *Personnel and Guidance Journal*, 1961, *39*, 466-471.

Fortner, Mildred L. Vocational choices of high school girls: can they be predicted? *Vocational Guidance Quarterly*, 1970, *18*, 203-206.

Fried, M. A. Is work a career? *Trans-action*, 1966, *3*, 42-47.

Friedlander, F. Importance of work versus nonwork among social and occupationally stratified groups. *Journal of Applied Psychology*, 1966, *50*, 437-441.

Friedman, P., and Phillips, G. M. Toward a rhetoric for the poverty class. Presented at Pa. Spch. Assn., Harrisburg, Pa., 1966.

Giuliani, B., and Centra, J. A. The woman veterinarian. *Personnel and Guidance Journal*, 1968, *46*, 971-975.

Greenhaus, J. H. An investigation of the role of career salience in vocational behavior. *Journal of Vocational Behavior*, 1971, *1*, 209-216.

Gribbons, W. D. and Lohnes, P. R. *Emerging Careers*. New York: Columbia University, Teachers College Press, 1968.

Gross, E. The worker and society. In Borow, H. (Ed.), *Man in a world at work*. Boston: Houghton Mifflin, 1964.

Gross, E. A sociological approach to the analysis of preparation for work life. *Personnel and Guidance Journal*, 1967, *45*, 416-423.

Grunes, Willa Freeman. On perception of occupations. *Personnel and Guidance Journal*, 1956, *34*, 276-279.

Gunderson, E. K. E., and Nelson, P. D. Socioeconomic status and Navy occupations. *Personnel and Guidance Journal*, 1965, *44*, 263-266.

Gysbers, N. C., Johnston, J. A., and Gust, T. Characteristics of homemakers and career-oriented women, *Journal of Counseling Psychology*, 1968, *15*, 541-546.

Harmon, Lenore W. Women's working patterns related to their SVIB housewife and "own" occupational scores. *Journal of Counseling Psychology*, 1967, *14*, 299-301.

Harmon, Lenore W. Predictive power over ten years of measured social service and scientific interests among college women. *Journal of Applied Psychology*, 1969, *53*, 193-198.

Harmon, Lenore W. Anatomy of career commitment in women. *Journal of Counseling Psychology*, 1970, *17*, 77-80.(a)

Harmon, Lenore W. Strong Vocational Interest Blank profiles of disadvantaged women. *Journal of Counseling Psychology*, 1970, *17*, 519-521.(b)

Harmon, Lenore W. The childhood and adolescent career plans of college women. *Journal of Vocational Behavior*, 1971, *1*, 45-56.

Harmon, Lenore W. Variables related to women's persistence in educational plans. *Journal of Vocational Behavior*, 1972, *2*, 143-154.

Hart, D. H., Rayner, K., and Christensen, E. R. Planning, preparation and chance in occupational entry. *Journal of Vocational Behavior*, 1971, *1*, 279-285.

Havighurst, R. J. Youth in exploration and man emergent. In Borow, H. (Ed.), *Man in a world at work*. Boston: Houghton Mifflin, 1964.

Hawley, Peggy. What women think men think: does it affect their career choice? *Journal of Counseling Psychology*, 1971, *18*, 193-199.

Helson, Ravenna. Personality characteristics and developmental history of creative college women. *Genetic Psychology Monographs*, 1967, *76*, 205-256.

Herr, E. L. Differential perceptions of "environmental press" by high school students. *Personnel and Guidance Journal*, 1965, *43*, 678-686.

Hewer, Vivian H. Vocational interests of college freshmen and their social origins. *Journal of Applied Psychology*, 1965, *49*, 407-411.

Hewer, Vivian H., and Neubeck, G. Occupations of fathers and mothers of entering University of Minnesota freshmen, fall, 1959. *Personnel and Guidance Journal*, 1962, *40*, 622-627.

Holland, J. L. A theory of vocational choice. *Journal of Counseling Psychology*, 1959, *6*, 35-45.

Hollingshead, A. B. *Elmtown's youth*. New York: Wiley, 1949.

Hornaday, J. A., and Kuder, G. F. A study of male occupational interest scales applied to women. *Educational and Psychological Measurement*, 1961, *21*, 859-864.

Hoyt, D. P., and Kennedy, C. E. Interest and personality correlates of career motivated and homemaking motivated college women. *Journal of Counseling Psychology*, 1958, *5*, 44-48.

Huxley, A. L. *Brave new world*. New York: Harper & Row, 1946.

Hyman, B. The relationship of social status and vocational interests. *Journal of Counseling Psychology*, 1956, *3*, 12-16.

Jenson, P. G., and Kirchner, W. K. A national answer to the question, "Do sons follow their fathers' occupations?" *Journal of Applied Psychology*, 1955, *39*, 419-421.

Kaldor, D. B., and Zytowski, D. G. A maximizing model of occupational decision-making. *Personnel and Guidance Journal*, 1969, *47*, 781-788.

Kriger, Sara Finn. Need achievement and perceived parental child-rearing attitudes of career women and homemakers. *Journal of Vocational Behavior*, 1972, *2*, 419-432.

Krippner, S. Junior high school students' vocational preferences and their parents' occupational levels. *Personnel and Guidance Journal*, 1963, *41*, 590-595.

Lauman, E. O., and Guttman, L. The relative associational contiguity of occupations in an urban setting. *American Sociological Review*, 1966, *31*, 169-178.

Lewis, E. C. *Developing women's potential*. Ames, Iowa: Iowa State University Press, 1968.

Lewis, E. C., Wolins, L., and Yelsma, Julia J. The academic interests of college women: a factorial study. *Personnel and Guidance Journal*, 1967, *46*, 258-262.

Levitt, Eleanor Sosnow. Vocational development of professional women: a review. *Journal of Vocational Behavior*, 1971, *1*, 375-385.

Lipsett, L. Social factors in vocational development. *Personnel and Guidance Journal*, 1962, *40*, 432-437.

Lunneborg, P. W., and Lunneborg, C. E. Roe's classification of occupations in predicting academic achievement. *Journal of Counseling Psychology*, 1968, *15*, 8-16.

Masih, L. K. Career saliency and its relation to certain needs, interests, and job values. *Personnel and Guidance Journal*, 1967, *45*, 653-658.

Matthews, Esther, and Tiedeman, D. V. Attitudes toward career and marriage and the development of life style in young women. *Journal of Counseling Psychology*, 1964, *11*, 375-383.

Maynard, P. E., and Hansen, J. C. Vocational maturity among inner-city youths. *Journal of Counseling Psychology*, 1970, *17*, 400-404.

Mead, Margaret. *Social organization of Manua.* Honolulu: Bernice P. Bishop Museum, 1930.

Mead, Margaret (Ed.). *Cooperation and competition among primitive groups.* New York: McGraw-Hill, 1937.

Mead, Margaret. *From the south seas.* New York: Morrow, 1939.

Mead, Margaret (Ed.). *Cultural patterns and technical change.* Paris: UNESCO, 1953.

Meir, E. I., Camon, A., and Sardi, Z. Prediction of persistence at work of women dentists. *Personnel and Guidance Journal*, 1967, *46*, 247-251.

Miller, D. C. Industry and the worker. In Borow, H. (Ed.), *Man in a world at work.* Boston: Houghton Mifflin, 1964.

Miller, D. C., and Form, W. H. *Industrial sociology.* New York: Harper & Row, 1951.

Mowsesian, R. Superior students' occupational preferences and their fathers' occupations. *Personnel and Guidance Journal*, 1966, *45*, 238-242.

Mulvey, Mary Crowley. Psychological and sociological factors in prediction of career patterns of women. *Genetic Psychology Monographs*, 1963, *68*, 309-386.

Murray, H. E. *Exploration in personality.* New York: Oxford, 1938.

Nagely, Donna L. Traditional and pioneer working mothers. *Journal of Vocational Behavior*, 1971, *1*, 331-341.

Neff, W. S. *Work and human behavior.* New York: Atherton, 1968.

Nolting, E., Jr. Vocational interests of women: a longitudinal study of the SVIB. *Journal of Applied Psychology*, 1970, *54*, 120-127.

O'Dowd, D. D., and Beardslee, D. C. College student images of a selected group of professions and occupations. Cooperative Research Project No. 562, U. S. Office of Education, Wesleyan University, Middletown, Connecticut, April, 1960.

Osipow, S. H. What do we really know about career development? In Gysbers, N., and Pritchard, D., (Eds.), Proceedings of the National Conference on Guidance, Counseling, and Placement in Career Development and Education-Occupational Decision-Making, Columbia, Missouri, 1969.(a)

Osipow, S. H. Student appraisal of a college preregistration counseling program. *Journal of College Student Personnel*, 1969, *10*, 47-51.(b)

Osipow, S. H., and Gold, J. A. Personal adjustment and career development. *Journal of Counseling Psychology*, 1968, *15*, 439-443.

Osipow, S. H., and Grooms, R. R. Behavior modification through situational manipulation. In Osipow, S. H., and Walsh, W. B. (Eds.), *Behavior change in counseling: Readings and cases.* New York: Appleton-Century-Crofts, 1970.

Osipow, S. H., and Phillips, G. M. Vocational development through the introductory speech class. *Vocational Guidance Quarterly*, 1967, *16*, 48-52.

Pace, C. R., and Stern, G. G. An approach to the measurement of psychological characteristics of college environment. *Journal of Educational Psychology*, 1958, *49*, 269-277.

Pallone, N. J., Rickard, F. S., and Hurley, R. B. Key influences of occupational preference among black youth. *Journal of Counseling Psychology*, 1970, *17*, 498-501.

Parker, Aileen W. Career and marriage orientation in the vocational development of college women. *Journal of Applied Psychology*, 1966, *50*, 232-235.

Pierce-Jones, J. Vocational interest correlates of socioeconomic status in adolescence. *Educational and Psychological Measurement*, 1959, *19*, 65-71.

Porter, J. R. Predicting vocational plans of high school senior boys. *Personnel and Guidance Journal*, 1954, *33*, 215-218.

Psathas, G. Toward a theory of occupational choice for women. *Sociology and Social Research*, 1968, *52*, 253-268.

Rand, Lorraine M. Masculinity or femininity? Differentiating career-oriented and homemaking-oriented college freshmen women. *Journal of Counseling Psychology*, 1968, *15*, 444-450.

Rand, Lorraine M., and Miller, Anna Louise. A developmental cross-sectioning of women's career and marriage attitudes and life plans. *Journal of Vocational Behavior*, 1972, *2*, 317-332.

Rezler, A. G. Characteristics of high school girls choosing traditional or pioneer vocations. *Personnel and Guidance Journal*, 1967, *45*, 659-665.

Roe, Anne. *The psychology of occupations.* New York: Wiley, 1956.

Roe, Anne. Early determinants of vocational choice. *Journal of Counseling Psychology*, 1957, *4*, 212-217.

Roe, Anne, and Siegelman, M. The origin of interests. *APGA Inquiry Series* No. 1, Washington, D. C.: American Personnel and Guidance Association, 1964.

Rose, Harriet A., and Elton, C. F. Sex and occupational choice. *Journal of Counseling Psychology*, 1971, *18*, 456-461.

Rosenberg, M. *Occupations and values.* Glencoe, Illinois: The Free Press, 1957.

Ross, W. T., and Ross, G. V. B. Backgrounds of vocational choice: an Apache study. *Personnel and Guidance Journal*, 1957, *35*, 270-275.

Saleh, S. D., and Lalljee, M. Sex and job orientation. *Personnel Psychology*, 1969, *22*, 465-471.

Samler, J. Psycho-social aspects of work: a critique of occupational information. *Personnel and Guidance Journal*, 1961, *39*, 458-465.

Samson, Ruth, and Stefflre, B. Like father . . . like son? *Personnel and Guidance Journal*, 1952, *31*, 35-39.

Schissel, R. F. Development of a career orientation scale for women. *Journal of Counseling Psychology*, 1968, *15*, 257-262.

Schmieding, O. A., and Jensen, Shirley F. American Indian students: vocational development and vocational tenacity. *Vocational Guidance Quarterly*, 1968, *17*, 120-123.

Sewell, W. H., and Shah, V. P. Social class, parental encouragement, and educational aspirations. *American Journal of Sociology*, 1968, *73*, 559-572.

Shappell, D. L., Hall, L. G., and Tarrier, R. B. Perceptions of the world of work: inner-city versus suburbia. *Journal of Counseling Psychology*, 1971, *18*, 55-59.

Slater, M. Perception: a context for the consideration of persistence and attrition among college men. *Personnel and Guidance Journal*, 1957, *35*, 435-440.

Slocum, W. L. Occupational careers in organizations: a sociological perspective. *Personnel and Guidance Journal*, 1965, *43*, 858-866.

Slocum, J. W., and Strawser, R. H. Racial differences in job attitudes. *APA Experimental Publication System*, June, 1971, *12*, Ms. No. 471-12.

Smigel, E. O. Occupational sociology. *Personnel and Guidance Journal*, 1954, *32*, 536-539.

Stephenson, R. M. Realism of vocational choice: a critique and an example. *Personnel and Guidance Journal*, 1957, *35*, 482-488.

Stewart, L. H. Relationship of socioeconomic status to children's occupational attitudes and interests. *Journal of Genetic Psychology*, 1959, *95*, 111-136.

Stone, T. K., and Athlestan, G. T. The SVIB for women and demographic variables in the prediction of occupational tenure. *Journal of Applied Psychology*, 1969, *53*, 408-412.

Strauss, G. The personality-versus-organizational theory. In Sayles, L. R. (Ed.), *Individualism and big business.* New York: McGraw-Hill, 1963.

Super, D. E., and Bachrach, P. B. *Scientific careers and vocational development theory.* New York: Bureau of Publications, Teachers College, Columbia University, 1957.

Thistlethwaite, D. L. College press and changes in study plans of talented students. *Journal of Educational Psychology*, 1960, *51*, 222-234.

Thomas, A. H., and Stewart, N. R. Counselor response to female clients with deviate and conforming career goals. *Journal of Counseling Psychology*, 1971, *18*, 352-357.

Tyler, Leona E. The development of career interests in girls. *Genetic Psychology Monographs*, 1964, *70*, 203-212.

Vandenberg, S. G., and Stafford, R. E. Hereditary influences on vocational preferences as shown by scores of twins on the Minnesota Vocational Interest Inventory. *Journal of Applied Psychology*, 1967, *51*, 17-19.

Vander Well, A. R. Influences of financial need on the vocational development of college students. ACT Research Report No. 36, Iowa City, Iowa: American College Testing Program, 1970.

Vriend, J. Vocational maturity ratings of inner-city high school seniors. *Journal of Counseling Psychology*, 1969, *16*, 377-384.

U. S. Department of Labor, *Sociological studies of occupations.* Washington, D.C.: Manpower Division, U. S. Government Printing Office, 1965.

Wagman, M. Interests and values of career and homemaking-oriented women. *Personnel and Guidance Journal*, 1966, *44*, 794-801.

Walsh, W. B., and Barrow, Cynthia A. Consistent and inconsistent career preferences and personality. *Journal of Vocational Behavior*, 1971, *1*, 271-278.

Watley, D. J., and Kaplan, Rosalyn. Career or marriage: aspirations and achievements of able young women. *Journal of Vocational Behavior*, 1971, *1*, 29-43.

Werts, C. E. Paternal influence on career choice. *Journal of Counseling Psychology*, 1968, *15*, 48-52.

White, Martha S. Psychological and social barriers to women in science. *Science*, 1970, *170*, 413-416.

Whitehill, A. M. Cultural values and employee attitudes: United States and Japan. *Journal of Applied Psychology*, 1964, *48*, 69-72.

Whyte, W. F. *The organization man.* New York: Simon & Schuster, 1956.

Wilensky, H. L. Varieties of work experience. In Borow, H. (Ed.), *Man in a world at work.* Boston: Houghton Mifflin, 1964.

Wolkon, K. A. Pioneer versus traditional: two distinct vocational patterns of college alumnae. *Journal of Vocational Behavior*, 1972, *2*, 275-282.

Young, M. D. *The rise of the meritocracy.* Baltimore: Penguin, 1961.

Zytowski, D. G. Toward a theory of career development for women. *Personnel and Guidance Journal*, 1969, *47*, 660-664.

# 8

# A Comparison
# of the Theories

We have now examined in considerable detail major viewpoints concerning the process of vocational decision making and subsequent career behavior. In doing so, the theories have been scrutinized, the relevant research described and its implications for the theories considered, and applications of the theories to the problems of human career behavior discussed. The next objective is to contrast the various theories with regard to their strengths and weaknesses according to a variety of criteria. As a result of such a comparison, it might be possible to reach some conclusions, not about which theory is "best" but rather under what conditions one theory might be more useful than another as a conceptual guide. Furthermore, such a comparison might be a useful stepping stone to the consideration of a synthesis of the theories and directions for future theorizing about career behavior. In this chapter we will compare the theories with regard to two general criteria: the formal adequacy of each theory as a theory and the adequacy of each theory in contributing to the understanding and facilitation of career development.

## FORMAL ADEQUACY

Theories may be assessed according to a number of criteria. In this book, we have chosen to consider theories in terms of their explanatory adequacy; the degree to which they are supported empirically; how general they are, that is, how broadly they are related to other bodies of scientific literature, data, and observation; the simplicity or parsimony of their concepts; how operational they are with respect to translations into both research and practice; and how logically consistent or inconsistent they are.

**Explanatory Adequacy**

Explanation in science characteristically accounts for phenomena at increasingly detailed levels of observation or introduces hypothetical concepts which relate events and describe the nature of the functional relationship between two sets of observations. The first kind of explanation is commonly called reductionistic, the second type constructive. Examination of the theories reveals that all are constructive in their explanation of the phenomena of career behavior. The theories offer little in the way of reductionistic explanation. Nevertheless, there is some variation among them. For example, Holland's theory (1959) identifies the function of constructs which underlie vocational behavior, while most of the other theories describe both the *development* and *functioning* of vocationally relevant constructs.

The trait-factor approach, similar to Holland's theory in conception, explains little about vocational behavior, relying more on description than explanation. Similarly, the sociological thinking about career development is mostly descriptive in nature and attempts to illustrate the situational parameters that influence vocational behavior. Only the need theories have any substantial degree of reductionism inherent in their explanation of career behavior. Since needs include a physiological component, the needs theory approach to occupational behavior can be viewed as reductionistic to the degree that physiological needs may be reduced through vocational activity, such as food earned and ingested to reduce hunger or sexual energy sublimated through vocational activity.

Most of the theories, thus, are clearly constructive, ranging from Holland (see Chapter 2), who identifies constructs which underlie vocational behavior, to Super (see Chapter 5), who postulates hypothetical constructs and processes, such as the self-concept and the interaction with situational events, to account for career behavior. In general, there seems to be little to choose among the theories as to explanatory adequacy because of their great similarity in explanatory approach. The theories are generally descriptive rather than explanatory. Only the more recent writings of Super (Super et al., 1963b) seem detailed and explicit enough to provide the basis of an *explanation* of the career development process.

**Empirical Support**

While the explanatory modes of behavior are very similar among the theories, the range of empirical support is wider and more varied. Some data exist on which to assess all the theories, but variations exist even in the degree to which different theoretical points of view have stimulated research. With a few exceptions, the research on career behavior has not been experimental in nature. Ordinarily, research designs have used convenient samples and have observed the behavior of subjects over a period of time, concentrating on possible differences in vocational behavior as a function of the original sorting into groups. For example, groups sorted on childhood experiences are expected to enter predictably different occupations, or students scoring in certain ways on personality instruments are expected to express vocational preferences of a predictably different kind than other students with somewhat different personality traits. Only rarely have conditions similar to those of an experiment been arranged.

In addition, the research has gradually been shifting from an emphasis on the testing of response-response laws to the examination and production of hypothetical constructs (Borow, 1960). The theories of career development have played a significant role in stimulating this change in research activity, since the theories have provided guides in the development of predictions and hypotheses and in the identification of profitable areas of investigation.

A considerable proportion of research based on Super's theory has resulted in empirical confirmation of the two fundamental aspects of his theory: that career choice is seen by the chooser as a way in which to implement his self-concept and that throughout life one is confronted with a series of career developmental tasks which specify the particular vocational decisions that must be made. Although a wider occupational base than now exists would be desirable, a number of recent research efforts have moved the data base from only those occupations possessing obvious potential for self-concept implementation (e.g., nursing) to others of a more dubious nature.

The behavioral style approach to personality and career has strong empirical support, but it has been applied to a very limited range of career situations. As for Holland's theory, the descriptive elements have had some experimental validation, but the results have by no means uniformly indicated the validity of Holland's personality types and their relation to career membership or goals. Thus, Holland's theory needs to reconcile the discrepancies that exist between measured personality style and the model personality required for satisfied functioning in a given occupation. On the positive side, Holland's theory has been well integrated into other major instrumentation and classification systems (e.g., the SVIB and the *Dictionary of Occupational Titles*).

Psychoanalytic concepts have received mixed empirical support because of the wide variety of specific approaches and variations in their translation into operational terms. Thus, some concepts, like the role of identification with appropriate adult models in career development, have received considerable empirical support, whereas the notion that psychic energy may be sublimated in vocational activity has received little support, because it is difficult, if not impossible, to make the latter problem explicit enough for research.

Needs theory, personal values, and the Ginzberg group approaches all have some empirical support, but the relevant data suffer from serious deficiencies. The needs and values data are too dependent upon paper-and-pencil tests and produce data which are largely of a response-response type. These data are subject to interpretations in addition to those consistent with the theory under discussion. The Ginzberg group produced data relevant to its theory, but the sampling limitations of the study very seriously interfere with the inferences that may be drawn from the study.

The sociological theories set out to be more descriptive in nature than the other approaches, so the application of a criterion of empirical support is not as legitimate for them as for the other approaches. In a similar way, because of its heuristic conception, the trait-factor approach is strictly empirical and, thus, the data obtained in the trait-factor frame of reference can only be supportive, or it would be excluded from the trait-factor frame of reference. Only one theory has consistently failed to be empirically supported. Though the research design is open to some criticisms, the investigations testing Roe's theory have almost uniformly failed to provide validation; exceptions to this failure to support Roe's theory have occurred in one or two recent studies, but the overwhelming weight of the evidence casts doubt on the validity of the theory.

### Generality

Several distinctive referents in basic psychological literature have served as anchors for the theories of career development. Virtually all the theories have roots in personality theory to some extent. The range has varied from the one extreme of a mere nod in the direction of personality theory, illustrated by the needs or values approaches, to the other extreme of the development of a miniature personality theory, exemplified by the work of Holland (1959) or Roe (1957).

In addition to personality theory, however, other streams of thought have influenced career development theory. Principal among these has been developmental psychology. The influence of developmental concepts has been strongly felt in the work of Super (1963a), for example, in the concepts of the vocational developmental task and in that of Roe (1957) in the emphasis she has placed on the role of early family experiences on the development of childhood personality traits.

Psychoanalytic thought has permeated psychology in many ways, and in addition to the explicitly analytic theories of career development, it has influenced the work of Roe, Ginzberg and associates (1951), and the social systems line of thought (see Chapter 7). Because of its emphasis on the role of childhood in shaping personality, psychoanalytic thinking has injected another aspect of developmental psychology into career development theory. Learning, too, has been superimposed with personality theory in the behavioral style stream of research on personality and career. Motivation and reinforcement are brought into the analysis of career behavior in the consideration of the way in which personality styles develop and are maintained, and in a sense, the personality style line of thought about careers is more closely attuned to psychological concepts in general than the other theories.

Somewhat more divorced from the center of psychological theory are the needs and values approaches to career development and the trait-factor and Holland approaches. The latter two theories share a dependence on the testing movement, to which Holland's theory adds a dash of Spranger's (1928) "types of man" approach. Despite their basis in personality theory, the needs and values approaches applied to career development have taken an empirical form and consequently are distantly related to psychological theorizing in general and instead have become heuristic.

### Parsimony

Most of the theories are more than adequate on the criterion of the parsimony of the concepts they introduce to describe and explain vocational behavior. Some of the theories may be even too parsimonious with the concepts they employ. The trait-factor personality approach (see Chapter 6) is almost a nontheory since it is basically empirical in nature. The viewpoint merely proposes that certain personality traits are more likely to be associated with some occupations than others. The needs and values approaches (see Chapter 6) go one step beyond the trait-factor theory, adding the postulate that the particular values and needs (constructs in themselves) a person has influence his choice of career, his behavior in it, and the degree to which the career satisfies him.

The Ginzberg (1951), Super (1953; 1963b), and personality style (see Chapter 6) models are essentially simple proposals. In the Ginzberg and Super approaches, the principles of developmental psychology play a major role. Neither theorist has significantly embellished those principles. The personality style system actually extends the needs approach since it generates principles to describe the way needs motivate human behavior in a vocational setting. Roe and Holland have also built their theories on only a few major concepts. Personality types, the level hierarchy, and environmental factors form the basis of the Holland theory, while genetic factors and family experiences are fundamental to Roe's theory.

### Operational Adequacy

The question of how operational the theories are must be considered in two parts, that is, the ease with which the theories lead to research applications and their relevance to program development and counseling. Generally, the theories appear to be more adequate when their research applications are stressed than when they are examined for counseling applications. Among the theories easiest to convert into research terms are the personality style, Super, trait-factor, needs, and Holland theories.

The trait-factor, needs, and Holland theories are similar as far as research is concerned. Fundamentally empirical in nature, their hypothetical concepts (if any) are close to the descriptive level of behavior, and hence, translation into research follows rather easily. The occupational preferences, persistence, or satisfaction of a population, sorted by needs, personality, or some other variable is observed and related to the theory.

Super and the personality style approaches form another set. They are not as easy to translate into research terms, not because their concepts are more comprehensive, but rather because the interrelation between the concepts is complex and requires sophisticated research procedures. The personality style approach lends itself, better than all the other views of career decision-making and behavior, to the experimental method. Super's theory, on the other hand, seems best suited to longitudinal research concerning patterns of career behavior over long periods of time.

The remaining theories (Ginzberg, psychoanalytic, social systems, Roe, and values) are difficult to implement in research terms. The difficulty lies primarily in the diffuseness of the concepts they employ (cf. psychoanalytic, Ginzberg, values), or in the relative inaccessibility of the important data (cf. Roe, social systems). Only the psychoanalytic theories of career development are contorted and exaggerated. These approaches have typically introduced the complex concepts of psychoanalytic theory in general to describe career development.

Another aspect of operational adequacy to be considered is the instrumentation associated with each of the theories. Holland has consistently paid attention to the development of means to measure personal attributes associated with the constructs in his theory. The Vocational Preference Inventory has been revised numerous times in this effort, and, more recently, the Self-Directed Search has been published, a measure which combines personality assessment with self-reported estimates of competencies. In addition, as noted in Chapter 2, a number of recent efforts have been made by Holland and others to integrate his system into other systems, with the result that the Strong Vocational Interest Blank, for example, now has an operational relationship with the theory, as does the Dictionary of Occupational Titles classification system.

Lofquist and Dawis (1969), in the development of their adjustment to work approach, have also generated a number of instruments especially tailored to use in connection with their theory. These instruments include the Minnesota Satisfaction Questionnaire, the Minnesota Satisfactoriness Scales, the Minnesota Importance Questionnaire, and the Job Description Questionnaire.

Super has directed less energy himself in the development of instruments to measure constructs associated with his theory than other investigators. He is responsible, however, for the Work Values Inventory, which measures one aspect of personality implementation in career, and is senior author of the Career Questionnaire, a measure of vocational maturity, another construct which grows out of his theory. Others, such as Crites, Gribbons and Lohnes, and Westbrook, have developed instruments designed to measure vocational maturity. Measures of the implementation of the self-concept have been less common, and most scales have been developed in connection with specific research projects. Nevertheless, both the developmental and self-concept aspects of Super's theory lend themselves well to instrumentation, and more can be expected from this quarter in the future.

Roe has not extended much energy in developing instruments, but the Parent Attitude Research Instrument is an example of one attempt to provide instrumentation for her theory, and the Hall Occupational Interest Inventory represents an independent effort to measure interests within the frame of reference described by Roe's theory.

The general personality approaches are relatively well represented in instruments: needs relative to occupations can be measured by the Adjective Check List, the Edwards Personal Preference Schedule, and the Minnesota Importance Questionnaire, for example; occupational values are frequently measured by the Work Values Inventory or the Allport-Vernon-Lindzey Study of Values; and general personality traits are frequently measured for their occupational relevance by means of the Minnesota Multiphasic Personality Inventory, the California Psychological Inventory, the Omnibus Personality Inventory, Cattell's 16 PF, and many others.

Only the psychoanalytic, social systems, and Ginzberg approaches have little instrumentation associated with them, and the reasons for this seem evident: psychoanalytic theory in general avoids psychometric evaluation, the social systems model tends to be descriptive rather than clinical or experimental in application, and the Ginzberg approach in many significant ways is a precursor (at least with respect to the emphasis on developmental aspects of careers) of the approach described by Super. As such, the Ginzberg approach has had little development since its initial formulation and presentation, and efforts along developmental lines associated with career growth have tended to be investigated in the context of the general ideas proposed by Super.

## Logical Consistency

Only two of the theories have serious problems of internal inconsistency. Roe's failure to deal adequately with the effects of changing family environments on personality development poses a problem. Children are not always treated the same by their parents; two parents may have different styles of child rearing; parents may react to children differently at different ages; a parent may die. All of these introduce apparently insoluble difficulties for Roe's theory. Explaining adult behavior in terms of childhood environment under these circumstances is nearly impossible. In a similar vein, the Ginzberg theory suffers from some logical difficulties by introducing pseudoconcepts which can easily serve as explanatory loopholes if events do not occur as predicted.

# THE PROCESS OF CAREER DEVELOPMENT

## Normal Development

The main thrust of several of the theories is in the descriptions of how the career decisions of normally developing people evolve. The theoretical treatment given to normal career development seems to follow one of three general lines of thought. Roe (1957), Super (1953; 1963a), Ginzberg and associates (1951), and psychoanalytic thought all describe career behavior fundamentally in terms of general concepts of human development. Super emphasizes how the self-concept is shaped. According to Super, each phase of life exerts its own particular emphasis on human behavior, including individual vocational behavior. It is thus possible to chart, in general terms, the activities of a vocational sort that are to be expected to an individual living in Western culture.

The Ginzberg approach, similar to Super's, describes career development as a series of events in a predictable sequence. Each aspect of the sequence presents the individual with a particular set of problems to be solved. Thus, in the vocational realm, the Ginzberg theory attempts to predict the sequence of behavior relevant to career decision-making. Ginzberg's approach does not lead to the prediction of occupation as much as it allows one to anticipate the vocationally relevant behavior an individual will engage in.

The developmental flavor is also prominent in the psychoanalytic approach to career behavior. While the developmental phases of analytic theory are not as closely attuned to career behavior, the analytic approach places a heavy emphasis on the idea that personality development is crucially related to the events of early childhood and that the ensuing personality causes the kind of occupational behavior that may be seen later.

Roe's description of the normal career development process is not as explicit as Super's description. She assumes that individuals differ physically and psychologically at birth. Added to these differences are the effects of parental attitudes and behavior styles which lead the maturing child to favor one of a number of interpersonal styles of behavior. The combination of the genetic features and the familial patterns lead to the prediction of general vocational behavior. Roe's theory is primarily concerned with predicting what kind of occupation a person will choose, but says little about vocational development subsequent to the choice.

Both the Holland and social systems approaches emphasize the view that vocational behavior is situationally bound. In the social systems approach, normal career development must be viewed in the context of its situational determinants, such as social class membership, economic opportunities, and the organization of the world of work. For Holland, the important situational determinants seem to lie more in the individual's organization of his perceptions of the vocational world and how he might best interact with it. Thus, the youth, according to Holland, might develop images (or stereotypes) of the activities involved in a variety of kinds of work and then try to integrate these images into his own view of how he fits into the world. The determinants of his view, of course, probably include factors such as social class membership and personality development as emphasized by the other theorists.

The other personality approaches, trait-factor, personal style, needs, and values, are really weak conceptually in their characterization of normal career development. The only generalized view expressed by any of these approaches is that of the trait-factor group, that people with certain traits in common will be engaged in occupations similar to one another. It fails, however, to describe how these people came to resemble one another. These approaches, rather, are likely to be built upon one of the developmental lines of thought concerning career behavior. They illustrate how personality might influence or be related to career behavior once the personality pattern of the individual has developed.

Our review of the theoretical views of normal career development reveals several significant attitudes. Rarely does a theory attempt to predict a specific occupational choice. More typically, the theories predict entry into general vocational areas, personality requirements of general career areas, influences that may shape personality in vocationally relevant ways, and age level behaviors of importance to career development. In effect, the theories emphasize all the nonability aspects of human behavior that relate to vocational preference, selection, attainment, and satisfaction, and pay very little direct attention to the role of aptitudes in career behavior.

### Problems in Career Development

Before one can consider how career development can go awry, some clear idea about the meaning of misdirected career development must be developed. For example, it might refer to vocational indecision, conflict, or failure, or to a choice that is not consistent with information about the individual. In fact, depending upon the theory under consideration, it might be any of these. According to the developmental theorists, career development goes awry when individuals fail to keep pace with the demands of their culture or their age mates. Ginzberg's group specifically points to several behaviors that must develop in order for mature career behavior to occur. The ability to perform the reality testing task, the development of a mature time perspective, the ability to delay the gratification of desires, the ability to compromise, and the ability to identify with appropriate adult models are all important. If these abilities fail to materialize during the adolescent period, career decisions will be inadequate and the individual will continue to be employed in a career in which he is dissatisfied or he will engage in numerous unsatisfying occupational pursuits.

The Ginzberg group also specifically related the ability to make good vocational choices to emotional stability, a relationship that most of the theorists seem to regard as valid but which has only on occasion been made explicit, notably by Super and by psychoanalytic authors writing about careers. In general, it is agreed that if the psychological development of the individual is not adequate, career development will not progress smoothly. Unfortunately, many theories have failed to show how career development can become misdirected in theoretical terms.

Roe and Super are not explicit about how career development can go wrong.

It is possible, however, to infer from Super's writings that problems of maturation in general are related to the proper performance of the vocational developmental tasks required at a given age level, much in the way the Ginzberg group suggests. Similarly, in describing the shaping of the self-concept, Super leaves the way open for inferences to be drawn about what factors might create distortions in self-concept and what effects these distortions might have on career behavior. For Roe, the question of misdirected career choice is not appropriate since she has described how choices are made without seriously trying to evaluate their adequacy.

Holland's theory is very explicit about how poor career choices may be made. Holland discusses this problem in terms of conflict or indecision in career matters. If the modal personality style leads to an occupational decision that is blocked and there is no strong second modal personal orientation, vocational indecision will be observed. Similarly, if two orientations are nearly equal in strength, conflict in vocational decision will occur. In terms of abilities, a poor choice could be made if the individual did not evaluate his talents accurately and thus his level hierarchy was over- or underinflated. In that case, the individual would either be observed to aspire to a career which might be consistent with his modal orientation but too difficult for him, or choose one that failed to use his talents sufficiently.

The theories rely on four main factors to account for misdirected career development. Most prominent of the four is the likelihood of a retarded rate of development in general which causes an individual to fail to have the skills necessary to cope with the vocational developmental tasks relevant to his age and position level. The other three factors, inadequate emotional adjustment, inaccurate self-evaluation, and frozen behavior between two attractive behavior sequences, are seen as possible sources of difficulty but do not seem to be viewed as pervasive in causing difficulties in career development.

### Facilitation or Modification of Career Behavior

Of all the theorists, only Super has written extensively about how career development may be corrected if it has gone astray or how it might be facilitated in the normally developing individual. Given Super's emphasis on the total life span, it is not surprising that he has devoted attention to the applications of career development theory to practice. The vocational developmental tasks enumerated by Super point the way to programmatic and individual approaches to correct and facilitate career development. According to Super, specific programs for adolescents should expose them to the necessary information for making the decisions required of them at that stage of development in order to avoid future errors or to correct past decisions. All through the life cycle, programs may be developed to enable people to make these decisions on a sounder basis.

While interviewing represents only one aspect of Super's approach to the facilitation or correction of career behavior, for most of the theorists, interviewing remains a primary procedure. The Ginzberg group generally proposes that if career development is not proceeding as it should in an adolescent, efforts should be directed toward the identification of his present stage of development, and experiences should be provided which accelerate the individual through previous periods of development and bring him to his appropriate level.

Aside from interviews designed to provide more insight into an individual's personal orientation, Holland's theory might lead to the proposal to exert more efforts toward the identification of satisfactions to be obtained in various work environments, as well as instruction for the individual to help him exert more control over life situations open to him. Picking the "right" school or industrial organization should provide a work atmosphere conducive to vocational satisfaction.

Since psychoanalytically oriented career counselors devote their energies to the identification of how and where an individual's impulses may be expressed vocationally with the greatest adequacy, their main efforts are devoted to interviewing procedures which attempt to lead to greater awareness of impulses and the identification of wholesome ways to express them in general. Roe's theory, too, leads the counselor to help his client in trying to understand the forces that shaped his personality and better identify the conditions under which he might work with the greatest satisfaction.

### Critical Periods and Critical Agents in Career Development

Once again, several distinctive lines of thought about when the most significant experiences for career development occur and what the critical sources of influence are emerge upon examination of the theories. The Ginzberg group and Super fall into one category. These writers agree that among the most critical agents influencing career development are the kind of adult models available during youth and adolescence, and for Super, models continue to be important. According to Super, many important periods of life exist for career development, largely because there are numerous points in the life span when critical decisions affecting careers must be made. The Ginzberg theory emphasizes the age range from about 10 to 24 years, since it is during this period that educational and vocational decisions are made affecting one's entry job.

Roe and the psychoanalytic writers seem to form a second category of thought about important periods and influences on career behavior. Both of these views emphasize the role of parents during early childhood in the shaping of mature personality. According to both of these approaches, later events exert a less significant impact on occupational behavior. Holland, personal values, personality behavior style, and the social systems approach form a third view. Although none of these treat any particular period of development as crucial, they do have something to say about the source of influence on decisions. For Holland, family factors, left unspecified, and social institutions are highly critical in the development of personality types and occupational images as well as opportunities. Similarly, the social systems view places a heavy emphasis on family variables such as social class, education, and income, in combination with economic opportunities and social and industrial organization, as major forces which shape the individual's vocational development. To a less explicit extent, the personal values line of thought sees family and cultural factors as forces which shape values. Finally, the behavioral style approach necessarily assumes the importance of situational variables in determining the behavioral styles an individual learns, as well as providing a basis for eliciting these styles. Although not a category because they say nothing about either critical periods or critical agents, the trait-factor approaches form a final unit. This line of thought has nothing explicit to say about the forces which shape occupational behavior.

## The Role of Interests in Career Development

Interests play an intimate role in career development theory, but the particular role is not typically stated in an explicit fashion in the theories of career development. Some theorists, like the Ginzberg group, assign interests a significant role at a particular age period. Others, like Super and Roe, tie interests more directly to occupational behavior. Super's theory views interests as an aspect of the self-concept, whereas in Roe's theory interests derive from psychic energy and lead to one's fundamental orientation toward or away from people. Interests are seen as growing out of individual need hierarchies by the needs theorists; to the trait-factor theorists and Holland, interests are another aspect of the person-occupation equation, something to be assessed but not necessarily analyzed. The social systems and values approaches are likely to view interests as reflections of the forces of society and family.

## The Role of Aptitudes in Career Development

Aptitudes are given varying emphasis by the theories. To the trait-factor theorists, including Holland, aptitudes comprise part of the equation involved in choice. Roe and the social systems approaches view aptitudes as genetically determined, and thus achievement is partly a function of heredity, but also the result of culture and environment. Neither Holland, Roe, nor the social systems view emphasizes the role of aptitudes in career development, however. On the other hand, Super sees aptitudes as a factor to be considered in career decision-making, an entity to be assessed and tested against reality. The needs and values approaches simply view the role of aptitudes in career development as a factor which interacts with the more critical variables, that is, needs or values. To the behavioral style theorist, aptitudes are part of the situational context both contributing to the situation and interacting with it within which individuals' career behavior occurs. The work adjustment approach of Lofquist and Dawis fully includes performance and aptitude variables through the vehicle of job satisfactoriness, one of the independent variables used to predict job tenure. Finally, the Ginzberg group fails to consider aptitudes seriously, consistent with the psychoanalytic antecedents of its thought. Ginzberg and his associates do consider the role that unusual and highly specific talents play in overdetermining career development, such as the role of musical talent in the precocious musician's commitment to a musical career.

### The Role of the Family in Career Development

The personality approaches, represented by trait-factor thought, needs, values, and behavioral style, fail to discuss the role of family influences on career development in any distinctive manner. Values and needs are seen as being shaped in a vague way by the family context; the family contributes to the situational context as seen by the behavioral style approach and to the traits the individual develops with which the trait-factor theorist is concerned; not much more than passing attention is given to the family by proponents of these views.

The Ginzberg theory, Super, psychoanalytic thought, and social systems views concern themselves with the family in a slightly more explicit way. To Super, the family plays a critical role in the formation of the individual's self-concept and in the provision of a context for its implementation. Psychoanalytic thought sees psychosexual development significantly influenced by the family structure and interactions of its members. To Ginzberg and the social systems theorists, the family creates a highly significant situation which plays a major role in determining the specifics of the career decisions an individual will make. Factors associated with family membership determine an individual's social class, financial resources, and attitudes toward work. In the view of the Ginzberg theorists, a poor family will accelerate the career development of their offspring, but will not alter the sequence through which he goes in any significant way. In addition, the lower class family is likely to be more passive in its general behavior and attitudes than middle or upper class families and thus its members may try to exert less direct influence on their career patterns than upper or middle class people. Only Roe rests the hub of a theory on the family. To Roe, the family plays a crucial role in determining, in fairly specific ways, the kinds of interactions with people that the youth will learn to develop.

It seems obvious that familial factors are important to career decisions, both in the determination of the situational variables involved in career development (such as educational, economic, hygienic and medical resources, social support and reinforcement, and the provision of a context for work) and in the intra-individual variables (such as the physical and psychological characteristics that have a strong genetic component). It is striking that so little theorizing has been done to relate explicitly the role of the family to occupational behavior, particularly when extensive data exist showing how the family background influences the kind of initial choice made and the manner in which it is implemented.

TABLE 8.1. A Summary Comparison of Some Theories and Subtheories of Career Development with Respect to Some Key Aspects

| Theory | Explanatory Mode | Empirical Support | Generality | Complexity | Operationality | Key Variables |
|---|---|---|---|---|---|---|
| Roe | Attempts to be somewhat explanatory; predicts molar career decisions and process | numerous studies; mostly negative results | very broad in design; most applicable to upper level careers | many complex constructs | somewhat hard to make operational; instruments to assess major variables exist; occupational classification system helpful | family; experiences |
| Holland | mostly descriptive; predicts molecular decisions | numerous studies; mostly positive results | very broad applicability | relatively simple in conception | easy to make operational; instrumentation available; numerous practical applications | interests; occupational stereotypes; information about self and careers; environment |
| Super | mostly explanatory; predicts relatively molecular events, but also includes process predictions | numerous studies; mostly positive results | very broadly applicable | moderately complex in conception | potentially operational; instrumentation available; many practical applications | self-concept; developmental stages and tasks |
| Ginzberg et al. | mostly descriptive; process not product-oriented | few studies; some support for general structure | narrow in applicability | average complexity | not very operational nor practical | developmental stages; social variables |
| Psychoanalytic | mostly explanatory; predicts process, not product | some studies; numerous concepts have been supported | broad in design but narrow in practice | very complex constructs | hard to make operational; could lead to practice but hasn't reached potential | sublimation; ego; identification mastery |

| | | | | | | |
|---|---|---|---|---|---|---|
| Lofquist-Dawis | molecular; deductive | sparse to date (still new) but encouraging | very broad in scope; work-setting-oriented | numerous complex constructs and relationships | very operational; many instruments available; has some practical applications | needs; traits; satisfaction and satisfactoriness; job tenure |
| Trait-factor | molecular; empirical | many studies; results highly variable | potentially broad but narrow in execution | essentially empirical and not conceptual in nature | operationality varies with availability of personality-aptitude instruments, practical for selection purposes | personality traits; aptitudes; needs |
| Needs | explanatory but includes molecular predictions | many studies; results frequently support, but variable | broad in scope | relatively simple in concept | operationality varies with availability of instruments to measure needs; not very practical | needs and their satisfaction; needs hierarchies |
| Values | explanatory, process-oriented | many studies; results frequently support | broad in scope | relatively simple in concept | operationality varies with availability of instruments to measure values | values |
| Social systems | descriptive, process-oriented | many studies; results frequently support | very broad in scope | relatively simple concepts at times, empirical in nature rather than conceptual | not easy to make some aspects operational, though other aspects lend themselves to operational methods; not highly applied | social class, family; sex, age, race, culture; economy |

## SUMMARY

One conclusion to be drawn from the comparison of the theories we have just made is that the various theories differ not only because the thinking of their authors about careers is distinctive but also because they are trying to accomplish different objectives in their theorizing. Some theorists are trying to explain why people make the choices they do (e.g., Holland); others are emphasizing the development of career choices over time (e.g., Super). Further, some theorists seem to be working harder than others at providing practical techniques for facilitating vocational development, or attempting to examine the characteristics that differentiate members of occupations from one another. The theorists do, however, share a tendency to imply that their concepts are universally applicable. It is this implication that occasionally gets in the reader's way when he is trying to sift through the data and concepts of the theories to generate applications.

The theories' strength lies in their general explanation of the way career decision-making occurs. For formal adequacy as theories, much seems to be lacking. In general, the theories have failed to pay serious attention to the satisfaction of the criteria applied to the scientific evaluation of theory. There is a tendency to describe the career development process in very general terms, probably more general than is useful to researcher and practitioner alike. The major exceptions are Super's and Holland's revised theories, which have taken on an increasingly applied and operational appearance.

Considerable data pertinent to career development and occupational psychology have been accumulated in theoretical terms. If closer ties to basic psychological theory existed, the theories would be strengthened. Some signs of the development of closer ties exist, and these signs auger well for the increasing adequacy and potency of career development theory in years to come.

Generally, the similarities between the theories outweigh the differences; they emphasize the same kinds of critical agents and periods in career development. The differences between the theories lie in their choice of emphasis, the research methods suitable to each, and the degree to which they specify the relations between various events.

As a conceptual model, Super's theory seems to be the most highly developed and advanced. This is reflected in its explicitness, its fairly high degree of empirical support, and its substantially larger number of applications to human affairs. The personality style approach, on the other hand, seems to be the most amenable to the experimental and scientific method and the closest to basic psychological concepts, but still lacking in a wide base of empirical support.

Table 8.1 summarizes the status of ten of the theoretical approaches on a number of important dimensions. *Explanatory Mode* is designed to reveal the major style of explanation of the theory, that is, is it primarily attempting to predict specific career choices, describe the process of career development, or explain how choices come about. *Empirical Support* refers to the overall nature of the number of studies pertaining to a theory and their general results. *Generality* is a summary of the scope of the theory: does it aim and succeed in applying itself to workers in a broad array of jobs in various cultures, or is it mainly pointed to high level workers, college students and their choices, etc.? *Complexity* is a summary statement of the number and abstractness of the concepts used in the theory. *Operationality* refers to the ease with which the concepts of the theory may be translated into research hypotheses, instruments, and practical applications. Finally, *Key Variables* attempts to summarize the most important variables used in the theory to explain or describe career events.

# REFERENCES

Borow, H. Research programs in career development. *Journal of Counseling Psychology,* 1960, 7, 62-70.

Ginzberg, E., Ginsburg, S. W., Axelrad, S., and Herma, J. L. *Occupational choice: an approach to a general theory.* New York: Columbia University Press, 1951.

Holland, J. L. A theory of vocational choice. *Journal of Counseling Psychology,* 1959, 6, 35-45.

Lofquist, L. H., and Dawis, René V. *Adjustment to work: a psychological view of man's problems in a work oriented society.* New York: Appleton-Century-Crofts, 1969.

Roe, Anne. Early determinants of vocational choice. *Journal of Counseling Psychology,* 1957, 4, 212-217.

Spranger, E. *Types of men.* New York: Stechert, 1928 (translation).

Super, D. E. A theory of vocational development. *American Psychologist,* 1953, 8, 185-190.

Super, D. E. Self-concepts in vocational development. In Super, D. E., et al., *Career development: self-concept theory.* New York: CEEB Research Monograph No. 4, 1963.(a)

Super, D. E., Starishevsky, R., Matlin, N., and Jordaan, J. P. *Career development: self-concept theory.* New York: CEEB Research Monograph No. 4, 1963.(b)

# 9

# Perspective

On the basis of the previous chapters it is clear that many problems and unresolved issues remain in the theoretical structure of career development. This chapter aims to bring these issues into clearer focus. After examining the theories, as well as the research and applications that derive from them, several issues become prominent. It seems to be generally accepted that career choice is most profitably viewed as developmental in nature and based on principles of developmental psychology such as Beilin (1955) has explicated. Beilin has pointed out the tendency for human behavior to move from the general, dependent, self--oriented, and isolated to the specific, independent, social, and integrated. Career development has been construed by many writers to be one aspect of this maturing process.

Of course some dissenting voices may be heard. The dissenters are represented by writers such as Calia (1966), who point out the limitations of the developmental approach to careers and emphasize the indisputable fact that in practice, counselors rely heavily on the trait-factor approach despite its heuristic emphasis. A defense of the use of the trait-factor approach to career counseling appears to be especially apt in view of new procedures in automated data processing. Furthermore, Calia has criticized the career view because of the limitations that many unpredictable events impose on anticipating careers. How can a man anticipate the sudden illness of a superior which creates a premature advancement, or a technological development which makes an industry obsolete in a decade? Because there have been few attempts to translate career development theory into practice, the trait-factor approach continues to be the foundation of career counseling. Nevertheless, most writers prefer to view the trait-factor thought as one aspect to be considered in the analysis of the role of abilities, personality traits, interest, and family influences in the shaping of eventual career membership and occupational behavior. Most writers have chosen to emphasize the role of one or two of these variables over the others, but nearly all have acknowledged that many factors operate to influence career development.

Whether existing emphases will change in the years to come is debatable, though most theoretically oriented writers seem to assume that important changes will occur. Super (1972) has predicted that four major activities will exemplify career development work over the next 20 years: the development of career models by means of such devices as lattice theory, Markov chains, path analysis, and the career tree; extending our knowledge regarding exploratory behavior; developing better measures of vocational maturity; and extending self-concept theory. Holland (1972) and Roe (1972) hope for a greater investment of effort in the study of "important" problems and better interaction between the practitioner and researcher. Roe further sees more interdisciplinary research, more attention paid to vocational development in lower level occupations, and more longitudinal research. Tiedeman (1972) anticipates a greater impact for technology such as the computer in both research and vocational counseling. Osipow (1969) sees future developments largely in terms of increasing understandings about occupational effectiveness and satisfaction, in addition to predicting occupational membership by means of improved and novel techniques of measuring and observing vocationally related events. Others, such as Campbell (1969), have also anticipated a more comprehensive study of vocational development through "social systems" approaches, or, like O'Hara (1969), have called for an improved research base to apply to the practice of vocational counseling. Finally, the career education movement is likely to exert an influence in the direction of generating applications of theories of career development to programs and practice.

A growing emphasis has been placed on the impact of social forces in career development. It has become increasingly evident that when the situational determinants of career development are ignored, serious limitations are imposed on theoretical endeavors. In order to avoid limiting the impact of theory to this time and place, situational factors must be systematically built into career development theory. Often our theories, seeming to assume that career choice is static, appear designed to describe career development only in the context of mid-twentieth-century America. The question of career development in other cultures is ignored. What is career behavior like in Red China or the Soviet Union? What are the career patterns that emerge in developing nations? Attention to the problems of emerging nations might help us answer questions concerning the career development of disadvantaged Americans, who in many respects face career problems similar to those of individuals in newly developing countries. How does one quickly acquire modern attitudes to technological skills? Lyon (1965) has warned that current theories of career development will soon be obsolete if they continue to fail to take the social context into account in their formulations. Cultural patterns exert a strong influence on the interaction between personality and occupation. Lyon has pointed out that American culture is rapidly bringing to an end the day of "straight line" career, that is, the career which lasts from youth until death or retirement, and is replacing it with the "serial" career, in which one's occupational life occurs in phases, and one moves from one level and activity to another with increasing maturity and experience. Similarly, class differences in America are leveling, and the differences between class expectations regarding occupational activities are disappearing.

The process of career choice is so deeply imbedded in cultural and economic factors that it is unreasonable to try to develop a theory of vocational development without including those variables. Social and economic conditions have changed drastically in the United States between the 1930s and 1970s and so has career development. Thus, it is not unreasonable to expect significant changes in the economy and culture in the years ahead, bringing about concomitant changes in career development. Most (if not all) career theorists have recognized the impact of cultural change on career development and have used increasingly abstract concepts in their formulations of career behavior, with individual development given continuity by the notion of the implementation of a self-concept as a guiding factor in career behavior.

It seems to be growing increasingly clear that a theory of career decision-making and behavior must be developed which will possess the generality to deal effectively with environmental variables. Mierzwa (1963) has reported data illustrating the usefulness of the concept of multidetermination of career choice. He has proposed the use of a systems analysis for career behavior and counseling about vocations.

Thus, a systems view of career behavior is gradually emerging. The systems view explicitly recognizes that various situational and individual factors operate to influence career behavior in a broad way. With a highly sophisticated systems approach to career development, questions about the role of the biological, social, and situational factors in occupational behavior would become more explicit and hence more open to scrutiny, and understandings of the interactions between these views would be more likely to emerge as a consequence.

# THE SYSTEMS APPROACH

Applied to career development, the systems approach is most clearly seen in the analysis of decision-making. Decisions may be viewed as links in a chain. Each decision can be made only immediately prior to action, yet preparation for the act of deciding and plans for the implementation of the decision itself are necessary. Furthermore, even though decisions have immediate implications, the long-range effects of decisions and estimates of their effects on future decisions are to be considered even though not made final now. Figure 9.1 illustrates the process.

$T_1$ represents the present, $T_0$ the past, and $T_2$ the future. The lowercase letters a, b, c represent small decisions, and the uppercase letters A, B, C represent major decisions. On the basis of a network of decisions made during $T_0$, the

FIGURE 9.1. Schematic representation of a decision making network.

individual arrives at $T_1$, which may be the time of registration in college. At that time he makes a series of small decisions, a, b, and c, which may be to take math, English, and physics courses. The dotted lines represent potential avenues which for various reasons were not followed. They each have highly intricate potential networks for decision. These decisions lead to experiences which may be interpreted in a variety of ways at $T_1$ plus, which lead to more significant decisions, such as A and B. Eventually, after working through a multitude of such alternatives, the student emerges at another major decision point in his life, $T_2$, possibly college graduation. The previous experiences and decisions created the context in which a number of small decisions and a large decision could be made. In such a manner, then, the individual might go on making the decisions necessary to life. The role of the researcher is to identify the factors involved in influencing decisions at the numerous choice points; the role of the counselor is to help the individual cope with the discontinuities introduced at these junctures.

### Approaches to the Study of Decision-Making

A variety of somewhat sophisticated attempts to deal with decision-making has been made. Hsu (1970) describes a quantitative system, based on decision theory, designed to analyze the decision-making process. Included are what Hsu considers to be the essential variables involved in decision-making: outcomes, valances of outcomes, expectancies of outcomes, and possible alternatives. Hsu does not, however, present any data to accompany the model and the several formulae he proposes. Marshall (1967) has tried to show how Bayesian decision as opposed to classical decision-making can be applied to educational programming. Marshall's work has potential application to individual decision-making with regard to educational-vocational choice, but needs further elaboration to make it testable. Katz (1966) has elaborated his views about decision-making for careers, views which rest heavily on the role of values in career planning. Miller (1968) has attempted to show how learning theory might be applied to the study of vocational decisions, but his presentation does not really suggest practical applications of learning theory to the educational-vocational decision-making task.

A number of writers, notably Gelatt and Clarke (1967) and Thoresen and Mehrens (1967), have tried to apply the use of the concept of subjective probability estimates of success in vocational decision-making. In a review of research on preferences, gambling behavior, and level of aspiration, Gelatt and Clarke (1967) observe that it is possible to construe that what goes on in educational-vocational decision-making is a series of estimates of probability of success combined with the personal value of the activities available.

Career decision-making may be viewed as a kind of "increasing approximation" method (Gelatt, 1962). When confronted with a set of alternatives for an educational-vocational problem, an individual collects information designed either to lead to a plan to deal with the problem or to identify more information essential to solving the problem. The sequence is thus: collect information, assess the information and predict outcomes of various courses of action in terms of probability and desirability, identify alternatives, evaluate and select, and finally implement the decision. The implementation may either terminate the problem or be a preliminary solution designed to provide more information, in which case the process would be repeated.

Kaldor and Zytowski (1969) have described a system, which, in a complex way, appears to be a variant of subjective estimate of probabilities methods. Kaldor and Zytowski seem, in an implicit way, to go beyond the consideration of the utility of the outcome for the chooser as an important variable and, instead, include the effect that the "costs" to the individual interact with his estimates of probabilities of various outcomes. In other words, Kaldor and Zytowski imply that what an individual will choose depends on his estimates of the likelihood of various outcomes in combination with the expense in time, effort, etc., of producing each outcome.

Appel and Haak (1968) have presented a good analysis of assumptions underlying thinking about career decision-making and supporting data regarding these assumptions. According to Appel and Haak, it is assumed that the best vocational decisions have an informational base, but the data available do not necessarily support such assumptions, in fact, there is some reason to believe that an overload of information can interfere with good decision-making. Second, Appel and Haak suggest that evidence tends to support the notion that vocational decisions are best made when an individual is ready, not at some arbitrarily determined time. Not generally supported is the assumption that vocational choices are the result of a narrowing process; partially supported, in the view of

Appel and Haak, is the assumption that occupational attractiveness is a function of anticipated rewards rather than success; some people appear, however, to prefer safe goals to risky ones.

### Cognitive Dissonance in Career Decision-Making

Hilton (1962) chose to organize his thinking about career decision-making along the concept of cognitive dissonance. Cognitive dissonance (Festinger, 1957) is the discord introduced into one's perceptions of the world and his role in it by the observation of events that are grossly at variance with expectations. For example, a man who views his son as a brilliant student would experience cognitive dissonance were the boy to fail in his college studies. According to Festinger, attempts to reduce cognitive dissonance provide a very potent motivating agent behind human behavior. Thus, the father cited in our example would search for causes for the son's failure that did not detract from his son's brilliance as a student in order to reduce the very dissonant event of his failure in school.

Hilton summarizes his view of the process as follows: some event stimulates an individual's attention to the need to make a career decision. This stimulus may be the offer of a different job, the need for more money, the desire to live in a more agreeable climate, and so on. If the dissonance introduced by this stimulus is above the individual's ability to tolerate, he will reexamine and perhaps change his beliefs about himself and his work, and as an outgrowth of the reexamination, may change jobs. To the degree that the changes he initiates reduce the dissonance, he will continue along the new line or make further revisions.

In this scheme it becomes critical to identify the factors which can increase occupational dissonance. Some come readily to mind: occupational opportunities, institutional pressures, interpersonal conflicts. Nevertheless, the potential variety of factors for introducing dissonance is immense and must be identified specifically for each individual by the counselor. Furthermore, counselors must develop strategies to deal with dissonance. They may even want to consider the introduction of counter-dissonance agents, for example, suggesting to the ill-advised premedical student that physicians work too hard. A counselor might help a person avoid a premature identification with an educational or vocational plan because the need to modify the plan might create excessive dissonance for him and prevent an appropriate change later.

Hershenson and Roth have used cognitive dissonance in another way (1966). They have made explicit the notion that vocational decision-making reduces the range of subsequent vocationally related experiences and thus reduces the variety of career alternatives open to an individual. The range is reduced because the individual becomes attracted to a field by virtue of his experience, fails to know much about other possibilities, is too heavily committed to a course of action to change or recognize the need for a change, and is getting along reasonably well in the situation, uncomfortable as it may be. Thus, in order to avoid the disruptive effects of cognitive dissonance the more intent on a vocational objective or direction one becomes, the greater the likelihood is that he will interpret events, both consistent and inconsistent, as being in accordance with his current vocational plans and activities.

The above approaches are schematic and thus inadequate to identify the specific content involved in making decisions. Perhaps countering this deficiency is Fletcher's (1966) hypothesis that career decisions are based on the effect associated with the career at the time of decision and thus the adequacy of the decision is a function of the individual's breadth of experience, his realism, and his ability to resist irrelevant stimuli. These factors can explicitly be taken into account, and a counseling objective may be to increase the experience and realism of clients and strengthen their ability to identify and resist irrelevancies, preceded by an assessment of the clients' development in each of these three areas.

### Other Elements in the System

All the literature reviewed in this book suggests that there is an interdependence between personality variables, choice dimensions, and environmental conditions. One person, with a particular set of attributes in a given culture and operating under a special set of economic circumstances, will be confronted by a series of choice points which will lead to an idiosyncratic sequence of decisions. Vigorous, energetic, restless, intelligent young men in nineteenth-century America were attracted to entrepreneurial fields as a result of social and economic press. In twentieth-century America, such men may seek technological careers because they represent the same potential for achievement that entrepreneurial activities provided for their nineteenth-century counterparts.

Thus, it can be seen that individual A in culture B under economic conditions C will make a series of decisions $x$, $y$, and $z$. The situational variables B and C are interdependent and determine the specific nature of $x$, $y$, and $z$, which are sequential. What has typically been done in research on personality and career decision-making has been to examine the effects of individual variables, for example, the need for achievement, as if these variables have a constant value, while ignoring social and economic variables. Thus, it might be observed, as White (1963) did, that compulsive people tend to become bank tellers, without recognizing the possibility that compulsive people in another social and economic milieu may become mechanics or art critics.

What appears to be necessary is to study occupational behavior controlling two of the variables and varying the other. For example, if the effect of social forces on occupational membership within given personality types under constant economic conditions were studied, it might be observed that certain personality attributes are advantageous at one social level and troublesome at another.

## Moderator Variables

Also intriguing is the possibility that personality might have a different effect on behavior as social and economic factors vary. The functional relation between personality, economy, and society might be more explicit if empirical data were available to describe better the way they covary. The particular nature of the relationship of these variables to one another is very significant and suggests the use of the concept of the moderator variable to describe the role that personality plays in vocational development and decision-making.

Holland's theory of career choice (1959) represents a simplified version of the use of the moderator variable in vocational choice. The personality type provides the major source of impetus toward an occupational environment, but the specific choice is influenced by the level hierarchy. According to theory, it is the level hierarchy which dictates the specific occupation that will be selected within the personality mode appropriate to the major personal orientation to life. The level hierarchy, in turn, is a function of self-evaluation and intelligence. Thus, the eventual occupational choice is *moderated* by intelligence and self-evaluation.

## The Function of Moderator Variables

As an example of how they operate, let us imagine how conformity might serve to moderate the effect of intelligence in creative behavior. One might suppose that at low levels of intelligence and high levels of conformity little in the way of creative production would occur and that at high levels of intelligence and low levels of conformity creative potential would be at its maximum. However, the relationship between the two variables and creativity is not necessarily linear, and the concept of conformity as a moderating factor in creative behavior could be productive in the study of creativity.

## The Application of Moderator Variables to Vocational Behavior

For example, let us consider how age moderates career behavior. It seems very reasonable to expect that certain personal styles may lead to one kind of behavioral decision under one set of conditions and another quite different kind of decision under other conditions. Thinking in terms of career patterns, these decisions are likely to be affected by the age of the decision-maker. Furthermore, personality style may also be expected to affect an individual's cognitive structure as a function of his ability, his background, and so on.

Consider a young man, impulsive, lower middle class socially and economically, aspiring to upward mobility, confronted with a high risk but high payoff occupational decision. He can be expected to take the risk eagerly. Twenty years later, assuming the risk was taken and successfully managed, this same man has been affected by the consequences of his decision and should not be expected to behave the same way in risk-taking situations. He is not likely to behave impulsively and his tendency to take risks is likely to be reduced because he now has achieved many of his ambitions for upward mobility. Obviously, different predictions about his vocational behavior in a risk-taking situation will be made now than 20 years earlier. Looking at personality traits alone, one might overlook his changed status and make predictions about occupational behavior similar to those made earlier. The factors of economics and social standing will have altered weights in the behavioral equation of this man.

### Implications of Research and Counseling

What do moderator variables mean for career development? They mean more complex research designs, a need for better instruments to assess personality, and a revision of the concept of personality away from static traits (i.e., achievement and abasement needs, compulsive traits, and so on) toward a conception of personality style which allows the integration of the disparate traits inherent in the trait-factor approach into a *behavioral* (situational) context. It would also imply the development of instruments to assess personal style, socioeconomic factors that press on the individual, and ways of integrating this material and summarizing it so that it can be useful to the decision-maker.

### Summary

The systems approach is in a position to take the most useful concepts of each theory of career development and apply them to the understanding of individual behavior. Elements of the social, personal, and economic situation within which individuals operate may be more explicitly analyzed, and the relationship of the larger systems to one another may be more clearly understood than in the traditional approaches to behavior, which tend to emphasize only one major segment of either the individual or his environment.

# RESEARCH

The description of the research concerning career development has revealed a number of shortcomings. Most notable is the lack of experimentation and the heavy reliance on descriptions of career behavior based on observations of convenient samples. Meaningful research has also been seriously hampered by a lack of valid instruments to measure such concepts as personality traits, career satisfaction, needs, values, and family environment.

Thus far, career development research has primarily described the processes relevant to career behavior. What is needed is an "experimental vocational psychology" (Crites, 1965) which will lead to explanations as well as descriptions of vocational development. The goal should be to formulate lawful relationships and hypotheses concerning career behavior so that research data can be interpreted only in one way and not be subject to the wide variety of interpretations (or none at all), as is frequently the case now.

## How Data Are Obtained

One of the biggest problems facing the researcher in career development is collecting good data. As suggested above, a serious problem of instrumentation exists. Frequently, the information that seems significant is difficult to collect systematically and difficult to quantify. Typically, counselors are in a good position to assess concepts of career development because of the highly personal and relevant material that is discussed with them. Unfortunately, counselors are usually not interested in data collection for research, at least at the moment they are counseling. Then, too, counselors enter into the client's life as agents of change and thus become confounding agents in the events that should be observed by an experimenter.

Collection of the same kind of data by the inventory method which counselors normally obtain through interviews frequently results in sterile and invalid data which fail to answer the significant questions. The interview method provides the richest source of data, but the inventory method is the most objective and reliable. Researchers faced with this dilemma have often resolved it by collecting both kinds of data and using the best aspects of each. Concepts suggested by interview procedures are compared with the more stable observations revealed by inventories.

## Sampling

Most commonly, career development research has used student samples. It seems clear that students have been extensively studied at least partly because they are an accessible sample. The overemphasis of student-based career development research clearly places limitations on the generalizations that may be drawn from much of the data. It must be recognized, however, that there is a legitimate use of students in career development research. One of the most critical periods of career development occurs during the adolescent years, and many counselors are primarily concerned with the decisions made during that time. Thus, it is important to improve the accuracy with which students can be assisted in predicting the starting point of their careers, and student-based career development research contributes to that improvement.

A more significant research shortcoming lies in the lack of adequate follow-up data concerning differences between students whose later development continues to be smooth as opposed to those who encounter difficulties, as well as other data that might relate significant developmental trends in later life to behavior observed during student days. For example, it would be useful to observe a sample of prelaw students, investigate the details of their career development to the time of observation, follow them through law school and beyond, and then use the observations from that group to make predictions about and counsel a group of students starting their prelaw studies.

### Effects of Counseling on Educational-Vocational Adjustment

Most of the studies of the role of educational-vocational counseling in career decision (e.g., Gonyea, 1962; 1963; Hewer, 1966; Apostal, 1960; Marks, Ashby, and Zeigler, 1965; Marks, Ashby, and Noll, 1966; Hill and Grieneeks, 1966) have raised serious questions about the effect of counseling on educational performance or vocational decisions, or at least have challenged the common criteria called into use in evaluating counseling. Typically, criterion studies have compared the performance, or decisions, of groups of students receiving counseling with those who have not been counseled, or who might have been counseled in different ways. Inferences were drawn about the adequacy of the decisions or performance and the ways counseling may have contributed to the adequacy or shortcomings of the behavior observed.

Three problems seem to be inherent in this technique. First, the actual counseling procedures to which individuals are exposed are rarely described in an explicit fashion, and thus it becomes exceedingly difficult to identify genuine differences in experiences of counseled or noncounseled groups. Second, the outcomes are frequently evaluated in highly specific terms. Did the subject choose to major in engineering after counseling and was he an engineer five years after college? How many and what kinds of changes in academic major occurred after counseling? This type of question fails to recognize that entering engineering at college graduation may have been very appropriate at the time, but that in the normal process of career development, an individual may quite properly change to another field. One's exposure to engineering studies may contribute crucially to one's later career in city planning, in government, or in management.

A study by Hollender (1971) illustrates some of the problems involved in considering the outcomes of vocational counseling. Hollander examined the hypothesis that vocational decisiveness increases with age by studying a cross section of 5200 students in grades six through twelve. He found that about 30 percent of his sample entered adolescence undecided and about 30 percent finished high school undecided about vocational plans, and concludes that no change in decisiveness about career plans occurs during adolescence. The critical point is whether or not the same 30 percent are undecided entering adolescence as the 30 percent at high school graduation. Obviously, since Hollender's study is cross-sectional, the two are not the same, and in that light it is potentially misleading to draw the conclusion that no changes in decisiveness occur during adolescence. In a similar way, averaging outcomes regarding decisions about careers following counseling may mask important individual changes.

Third, the sources of judgments made introduce irrelevant bias. In Hewer's study (1966) it was observed that counselor judgments about the realism of client career choices made at the completion of counseling did not agree with student judgments about the appropriateness of their current work and the decisions they had made some years earlier. In fact, the clients saw more relation between their current jobs and past decisions than did the counselors, suggesting, quite reasonably, that they had sources of information connecting the events in their lives in a more meaningful way than did the counselors.

## Summary

Career development theory is intimately bound to research in career decision-making and its effectiveness. To improve current research efforts, a number of steps might be considered: first, a broadening of the sampling usually obtained and more follow-up data; second, greater willingness to use interview data in combination with more objective data collection techniques; third, the use of experimental designs which avoid the effects of biases in sampling resulting from the study only of people coming to counseling centers for help and which would also facilitate replication and allow the introduction of treatment procedures in sequence much as Crites (1964, p. 305) has suggested; finally, more explicit description of input variables, experimental conditions, and expected and observed outcomes.

# IMPLICATIONS FOR PRACTICE

The review of career development theory raises two questions with regard to applications to practical matters: what should vocational counseling attempt to accomplish, and how should it go about its tasks? Related to the first question is the additional question of the degree to which vocational counseling should attempt to be preventive and facilitative in nature versus corrective or rehabilitative. It would probably be widely agreed that the development of facilitative programs for career behavior is the most efficient approach in the long run, but given our imperfect world and its imperfect inhabitants, the fact is that the development of some people will become disrupted and efforts to correct problems in their development will be necessary.

Most career development theories are written descriptively so that either a facilitative or rehabilitative approach is possible. However, most counseling theorists have grown up in the tradition of problem-centered counseling and thus most thought has been given to the corrective aspects of career counseling. Many clinical techniques and concepts have been applied directly, and sometimes inappropriately, to the matters of career development.

## Clinical Procedures and Career Development

Ivey and Morrill (1968) have taken the interesting point of view that "career process" is an aspect of mental health and general development, and, as a result, suggest that counseling activities deemphasize career choice and intensify the emphasis placed on helping individuals become aware of the continuity that runs through their lives. The point of view expressed by Ivey and Morrill represents only one aspect of the impact on thinking about vocational counseling that clinical psychology has exerted. Also growing out of the clinical tradition is the recognition of the importance of identifying the client's problem and deciding what might be done to best resolve the difficulty. In simple terms, Pepinsky's (1948) list of client problems summarizes the variety of career problems presented to counselors. The problem areas, labeled lack of assurance, lack of information, lack of skill, dependence, self-conflict, and choice anxiety, are general in nature, yet suggestive of treatment procedures once the problem is clearly defined. In a more general way, Super (1957) has called for a three-pronged appraisal including assessment of the problem, the individual, and predictions about the outcome.

Many client problems fall under the rubrics suggested by the Pepinsky scheme: mistakes about the parameters of a career; discrepancies between anticipated rewards and actual events; inappropriate extrapolations of past experiences; misevaluation of skills; faulty labeling of interests; undifferentiated, multiple, adient, or avoidant interest patterns; and interests having no known vocational application. Once so assessed, however, these attitudes are resistant to change on the basis of information and frequently recur at later choice points. Many individuals fail to seek counseling help because they can live with the inefficient decisions they make. Furthermore, these assessment procedures fail to take into account the developmental nature of career behavior. Might it not be more profitable to develop programs that would educate people to career patterns and career decisions so that they make sound decisions and develop techniques to continue to make them as required during life?

Even though there may be a lack of research evidence to substantiate the use of the "dynamic" model of career counseling (McCabe, 1965) as compared to the trait-factor approach, it must be recalled that the trait-factor approach is limited to specific immediate decisions and that the "dynamic" models, building on the trait-factor approach, try to prepare the individual to make a series of specific decisions (Nachmann, 1965).

## Making Vocational Counseling Operational

That counseling is rapidly approaching the need to face the decision of *what* behavior should be changed is demonstrated by a study reported by Krumboltz and Schroeder (1965), who devised a way to assess the use of reinforcement counseling in educational-vocational information gathering. They found that the kind and amount of information-seeking behavior of a student could be influenced by the type of reinforcement procedure followed.

What is critical about this study is the fact that differences in behavior as a function of counseling techniques could be observed and measured. It appears to be possible to get people to change their behavior during interviews in a manner which influences their out-of-interview behavior in significant ways. Now that the rudiments of a technology to produce change exist, shall they be used to extend information-seeking behavior or on more socially significant and recurring patterns of behavior? Yabroff (1969), Magoon (1969), and Krumboltz and Sheppard (1969) have described applications of behaviorally oriented techniques to the process of vocational counseling and development. The behavioral methods generally deal with overt, explicit behaviors that can be measured and on which progress can be charted. In addition, the behavioral approaches frequently use simulation techniques to effect the desired growth in individual behavior. Crites' plan for the development of the Vocational Development Inventory (1961) represents another outline of a way that a concept critical to career development may be made operational in terms of expected tasks at discrete points in development.

Too often the implications of relevant observations from psychology at large have been overlooked. For example, Izard (1960) observed that individuals who score high on the personality traits of autonomy and dominance on the Edwards Personal Preference Schedule were unlikely to be convinced to change a concept. If the influence of such traits were found to be general, there might be implications for the development of different kinds of counseling procedures on the basis of the personality patterns of the clients even though the general reason the clients seek counseling might be the same.

Hershenson (1968) has attempted to integrate some of the developmental theories of vocational choice into a single framework. He suggests that five stages exist: an awareness stage, a control stage, a directed stage, a goal-directed stage, and an invested stage. Each of the five stages has a corresponding vocational mode, respectively: being, play, work, occupation, and vocation; the stages ask different questions, respectively "am I," "who am I," "what can I do," "what will I do," and "what meaning has it"; and finally, each stage is appropriately measured differently, again, respectively, by socialization, attitudes and values, abilities, interests, and satisfaction. In another paper, Hershenson (1969a) has tried to relate these life stages to specific vocational techniques designed to promote progress through the stages. However, a good data base underlying the stages appears to be lacking, and the methods themselves seem to be at a level of abstraction which makes them difficult to apply.

Morrill and Forrest (1970) have summarized approaches to counseling for careers by asserting that four types of methods seem feasible: counseling oriented toward producing a specific vocational decision (traditional counseling) counseling designed to teach decision-making skills so the individual can make good vocational choices throughout his life, counseling which views career development as a process rather than a point in time and focuses on continuity and growth rather than choice, and counseling oriented to help individuals use their assets to reach their own goals and influence the options open to them.

## Group Methods

Although group methods have a long history in counseling, some resistance has always been expressed to their use, since counseling has been seen as a way to individualize large and impersonal educational institutions. Nevertheless, some imaginative uses of group techniques have been suggested. Ford (1962) has pointed out that responses elicited from individuals by procedures in group settings may be modified in individual settings at a later time. In fact, there may even be some advantages to presenting information in one setting and modifying it in another. People might be inclined to dissociate the source of stimulation from the counselor who sees them later, and the time delay may provide a fruitful incubation period.

Courses dealing with the proper approaches to and information about career decision-making have been continually improved and may go a long way toward decision-making effectiveness (e.g., Salinger, 1966).

## Program Development

Ideas about group methods such as those suggested by Ford (1962) and Magoon (1964) suggest the development of programs designed to facilitate career development. Magoon (1964), concerned about both the shortage of counselors and the general inaccessibility of occupational information, has suggested some programmatic ways of disseminating career and educational information.

Following another tack, Ford (1962) has proposed that since educational-vocational counseling attempts to elicit responses relevant to the decision-making task and modify them through the use of the interview, it is theoretically feasible to elicit these responses and response modifiers in group settings, thus saving staff time. Furthermore, experience suggests that group approaches may have unique features which result in greater effectiveness in modifying responses than the individual interview. Other group members are often more potent response eliciters and modifiers than counselors.

Pritchard (1962) has suggested an approach to career decision-making that lends itself to program development. Discarding the use of tests and checklists because they are too stimulus bound, he suggests instead a greater emphasis on occupational sociology to provide information about work settings. A program derived from his approach would emphasize the choice process rather than the choice and would aim for closer agreement between occupational and self-exploration by means of real or vicarious work experiences. Such a program would necessarily result in an increasing emphasis on the differences of work settings *within* occupations to bring about a greater tolerance between client and career. Procedures showing people how their general goals might be implemented personally would be a strong move in the direction of increasing individual control over the career development process.

Similarly, programs aimed at prevention of error, correction of difficulties, and the facilitation of growth through planned professional intervention should be developed. For example, at Pennsylvania State University a preregistration counseling program requires each student to participate in a reassessment of his academic plans at the time of his entrance into college, and the counseling division can provide a student with great flexibility and latitude in the modification of his plans should that become necessary later on. In such a way the university has introduced procedures and programs designed to encourage students to find and express their special talents and interests, recognizing that young college freshmen are frequently unsettled in their educational and vocational objectives.

A significant programmatic development occurring presently is the career education movement. In part, this movement is the result of efforts at theory building in career development, and draws heavily on research and ideas in career development theory. Career education is designed to be a system-wide, kindergarten through college, education that has vocational choice and development at its heart. The rationale is to make education relevant to career life. Part of the implementation of this rationale involves enhancing career and self-exploration, awareness, and attitude development during childhood and adolescence, the shaping of decision-making as well as educational and career-related skills, training, and eventually job placement, all within the context of the curriculum. Formerly, such efforts, where they occurred, tended to be outside the mainstream of school activities. Career education as yet is not fully open to evaluation, but it seems likely it will exert a press on those working in the field of career development theory to extend the data base of their work as well as to make their efforts increasingly applied in nature. It is entirely possible that the effects of career education will change the shape of thinking about career development.

## Summary

Career development theory and practice have developed in the context of a clinical tradition. This tradition has led to some misleading and unproductive efforts because of its overemphasis on diagnosis of problems at the expense of the development of special techniques and programs to facilitate growth. Rather than emphasize stereotyped occupational information, counselors should focus their efforts on the identification and encouragement of desirable career development patterns and provide experiences to facilitate them. In doing so, there should be a greater emphasis on programmatic approaches to counseling. In addition, more realistic career experiences, perhaps with the use of simulation techniques possible through computer technology, should be developed. The goal of career development counseling should be to make career development a more rational and systematic process, as much under the control of the individual as possible.

## CONCLUDING SUGGESTIONS

It becomes clear, as the assessment of career development theory is concluded, that several shortcomings exist. Crites (1969) talks about theories of vocational choice and theories of vocational adjustment, and of psychological, nonpsychological, and general theories within the adjustment and choice categories. The approach in the present work takes the stance that the theories described are theories of career development, combining both choice and adjustment. While most of the theories seem to emphasize vocational choice, the developmental aspect is implicit, and sometimes explicit, in all of them, and is due for increasing attention.

An aspect of the theories that is open to criticism has to do with technical construction. Carkhuff, Alexik, and Anderson (1967) have taken issue with the theories in terms of their formal adequacy. Crites (1969), in a more detailed analysis of theory construction in the terms proposed by Marx (1963), has elaborated upon the differences between models (designed to fit observations), deductive theories (which go from concepts to data), functional theories (where a continuous interaction between data and concepts occurs), and inductive theories (which go from data to empirical relationships). To some extent, the theories represent all the various approaches to concept development, though few, if any, of the theories conform closely to a systematic way of theory building. In an effort to introduce greater rigor and systematically integrate research and writing in the study of work behavior, Hershenson (1969b) has suggested a series of definitions to be accepted by scientists and practitioners dealing with the science of "ergology."

Overall, the theories appear to be much too broad in scope and generally too skimpy in detail. What vocational psychology needs at the present time is a collection of miniature theories, each dealing with circumscribed, explicit segments of vocational behavior, to be woven into a broad theory after the smaller theories have been shaped by empirical findings. A miniature theory describing the decision-making process, a theory explaining job satisfaction, a theory explaining how career development is related to self-concept implementation, could all be developed independently, and when the details are in order, connected by other theoreticians to a larger conception of how the human personality develops and functions.

Another difficulty in the understandings about career development lies in one of the central assumptions most investigators make and questioned only by an occasional writer (e.g., Ginzberg et al., 1951; Zytowski, 1965). It is generally assumed that all men want to work and desire vocational activities. Seldom is any consideration given to the likelihood that a given individual may have negative attitudes toward work. It is entirely possible that the idea of becoming involved in a career could acquire fearful stimulus properties which lead to the avoidance of occupationally related behavior and which could account for some of the difficult-to-understand behavior concerning career decisions that is sometimes observed in reasonably well-endowed individuals.

A third problem lies in the treatment of female career development by the theories. Few special explanations or concepts have been devised to deal with the special problems of the career development of women, yet all who have observed or counseled women with respect to their career behavior realize that special problems exist for them as opposed to men and that most of the masculine-based tests and theories fail to provide a useful vehicle for the understanding of the career development of women.

The concept of interest in career development has been overemphasized, and in its traditional guise, it is not really very helpful either in understanding career development or in helping people to make sound educational-vocational decisions. It is a static concept as now used, representing the current state of a person's development without the recognition that interests change, that job settings change, and that there is considerably more in career satisfaction than finding "interesting" work. The limitations of the concept of interest are implicitly recognized by the failure of any of the theories of career development to use the concept directly; in fact, the theories represent attempts to go beyond the traditional and limiting notion of interest to uncover its ingredients. It would be appropriate to try to salvage the concept by redefining it and by rethinking factors that account for the development of interests. What is the role personality plays in the development of interest? How are interests acquired? Are they, as Strong (1943) has suggested, the result of the reward of effective abilities put to good use?

In redefining interest, care must be taken to differentiate kinds of interest (Super and Crites, 1962). The failure to do this has contributed to the devitalization of the concept. First, there is tested interest, which can be measured by testing knowledge that reflects involvement in an activity. Interest in mechanical matters can be tested by administering a test assessing mechanical knowledge. Inventoried interest is measured by asking individuals to tell, in various ways, what it is they like to do. The Kuder Preference Record and the SVIB are examples of such instruments. Finally, there is manifest interest, which may be inferred by observing what a person chooses to do when he has a relatively free choice. Presumably, although all three of these interests are related to one another, they are not identical. Hence, when interests are discussed without specification about what kind of interest is under discussion, some error in communication is likely to result.

Related to the impotence of the concept of interest has been its close relationship to the trait-factor approach to careers, that is, predictions about the field of job entry. Interests have been used to make these predictions, and the two concepts have become involved in an unfruitful static attempt to preduct a one-shot event, when in fact interests and jobs are really constantly changing. Differentiating between educational and vocational decisions is another but similar problem. The two are not the same, yet are often discussed as if they are and as if educational choices lead irrevocably to specific careers, when the fact is that relatively little connection exists between the two.

It is behavior that needs to be predicted. The particular behaviors that are of concern to career development theory need to be identified. Manifested interests, to be sure, must be one of these behaviors. The behaviors of relevance to career development should be observed and related to environmental conditions, thus minimizing chance effects.

The fruitful career development theory will take shape within the larger context of human development and behavior theory. The role of vocational psychology should be to devise subtheories to deal with special areas of behavior of particular interest to vocational psychologists, these areas to be defined along the lines Borow (1964) has suggested. For example, areas of interest to career psychologists may be developed along the lines of either process variables or agents of behavior. The process variables might focus on, for example, the career development of men by social class, differentiation of abilities, personality, and the interaction of the above. Or theory might examine the process of occupational satisfaction or of behavior in the job setting along similar lines. Focusing on the agents involved in career behavior would lead to attention to the effects of familial, social, situational, and age variables on career behavior. Ultimately, the aim would be to relate these separate endeavors at a higher level of abstractions to concrete events.

Whatever may occur, it must be kept in mind that in a highly complex society, counseling represents an attempt to individualize group processes. Counselors in educational settings are in a particularly favorable position to take account of the individual differences among people which are so important to the development and effective application of human resources. Effective concepts must be devised to guide the efforts to help people use their special characteristics well.

# REFERENCES

Appel, V. H., and Haak, Ruth A. Decision-making process: a basis for the reappraisal of vocational counseling. Presented at the APA Convention, San Francisco, 1968.

Apostal, R. A. Two methods of evaluating vocational counseling. *Journal of Counseling Psychology*, 1960, 7, 171-175.

Beilin, H. The application of general developmental principles to the vocational area. *Journal of Counseling Psychology*, 1955, 2, 53-57.

Borow, H. An integral view of occupational theory and research. In Borow, H. (Ed.), *Man in a world at work*. Boston: Houghton Mifflin, 1964.

Calia, V. F. Vocational guidance: after the fall. *Personnel and Guidance Journal*, 1966, 45, 320-327.

Campbell, R. E. Vocational ecology: a perspective for the study of careers. *The Counseling Psychologist*, 1969, 1, 20-23.

Carkhuff, R. R., Alexik, Mae, and Anderson, Susan. Do we have a theory of vocational choice? *Personnel and Guidance Journal*, 1967, 46, 335-345.

Crites, J. O. A model for the measurement of vocational maturity. *Journal of Counseling Psychology*, 1961, *8*, 255-259.

Crites, J. O. Proposals for a new criterion measure and improved research design. In Borow, H. (Ed.), *Man in a world at work*. Boston: Houghton Mifflin, 1964.

Crites, J. O. The vocational development project at the University of Iowa. *Journal of Counseling Psychology*, 1965, *12*, 81-86.

Crites, J. O. *Vocational psychology*. New York: McGraw-Hill, 1969.

Festinger, L. *A theory of cognitive dissonance*. Stanford, California: Stanford University Press, 1957.

Fletcher, F. M. Concepts, curiosity, and careers. *Journal of Counseling Psychology*, 1966, *13*, 131-138.

Ford, D. H. Group and individual counseling in modifying behavior. *Personnel and Guidance Journal*, 1962, *40*, 770-773.

Gelatt, H. B. Decision-making: a conceptual frame of reference for counseling. *Journal of Counseling Psychology*, 1962, *9*, 240-245.

Gelatt, H. B., and Clarke, R. B. Role of subjective probabilities in the decision process. *Journal of Counseling Psychology*, 1967, *14*, 332-341.

Ginzberg, E., Ginsburg, S. W., Axelrad, S., and Herma, J. I. *Occupational choice: an approach to theory*. New York: Columbia University Press, 1951.

Gonyea, G. G. Appropriateness of vocational choice as a criterion of counseling outcome. *Journal of Counseling Psychology*, 1962, *9*, 213-219.

Gonyea, G. G. Appropriateness of vocational choices of counseled and uncounseled college students. *Journal of Counseling Psychology*, 1963, *10*, 269-275.

Hershenson, D. B. Life-stage vocational development system. *Journal of Counseling Psychology*, 1968, *15*, 23-30.

Hershenson, D. B. Techniques for assisting life-stage vocational development. *Personnel and Guidance Journal*, 1969, *47*, 776-780.(a)

Hershenson, D. B. Toward a science of ergology. *Journal of Counseling Psychology*, 1969, *16*, 458-459.(b)

Hershenson, D. B., and Roth, R. M. A decisional process model of vocational development, *Journal of Counseling Psychology*, 1966, *13*, 368-370.

Hewer, Vivian H. Evaluation of a criterion: realism of vocational choice. *Journal of Counseling Psychology*, 1966, *13*, 289-294.

Hill, A. H., and Grieneeks, Laurabeth. Criteria in the evaluation of educational and vocational counseling in college. *Journal of Counseling Psychology*, 1966, *13*, 189-201.

Hilton, T. L. Career decision-making. *Journal of Counseling Psychology*, 1962, *9*, 291-298.

Holland, J. L. A theory of vocational choice. *Journal of Counseling Psychology*, 1959, *6*, 35-45.

Holland, J. L. The future of vocational development theory and its practical implications. In Whiteley, J. M., and Resnikoff, A. (Eds.), *Perspectives on vocational development*. Washington, D.C.: American Personnel and Guidance Association, 1972.

Hollender, J. W. Development of vocational decisions during adolescence. *Journal of Counseling Psychology*, 1971, *18*, 244-248.

Hsu, Ching-Yang C. A conceptual model of vocational decision-making. American Psychological *Experimental Publication System*, October, 1970, *8*, Ms No. 270-6.

Ivey, A. E., and Morrill, W. H. Career process: a new concept for vocational behavior. *Personnel and Guidance Journal*, 1968, *46*, 644-649.

Izard, C. E. Personality characteristics associated with resistance to change. *Journal of Consulting Psychology*, 1960, *24*, 437-440.

Kaldor, D. B., and Zytowski, D. G. A minimizing model of occupational decision-making. *Personnel and Guidance Journal*, 1969, *47*, 781-788.

Katz, M. R. A model of guidance for career decision-making. *Vocational Guidance Quarterly*, 1966, *15*, 2-10.

Krumboltz, J. D., and Schroeder, W. W. Promoting career planning through reinforcement. *Personnel and Guidance Journal*, 1965, *44*, 19-26.

Krumboltz, J. D., and Sheppard, L. E. Vocational problem solving experience. In Krumboltz, J. D., and Thoresen, C. E. (Eds.), *Behavioral counseling: cases and techniques*. New York: Holt, Rinehart, and Winston, 1969.

Lyon, R. Beyond the conventional career: some speculations. *Journal of Counseling Psychology*, 1965, *12*, 153-158.

McCabe, S. P. Hazards in the use of clinical techniques in vocational counseling. *Personnel and Guidance Journal*, 1965, *43*, 879-881.

Magoon, T. M. Innovations in counseling. *Journal of Counseling Psychology*, 1964, *11*, 342-347.

Magoon, T. M. Developing skills for educational and vocational problems. In Krumboltz, J. D., and Thoresen, C. E. (Eds.), *Behavioral counseling: cases and techniques*. New York: Holt, Rinehart & Winston, 1969.

Marks, E., Ashby, J. D., and Noll, G. A. Recommended curricular change and persistence in college. *Personnel and Guidance Journal*, 1966, *44*, 974-977.

Marks, E., Ashby, J. D., and Zeigler, M. L. Recommended curricular change and scholastic performance. *Journal of Counseling Psychology*, 1965, *12*, 17-22.

Marshall, J. C. Bayesian decision. *Journal of Counseling Psychology*, 1967, *14*, 342-345.

Marx, M. H. (Ed.). *Theories in contemporary psychology*. New York: Macmillan, 1963.

Mierzwa, J. A. Comparison of systems of data for predicting career choice. *Personnel and Guidance Journal*, 1963, *42*, 29-34.

Miller, A. W. Learning theory and vocational decisions. *Personnel and Guidance Journal*, 1968, *47*, 18-23.

Morrill, W. H., and Forrest, D. J. Dimensions of counseling for career development. *Personnel and Guidance Journal*, 1970, *49*, 299-305.

Nachmann, Barbara. Some comments on clinical appraisal in vocational counseling. *Personnel and Guidance Journal*, 1965, *43*, 884-885.

O'Hara, R. P. Comment on Super's papers. *The Counseling Psychologist*, 1969, *1*, 29-31.

Osipow, S. H. Some revised questions for vocational psychology. *The Counseling Psychologist*, 1969, *1*, 17-19.

Pepinsky, H. B. The selection and use of diagnostic categories in clinical counseling. *Applied Psychological Monograph*, No. 15, 1948.

Pritchard, D. H. The occupational exploration process: some operational implications. *Personnel and Guidance Journal*, 1962, *40*, 674-680.

Roe, Anne. Prospectus. In Whiteley, J. M., and Resnikoff, A. (Eds.), *Perspectives on vocational development*. Washington, D.C.: American Personnel and Guidance Association, 1972.

Salinger, M. D. Adapting a college-level occupations course to meet expressed student needs. *Personnel and Guidance Journal*, 1966, *45*, 272-275.

Strong, E. K., Jr. *Vocational interests of men and women*. Stanford, California: Stanford University Press, 1943.

Super, D. E. The preliminary appraisal in counseling. *Personnel and Guidance Journal*, 1957, *36*, 154-161.

Super, D. E. Vocational development in 20 years: how will it come about? In Whiteley, J. M., and Resnikoff, A. (Eds.), *Perspectives on vocational development*. Washington, D.C.: American Personnel and Guidance Association, 1972.

Super, D. E. and Crites, J. O. *Appraising vocational fitness* (Rev. ed.). New York: Harper & Row, 1962.

Thoresen, C. E., and Mehrens, W. A. Decision theory and vocational counseling. *Personnel and Guidance Journal*, 1967, *46*, 165-172.

Tiedeman, D. V. A machine for the epigenesis of self-realization in career development: description, subsequent development, and implications. In Whiteley, J. M., and Resnikoff, A. (Eds.), *Perspectives on vocational development*. Washington, D.C.: American Personnel and Guidance Association, 1972.

White, J. C. Cleanliness and successful bank clerical personnel — a brief. *Journal of Counseling Psychology*, 1963, *10*, 192.

Yabroff, W. Learning decision-making. In Krumboltz, J. D., and Thoresen, C. E. (Eds.), *Behavioral counseling: cases and techniques*. New York: Holt, Rinehart & Winston, 1969.

Zytowski, D. G. Avoidance behavior in vocational motivation. *Personnel and Guidance Journal*, 1965, *43*, 746-750.

# Name Index

313

# Subject Index